ORTHODOX CHRISTIANITY, Volume I

THE ECUMENICAL PATRIARCHATE

A History of Its Metropolitanates
with Annotated Hierarch Catalogs

by

Demetrius Kiminas

THE BORGO PRESS

An Imprint of Wildside Press LLC

MMIX

FIRST EDITION

CONTENTS

DEDICATION

To His All Holiness, BARTHOLOMEW I,

Archbishop of Constantinople, New Rome and Ecumenical Patriarch

and

To the Reposed Hierarchs, Their Memory Eternal

PREFACE

The history of the Ecumenical Patriarchate is a significant and inseparable part of the history of Christianity. This publication aspires to present the history of all Metropolitanates remaining under the jurisdiction of the Ecumenical Patriarchate today, and to present lists of the Hierarchs who have shepherded them in a concise and comprehensive form.

It is hoped that this work will be the first of more publications of the same nature, covering the other Orthodox Patriarchates and Autocephalous Churches in exactly the same way. The material needed for these remaining publications has already been assembled, with only its organization into book form remaining. It will all depend on the kind of reception this first book receives.

Although every possible care has been taken to remove errors, the heavy presence of dates and names in this work means their presence is unavoidable. I apologize in advance for any errors that may have crept in the following pages, and would appreciate any corrections, at my e-mail address, **constantinople@gmx.net**.

I would like to thank Professor Emeritus Michael Burgess for nudging me to proceed with this publication, and, in fact, altering my initial decision of pursuing only a Greek edition.

—Demetrius Kiminas
Athens, Greece
January 2009

PART I

THE ECUMENICAL PATRIARCHATE

A SHORT HISTORY

The Greek colony of Byzantium was established by an expedition led by the citizens of Megara[1] inside the Bosporus Strait circa 657 BC; its name was derived from the leader of the expedition, Byzas. The city came under Persian rule in 512 BC, but was freed by an expedition from Sparta in 477 BC. It allied itself with the Macedonian Greeks at the time of Alexander the Great, securing its independence during the time of the Hellenistic Empires.

After Greece became a Roman province in 146 BC, Roman influence spread in Byzantium, although the city remained free. In 64 BC the Asian side of Bosporus became part of the Roman province of Bithynia, and Byzantium became in essence part of the Roman Empire, although it nominally remained a free city, with brief interruptions, until 196 AD.

According to written sources from the 4th century AD, Apostle Andrew visited Byzantium circa 36 AD, and two years later consecrated one of the Seventy Apostles as its first Bishop—St. Stachys.

During the early Roman era, Christians in the Roman Empire were persecuted as criminals. This policy changed by a decision taken at Mediolanum (Milano, Italy) in February, 313 AD by the Western Emperor, Constantine I (reigned 307-337), and his Eastern colleague, Emperor Licinius (308-324). The Christians were granted equal status with the adherents of the Empire's other religions.

Constantine became sole ruler of the Roman Empire on September 18, 324, and soon afterwards initiated a plan to move the Empire's capital from Rome to the east, choosing the city of Byzantium as its new site. The foundation stone for the new city was set on November 3, 324.

Soon afterwards, the First Ecumenical Council (June 19-August 25, 325) was convened by Emperor Constantine I in nearby Nicaea (today, Iznik in northwestern Asia Minor); this condemned the Arian heresy and decreed the Symbol of Faith, subsequently known as the Nicene Creed. It also established the system of ecclesiastical division through Metropolitanates, each having a number of Dioceses under its jurisdiction—a system that was geographically based on the then political division of the Roman Empire in eparchies. Byzantium thus became a Diocese under the Metropolitanate of Heraclia (today Marmaraereglisi in Eastern Thrace). The Sees of Alexandria, Rome, and Antioch were recognized as having a primacy of honor among the other Metropolitanates. The Council was presided over by the Emperor himself.

The inauguration ceremony of "New Rome," "Constantine's City" (Konstantinou Polis, later Konstantinoupolis, westernized as Constantinople), was held on May 1, 330. At the same time the former Diocese of Byzantium became the ecclesiastically independent Archdiocese of Constantinople.

Christianity was becoming predominant in the Roman Empire. Western Emperor Gratianus refused in 375 to don the robes of the Pontifex Maximus (head of the pagan religion in the Empire). Gratianus appointed Theodosius I as Emperor in the East, and together on February 27, 380 they decreed the adoption of Christianity as the official religion of the Roman Empire.

In May 381 the Emperor Theodosius I (379-395) convened the Second Ecumenical Council in Constantinople. During its sessions (which ended on July 9, 381) it condemned the heresies of Arianism, Macedonianism, and Apollinarianism, modified and appended the Nicene Creed (which reached the form used today in the Eastern Orthodox Church), and recognized the See of Constantinople as having the primacy of honor, ranking it second in importance after the See of Rome. The Council was presided by the Patriarch of Antioch, Meletius I (360-381) until his sudden death in May 381. The presidency was then held by the newly elected Patriarch of Constantinople, Gregory I, until his resignation in June, and finally by his successor, the Patriarch of Constantinople, Nectarius (381-397).

Indeed, after the Second Ecumenical Council, the Sees of honorary primacy (Rome, Constantinople, Alexandria, and Antioch) used their rights of inspection over the affairs of the nearby Metropolitanates to slowly establish a form of control that later led to the system of five Patriarchates.

In 382 Gratianus renounced the title of Pontifex Maximus, and on February 24, 391 paganism was outlawed. Pagans were to be persecuted, and the practice of paganism, once the national religion, became a criminal offence.

During the period 382-90 the Patriarch of Rome, Damasus I, arranged for a new, more accurate translation of the New Testament's original Greek text into Latin, in order to replace the numerous Latin versions that circulated at the time, some of them containing significant errors. (Today, the original God-inspired Greek text of the New Testament is used in the Liturgy by the Ecumenical Patriarchate, Patriarchate of Alexandria, Patriarchate of Jerusalem, Church of Cyprus, and Church of Greece.)

The Third Ecumenical Council was convened by Emperor Theodosius II (408-50) in Ephesus (today, Selçuk in western Asia Minor) from June 22-July 31, 431. It condemned the heresy of Nestorianism, and reaffirmed the Nicene Creed, stating that any alteration to its text in the future was forbidden by the punishment of defrocking for the clergy and excommunication for the laity.[2] Protests by the Metropolitanate of Cyprus over the ever-increasing control of the See of Antioch led to the declaration of the Cypriot Church as autocephalous (self-ruled). The Council was presided by the Patriarch of Alexandria, Cyril I (414-44).

The Fourth Ecumenical Council was convened by Emperor Marcian (450-57) in Chalcedon (a city in the Asian side of the Bosporus Strait opposite Constantinople, today called Kadikoy) between October 9-November 1, 451. It condemned the heresy of Monophysitism, leading to the schism in the Patriarchate of Alexandria that created the Coptic Patriarchate of Alexandria. The Sees of Rome, Constantinople, Alexandria, Antioch, and Jerusalem were officially declared "Patriarchates," with all the ecclesiastic eparchies in the Empire subordinated under them according to geographic criteria. It was also stated that Rome and Constantinople, being the Old and New Rome, would have equal honorary primacy. The Council was jointly presided over by the Bishop of Lilybaeum (today Marsala in west Sicily, Italy), Paschasinus (the representative of the Patriarch of Rome), and by the Patriarch of Constantinople, Anatole (449-58).

The Patriarchate of Constantinople was given jurisdiction over the Metropolitanates in the greater part of Asia Minor (only southeastern Asia Minor was given to the Patriarchate of Antioch), Thrace, the Aegean Islands, and the barbaric lands that surrounded the Empire. The area of East Illyricum (including most of present-day Greece), which was claimed by both Rome and Constantinople, was left out of any Patriarchal jurisdiction (the Metropolitan of Thessalonica exercised honorary primacy over the Metropolitanates of that area). Only in the year 535 was the area of East Illyricum subordinated to the Patriarchate of Rome by decree of Byzantine Emperor Justinian I (527-65).

The deposition of the last Emperor in the West, Romulus Augustus, on September 4, 476 by the Gothic ruler Odoacer marked the end of the Western Roman State. At that date the Patriarchate of Rome ceased to be located within the borders of the Empire. Some decades later, however, East Roman Emperor Justinian I managed to annex part of the former Western Empire, including Italy. Justinian's armies entered Rome on December 9, 536, after sixty years of Gothic occupation. It was retaken by the Goths on December 17, 546, but they abandoned it a few months later, and had to retake it from the Romans on January 16, 550. The Roman Empire finally reconquered the city in June 552.

During this era the Patriarch of Constantinople began to be addressed as the "Ecumenical Patriarch", with the first known use of the title being recorded at the time of Patriarch Acacius (472-89). In the major Church Council held in Constantinople in 536, the Patriarchs of Constantinople John II (518-20), Epiphanius (520-35), Anthimus I (535-36), and Menas (536-52) were referred to as "Ecumenical Patriarchs" in the presence of representatives from the other four Patriarchates. The widespread use of the title is confirmed by its presence in official documents—for example, in the laws issued by the Emperor Justinian I.

The Fifth Ecumenical Council was convened by Emperor Justinian I in Constantinople between May 5-June 2, 553. It condemned the heresies of Nestorianism, Monophysitism, and Origenism. The Council was presided by the Patriarch of Constantinople, Eutychius (552-65, 577-82).

A Council held in Constantinople in 587 regarding the Patriarch of Antioch, Gregory I (570-93), officially bestowed the title "Ecumenical Patriarch" on Constantinople Patriach John IV (582-95). This action caused Patriarch of Rome, Pelagius II (579-90), to sever his communion with Constantinople, while his successor, Gregory I (590-604), sent letters of protest to both Patriarch John IV and Emperor Mauricius (582-602)—but with no results. Henceforth all Patriarchs of Constantinople were officially addressed as Ecumenical Patriarchs.

In 605 the great war with the Persian Empire began, with the Persians conquering Syria (Antioch fell in 611), Palestine (Jerusalem fell in May 614), and Egypt (Alexandria fell in 617). The war ended in September 629, when the Persians were forced to evacuate the occupied territories; the conflict exhausted the armies and infrastructure of both the Byzantines and the defeated Persians. Victorious Emperor Heraclius I (610-41), referred by some scholars as the first crusader, recovered the Holy Cross from the Persians and reinstored it to Jerusalem on March 21, 631, an event annually commemorated by the Orthodox Church.

But before the war-devastated Empire could be reorganized, a new, more powerful force invaded its borders. The Arabs, taking advantage of the weakened state of the Empire, and motivated by a new religion (initially regarded as a new Christian heresy by the Romans), invaded Syria in February 634. They took Damascus in September 635, Antioch in 637, Jerusalem in March 638, and Alexandria in September 642. Three of the five Patriarchates ceased being located within the borders of the Roman Empire.

The Sixth Ecumenical Council was convened by Emperor Constantine IV (668-85) in Constantinople between November 7, 680 and September 16, 681. It condemned the heresy of Monothelitism, and anathematized the Patriarchs of Constantinople, Sergius (610-38), Pyrrhus (638-41 and 654), Paul II (641-53), and Peter (654-66); the Patriarch of Alexandria, Cyrus (630-43); and the Patriarch of Rome, Honorius I (625-38), as Monothelite heretics. Emperor Constantine IV presided over the first eleven sessions of the

Council and the last (eighteenth) session, while the Patriarch of Constantinople, George I (679-86), presided over sessions 12-17.

The decisions of the Fifth and Sixth Ecumenical Councils were reaffirmed in the so-called Penthekti or Quinsext (Fifth-Sixth) Council which was convened by Emperor Justinian II (685-95, 705-11) in Constantinople between September 1, 691-August 31, 692. It formulated cannons that resolved the issues raised in the two previous Councils, and was presided over by the Patriarch of Constantinople, Paul III (688-93).

The Iconoclast movement, although a minority in the Empire, was embraced by Emperor Leo III (717-41), who decreed in 730 that icon veneration was a pagan remnant, and ordered all the icons in the Empire to be destroyed (representations of Saints by statues were avoided in the Eastern Empire, and remain so in the Orthodox tradition, due to the statues' association with paganism).

This new policy led to persecutions of all Orthodox hierarchs, monks, and laity who resisted it. Insurrections appeared all over the Empire, and the Patriarch of Rome refused to accept the Emperor's decision, condemning the Emperor's interference in religious matters. In retaliation, Emperor Leo removed East Illyricum, southern Italy, and Sicily from the jurisdiction of the Patriarchate of Rome, and attached them to the Patriarchate of Constantinople. The relations of the Patriarchate of Rome with the Byzantine Empire never recovered after this blow. Further, the Patriarchate of Rome lost contact with its Greek-speaking eparchies, and gradually estranged itself from Eastern Church traditions.

Ravenna, the administrative center of the Roman Empire in Italy, fell to the invading Lombards in 751. The Patriarch of Rome, knowing that he could not count on the Empire for help, since its armies were occupied on the Eastern borders with wars against the Arabs, sought the assistance of the Frankish kingdom. The Franks invaded Italy, taking Ravenna in 754, and gave most of the conquered territory to the Patriarchate of Rome. Henceforth a new "Papal State" was created, with the Patriarchate of Rome becoming politically independent from the Roman Empire.

The Seventh Ecumenical Council was convened by Emperor Constantine VI (780-97) in Nicaea between September 24-October 13, 787. In reality, however, the Council was convened by the Emperor's mother Irene, who later ruled as Empress (797-802). It condemned the heresy of Iconoclasm, putting an end to the conflict that had raged in the Empire for the past 57 years. It decreed that icon veneration was an integral part of the Christian faith, distinguishing it from icon adoration, still regarded as a sin. The Council was presided over by the Patriarch of Constantinople, Tarasius (784-806).

Due to a widespread tendency in the west to alter the Nicene Creed by adding the "filioque" clause[2], the Patriarch of Rome, Leo III (795-816), specifically forbad that practice, and had the unaltered Nicene Creed engraved in silver tablets displayed over the tomb of Apostle Peter for all to see.

The new Emperor, Leo V (813-20), held another Iconoclastic council in Constantinople on April 815, and once again forbad the veneration of icons in the Empire. This second era of Iconoclasm lasted until March 843, when icons were gloriously reinstated. The reinstatement event is commemorated by the Orthodox Church on the First Sunday of Feasting annually, henceforth called "Sunday of Orthodoxy."

A council that is regarded by some Orthodox scholars as an Eighth Ecumenical Council (although the Orthodox Church officially recognizes only the first seven Ecumenical Councils) was convened by Emperor Basil I (867-86) in Constantinople between November 879-March 3, 880. It restated that the Nicene Creed should not be altered in any way, resolved issues between the Patriarchates of Rome and Constantinople regarding the church of Bulgaria, annulled local councils held in the past in both Constantinople and Rome against Ecumenical Patriarch Photius I (858-67, 877-86), and decreed that excommunications by Constantinople should be recognized by Rome, and vice versa. The Council was presided by Ecumenical Patriarch Photius I.

The growing strength of the Bulgarian state in the Balkans enabled it to unilaterally declare the Metropolitan of Preslav a Patriarch in 911. This move was not recognized by Constantinople, but in 927 the creation of a Bulgarian Patriarchate with its seat in the northern city of Dorostolum (later Dristra, today Silistra, a city on the Danube river) was agreed to by treaty.

Emperor Nicephorus II Phocas (963-69) conquered Antioch on October 28, 969. After 332 years inside Arab territory, the See of the Patriarchate of Antioch came back within the borders of the Roman Empire.

The Bulgarian Patriarchate was abolished when Emperor John I Tzimiskes (969-76) dissolved the Bulgarian state in 971. However, a new center of Bulgarian resistance in the west resulted in the unilateral re-establishment of the Bulgarian Patriarchate in Ohrid (city situated on the lake of the same name near the Albanian border) a few years later (976). Around this time the evangelization of the Russian people had sufficiently spread that in 988 a new Metropolitanate of the Ecumenical Patriarchate was established in Kiev.

In 1012 the Metropolitan of Iberia (today Georgia in the Caucasus region) unilaterally adopted the title of Catholicus-Patriarch. (The Church of Iberia had been given Autonomy by the Patriarchate of Antioch in 467.)

When Emperor Basil II Boulgaroktonus (976-1025) dissolved the new Bulgarian state in 1018, he abolished the Bulgarian Patriarchate, and replaced it with an Autocephalous Archdiocese with its seat in Ohrid. After Basil's death, the Archdiocese of Ohrid lost its Bulgarian nature, and its hierarchs and Archbishops were mostly of Greek nationality.

Various alterations in the liturgy which had recently appeared in Rome (for example, the use of unleavened bread in mass, which started in the ninth century) complicated its relations with the other four Patriarchates. However, when the Patriarch of Rome, Sergius IV (1009-12), added the "filioque" clause in the Nicene Creed to the formal papers announcing his election to the Patriarch of Constantinople, Ecumenical Patriarch Sergius II (1001-19) deemed this act a direct violation of the Ecumenical Councils, and severed communion with Rome (the schism of the two Sergiuses).

Although efforts were undertaken to restore communion, the successor of Sergius IV, Benedict VIII (1012-24) again submitted the Creed with the "filioque" clause. The Roman envoys who arrived in Constantinople at the time of Patriarch Michael I Cerularius (1043-58), headed by Cardinal Hubert, advised that "Only Rome has the right to teach and will not accept to be taught. Only Rome has the right to judge and will not accept to be judged." Hubert then accused the Orthodox church of removing the "filioque" clause from the Nicene Creed, adding that Rome had justly restored it.

Tensions between the two churches continued to rise, and on Saturday, July 16, 1054, Cardinal Hubert entered the Cathedral of Hagia Sophia during the evening liturgy, and left a letter on the altar which anathematized the Patriarch of Constantinople and all who agreed with him. The letter repeated the false claim that the Eastern Church had removed the "filioque" clause from the Nicene Creed. Patriarch Michael Cerularius convened a local council on Sunday, July 17, 1054, which, after reading the decisions of the Ecumenical Councils that forbad any change to the Nicene Creed, anathematized the letter, its authors, and its couriers. The letter was then cast into fire as a work of heretics.

The decisions of this council were communicated to the Patriarchs of Antioch, Alexandria, and Jerusalem, with the request that they too remove the name of the Patriarch of Rome from their diptychs due to his fall into heresy. Although at the time the schism was not regarded as permanent (various east-west schisms had occurred in previous centuries and were later healed), it continues to this day.

The catastrophic defeat of the Roman army by a new enemy, the Seljuk Turks, in a battle near the city of Manzikert (today Malazgirt in eastern Asia Minor, north of lake Van) on August 26, 1071 heralded the unobstructed influx of the Muslim Turks into Christian Asia Minor. The Seljuks conquered Antioch in 1084.

In 1073 the new Patriarch of Rome, Gregory VII (1073-85), restricted the use of the title "Pope" (used in the west to address all the bishops at the time), to the Patriarch of Rome. This caused the title of Pope to gradually replace the title Patriarch of Rome or Patriarch of the West. In March 1075 Gregory VII unilaterally decreed that the Pope had Universal Jurisdiction over the Christian Church, including over the other Patriarchs, instead of the Honor of Primacy held by his predecessors. This teaching was viewed by the Orthodox as a further fall of Rome into heresy.

When the armies of the First Crusade arrived from the west, they were offered safe passage through the Roman Empire by Emperor Alexius I Comnenus (1081-1118). The Crusader armies conquered Antioch in 1098, Jerusalem in 1099, and established the so-called Crusader states in the area. All Byzantine attempts to expel the Turks from Asia Minor ended with the Romans' disastrous defeat in Myriocephalon, southeast of Ankara, in September 1176. Few years later, in 1187, the Turks took Jerusalem from the Crusaders.

In 1185 the Bulgarians rebelled against the Romans and succeeded in regaining their independence. The next year they unilaterally established an Autocephalous Archdiocese, with its seat at Turnov (today Veliko Tarnovo in central Bulgaria).

On April 12, 1204, the army of the Fourth crusade conquered and pillaged Constantinople, still the largest and richest city in Europe. The ferocity of the atrocities stigmatized the western world in the hearts of the Orthodox. This event and the persecution of the Orthodox clergy during the western rule that followed it, extinguished any honest hope of eventual reunification that remained in the Eastern Roman Empire.

The crusaders set up a Latin Empire of Constantinople that included a Latin "Patriarch of Constantinople," while the Orthodox Byzantine Emperor moved his capital to Nicaea in northwestern Asia Minor, the site of two Ecumenical Councils. The Patriarchate of Constantinople was also forced to relocate there.

On August 16, 1219, the Ecumenical Patriarch granted Autocephaly to the Serbian church, with its seat in Peć (a city in western Kosovo, Serbia).

After an alliance was formed between the Byzantines and the Bulgarians, in 1234 the Autocephaly of the Archdiocese of Turnov was recognized by the Ecumenical Patriarch, who the very next year granted it the title of Patriarch.

In 1229 the crusaders regained Jerusalem, but in 1239 the Turks retook the city. The last conquest of Jerusalem by the crusaders occurred in 1243, only to be retaken by the Turks in 1244. (The crusader state of Antioch was conquered by the Mamluks in 1268.) In 1260 the crusader rulers of the island of Cyprus abolished its Orthodox hierarchy.

On July 25, 1261, Emperor Michael VIII Paleologus (1258-82) retook Constantinople from the Latins. The capital of the Byzantine Empire now returned to its ancient site, but the Empire never recovered from the devastation of 1204.

Emperor Michael VIII, eager to consolidate his realm now that its capital was back in Constantinople, arranged in 1274 for an Orthodox delegation to attend the Latin Council of Lyons, where on July 6, 1274 a union of the Latin and Orthodox churches was proclaimed, after the Orthodox delegation was forced by the Emperor to accept all alterations in the faith that had occurred in the western church. This unconditional "union," which caused waves of protest in the Empire and the Orthodox world, collapsed in 1281 when the new Pope excommunicated the Byzantine Emperor during an attempt to gather a Latin force for retaking Constantinople.

In 1318 the seat of the Ecumenical Patriarchate's Metropolitanate of Russia was transferred from the city of Kiev to the city of Moscow (Moskva).

In 1324, the Greek scholar Nicephorus Gregoras, who had noted the deficiencies of the Julian calendar, proposed to Emperor Andronicus II Paleologus (1282-1328) a plan for its correction. However, the Empire was too weak at the time and the Emperor rejected the plan, fearing that it would confuse the people, and that the Empire could not impose it on the Western European states.

On April 11, 1346 a council of the Serbian church (the Serbian state being then in war with the Byzantine Empire) unilaterally elevated the See of Peć to Patriarchate status. The Patriarch later (after the Serbian state had annexed areas of Greece), claimed to be Patriarch of "the Serbs and the Romans" in empathy with the Serbian Emperor's pretensions. This caused the Ecumenical Patriarch to declare the Serbian Church schismatic in 1353, and anathematize the Serbian king and hierarchs.

A series of councils that are collectively regarded by some Orthodox scholars as a Ninth Ecumenical Council were held in Constantinople between June 10-August 1341, February 1347, and May 27-July 1351. They condemned the heresy of Augustinianism, and approved the form of religious prayer known as Hesichasm. The initial Council of 1341 was convened by Emperor Andronicus III (1328-41), and was presided over by Ecumenical Patriarch John IV (1334-47); the Council of 1347 was convened and presided over by Emperor John V (1341-76, 1379-91); and the Council of 1351 was convened by Emperor John VI (1347-54), and was presided over by Ecumenical Patriarch Callistus I (1350-53, 1355-63).

In 1359 the new Metropolitanate of Hungaro-Walachia in the Ecumenical Patriarchate was established in the capital of Walachia, Curtea de Arges (in present-day Romania). The See of the Patriarchate of Antioch was transferred from ruined Antioch to Damascus circa 1360. In 1375 the anathema on the Serbian church was lifted, the schism was healed, and the title of Patriarch was bestowed on the Archbishop of Peć by the Ecumenical Patriarch. In 1392 a new Metropolitanate of Moldavo-Walachia was established by the Ecumenical Patriarchate with its See in the capital of Moldavia, Suceava (in present-day Romania).

After the conquest of most of the Balkan Peninsula by the Ottoman Turks, the Ecumenical Patriarchate abolished the Bulgarian Patriarchate in August 1394, with Turnov becoming one of its Metropolitanates. In 1394 the Ottomans occupied the last Roman cities in Thrace, reducing the area of the Byzantine Empire effectively to Constantinople and its suburbs, an area in southern Greece, and some scattered islands. The disastrous defeat of the Ottomans in Ankyra by Tamerlane's Mongol armies in 1402 enabled the Romans to regain Thessalonica and the seaside cities of Thrace in the Marmara Sea coast as far as Panidon (Grk Πάνιδον, Trk Barbaros), and on the Black Sea coast as far as Mesimvria (Grk Μεσημβρία, Bulg Nesebar) at the beginning of 1403. Many of these cities remained in Roman hands until the Empire's final days.

Emperor John VIII Paleologus (1425-48), desperate to receive military aid from the West, visited Italy with the Ecumenical Patriarch Joseph II (1416-39), together with many hierarchs and theologians whom he forced to accept union with the Western church. The Council of Ferrara-Florence, which was held from January 8, 1438-July 6, 1439, proclaimed this union by accepting all alterations in the faith that had occurred in the western church.

This union earned some western help for the Emperor's army, but caused great division in the people of the Empire, with most of the hierarchs and theologians renouncing their signatures when they returned to Constantinople, stating they had been forced to sign the documents against their will. (Patriarch Joseph II died in Florence on June 10, 1439, before signing the decrees of the council.) The Council resulted in the creation of the Uniate (or Eastern Rite) churches, which retain Orthodox liturgy, but are in union with the Patriarchate of Rome, and are thus considered heretical by the Orthodox. The existence of the Uniate churches remains to this date one of the main problems in the relations between the Catholic Church and the Orthodox Church.

In 1448 the Church of Russia unilaterally declared its Autocephaly to protest the Ferrara-Florence Council. Ecumenical Patriarch Gregory III (1443-50) left Constantinople in the summer of 1450 and sought refuge in Rome. Due to the critical military situation, the Emperor did not permit the election of an Orthodox successor.

Constantinople fell to the Ottoman Turks on Tuesday, May 29, 1453. The last Roman Emperor, Constantine XI Paleologus (1448-53), was slain on the city's walls while fighting against the invaders.[3] Ottoman Sultan Mehmet II, adding "Emperor" to his titles after his victory, allowed the election of a new Ecumenical Patriarch on January 6, 1454, to whom he granted the role of National Leader of the Orthodox inside the Ottoman Empire, the Patriarchate henceforth being referred to as the Roman Patriarchate (trk Rum Patrikhanesi) by the Ottoman authorities. The position of the Ecumenical Patriarch was thus regularized, with it gaining a far greater role over the lives of the Orthodox population in the Empire than it had had under the Byzantine Emperors.

In 1459, after the Serbian lands passed under the control of the Ottomans, the Patriarchate of Peć was abolished, its territories being annexed to the Archbishopric of Ohrid.

The practice of paying a large sum of money to the Sultan on the election of every new Ecumenical Patriarch began in 1465. An additional monetary contribution was imposed on the Patriarchate in 1474, required to be paid yearly. Additional contributions could be arbitrarily requested by the Sultan at any time. Failure of any Patriarch to meet the demands of the Ottomans led to his immediate deposition. These requirements caused frequent changes in the succession of the Ecumenical Patriarchs, with sometimes the same Hierarchs being re-elected Patriarchs in turn, since the authorities earned a respectable levy for each new election. The last Patriarch to be elected while not yet a Hierarch (and thus needing to be consecrated as a bishop after his election), was Maximus III (1476-82). All subsequent Patriarchs were already Hierarchs, being Metropolitans of the Ecumenical Patriarchate before their election.

A Council attended by the Orthodox Patriarchs, calling itself Ecumenical, convened in 1484 at Constantinople. Presided over by Ecumenical Patriarch Symeon (1466, 1471-75, 1482-86), it rejected the Council of Ferrara-Florence, and condemned the addition of the "filioque" to the Nicene Creed as heresy.

In 1517 the Ottomans conquered Damascus, Jerusalem, and Alexandria, thus bringing all of the Orthodox Patriarchates within the borders of a single state. The Ecumenical Patriarchate immediately began playing a significant role in safeguarding the other Patriarchates, which later extended to the election of the Patriarchs themselves. Specifically, the Synod of the Ecumenical Patriarchate elected the Patriarchs of Alexandria from 1620-1865, the Patriarchs of Antioch from 1724-1885, and the Patriarchs of Jerusalem from 1661-1845.

In 1557 the Serbian Patriarchate of Peć was re-established.

In 1571, after the conquest of Cyprus by the Ottomans, the Ecumenical Patriarchate restored the Orthodox hierarchy there and reasserted the Autocephaly of the Cypriot Church.

In July 1577 the See of the Metropolitanate of Philadelphia was transferred to the city of Venice in order to care for the Orthodox of Italy and Western Europe. The See remained there officially until June 1712.

In 1582 Pope Gregory XIII (1572-85) corrected the Julian calendar by adopting what came to be known as the Gregorian calendar. This was accomplished by skipping ten days, with October 4, 1582 being followed by October 15. Roman Catholic countries soon adopted the new calendar; however, there were difficulties in persuading the Orthodox and the Protestants to use it (for example, Great Britain adopted it in 1752).

On January 26 (Julian date)/February 5 (Gregorian date), 1589, the Metropolitan of Moscow, Job or Iov (1586-1605), was elevated to the rank of Patriarch by Ecumenical Patriarch Jeremias II (1572-79, 1580-84, 1587-95), who was then visiting Moscow. The establishment of the Patriarchate of Russia and the simultaneous granting of Autocephaly to the Church of Russia was confirmed on February 12/22, 1593 by a Pan-Orthodox Council convened in Constantinople and attended by the Orthodox Patriarchs. The same Council examined the Gregorian calendar's unilateral imposition in the west, and found Rome's use of the new calendar for the calculation of the Easter date to be in violation of the First Ecumenical Council. That Council had decreed that Christian Easter should not be celebrated on the same date as the Jewish Easter, nor before the Jewish Easter, something that was possible if the new Gregorian calendar was used to calculate Easter. Thus, this change in the calculation of Easter in the West was condemned as heretical. The western belief in the existence of "purgatory" (officially adopted by Rome as dogma in 1254) was also condemned as heretical.

In 1628 Patriarch Cyril I Loucaris (1620-35, 1637-38) abandoned the Eastern Roman dating system which counted years since the "beginning of creation"; thus, year 7136 from creation was replaced with Year of the Lord 1628 in official Patriarchal documents.

On February 14/25, 1721 the Russian Czar Peter I (1682-1725) abolished the Patriarchate of Moscow, establishing a ruling Synod for the Russian Church. Due to the aggressive actions of the Uniates in Halep (Aleppo, in Syria) that made it impossible for the Patriarch of Antioch to install an Orthodox Metropolitan in the city, the Patriarchate of Antioch transferred the Metropolitanate of Halep (ancient Beroea or Veria in Syria) to the jurisdiction of the Ecumenical Patriarchate in November 1757.

In May 1763 the absolute rule of the Ecumenical Patriarch since 1454 came to an end, with the establishment of what came to be known as Elderism (Grk. Γεροντισμός). The seal of the Patriarchate was divided in four parts, and three of the Elder Metropolitans held three of them. Thus, the Patriarch could not make decisions alone, but had to secure the approval of the Synod. If all the Elder Metropolitans agreed that a Patriarch was unworthy, they could now request his deposition by the Ottoman authorities. The title of Elder was bestowed on the Metropolitans of eight Metropolitanates: Kaisaria, Ephesos, Iraklia, Kyzikos, Nikaia, Nikomidia, Chalkidon, and Derki.

On September 11/22, 1766, at the request of its hierarchs, the Patriarchate of Peć was abolished by the Ecumenical Patriarchate.[4] On January 16/27, 1767, the Autocephalous Archdiocese of Ohrid was abolished at the request of its hierarchs.[5] Their Metropolitanates were added to the eparchies of the Ecumenical Patriarchate, with the unofficial exception of the Metropolitanate of Montenegro—since the small mountainous area of Montenegro was not under Ottoman control, after 1766 its Metropolitanate unilaterally declared itself Autocephalous, with its Hierarchs henceforth traveling to Russia for consecration. These requests were made due to the debts both Sees had accumulated over the years, which their Hierarchs were now unable to service. With the integration of these jurisdictions to the Ecumenical Patriarchate, the debts became the responsibility of the Mother Church. When the Russian Empire annexed Crimea in 1783, the Ecumenical Patriarchate transferred the Metropolitanate of the area to the Russian Church.[6]

THE PERIOD AFTER 1800

After the Russian Empire completed its annexation of most of the Georgian states in May 1810, the Russian authorities abolished the Autocephaly of the Georgian Church, unilaterally annexing it on June 30/July 12, 1811.

The Greek revolution against Ottoman occupation began on March 25/April 6, 1821, causing the execution of Ecumenical Patriarch Gregory V (1797-98, 1806-08, 1818-21) by the Ottoman Turks on April 10/22, 1821, together with numerous Orthodox hierarchs in the Ottoman Empire, including every Orthodox prelate on the islands of Crete and Cyprus. The Ecumenical Patriarchate arranged for new hierarchs to be consecrated on Cyprus in December 1821, again reasserting the Autocephaly of the Cypriot Church.[7]

An autonomous Serbian Principality was created within the Ottoman Empire in 1830, and the Ecumenical Patriarchate granted autonomy to the Serbian Church on August 17/29, 1831. The very next day Ecumenical Patriarch Constantius I (1830-34) consecrated the new Head of the Serbian Church.[8]

Meanwhile, the Greek revolution had resulted in the creation of an independent Kingdom of Greece in 1832, with a king elected from the ruling dynasty of Bavaria, and Bavarian ministers being appointed to the most important ministries of the government. The Bavarians severed all relations between the Greek Metropolitanates and the Ecumenical Patriarchate, accusing the latter of being influenced by the Ottoman government; the Greek Church was unilaterally declared Autocephalous on July 23/August 4, 1833. The Ecumenical Patriarchate finally granted Autocephaly to the Church of Greece on June 29/July 11, 1850, relinquishing its Metropolitanates in that area.[9] The new Greek state called its citizens Hellenes, the name that the Ancient Greeks called themselves, in order to distinguish them from the Romans (Greek Orthodox) who lived inside the Ottoman Empire. Since during the next century most of the remaining "Romans" relocated to Greece, the term was slowly replaced by the word "Hellenic" (it should be noted that the word "Byzantine" was invented by western scholars in the sixteenth century, and was never actually used by the citizens of the Eastern Roman Empire).

The Dogma of the Immaculate Conception, considered heretic by the Orthodox, was adopted by Rome on November 26/December 8, 1854.

In 1856 the Sultan decreed that all his subjects were equal before the law, regardless of religion. This had the positive effect of abolishing the annual monetary contributions paid by the Patriarchate, which had greatly multiplied over the years, as well as the large monetary contribution paid by each Patriarch after his election.

New rules in the Ottoman Empire regarding the government of the Orthodox population were imposed on July 6/18, 1860. Elderism was abandoned, and representatives of the laity now participated in the elections of Patriarchs. This new practice was first used in the election of Ecumenical Patriarch Joachim II (1860-63, 1873-78) on October 4/16, 1860. The rules caused unrest among the Bulgarian subjects of the Empire, who believed that they were underrepresented in the election of the Ecumenical Patriarch.

In 1861 the new state of Romania was created, and its Prince confiscated any land belonging to the church. On December 2/14, 1864 he unilaterally declared the Romanian Church Autocephalous. Great Britain ceded the Ionian Islands to Greece in 1864, and the Ecumenical Patriarchate transferred the Islands' Metropolitanates[10] to the jurisdiction of the Church of Greece in July 1865.

The Dogma of the Papal Infallibility, considered heretic and blasphemous by the Orthodox, was adopted by Rome on July 6/18, 1870.

Negotiations regarding the new election rules continued to be carried out in Constantinople between the Bulgarians and the Ecumenical Patriarchate. However, the Bulgarians finally requested the creation of a Bulgarian Exarchate that would incorporate the Bulgarian people in the Ottoman Empire, including those living in cities where the Greek and Serbian Orthodox were predominant. This caused a deadlock in the negotiations, and led the Ottoman government to accept a proposition by the Bulgarians to establish an Autocephalous Bulgarian Exarchate on February 27/March 11, 1870. However, the Exarchate was established only in areas where the Bulgarian Orthodox constituted a majority of the Orthodox population.[11]

The Ecumenical Patriarchate declared that the practices of the Bulgarian Exarchate amounted to a new heresy, "Ethnophyletism," and, after further unfruitful negotiations, decided to defrock the hierarchs who had taken part in its creation. Since the Bulgarian politicians regarded this matter from a political viewpoint and considered the Exarchate a precursor to the necessity of a future Bulgarian state, they refused to recognize Constantinople's actions. The Patriarchate then excommunicated the defrocked hierarchs and convened an Orthodox Council in Constantinople (attended by the Patriarchs of Constantinople, Alexandria, Antioch, Jerusalem, the Archbishop of Cyprus, and other hierarchs), which on September 6/18, 1872 declared that the defrocked and excommunicated Bulgarian hierarchs were to be regarded as schismatic, along with all the clergy who were ordained by them, and any laity who kept communion with them and accepted their liturgies and sacraments.

Serbia became fully independent and annexed additional territory from the Ottoman Empire in 1878. On February 1/13, 1879, the Ecumenical Patriarchate transferred its Metropolitanates in the new Serbian lands[12] to the jurisdiction of the Church of Serbia, and on October 20/November 1, 1879 granted Autocephaly to the Serbian Church. The Ottoman Empire ceded Thessaly to Greece in 1881, and the Ecumenical Patriarchate transferred the area's Metropolitanates[13] to the jurisdiction of the Church of Greece in early May 1882.

Great Britain occupied Alexandria on June 29/July 11, 1882, and Cairo on September 1/13, 1882, bringing the Patriarchate of Alexandria[14] outside the borders of the Ottoman Empire. In spite of its failure to secure compensation for the state-confiscated church lands, the Ecumenical Patriarchate officially granted Autocephaly to the Romanian Church[15] on April 25/May 7, 1885. It also returned the Metropolitanate of Halep to the Patriarchate of Antioch[16] in August 1888.

On December 9/21, 1898, the Island of Crete became an autonomous state under Ottoman suzerainty. An agreement was reached with the Ecumenical Patriarchate to grant semi-autonomous status to the Metropolitanate of Crete, with the Metropolitan being elected by the Ecumenical Patriarchate out of three candidates submitted by the island's political authorities. This went into effect on October 14/27, 1900. Bulgaria became fully independent on September 22/October 5, 1908 and deported the Greek population and the Hierarchs appointed by the Ecumenical Patriarchate, unilaterally annexing the four Metropolitanates that remained inside the Bulgarian state at the time.[17]

After the Balkan Wars of 1912-13, all of the Metropolitanates of the Ecumenical Patriarchate located in Western Thrace, Macedonia, Epirus, and the Aegean Islands were now inside the "New Lands" annexed by Greece, Serbia, and Bulgaria, plus the territory reserved for the new Principality of Albania.[18] The Ecumenical Patriarchate declined to transfer these jurisdictions to the churches of these countries. Nevertheless, all the Metropolitanates inside the new Bulgarian lands were unilaterally annexed by the schismatic Bulgarian Church.[19]

Following the fall of the Czar in Russia, and six months before the communists took control of the government, the Georgian Church[20] regained its Autocephaly on March 12/25, 1917, and the Russian Patriarchate was restored by the Russian Synod on August 28/September 10, 1917. During the First World War, an allied force under British command set out from Egypt, and captured Jerusalem on November 28/December 11, 1917, and Damascus on September 18/October 1, 1918, removing the Patriarchates of Jerusalem[21] and Antioch from the Ottoman Empire's control.

Meanwhile, civil war ensued in the former Russian Empire, causing large parts of it to be annexed by other countries or to become independent republics. The final communist victory led to violent persecutions of the clergy in Russia. Churches were destroyed, hierarchs were exiled or executed, and believers were ridiculed and discouraged from participating into religious life. The Russian Patriarchate, with Patriarch Tikhon I (1917-25) imprisoned, was suddenly unable to maintain control over or even communicate with its eparchies outside Russia. It was thus decided to accept the many requests for autonomy that came from abroad. Autonomy was granted to the Orthodox Church in Estonia on June 15/28, 1920, the Orthodox Church in Finland in February 1921, and the Orthodox Church in Latvia in July 1921, while the Orthodox Church in Poland was given semi-autonomy in the same year.

In the Balkans, emissaries of the Orthodox hierarchy from the newly formed Kingdom of Serbs, Croats, and Slovenes (later Yugoslavia) visited the Ecumenical Patriarchate, requesting the re-establishment of the Serbian Patriarchate and the transfer of the Ecumenical Patriarchate's ten remaining Metropolitanates in the former states of Serbia and Bosnia-Herzegovina to the Serbian Church.[22] The Holy Synod agreed to both requests on March 19/April 1, 1919, and the formal re-establishment of the Serbian Patriarchate occurred in Belgrade on August 30/September 12, 1920. The new Patriarchate also included the former unilaterally autonomous Metropolitanate of Montenegro. The official papers for the transfer of the ten Metropolitanates of the Ecumenical Patriarchate to the Serbian Church were signed on February 22/March 7, 1922, and for the elevation of the Serbian Church to Patriarchate status[23] on February 24/March 9, 1922.

The Church of the newly created state of Albania was unilaterally declared Autocephalous on September 12/25, 1922, and the Greek Metropolitans who had been expelled from the country a year earlier were never permitted to return. The end of the First World War signaled the breakdown of the Ottoman Empire. Constantinople was occupied by the Allies on October 30/November 12, 1918. In May 1919 the area of Asia Minor around Smyrna (Izmir) was occupied by Greek forces, and on July 28/August 10, 1920 the area of Thrace (both East and West) was officially annexed by Greece. The Greek-Turkish border was only 50 kilometers from Constantinople.

Greek forces had occupied most of Eastern Asia Minor (including Eskisehir and Afyon Karahisar, 200 kilometers from the Turkish headquarters in Ankara), when a devastating counteroffensive by the Turkish forces on August 15/28, 1922 broke through the Greek/Turk front, causing its collapse. The evacuation of Greek forces from Asia Minor followed, accompanied by a large part of the Orthodox population who lived in those areas. Any Orthodox who remained in the former Greek-occupied areas were executed or imprisoned by the advancing Turkish army. Negotiations for a peace treaty between Greece and the new Turkish republican government ensued, leading to an agreement which returned Eastern Thrace and the Aegean Islands of Imvros (today Gokceada) and Tenedos (today Bosca Ada) to Turkey. The Greek Orthodox population of Eastern Thrace was relocated to Greece in October, and the area was delivered to Turkey on November 12/25, 1922.

The new Turkish government abolished the Sultanate on October 19/November 1, 1922, and the last Sultan, Mehmet VI, left the country on November 4/17, 1922. The Allies finally evacuated Constantinople on September 23, 1923, and Turkish forces entered the city on October 6. The declaration of the new Turkish Republic followed on October 29, 1923, with its capital in Ankara, a city in the heart of Asia Minor.

Since the Metropolitanates of the Ecumenical Patriarchate were diminishing rapidly in number, new Metropolitanates for the Orthodox Diaspora were established abroad. The Metropolitanate of Thyatira and Great Britain was established on March 24/April 6, 1922 (promoted to an Archdiocese in 1954) to serve the Orthodox in Western Europe, the Autonomous Archdiocese of North and South America was established on April 26/May 9, 1922, and the Metropolitanate of Australia was established on March 7, 1924 (promoted to the Archdiocese of Australia and New Zealand on August 25, 1959).

At the same time, one after another, the Churches of the newly created European states were asking to be placed under the protection of the Ecumenical Patriarchate. The Church of Czechoslovakia was declared Autonomous on March 3, 1923, the Churches of Finland and Estonia were accepted as Autonomous under the jurisdiction of the Ecumenical Patriarchate on July 7, 1923, and the Church of Poland[24] was declared Autocephalous on November 13, 1924.

In 1923 an agreement between the Greek and Turkish government led to a mutual exchange of population. All remaining Orthodox living in Turkey were relocated to Greece, and all Muslims living in Greece were moved to Turkey. The two exceptions were the Greeks living in Constantinople proper and also on the Aegean islands of Imvros and Tenedos, who would remain under Turkish jurisdiction; and the Muslims of Western Thrace, who would remain in Greece. After this agreement, the Turkish government ceased to recognize the "Ecumenical" status of the Patriarchate, maintaining that the "Roman Patriarch" was only the leader of the few thousand Orthodox remaining in Turkey. This relocation left thirty-eight of the Patriarchate's forty-two Metropolitanates in Asia Minor and Eastern Thrace without a flock;[25] their Metropolitans were forced to stay in Constantinople or relocate to Greece. The hostile policy adopted by the Turkish state towards its remaining Greek Orthodox population after 1955, the year when Greek-Turkish relations deteriorated over the issue of Cyprus, led to the further dimunition in the Ecumenical Patriarchate's local flock, with an estimated population of just 3,500 communicants remaining today.

On October 1924 the Ecumenical Patriarchate created fourteen new temporal Metropolitanates inside the New Lands of Greece in order to accommodate its hierarchs who were forced to relocate to Greece. This was accomplished by dividing some of its existing Metropolitanates into two parts, but most of these new jurisidictions were abolished in later years.[26]

In an attempt to achieve a common calendar worldwide, political authorities in the Orthodox countries began to adopt the Gregorian calendar. Thus, in Bulgaria March 31, 1916 was followed by April 14, in Russia January 31, 1918 was followed by February 14, in Romania March 31, 1919 was followed by April 14, and in Greece February 15, 1923 was followed by March 1 (Serbia also made the change in 1919). Turkey abolished the Islamic calendar and officially adopted the Gregorian calendar on January 1, 1927. Since some political and Orthodox feasts in Greece were interconnected and customarily co-celebrated, their ensuing separation due to the use of different calendars by the political authorities and the Greek Orthodox Church became a cause of great concern.

An All-Orthodox Council was convened in Constantinople between May 10-June 8, 1923 in order to address the issue (the Russian Church was represented by Anastasy of Kisinov, today Chisinau in Moldova, and Alexander of North America). The Council decreed that the Orthodox Churches were permitted to adopt the New Calendar, so long as they retained the Julian calendar for the calculation of the date of Easter, as required by the First Ecumenical Council. On February 23, 1924, the Ecumenical Patriarchate notified the other Churches that its Synod had decided to adopt the New Calendar on March 10, 1924. Thus, in the Patriarchate of Constantinople, the Church of Greece, and the Church of Cyprus, March 9, 1924 was followed by March 23. (However, the Autonomous Monks' State of Mount Athos was excluded from the change, and still uses the Julian calendar.)

In the Church of Romania, September 30, 1924 was followed by October 14, in the Patriarchate of Alexandria, September 30, 1928 was followed by October 14, and in the Patriarchate of Antioch, September 30, 1929 was followed by October 14. The Church of Bulgaria (which was not invited to the Pan-Orthodox Council of 1923 due to its Schismatic status at the time) adopted the New Calendar in 1968. The Church of Serbia initially agreed to adopt the New Calendar, but although Patriarch Dimitrije informed the Ecumenical Patriarchate of his Church's decision in his letter of January 18, 1924, the Patriarchate of the Serbs continues to use the Julian calendar to this day.

In the Church of Russia, Patriarch Tikhon tried to adopt the New Calendar, but, with the Church being persecuted by the communists, the change could not be made universally, and after Tikhon's repose on April 7, 1925 the effort was abandoned, with any areas that had adopted the New Calendar reverting back to the Julian Calendar. The Church of Russia still uses the Julian calendar today. Also under communist persecution, the Church of Georgia tried to adopt the New Calendar twice, in 1923 and 1927, but on both occasions the negative reaction of the believers forced it to re-adopt the Julian Calendar, which it still uses today. The Patriarchate of Jerusalem refused to adopt the New Calendar on the grounds that this could cause problems in the delicate balance with other denominations over the use of the Holy Shrines, and continues to use the Julian calendar to this day.

On February 4, 1925, in coordination with the Ecumenical Patriarchate, the Autocephalous Church of Romania was raised to the status of Patriarchate.[27] In 1926 the Turkish authorities officially changed the name of Constantinople to Istanbul, as part of a policy to erase all Greek city names still used in the country. "Istanbul" is a corruption of the Greek phrase "is tin Polin," meaning "to the City"[28]. On September 4, 1928, the management of all of the Ecumenical Patriarchate's Metropolitanates located inside the New Lands of the Greek state were entrusted to the Church of Greece.[29]

On December 14, 1930, some of the Ukrainian Parishes in the USA accepted the jurisdiction of the Ecumenical Patriarch. On January 10, 1931 due to the internal discord which then impeded the normal functioning of the Archdiocese of North and South America, its Autonomy was abolished by the Ecumenical Patriarchate. On February 17, 1931, the Russian Exarchate of Western Europe accepted the jurisdiction of the Ecumenical Patriarch.

In 1932 negotiations between the Ecumenical Patriarchate and the Schismatic Bulgarian Church were held in Jerusalem, and the two churches reached an agreement for healing the schism. However, the Bulgarian state backed away from the agreement in 1934 due to political reasons. In February 1936, the Church of Latvia was accepted as Autonomous under the jurisdiction of the Ecumenical Patriarchate. On January 28, 1937, a Ukrainian Diocese in the USA accepted the jurisdiction of the Ecumenical Patriarch. On March 30, 1937, after lengthy negotiations, the Orthodox Church of Albania was declared Autocephalous by the Ecumenical Patriarchate. On September 14, 1938, the Carpatho-Russian parishes in the USA, which had previously recognized the Pope, returned to Orthodoxy, accepting the jurisdiction of the Ecumenical Patriarch.

After the annexation of Estonia and Latvia by the Soviet Union in 1941, the Autonomies of their Churches were abolished in March 30, 1941. The occupation of these countries by Germany enabled Estonia to regain its Autonomy on June 30, 1941 and Latvia on July 20, 1941. After the Soviet Union expelled the Germans, Latvian Church lost its Autonomy again on July 15, 1942, and the Estonians on March 9, 1945. The Heads of these Autonomous Churches lived in exile for the rest of their lives.

After the fascist government fell in Bulgaria, negotiations resumed in February 1945 between the Ecumenical Patriarchate and the Schismatic Church of Bulgaria, based on the previous negotiations of 1932. Agreement was reached in just a few days, and on February 22, 1945, the Ecumenical Patriarchate annulled the Schism of the Bulgarian Church and declared it Autocephalous. After Bulgarian forces evacuated the Yugoslavian state of Macedonia in 1945, the new communist government of Yugoslavia refused to permit the Serbian Hierarchs who had been expelled by the Bulgarians to return, pressuring the Serbian Patriarchate to create an Autonomous Church there.

On April 17, 1947, the new communist government in Poland deposed the Orthodox Metropolitan and forced the Orthodox Church to revert to Russian control. On June 22, 1948, the Patriarchate of Moscow declared the Church of Poland to be Autocephalous and arranged the election of a new Metropolitan. In 1948 the new communist government in Czechoslovakia forced the Archbishop of the Autonomous Orthodox Church to retire and dissolved the Archdiocese. On August 31, 1950 an Albanian Diocese in the USA accepted the jurisdiction of the Ecumenical Patriarch. On November 23, 1951, the Patriarchate of Moscow declared the Orthodox Church of Czechoslovakia as Autocephalous and appointed a new Archbishop. The Ecumenical Patriarchate did not recognize this act, and continued to regard the Church there as Autonomous.

On May 10, 1953, the Bulgarian Church was unilaterally elevated to Patriarchal status. The Ecumenical Patriarchate refused to recognize this action. On October 6, 1958, under pressure from the political authorities of Yugoslavia, the Serbian Patriarchate granted Autonomy to the Orthodox Church in the Yugoslav Republic of Macedonia by creating the Autonomous Archdiocese of Ohrid and Scopje. On July 27, 1961, after an official Bulgarian request, the Ecumenical Patriarchate formally bestowed the title of Patriarch on the head of the Church of Bulgaria.[30]

On February 5, 1963 the Archdiocese of Thyatera and Great Britain was divided into three parts: the Metropolitanate of Thyatera and Great Britain, the Metropolitanate of France, and the Metropolitanate of Germany. Few days later, on February 17, 1963, a Metropolitanate of Austria and Hungary was created.

On January 5, 1964, Ecumenical Patriarch Athenagoras I (1948-72) met with Pope Paul VI (1963-78) in Jerusalem. This was the first such meeting in 525 years. The two Patriarchs declared that the mutual anathemas of 1054 should be annulled. Thus, after 911 years, on December 7, 1965, during simultaneous ceremonies held in Rome and Constantinople, the anathemas exchanged between the two senior Patriarchates of Christianity were finally revoked. An exchange of visits followed, with Pope Paul VI (visiting Constantinople on July 25, 1967, and Ecumenical Patriarch Athenagoras visiting Rome on October 26 of the same year. The last Patriarch of Rome to visit Constantinople had been Constantine I (708-15), who had met with Ecumenical Patriarch Cyrus (705-11) in 710 and 711—1256 years earlier!

On July 16, 1967, the Autonomous Orthodox Church in the Yugoslavian Republic of Macedonia unilaterally declared itself Autocephalous; it was declared schismatic by the Serbian Patriarchate, and the other Orthodox Churches then ceased communion with the Archdiocese of Ohrid and Scopje, a state which continues to this day.

On November 22, 1967, the communist government in Albania outlawed all religious practices in the country. All hierarchs and clergy were imprisoned, all churches closed, and the official structure of the Orthodox Church in Albania was completely annihilated. Even the simple gesture of making the sign of the cross could now led to multi-year prison sentences. The last previous official persecution of Christians in the area had occurred at the time of the Roman Emperor Diocletian (284-305)!

On February 24, 1968, the Metropolitanate of Thyatera and Great Britain was again promoted to an Archdiocese. The Metropolitanate of Belgium and the Metropolitanate of Sweden were established on August 12, 1969, the Metropolitanate of New Zealand on January 1, 1970, and the Metropolitanate of Helvetia (Switzerland) on October 2, 1982. On March 3, 1990, the Ecumenical Patriarchate formally bestowed the status of Patriarchate to the Church of Georgia.[31] On April 1, 1990 the Ukrainian Orthodox Church of Canada, and on March 11, 1995 the Ukrainian Orthodox Church of America, Australia, and Western Europe accepted the jurisdiction of the Ecumenical Patriarch.

On October 1, 1990, the Patriarchate of Moscow[32] granted Autonomy to the Church of Ukraine; however, part of the Ukrainian Church unilaterally declared itself Autocephalous in June 1990, and another part declared itself Autocephalous in April 1992. The division in the Ukrainian Church remains unhealed to this day.

On November 7, 1990 the government of Albania relaxed the enforcement of its laws against religious practice in the country. On January 8, 1991 the Ecumenical Patriarchate appointed Anastasius, Titular Bishop of Androusa, previously head of the missionary activities of the Patriarchate of Alexandria in Kenya, as its Exarch in the country, entrusting him with overseeing the re-establishment of the Autocephalous Church in Albania. On April 29, 1991 a provisional constitutional law allowing free religious practice came into effect. The Exarch secured permission to enter Albania in July 1991, and his tireless work and zeal for the resurrection of the Church led to his election as Archbishop of the Albanian Orthodox Church on June 24, 1992. The work carried out since that date for the reorganization of the Albanian Church has been phenomenal.[33]

On November 5, 1991 the Metropolitanate of Italia was established (being renamed Metropolitanate and Italia and Malta on April 20, 2005). On February 22, 1996, following the renewed independence of Estonia and at the request of the Estonian Orthodox, the Ecumenical Patriarchate restored the Autonomy of the Estonian Orthodox Church; however, the Patriarchate of Moscow did not recognize this action, and still maintains its own jurisdiction in Estonia.

On July 30, 1996, the Archdiocese of North and South America was divided into four parts: the Archdiocese of America, the Metropolitanate of Toronto for the Orthodox of Canada, the Metropolitanate of Buenos Aires for the Orthodox in South America, and the Metropolitanate of Panamá for the Orthodox of Central America and the islands of the Caribbean Sea (renamed Metropolitanate of México on October 13, 2005). On the same date the Metropolitanate of Hong Kong for the Orthodox of the Far East was created.

On August 27, 1998, the Ecumenical Patriarchate granted Autocephaly to the Orthodox Church of the Czech Lands and Slovakia.[34] On January 20, 2003 the Metropolitanate of Spain and Portugal was established, and on April 20, 2004, the Metropolitanate of Korea (including Japan). On January 9, 2008 the Metropolitanate of Singapore was established.

On May 24, 2005 the Serbian Patriarchate re-established the Autonomous Archdiocese of Ohrid in the Former Yugoslav Republic of Macedonia, appointing new hierarchy in opposition to the Schismatic Church. The local authorities supported the schismatics, however, and proceeded to arrest the canonical head appointed by the Serbian Patriarchate and to demolish the churches under his jurisdiction.

The most significant problem that the Ecumenical Patriarchate faces today is the policies of the Turkish authorities, which continue to hinder its operation. Turkey does not recognize the Patriarchate's Ecumenical role; it maintains that it serves only the handful of adherents that have remained in Turkey, and imposes political standards on a religious issue. All future Patriarchs are required by law to be Turkish citizens, making it almost impossible for Hierarchs from the worldwide eparchies of the Ecumenical Patriarchate to be considered in the election process. Thus, with the numbers of Orthodox citizens in Turkey ever dwindling, the future presence of the Patriarchate in the country becomes endangered. Furthermore, most of the Church lands of the Ecumenical Patriarchate in Turkey have been confiscated, and its few remaining properties in Istanbul face the prospect of expropriation. In August 1971 the Turkish authorities closed the Theological Seminary of Halki Island (Trk Heybeli Ada), once attended by students from all the Orthodox Churches in the area, making it impossible for the Patriarchate to educate its future Hierarchs without sending them abroad (few of these students return to Turkey). Despite repeated requests to the Turkish government by the Patriarchate and significant pressure from the European Union and the United States, the Halki Seminary remains closed.

The Patriarchate remains today the only institution inside the Turkish Republic that existed before the establishment of the Ottoman Empire. The Orthodox hope that the Turkish authorities will realize that the presence of the Ecumenical Patriarchate enriches Turkey and does not constitute any threat to the Turkish state. By embracing the Patriarchate and allowing it to perform its religious functions freely, Turkey will bury the ghosts of the past, and demonstrate its willingness to become part of the European family of nations.

NOTES

1. The town of Megara is located in Attica, Central Greece, 40 km west of Athens.
2. The unilateral alteration of this Creed by the Patriarchs of Rome due to the addition of the "filioque" clause led to schism in 1054. (The filioque clause is the phrase "and from the Son", added to the Nicene Creed verse which states that the Holy Spirit proceeds from the Father.)
3. Tuesday remains up to this day an unlucky day in Greek folklore.
4. The eleven Metropolitanates added to the Ecumenical Patriarchate from the Patriarchate of Peć were: Veligradion (Belgrade), Ouzitsa (Užice), Nyssa (Niš), Novipazarion (Novi Pazar) [these are today inside Serbia]; Prezreni (Prizren) [today inside Kosovo]; Vosna (Bosnia), Ersekion (Herzegovina), Svornikion (Zvornik) [today inside Bosnia-Herzegovina]; Skopia (Skopje) [today inside the Former Yugoslav Republic of Macedonia]; Samokovion (Samokov), Kestentilion (Kyustendil) [today inside Bulgaria].
5. The thirteen Metropolitanates added to the Ecumenical Patriarchate from Archdiocese of Ohrid were: Kastoria, Vodena (Edessa), Moglena (Florina), Sisanion, Grevena (today inside Greece); Prespes and Ohrid (Ochrid), Pelagonia (Bitola), Devres (Debar), Velissos (Veles), Stromnitsa (Strumica) [today inside the Former Yugoslav Republic of Macedonia]; Gkora and Dyrachion (Durrës), Velegrades (Berat), Koritsa (Korçë) [today inside Albania].
6. The Metropolitanate of Gothia and Kaphas.
7. Today the Church of Cyprus encompasses nine Metropolitanates and three Dioceses.
8. The Ecumenical Patriarchate created the Autonomous Serbian Church by relinquishing two of its Metropolitanates: Veligradion (Belgrade) and Ouzitsa (Užice), with its subordinate Diocese of Sapaski (Šabac).
9. The twenty-one Metropolitanates, one Archdiocese and twenty-two Dioceses of the Ecumenical Patriarchate that were seized by the new Greek Kingdom in 1833 were as follows: in central Greece: Metropolitanate of Athens and Levadia with its subordinate five Dioceses: Skyros, Talantion and Diavlia, Karystos, Mendenitsa, Salona (Amfissa); Metropolitanate of Thiva (Thebes); Metropolitanate of New Patra (Ypati); Metropolitanate of Evripos (Euboea); the Nafpaktos part of the Metropolitanate of Nafpaktos and Arta; three Dioceses (and part of a fourth) of the Metropolitanate of Larissa: part of Zitounion (Lamia) and Almyros, Litza and Agrapha, Skiathos and Skopelos, Lidorikion. In the Peloponnese: Metropolitanate of Korinthos (Corinth) with its subordinate Diocese of Damala and Polyfengon; Metropolitanate of Old Patra with its three subordinated Dioceses: Koroni, Kernitzi and Kalavryta, Methoni; Metropolitanate of Monemvasia with its seven subordinated Dioceses: Androuvista, Androussa, Lagia, Mani, Milea, Platza, Elos; Metropolitanate of Lakedaimonia (Lacedaemon) with its four subordinated Dioceses: Vrestheni, Karyoupolis, Maltzini, Nafplion and Argos; Metropolitanate of Tripolis and Amykles; Metropolitanate of Christianoupolis; Metropolitanate of Zarnata; Metropolitanate of Oleni (Ilia); Metropolitanate of Reontas and Prastos; Archdiocese of Dimitsana. In the South Aegean Islands: Metropolitanate of Aigina, Ydra and Poros; Metropolitanate of Andros; Metropolitanate of Tinos; Metropolitanate of Santorini (Thira); Metropolitanate of Tzia and Thermia (Kea and Kythnos); Metropolitanate of Paronaxia (Paros and Naxos); Metropolitanate of Sifnos and

Milos. Note that the new Autocephalous Church of Greece abandoned the above ecclesiastical structure on November 20/December 2, 1833 and replaced it with a new system of ten permanent and thirty temporary Dioceses. This was again changed on July 10/22, 1852 to a system of ten Archdioceses and thirteen Dioceses. Today the Church of Greece encompasses eighty Metropolitanates, thirty-six of which are Metropolitanates of the New Lands (see note 29).

10. The four Metropolitanates, one Archdiocese and two Dioceses of the Ecumenical Patriarchate in the Ionian Islands were: Metropolitanate of Kerkyra (Corfu), with its subordinate Diocese of Paxi; Metropolitanate of Lefkas and Agia Mavra; Metropolitanate of Kephallinia, with its subordinate Diocese of Ithaki; Metropolitanate of Zakynthos; and the Archdiocese of Kythira.

11. The eleven Metropolitanates and one Diocese of the Ecumenical Patriarchate which were seized by the Bulgarian Exarchate were: Metropolitanate of Tornovo (Veliko Tarnovo), with its two subordinate Dioceses of Vratsa and Loftsa (Lovech); Metropolitanate of Sophia (Sofia); Metropolitanate of Vidyni (Vidin); Metropolitanate of Drystra (Silistra); Metropolitanate of Tzervenos (Cherven); Metropolitanate of Samakovion (Samokov); Metropolitanate of Preslava (Preslav); Metropolitanate of Kestentilion (Kyustendil); Metropolitanate of Nyssa (Niš); and Metropolitanate of Nyssava (Pirot). They were canonically relinquished to the Bulgarian Church only in 1945, when the Schism was healed (except Nyssa and Nyssava—see note 12).

12. The Ecumenical Patriarchate had two Metropolitanates in the new Serbian lands: The Metropolitanates of Nyssa (Nis) and of Nyssava (Pirot). However they both were ruled by a hierarch belonging to the schismatic Bulgarian Exarchate. The Hierarch announced his repentance and requested to be accepted by the Serbian Church. The Serbian Church agreed to his request and after acquiring the permission of the Ecumenical Patriarchate, received the Hierarch under its jurisdiction.

13. The four Metropolitanates and five Dioceses of the Ecumenical Patriarchate in Thessaly were: Metropolitanate of Larissa, with its four subordinate Dioceses of Trikki (Trikala), of Stagi, of Thavmakos, and of Gardikion; Metropolitanate of Demetrias (Volos) and Zagora; Metropolitanate of Phanariofersala (Phanarion and Fersala); Metropolitanate of Arta; and the Diocese of Platamon (subordinated to the Metropolitanate of Thessaloniki).

14. For long periods during the Arab and Ottoman occupation the only Hierarch in the Patriarchate of Alexandria was its Patriarch. Although titular Hierarchs appeared intermittently as his assistants, the first actual Metropolitanates in the modern era were established in 1908. Today the Patriarchate of Alexandria encompasses eighteen Metropolitanates and seven Dioceses scattered over the African continent (with five of its Metropolitanates located inside Egypt).

15. The Ecumenical Patriarchate created the new Autocephalous Romanian Church by relinquishing two of its Metropolitanates: Oungrovlachia (Hungaro-Walachia), with its three subordinate Dioceses of Rimnikon (Ramnic), of Bozeou (Buzau), and of Artzi (Arges); and the Metropolitanate of Moldavia with its three subordinate Dioceses of Romanon (Roman), of Chousion (Husi), and of Radaouzion (Radauti).

16. Today the Patriarchate of Antioch encompasses five Metropolitanates in Syria, six in Lebanon, one in Iraq, and three in Turkey (which have remained vacant for nine decades).

17. The four Metropolitanates of the Ecumenical Patriarchate seized by the Bulgarian Exarchate in 1908 were: Philippoupolis (Plovdiv), Mesimvria (Nesebur), Anchialos (Pomorie), and Varna.

18. The Dodecanese Islands in the southeastern Aegean were occupied by Italy and annexed by Greece after World War II. Their Metropolitanates still remain under the jurisdiction of the Ecumenical Patriarchate.

19. The two Metropolitanates of the Ecumenical Patriarchate seized by the Bulgarian Exarchate in 1913 were: Sozoagathopolis (Sozopol and Akhtopol) and Lititza (Ivaylovgrad).

20. The Russian Church finally recognized Georgian Autocephaly on October 31, 1943.

21. The Patriarchate of Jerusalem encompasses today two Metropolitanates in Israel, one Metropolitanate in Jordan, and the Autonomous Archdiocese of Mount Sinai in Egypt. The Brotherhood of the Holy Sepulchre is currently headed by ten Metropolitans (seven of them titular) and ten Archbishops (all titular).

22. The ten Metropolitanates of the Ecumenical Patriarchate that were transferred to the jurisdiction of the Serbian Church in 1920 were: Bosnia, Herzegovina, Zvornik, Banja Luka and Bihac (all these are today inside Bosnia-Herzegovina); Raskoprezreni (Raska and Prizren, today inside Kosovo); Skopia (Skopje), Prespes and Ochrid (Krusevo), Pelagonia (Bitola), Devres (Debar) and Velissos (Veles), Stromnitsa (Strumica), the northern part of Vodena (Edessa), the northern part of the Diocese of Polyani (Dojran) (all these are today inside the Former Yugoslav Republic of Macedonia).

23. Today the Patriarchate of the Serbs encompasses thirteen Dioceses in Serbia, four Dioceses and one Metropolitanate in Croatia, four Dioceses and one Metropolitanate in Bosnia-Herzegovina, one Diocese and one Metropolitanate in Montenegro, plus four Dioceses under the Autonomous Archdiocese of Ohrid inside the Former Yugoslav Republic of Macedonia.

24. The Orthodox Church of Poland today encompasses five Dioceses.

25. The Metropolitanates of the Ecumenical Patriarchate inside the borders of today's Turkey which still have Orthodox flock, and whose Metropolitans are permitted by the Turkish authorities to reside in their Sees, are: Derki (in Eastern Thrace, comprising part of the suburbs of modern Istanbul), Chalkidon (in Asia Minor, comprising part of the suburbs of modern Istanbul, on the Asian side of the Bosporus strait), Imvros and Tenedos (islands of the Northern Aegean, renamed Gokceada and Bosca Ada by the Turkish authorities), Pringiponnisa (Princes' Islands, renamed Kuzil Adalar by the Turkish authorities, a small cluster of islands inside the Sea of Marmara, near the Bosporus Strait).

26. The temporary Metropolitanates established in October 1924 were: in Epirus: Metsovon (an additional temporary Metropolitanate of Philiatai and Giromerion was established in September 3, 1925). In Macedonia: New Pelagonia, Giannitsa and Goumenissa, Langada, Ardamerion, Nigrita, Zichna, Kavala. In Western Thrace: New Orestias, Souflion. In the North Aegean Islands: Thasos, Plomarion, Kardamyla, Ikaria.

27. Today the Patriarchate of Romania encompasses six Metropolitanates, four Archdioceses, and twenty Dioceses in Romania, plus one Metropolitanate and three Dioceses in Moldova.

28. The Eastern Romans in their everyday speech abbreviated the name "Konstantinoupolis" to just Polis (City), using phrases like "we will go to the City" when referring to their capital. The last part of that phrase, "to the City" or in Greek, "is tin Polin," was adopted by the Arabs, who started calling the Roman capital "Istinpolin." In the following centuries the name was further corrupted to "Istanbul."

29. There were forty-seven Metropolitanates in the New Lands at that time, due to the creation of some temporary Metropolitanates a few years ago (see note 26). Today the thirty-six Metropolitanates of the New Lands are as per the list in SECTION P.

30. The Patriarchate of Bulgaria today encompasses twelve Metropolitanates inside Bulgaria.

31. The Patriarchate of Georgia today encompasses thirty-six eparchies inside Georgia.

32. The Patriarchate of Russia today encompasses: forty-six eparchies in European Russia, twenty-two eparchies in Siberia, eleven eparchies in Belarus, three eparchies in Kazakhstan, six eparchies in Moldova, forty-four eparchies in Ukraine, and one each in Lithuania, Latvia, Estonia, Azerbaijan, and Uzbekistan. It should be noted that in the Patriarchates of Russia and Georgia, Hierarchs of Eparchies are usually consecrated initially as Bishops, and later promoted (in some cases) to Archbishops and/or Metropolitans, according to seniority and merit. Thus, these Churches are divided into "Eparchies," the titles of their Hierarchs alternating between Bishop, Archbishop, and/or Metropolitan.

33. The Orthodox Church of Albania today encompasses three Metropolitanates.

34. The Orthodox Church of Czechia and Slovakia today encompasses two Dioceses in the Czech Republic and two Dioceses in Slovakia.

THE ECUMENICAL PATRIARCHS: A CATALOGUE

Archbishops of Constantinople, New Rome, and Ecumenical Patriarchs

The treatment given to the catalogs of Metropolitans, as mentioned in the Preface to Part II, apply to this list as well, with the following modifications: the previous positions of Patriarchs are mentioned even if they were not hierarchs prior to their election (*i.e.*, monks, deacons, priests). The full secular name of each Patriarch is also listed, when known, instead of just the surname. The following abbreviations are used: c. (circa), b. (beginning), m. (middle), e. (end). Further information pertaining to specific sections of the catalog is included as notes.

A. BISHOPS OF BYZANTIUM

1. Andrew (Apostle)	Ανδρέας ο Απόστολος	c.36 – c.38	d. 60/70
2. Stachys	Στάχυς	c.38 – c.54+	d. 54?
3. Onesimus	Ονήσιμος	c.54 – c.68+	d. 68?
4. Polycarp I	Πολύκαρπος Α'	c.71 – c.89+	d. 89?
5. Plutarch	Πλούταρχος	c.89 – c.105+	d. 105?
6. Sedecion	Σεδεκίων	c.105 – c.114+	d. 114?
7. Diogenes	Διογένης	c.114 – c.129+	d. 129?
8. Eleutherius	Ελευθέριος	c.129 – c.136+	d. 136?
9. Felix	Φήλιξ	c.136 – c.141+	d. 141?
10. Polycarp II	Πολύκαρπος Β'	c.141 – c.144+	d. 144?
11. Athenodorus	Αθηνόδωρος	c.144 – c.148+	d. 148?
12. Euzoius	Ευζώιος	c.148 – c.154+	d. 154?
13. Laurentius	Λαυρέντιος	c.154 – c.166+	d. 166?
14. Alypius	Αλύπιος	c.166 – c.169+	d. 169?
15. Pertinax	Περτίναξ	c.169 – c.187+	d. 187?
16. Olympianus	Ολυμπιανός	c.187 – c.198+	d. 198?
17. Mark I	Μάρκος Α'	c.198 – c.211+	d. 211?
18. Philadelphus	Φιλάδελφος	c.211 – c.217+	d. 217?
19. Cyriacus I	Κυριακός Α'	c.217 – c.233+	d. 233?
20. Castinus	Καστίνος	c.233 – c.240+	d. 240?
21. Eugene I	Ευγένιος Α'	c.240 – c.265+	d. 265?
22. Titus	Τίτος	c.265 – c.271+	d. 271?
23. Dometius	Δομέτιος	c.271 – c.284+	d. 284?
24. Rufinus	Ρουφίνος	c.284 – c.293+	d. 293?

25. Probus	Πρόβος		c.293 – c.306+	d. 306?
26. Metrophanes I	Μητροφάνης Α'		c.306 – 4 Jun 314+	d. 314
see note 1				

B. ARCHBISHOPS OF CONSTANTINOPLE

27. Alexander	Αλέξανδρος		c.summer 314 – Aug 337+	d. 337
(ex priest) Archbishop of Constantinople after 1 May 330				
28. Paul I	Παύλος Α'	(1st time)	autumn 337 – end 339	d. 351?
(ex priest) deposed and exiled				
29. Eusebius	Ευσέβιος		end 339 – end 341+	d. 341
(ex b.Nikomidia) Arian				
---. Paul I	Παύλος Α'	(2nd time)	end 341 – beg 342	d. 351?
(ex former a.Constantinople) deposed and exiled				
30. Macedonius I	Μακεδόνιος Α' (1st time)		beg 342 – beg 346	d. 364?
(ex deacon) Arian, deposed				
---. Paul I	Παύλος Α'	(3rd time)	beg 346 – c.Sep 351	d. 351?
(ex former a.Constantinople) deposed and exiled to Armenia, possibly Nov 351++ see note 2				
---. Macedonius I	Μακεδόνιος Α' (2nd time)		c.Sep 351 – 27 Jan 360	d. 364?
(ex former a.Constantinople) Arian, deposed				
31. Eudoxius	Ευδόξιος		27 Jan 360 – beg 370+	d. 370
(ex a.Antioch) Arian				
32. Demophilus	Δημόφιλος		beg 370 – 27 Nov 380	d. 385?
(ex b.Veria) Arian, deposed				
33. Evagrius	Ευάγριος		beg 370	d. 374?
(ex priest?) in opposition to Demophilus, deposed and exiled to Kyzikos or Vizyi				
34. Maximus I	Μάξιμος Α'		end 379/beg 380	d≥382
Cynic (ex priest) deposed, see note 3				

C. PATRIARCHS OF CONSTANTINOPLE

35. Gregory I	Γρηγόριος Α'		May 381 – Jun 381	d. 391?
Theologos (ex former b.Sassima) acting from spring 379, resigned, see note 4				
36. Nectarius	Νεκτάριος		Jun 381 – 27 Sep 397+	d. 397
(ex laity)				
37. John I	Ιωάννης Α'		26 Feb 398 – 20 Jun 404	d. 407
Chrysostomos (ex priest) deposed and exiled to Armenia, 14 Sep 407+				
38. Arsacius	Αρσάκιος		27 Jun 404 – 11 Nov 405+	d. 405
(ex priest)				
39. Atticus	Αττικός		b.Mar 406 – 10 Oct 425+	d. 425
(ex priest)				
40. Sisinnius I	Σισίννιος Α'		28 Feb 426 – 24 Dec 427+	d. 427
(ex priest)				
41. Nestorius	Νεστόριος		10 Apr 428 – 11 Jul 431	d≥451
(ex priest) heresiarch of Nestorianism, deposed and exiled to Antioch				
42. Maximianus	Μαξιμιανός		25 Oct 431 – 12 Apr 434+	d. 434
(ex priest)				
43. Proclus	Πρόκλος		12/13 Apr 434 – 12 Jul 446+	d. 446
(ex former m.Kyzikos)				

44. Flavian	Φλαβιανός		Jul 446 – 11 Αυγ 449++	d. 449
(ex priest) see note 5				
45. Anatole	Ανατόλιος		Nov 449 – 3 Jul 458+	d. 458
(ex deacon)				
46. Gennadius I	Γεννάδιος Α΄		Aug/Sep 458 – 20 Nov 471+	d. 471
(ex priest)				
47. Acacius	Ακάκιος		Feb 472 – 26 Nov 489+	d. 489
(ex priest)				
48. Fravitas	Φράβιτας		Dec 489 – Mar 490+	d. 490
(ex priest)				
49. Euphemius	Ευφήμιος		spring 490 – spring 496	d. 515?
(ex priest) secular name Epiphanios, deposed and exiled to Euchaïta				
50. Macedonius II	Μακεδόνιος Β΄		Jul 496 – 11 Aug 511	d. 516?
(ex priest) deposed and exiled to Euchaïta				
51. Timothy I	Τιμόθεος Α΄		Oct 511 – 5 Apr 518+	d. 518
(ex priest) monophysite				
52. John II	Ιωάννης Β΄		17 Apr 518 – Feb 520+	d. 520
(ex priest)				
53. Epiphanius	Επιφάνιος		25 Feb 520 – 5 Jun 535+	d. 535
(ex priest)				
54. Anthimus I	Άνθιμος Α΄		Jun 535 – Mar 536	d. 548
(ex b.Trapezous) monophysite, deposed				
55. Menas	Μηνάς		13 Mar 536 – 24 Aug 552+	d. 552
(ex priest)				
56. Eutychius	Ευτύχιος	(1st time)	e.Aug 552 – 22/31 Jan 565	d. 582
(ex priest) deposed				
57. John III	Ιωάννης Γ΄		31 Jan 565 – 31 Aug 577+	d. 577
(ex priest)				
---. Eutychius	Ευτύχιος	(2nd time)	3 Oct 577 – 6 Apr 582+	d. 582
(ex former p.Constantinople)				

D. ECUMENICAL PATRIARCHS

58. John IV	Ιωάννης Δ΄		12 Apr 582 – 2 Sep 595+	d. 595
(ex deacon) synodically acquired the title of Ecumenical Patriarch in 587				
59. Cyriacus II	Κυριακός Β΄		c.Feb 596 – 29 Oct 606+	d. 606
(ex priest)				
60. Thomas I	Θωμάς Α΄		23 Jan 607 – 20 Mar 610+	d. 610
(ex deacon)				
61. Sergius I	Σέργιος Α΄		18 Apr 610 – 9 Dec 638+	d. 638
(ex deacon) monothelite				
62. Pyrrhus	Πύρρος	(1st time)	20 Dec 638 – 29 Sep 641	d. 654
(ex Abbot of Theotocos Monastery) monothelite, resigned				
63. Paul II	Παύλος Β΄		1 Oct 641 – 27 Dec 653+	d. 653
(ex priest?)				
---. Pyrrhus	Πύρρος	(2nd time)	8/9 Jan 654 – 1 Jun 654+	d. 654
(ex former p.Constantinople) monothelite				
64. Peter	Πέτρος		8 Jun 654 – c.12 Oct 666+	d. 666
(ex deacon or priest) monothelite				
65. Thomas II	Θωμάς Β΄		17 Apr 667 – 15 Nov 669+	d. 669
(ex deacon)				

66. John V   Ἰωάννης Ε΄   e.Nov 669 – 18? Aug 675+   d. 675?
(ex priest) probably died

67. Constantine I   Κωνσταντίνος Α΄   2 Sep 675 – 9 Aug 677+   d. 677
(ex deacon)

68. Theodore I   Θεόδωρος Α΄   (1ˢᵗ time)   Aug/Sep 677 – Nov/Dec 679   d. 687
(ex priest) deposed

69. George I   Γεώργιος Α΄   Nov/Dec 679 – Jan/Feb 686   d. ?
(ex priest?) probably deposed

---. Theodore I   Θεόδωρος Α΄   (2ⁿᵈ time)   Jan/Feb 686 – 28 Dec 687+   d. 687?
(ex former p.Constantinople) probably died

70. Paul III   Παῦλος Γ΄   Jan 688 – 20 Aug 693+   d. 693
(ex laity)

71. Callinicus I   Καλλίνικος Α΄   Aug/Sep 693 – Aug 705   d. 711
(ex priest) deposed and exiled to Rome, Nov 711+ see note 6

72. Cyrus   Κύρος   Sep 705 – Dec 711   d. ?
(ex monk) deposed

73. John VI   Ἰωάννης ΣΤ΄   Dec 711 – Jul/Aug 715+   d. 715
(ex deacon) monothelite

74. Germanus I   Γερμανός Α΄   11 Aug 715 – 17 Jan 730   d. 742
(ex m.Kyzikos) resigned

75. Anastasius   Ἀναστάσιος   22 Jan 730 – Jan 754+   d. 754
(ex priest?) iconoclast

76. Constantine II   Κωνσταντίνος Β΄   8 Aug 754 – 30 Aug 766   d. 768
(ex b.Sylaion) iconoclast, deposed, 7 Oct 768++ see note 7

77. Nicetas I   Νικήτας Α΄   16 Nov 766 – 6 Feb 780+   d. 780
(ex priest) iconoclast

78. Paul IV   Παῦλος Δ΄   20 Feb 780 – 31 Aug 784   d. 784
(ex lector) resigned, Oct/Nov 784+

79. Tarasius   Ταράσιος   25 Dec 784 – 18 Feb 806+   d. 806
(ex laity)

80. Nicephorus I   Νικηφόρος Α΄   12 Apr 806 – 13 Mar 815   d. 828
(ex laity, elected 5 Apr) deposed and exiled to Prikonnisos

81. Theodotus I   Θεόδοτος Α΄   1 Apr 815 – c.Jan 821+   d. 821
Melissinos/Kassitiras (ex monk) iconoclast

82. Anthony I   Ἀντώνιος Α΄   c.Jan 821 – Jan 837+   d. 837
Constantine Kassymatas (ex b.Sylaion) iconoclast

83. John VII   Ἰωάννης Ζ΄   21 Jan 837 – 4 Mar 843   d. ?
Morocharzianos (ex Abbot of Saints Sergius and Bacchus Monastery) iconoclast, deposed

84. Methodius I   Μεθόδιος Α΄   11 Mar 843 – 14 Jun 847+   d. 847
(ex monk and former Monastery Abbot, elected 4 Mar)

85. Ignatius   Ἰγνάτιος   (1ˢᵗ time)   4 Jul 847 – 23 Oct 858   d. 877
Nicetas Rangave (ex Abbot of Archistratigos Monastery) deposed

86. Photius I   Φώτιος Α΄   (1ˢᵗ time)   25 Dec 858 – 23 Sep 867   d≥893
(ex laity) deposed

---. Ignatius   Ἰγνάτιος   (2ⁿᵈ time)   23 Nov 867 – 23 Oct 877+   d. 877
Nicetas Rangave (ex former p.Constantinople)

---. Photius I   Φώτιος Α΄   (2ⁿᵈ time)   26 Oct 877 – 29/30 Sep 886   d≥893
(ex former p.Constantinople) deposed

87. Stephen I   Στέφανος Α΄   18 Dec 886 – 17/18 May 893+   d. 893
Macedon (ex subdeacon)

88. Anthony II	Αντώνιος Β΄		Aug 893 – 12 Feb 901+	d. 901
Kavleas (ex Abbot of a Monastery in Constantinople)				
89. Nicholas I	Νικόλαος Α΄	(1st time)	1 Mar 901 – Feb 907	852-925
Mystikos (ex monk) deposed				
90. Euthymius I	Ευθύμιος Α΄		Feb 907 – 15 May 912	d. 917
(ex Abbot of a Monastery at Psamathia) deposed				
---. Nicholas I	Νικόλαος Α΄	(2nd time)	15 May 912 – 15 May 925+	852-925
Mystikos (ex former p.Constantinople)				
91. Stephen II	Στέφανος Β΄		29 Jun 925 – 18 Jul 927+	d. 927
(ex m.Amasia)				
92. Tryphon	Τρύφων		14 Dec 927 – Aug 931	d. ?
(ex monk) deposed				
93. Theophylactus	Θεοφύλακτος		2 Feb 933 – 27 Feb 956+	917-956
Lekapinos (ex subdeacon)				
94. Polyeuctus	Πολύευκτος		3 Apr 956 – 5 Feb 970+	d. 970
(ex monk)				
95. Basil I	Βασίλειος Α΄		13 Feb 970 – Aug/Nov 973	d. ?
Skamandrinos (ex monk) deposed and exiled to Skamandros				
96. Anthony III	Αντώνιος Γ΄		Dec 973 – Jun 978	d. 983
(ex monk) resigned				
97. Nicholas II	Νικόλαος Β΄		Apr/May 980 – 16 Dec 991+	d. 991
Chrysovergis (ex monk) see note 8				
98. Sisinnius II	Σισίννιος Β΄		12 Apr 996 – 24 Aug 998+	d. 998
(ex laity)				
99. Sergius II	Σέργιος Β΄		Jun/Jul 1001 – Jul 1019+	d. 1019
(ex Abbot of Taxiarchon Monastery)				
100. Eustace	Ευστάθιος		Jul 1019 – Nov/Dec 1025+	d. 1025
(ex priest)				
101. Alexius	Αλέξιος		15 Dec 1025 – 20 Feb 1043+	d. 1043
(ex Abbot of Stoudiou Monastery)				
102. Michael I	Μιχαήλ Α΄		25 Mar 1043 – 2 Nov 1058	d. 1059
Kiroularios (ex monk) deposed and exiled to Prikonnisos, 21 Jan 1059+				
103. Constantine III	Κωνσταντίνος Γ΄		2 Feb 1059 – 9/10 Aug 1063+	d. 1063
Lichoudis (ex monk)				
104. John VIII	Ιωάννης Η΄		1 Jan 1064 – 2 Aug 1075+	1006-1075
Xifilinos (ex monk)				
105. Cosmas I	Κοσμάς Α΄		Aug 1075 – 8 May 1081	d. 1082?
Ierosolymitis (ex monk) resigned				
106. Eustratius	Ευστράτιος		May 1081 – Jul 1084	d. ?
Garidas (ex monk) deposed				
107. Nicholas III	Νικόλαος Γ΄		Aug 1084 – Apr/May 1111+	d. 1111
Kyrdiniatis (ex monk)				
108. John IX	Ιωάννης Θ΄		24 May 1111 – e.Apr 1134+	d. 1134
Agapitos (ex deacon)				
109. Leo	Λέων		May 1134 – Jan 1143+	d. 1143
Styppis (ex priest)				
110. Michael II	Μιχαήλ Β΄		Jul 1143 – Mar 1146	d. ?
Kourkouas (ex Abbot of Archangel Michael Monastery) resigned				
111. Cosmas II	Κοσμάς Β΄		e.Apr 1146 – 26 Feb 1147	d. ?
Attikos (ex deacon) deposed				

112. Nicholas IV   Νικόλαος Δ΄   Dec 1147 – Mar/Apr 1151   d. 1152
Mouzalon (ex former a.Cyprus) resigned

113. Theodotus II   Θεόδοτος Β΄   Mar 1151/Apr 1152 – Oct 1153/Oct 1154+ d. 1153/4
(ex Abbot of Anastaseos Monastery) died after two years and 6 months

114. Neophytus I   Νεόφυτος Α΄   Oct 1153/Nov 1154   d. ?
(ex monk) resigned less than a month after his election, not consecrated

115. Constantine IV   Κωνσταντίνος Δ΄   Nov 1154 – e.May 1157+   d. 1157
Chliarinos (ex deacon)

116. Luke   Λουκάς   Aug/Oct 1157 – winter 1169/70+   d. 1169/70
Chrysovergis (ex monk)

117. Michael III   Μιχαήλ Γ΄   Jan 1170 – Mar 1178+   d. 1178
(ex deacon)

118. Chariton   Χαρίτων   Mar/Aug 1178 – Feb/Jul 1179+   d. 1179
Evgeniotis (ex Abbot of Manganon Monastery) died after 11 months

119. Theodosius I   Θεοδόσιος Α΄   Feb/Jul 1179 – Aug 1183   d≥1191
Vorradiotis (ex monk) deposed and exiled to Terevinthos

120. Basil II   Βασίλειος Β΄   Aug 1183 – Feb 1186   d≥1191
Kamatiros (ex deacon) deposed

121. Nicetas II   Νικήτας Β΄   Feb 1186 – Feb 1189   d≥1191
Mountanis (ex deacon) deposed

122. Leontius   Λεόντιος   Feb/Mar 1189 – Sep/Oct 1189   d≥1191
(ex Abbot of Saint Apostles Monastery) deposed

123. Dositheus   Δοσίθεος   Sep/Oct 1189 – 10 Sep 1191   d. ?
(ex p.Jerusalem) resigned, see note 9

124. George II   Γεώργιος Β΄   10 Sep 1191 – 7 Jul 1198+   d. 1198
Xiphilinos (ex priest?)

125. John X   Ιωάννης Ι΄   5 Aug 1198 – Apr/May 1206   d. 1206
Kamatiros (ex deacon) resigned, 26 Jun 1206+ see note 10

126. Michael IV   Μιχαήλ Δ΄   20 Apr 1208 – 26 Aug 1214+   d. 1214
Autorianos (ex priest) in Nicaea

127. Theodore II   Θεόδωρος Β΄   *28 Sep* 1214 – 31 Jan 1216+   d. 1216
Irinikos (ex priest) in Nicaea

128. Maximus II   Μάξιμος Β΄   *3 Jun* 1216 – Dec 1216+   d. 1216
(ex monk) in Nicaea

129. Manuel I   Μανουήλ Α΄   Mar 1217 – autumn 1222+   d. 1222
Sarantinos/Charitopoulos (ex deacon) in Nicaea

130. Germanus II   Γερμανός Β΄   4 Jan 1223 – Jun 1240+   d. 1240
(ex monk) in Nicaea, see note 11

131. Methodius II   Μεθόδιος Β΄   c.summer 1240 – c.autumn 1240+   d. 1240
(ex Abbot of Yakinthos Monastery) in Nicaea, died after 3 months

132. Manuel II   Μανουήλ Β΄   Aug/Oct 1243 – Oct 1254+   d. 1254
(ex priest) in Nicaea, see note 12

133. Arsenius   Αρσένιος   (1st time)   Nov 1254 – Feb/Mar 1260   d. 1273
George Autorianos (ex monk) deposed (to former, to p.Constantinople)

134. Nicephorus II   Νικηφόρος Β΄   c.Mar 1260 – c.Feb 1261+   d. 1261
(ex m.Ephesos) in Nicaea

-----. Arsenius   Αρσένιος   (2nd time) May/Jun 1261 – May/Jun 1264   d. 1273
George Autorianos (ex former p.Constantinople) deposed and exiled, 30 Sep 1273+ see note 13

135. Germanus III   Γερμανός Γ΄   28 May 1265 – 14 Sep 1266   d≥1274
Gavras, referred to mockingly as Markoutzas (ex m.Adrianoupolis) resigned

136. Joseph I   Ιωσήφ Α΄   (1st time)   1 Jan 1267 – 9 Jan 1275   d. 1283
(ex Abbot of Lazaros Monastery, elected 28 Dec 1266) deposed (to former, to p.Constantinople)

137. John XI   Ιωάννης ΙΑ΄   2 Jun 1275 – 26 Dec 1282   d. 1297
Vekkos (ex priest?, elected 26 May) uniate, deposed, Mar 1297+

-----. Joseph I   Ιωσήφ Α΄   (2nd time)   31 Dec 1282 – 23 Mar 1283+   d. 1283
(ex former p.Constantinople)

138. Gregory II   Γρηγόριος Β΄   11 Apr 1283 – Jun 1289   d. 1290
George Kyprios (ex laity, elected 28 Mar) resigned

139. Athanasius I   Αθανάσιος Α΄   (1st time)   *14 Oct* 1289 – 16 Oct 1293   d. 1315?
(ex monk) resigned (to former, to p.Constantinople)

140. John XII   Ιωάννης ΙΒ΄   1 Jan 1294 – 21 Jun 1303   d≥1308
(ex Abbot of Pammakaristos Monastery) secular name Kosmas, resigned

-----. Athanasius I   Αθανάσιος Α΄   (2nd time)   23 Jun 1303 – c.Sep 1309   d. 1315?
(ex former p.Constantinople) resigned

141. Niphon I   Νήφων Α΄   9 May 1310 – 11 Apr 1314   d. 1328
(ex m.Kyzikos) deposed, 3 Sept.1328+

142. John XIII   Ιωάννης ΙΓ΄   12 May 1315 – 11 May 1319   d. 1320?
John Glykys (ex laity) resigned

143. Gerasimus I   Γεράσιμος Α΄   21 Mar 1320 – 20 Apr 1321+   d. 1321
(ex Abbot of Manganon Monastery)

144. Isaiah   Ησαΐας   11 Nov 1323 – 13 May 1332+   d. 1332
(ex monk) see note 14

145. John XIV   Ιωάννης ΙΔ΄   Feb 1334 – 2 Feb 1347   1283-1347
Kalekas (ex m.Thessaloniki) deposed, 29 Dec 1347+

146. Isidore I   Ισίδωρος Α΄   17 May 1347 – Feb/Mar 1350+   d. 1350
Vouchiras (ex former m.Monemvasia)

147. Callistus I   Κάλλιστος Α΄   (1st time)   *10 Jun* 1350 – 15 Aug 1353   d. 1363
(ex monk) deposed (to former, to p.Constantinople) see note 15

148. Philotheus   Φιλόθεος   (1st time)   e.Aug 1353 – Nov/Dec 1354   d. 1379
Kokkinos (ex m.Iraklia) deposed (to former, to president m.Iraklia)

-----. Callistus I   Κάλλιστος Α΄   (2nd time)   Jan 1355 – Aug 1363+   d. 1363
(ex former p.Constantinople)

-----. Philotheus   Φιλόθεος   (2nd time)   8 Feb 1364 – c.Aug 1376   d. 1379
Kokkinos (ex former p.Constantinople) deposed, see note 16

149. Macarius   Μακάριος   (1st time)   c.Jun 1377 – Jul 1379   d≥1391
(ex m.Sevastia) deposed (to former, to p.Constantinople) see note 17

150. Nilus   Νείλος   Mar/Apr 1380 – 1 Feb 1388+   d. 1388
Neophytus Kerameus (ex Abbot of Charsianiton Monastery)

151. Anthony IV   Αντώνιος Δ΄   (1st time)   Jan 1389 – Jul 1390   d. 1397
(ex monk) deposed (to former, to p.Constantinople)

-----. Macarius   Μακάριος   (2nd time)   30 Jul 1390 – e.Sep 1390   d. ?
(ex former p.Constantinople) probably deposed, see note 17

-----. Anthony IV   Αντώνιος Δ΄   (2nd time)   c.Sep 1390 – May 1397+   d. 1397
(ex former p.Constantinople) see note 17

152. Callistus II   Κάλλιστος Β΄   17 May 1397 – c.Aug 1397+   d. 1397
(ex monk)

153. Matthew I   Ματθαίος Α΄   Oct 1397 – 10 Aug 1410+   d. 1410
(ex m.Kyzikos) see note 18

154. Euthymius II   Ευθύμιος Β΄   25/26 Oct 1410 – 29 Μαρτίου 1416+   d. 1416
(ex Abbot of Stoudiou Monastery)

155. Joseph II (ex m.Ephesos)	Ιωσήφ Β΄		21 May 1416 – 10 Jun 1439+	d. 1439
156. Metrophanes II (ex m.Kyzikos) uniate	Μητροφάνης Β΄		4/5 May 1440 – 1 Aug 1443+	d. 1443
157. Gregory III Mellisinos, referred mockingly as Mammi (ex monk) uniate, deposed, see note 19	Γρηγόριος Γ΄		summer 1445 – c.summer 1450	d. 1459
158? Athanasius II (ex Abbot of Perivleptos Monastety) existence contested, see note 19	Αθανάσιος Β΄		c.summer 1450	d. ?
159. Gennadius II George Scholarios (ex monk) resigned (to former, to p.Constantinople) see notes 20, 21.1	Γεννάδιος Β΄	(1st time)	6 Jan 1454 – 6 Jan 1456	d. 1472?
160. Isidore II (ex Abbot of Xanthopoulon Monastery) see note 21.2	Ισίδωρος Β΄		Jan 1456 – 31 Mar 1462+	d. 1462
161. Joasaph I Kokkas (ex monk) deposed, see note 21.3	Ιωάσαφ Α΄		1 Apr 1462 – 10 Apr 1463	d. ?
-----. Gennadius II George Scholarios (ex former p.Constantinople) resigned (to former, to p.Constantinople) see note 21.4	Γεννάδιος Β΄	(2nd time)	Apr 1463 – c.Jun 1463	d. 1472?
162. Sophronius I Syropoulos (ex monk) resigned, see note 21.5	Σωφρόνιος Α΄		Jun 1463 – b.Aug 1464	d. ?
-----. Gennadius II George Scholarios (ex former p.Constantinople) resigned, see note 21.6	Γεννάδιος Β΄	(3rd time)	b.Aug 1464 – autumn 1465	d. 1472?
163. Mark II Xylokaravis (ex monk) deposed (to former, to president a.Ohrid) see note 21.7	Μάρκος Β΄		autumn 1465 – autumn 1466	d. ?
164. Symeon Trapezountios (ex monk) deposed (to former, to p.Constantinople) see note 21.8	Συμεών	(1st time) autumn 1466 – end 1466		d. 1486
165. Dionysius I (ex m.Philippoupolis) resigned (to former, to p.Constantinople) see note 21.9	Διονύσιος Α΄	(1st time)	end 1466 – end 1471	d. 1492
-----. Symeon Trapezountios (ex former p.Constantinople) resigned (to former, to p.Constantinople)	Συμεών	(2nd time)	end 1471 – beg 1475	d. 1486
166. Raphael I (ex monk) died in prison	Ραφαήλ Α΄		beg 1475 – beg 1476++	d. 1476
167. Maximus III Manuel Christonymos (ex laity), see note 22	Μάξιμος Γ΄		spring 1476 – 3 Apr 1482+	d. 1482
-----. Symeon Trapezountios (ex former p.Constantinople), see note 22	Συμεών	(3rd time)	Apr 1482 – autumn 1486+	d. 1486
168. Niphon II (ex m.Thessaloniki) deposed (to former, to p.Constantinople)	Νήφων Β΄	(1st time)	end 1486 – beg 1488	d. 1508
-----. Dionysius I (ex former p.Constantinople) resigned	Διονύσιος Α΄	(2nd time)	Jul 1488 – end 1490	d. 1492
169. Maximus IV former name: Manasses (ex m.Serres) resigned, see note 23	Μάξιμος Δ΄		beg 1491 – beg 1497	d. ?
-----. Niphon II (ex former p.Constantinople) resigned (to former, to p.Constantinople)	Νήφων Β΄	(2nd time) summer 1497 – c.Aug 1498		d. 1508
170. Joachim I (ex m.Drama) deposed (to former, to p.Constantinople)	Ιωακείμ Α΄	(1st time) autumn 1498 – spring 1502		d. 1504
-----. Niphon II (ex former p.Constantinople) resigned (to former, to president m.Oungrovlachia) 11 Aug 1508+	Νήφων Β΄	(3rd time)	spring 1502	d. 1508
171. Pachomius I (ex m.Zichna) deposed (to former, to p.Constantinople)	Παχώμιος Α΄	(1st time)	beg 1503 – beg 1504	d. 1513
-----. Joachim I (ex former p.Constantinople)	Ιωακείμ Α΄	(2nd time)	beg 1504 – autumn 1504+	d. 1504

-----. Pachomius I   Παχώμιος Α'   (2nd time)   autumn 1504 – beg 1513+   d. 1513
(ex former p.Constantinople)

172. Theoleptus I   Θεόληπτος Α'   mid 1513 – Dec 1522+   d. 1522
(ex m.Ioannina)

173. Jeremias I   Ιερεμίας Α'   (1st time)   31 Dec 1522 – Apr/May 1524   d. 1546
(ex m.Sophia) deposed (to former, to p.Constantinople) see note 24

174. Johnnicius I   Ιωαννίκιος Α'   Apr/May 1524 – 24 Sep 1525   d. 1526?
(ex m.Sozopolis) deposed, see note 24

-----. Jeremias I   Ιερεμίας Α'   (2nd time)   24 Sep 1525 – 13 Jan 1546+   d. 1546
(ex former p.Constantinople)

175. Dionysius II   Διονύσιος Β'   17 Apr 1546 – Jul 1556+   d. 1566
(ex m.Nikomidia) see note 25

176. Joasaph II   Ιωάσαφ Β'   Jul/Aug 1556 – Jan 1565   d≥1566
(ex m.Adrianoupolis) deposed, see note 26

177. Metrophanes III   Μητροφάνης Γ'(1st time)   Jan/Feb 1565 – 4 Μαϊου 1572   d. 1580
(ex m.Kaisaria) resigned (to president m.Chios)

178. Jeremias II   Ιερεμίας Β'   (1st time)   5 May 1572 – 23 Nov 1579   d. 1595
Tranos (ex m.Larissa) deposed (to former, to p.Constantinople) see note 27

-----. Metrophanes III   Μητροφάνης Γ'(2nd time)   23 Nov 1579 – 9 Aug 1580+   d. 1580
(ex former p.Constantinople), see note 27

-----. Jeremias II   Ιερεμίας Β'   (2nd time)   Aug 1580 – 22 Feb 1584   d. 1595
Tranos (ex former p.Constantinople) deposed and exiled to Rhodes (to former, to p.Const) see note 28

179. Pachomius II   Παχώμιος Β'   22 Feb 1584 – m.Feb 1585   d≥1586
Patestos (ex m.Kaisaria) deposed, see notes 28, 29

180. Theoleptus II   Θεόληπτος Β'   16 Feb 1585 – May 1586   d≥1591
(ex m.Philippoupolis) deposed, see notes 29, 30

-----. Jeremias II   Ιερεμίας Β'   (3rd time)   Apr 1587 – end 1595+   d. 1595
Tranos (ex former p.Constantinople) see note 31

181. Matthew II   Ματθαίος Β'   (1st time)   b.Feb 1596 – e.Feb 1596   d. 1603
(ex m.Ioannina) deposed after 20 days (to former, to p.Constantinople)

182. Gabriel I   Γαβριήλ Α'   c.Mar 1596 – Aug 1596+   d. 1596
(ex m.Thessaloniki)

183. Theophanes   Θεοφάνης   e.Feb 1597 – 26 Mar 1597+   d. 1597
Karykis (ex m.Athina) see note 32

184. Meletius I   Μελέτιος Α'   27 Mar/2 Apr 1597 – Mar/Apr 1598   1549-1601
Pigas (Patriarch of Alexandria and Caretaker of the Ecumenical See) resigned, 12 Sep 1601+

-----. Matthew II   Ματθαίος Β'   (2nd time)   Apr 1598 – c.Jan 1602   d. 1603
(ex former p.Constantinople) resigned (to former, to p.Constantinople)

185. Neophytus II   Νεόφυτος Β'   (1st time)   b.Feb 1602 – m.Jan 1603   d≥1612
(ex m.Athina) deposed and exiled to Rhodes (to former, to p.Constantinople)

-----. Matthew II   Ματθαίος Β'   (3rd time)   m.Jan 1603 – b.Feb 1603+   d. 1603
(ex former p.Constantinople) died after 17 days

186. Raphael II   Ραφαήλ Β'   b.Feb 1603 – m.Oct 1607   d. 1607/8
(ex m.Mithymna) resigned, end 1607/beg 1608+ (before 20 Apr 1608)

-----. Neophytus II   Νεόφυτος Β'   (2nd time)   15 Oct 1607 – Oct 1612   d. ?
(ex former p.Constantinople) deposed and exiled to Rhodes

187. Cyril I   Κύριλλος Α'   (1st time)   Oct 1612 – Oct/Nov 1612   1572-1638
Loukaris (Patriarch of Alexandria and Caretaker of the Ecumenical See) resigned after 21 days

188. Timothy II   Τιμόθεος Β'   Oct/Nov 1612 – 3 Sep 1620+   d. 1620
Marmarinos (ex m.Old Patra)

-----. Cyril I   Κύριλλος Α΄   (2nd time)   4 Nov 1620 – 12 Apr 1623   1572-1638
Constantine Loukaris (ex p.Alexandria) deposed (to former, to p.Constantinople)

189. Gregory IV   Γρηγόριος Δ΄   12 Apr 1623 – 18 Jun 1623   d. ?
(ex m.Amasia) deposed and exiled to Rhodes

190. Anthimus II   Άνθιμος Β΄   18 Jun 1623 – 22 Sep 1623   d. 1628
(ex m.Adrianoupolis) resigned

-----. Cyril I   Κύριλλος Α΄   (3rd time)   22 Sep 1623 – 4 Oct 1633   1572-1638
Constantine Loukaris (ex former p.Constantinople) deposed (to former, to p.Const see note 33

191. Cyril II   Κύριλλος Β΄   (1st time)   4 Oct 1633 – 11 Oct 1633   d. 1640
Kontaris (ex m.Veria) deposed and exiled to Tenedos (to former, to president m.Veria)

-----. Cyril I   Κύριλλος Α΄   (4th time)   11 Oct 1633 – 25 Feb 1634   1572-1638
Constantine Loukaris (ex former p.Constantinople) deposed (to former, to p.Constantinople)

192. Athanasius III   Αθανάσιος Γ΄   (1st time)   25 Feb 1634 – b.Apr 1634   d. 1654
Patellarios (ex m.Thessaloniki) deposed (to former, to president m.Thessaloniki)

-----. Cyril I   Κύριλλος Α΄   (5th time)   b.Apr 1634 – b.Mar 1635   1572-1638
Constantine Loukaris (ex former p.Constantinople) deposed (to former, to p.Constantinople)

-----. Cyril II   Κύριλλος Β΄   (2nd time)   b.Mar 1635 – m.Jun 1636   d. 1640
Kontaris (ex president m.Veria) deposed and exiled to Rhodes (to former, to p.Constantinople)

193. Neophytus III   Νεόφυτος Γ΄   m.Jun 1636 – b.Mar 1637   d. ?
(ex m.Iraklia) resigned

-----. Cyril I   Κύριλλος Α΄   (6th time)   b.Mar 1637 – 20 Jun 1638   1572-1638
Constantine Loukaris (ex former p.Constantinople) deposed, 27 Jun 1638++ see note 34

-----. Cyril II   Κύριλλος Β΄   (3rd time)   20 Jun 1638 – e.Jun 1639   d. 1640
Kontaris (ex former p.Constantinople) deposed and exiled to Tunis, 24 Jun 1640++ see note 35

194. Parthenius I   Παρθένιος Α΄   1 Jul 1639 – b.Sep 1644   d. 1646
(ex m.Adrianoupolis) deposed and exiled to Cyprus

195. Parthenius II   Παρθένιος Β΄   (1st time)   8 Sep 1644 – 16 Nov 1646   d. 1651
(ex m.Adrianoupolis) deposed and exiled to Cyprus (to former, to p.Constantinople)

196. Johnnicius II   Ιωαννίκιος Β΄   (1st time)   16 Nov 1646 – 28 Oct 1648   d. 1659/60
Lindios (ex m.Iraklia) deposed (to former, to p.Constantinople)

-----. Parthenius II   Παρθένιος Β΄   (2nd time)   29 Oct 1648 – 16 May 1651++   d. 1651
(ex former p.Constantinople) see note 36

-----. Johnnicius II   Ιωαννίκιος Β΄   (2nd time)   b.Jun 1651 – m.Jun 1652   d. 1659/60
Lindios (ex former p.Constantinople) deposed (to former, to p.Constantinople)

197. Cyril III   Κύριλλος Γ΄   (1st time)   m.Jun 1652 – e.Jun 1652   d≥1655
Spanos (ex m.Tornovo) deposed after 8 days (to former, to p.Constantinople)

-----. Athanasius III   Αθανάσιος Γ΄   (2nd time)   e.Jun 1652 – b.Jul 1652   d. 1654
Patellarios (ex former p.Constantinople) resigned after 15 days, 5 Apr 1654+

198. Païsius I   Παΐσιος Α΄   (1st time)   b.Jul 1652 – b.Apr 1653   d≥1672
(ex m.Larissa) resigned (to former, to p.Constantinople)

-----. Johnnicius II   Ιωαννίκιος Β΄   (3rd time)   b.Apr 1653 – b.Mar 1654   d. 1659/60
Lindios (ex former p.Constantinople) deposed (to former, to p.Constantinople)

-----. Cyril III   Κύριλλος Γ΄   (2nd time)   b.Mar 1654 – m.Mar 1654   d≥1655
Spanos (ex former p.Constantinople) deposed after 14 days and exiled to Cyprus

-----. Païsius I   Παΐσιος Α΄   (2nd time)   m.Mar 1654 – Mar 1655   d≥1672
(ex former p.Constantinople) deposed (to former, to president m.Kyzikos)

-----. Johnnicius II   Ιωαννίκιος Β΄   (4th time)   Mar 1655 – e.Jul 1656   d. 1659/60
Lindios (ex former p.Constantinople) deposed (to former, to president a.Tzia)

199. Parthenius III   Παρθένιος Γ΄   26 Jul 1656 – 24 Mar 1657++   d. 1657
(ex m.Chios) see note 37

200. Gabriel II   Γαβριήλ Β΄   23 Apr 1657 – 30 Apr 1657   d. 1659
    (ex m.Ganos) deposed (to former, to president m.Prousa) 3 Dec 1659++ see note 38

201. Parthenius IV   Παρθένιος Δ΄   (1st time)   1 May 1657 – e.Jun 1662   d≥1685
    Mogilalos (ex m.Prousa) resigned (to president m.Prousa) see note 39

202. Dionysius III   Διονύσιος Γ΄   29 Jun 1662 – 21 Oct 1665   d. 1696
    Vardalis (ex m.Prousa) deposed (to former, to president m.Thessaloniki) 28 Aug 1696+

-----. Parthenius IV   Παρθένιος Δ΄   (2nd time)   21 Oct 1665 – 9 Sep 1667   d≥1685
    Mogilalos (ex president m.Prousa) deposed and exiled (to former, to president m.Proilavos)

203. Clement   Κλήμης   9 Sep 1667 – 5 Jan 1668   d. ?
    (ex m.Ikonion) deposed and exiled to unknown location, see note 40

204. Methodius III   Μεθόδιος Γ΄   5 Jan 1668 – b.Mar 1671   d. 1679
    Moronis (ex m.Iraklia) resigned (to former, to president m.Philadelphia)

-----. Parthenius IV   Παρθένιος Δ΄   (3rd time)   b.Mar 1671 – 7 Sep 1671   d≥1685
    Mogilalos (ex former p.Constantinople) deposed and exiled to Cyprus (to former, to p.Const)

205. Dionysius IV   Διονύσιος Δ΄   (1st time)   8 Nov 1671 – 25 Jul 1673   d. 1696
    Komninos (ex m.Larissa) deposed (to former, to president m.Philippoupolis)

206. Gerasimus II   Γεράσιμος Β΄   25 Jul 1673 – e.Dec 1674   d. 1689
    Kakavelas (ex m.Tornovo) deposed (to former, to president m.Chios) 6 Feb 1689+

-----. Parthenius IV   Παρθένιος Δ΄   (4th time)   1 Jan 1675 – 29 Jul 1676   d≥1685
    Mogilalos (ex former p.Constantinople) deposed (to former, to president m.Anchialos)

-----. Dionysius IV   Διονύσιος Δ΄   (2nd time)   29 Jul 1676 – 30 Jul 1679   d. 1696
    Komninos (ex president m.Philippoupolis) deposed (to former, to president m.Philippoupolis)

207. Athanasius IV   Αθανάσιος Δ΄   30 Jul 1679 – 10 Aug 1679   d. ?
    (ex former b.Raidestos) deposed and exiled to unknown location

208. Jacob   Ιάκωβος   (1st time)   10 Aug 1679 – 30 Jul 1682   d. 1690
    (ex m.Larissa) resigned (to former, to p.Constantinople)

-----. Dionysius IV   Διονύσιος Δ΄   (3rd time)   30 Jul 1682 – 10 Mar 1684   d. 1696
    Komninos (ex president m.Philippoupolis) deposed (to former, to president m.Chalkidon)

-----. Parthenius IV   Παρθένιος Δ΄   (5th time)   10 Mar 1684 – 20 Mar 1685   d. ?
    Mogilalos (ex president m.Anchialos) resigned (to president m.Vidyni)

-----. Jacob   Ιάκωβος   (2nd time)   20 Mar 1685 – e.Mar 1686   d. 1690
    (ex former p.Constantinople) deposed (to former, to p.Constantinople)

-----. Dionysius IV   Διονύσιος Δ΄   (4th time)   e.Mar 1686 – 12 Oct 1687   d. 1696
    Komninos (ex president m.Chalkidon) deposed (to former, to p.Constantinople)

-----. Jacob   Ιάκωβος   (3rd time)   12 Oct 1687 – 3 Mar 1688   d. 1690
    (ex former p.Constantinople) resigned, Mar 1690+

209. Callinicus II   Καλλίνικος Β΄   (1st time)   3 Mar 1688 – 27 Nov 1688   c.1630-1702
    Akarnan (ex m.Prousa) deposed (to former, to p.Constantinople)

210. Neophytus IV   Νεόφυτος Δ΄   27 Nov 1688 – 7 Mar 1689   d. ?
    Philaretos (ex former m.Adrianoupolis) deposed

-----. Callinicus II   Καλλίνικος Β΄   (2nd time)   7 Mar 1689 – Jul/Aug 1693   c.1630-1702
    Akarnan (ex former p.Constantinople) deposed (to former, to p.Constantinople)

-----. Dionysius IV   Διονύσιος Δ΄   (5th time)   Aug 1693 – Apr 1694   d. 1696
    Komninos (ex former p.Constantinople) deposed, 23 Sep 1696+

-----. Callinicus II   Καλλίνικος Β΄   (3rd time)   Apr 1694 – 8 Aug 1702+   c.1630-1702
    Akarnan (ex former p.Constantinople)

211. Gabriel III   Γαβριήλ Γ΄   m.Aug 1702 – 17 Oct 1707+   d. 1707
    (ex m.Chalkidon)

212. Neophytus V   Νεόφυτος Ε΄   20 Oct 1707 – 25 Oct 1707   d. 1711?
    (ex m.Iraklia) his election was not accepted by the Turkish authorities (to m.Iraklia)

213. Cyprian   Κυπριανός   (1ˢᵗ time)   25 Oct 1707 – e.May 1709   d≥1720
(ex m.Kaisaria) deposed and exiled to Athos (to former, to president m.Ephesos)

214. Athanasius V   Αθανάσιος Ε'   e.May 1709 – b.Dec 1711   d≥1718
Margounios (ex m.Adrianoupolis) resigned

215. Cyril IV   Κύριλλος Δ'   b.Dec 1711 – b.Nov 1713   d. 1728
(ex m.Kyzikos) resigned

-----. Cyprian   Κυπριανός   (2ⁿᵈ time)   b.Nov 1713 – 28 Feb 1714   d≥1720
(ex former p.Constantinople) resigned

216. Cosmas III   Κοσμάς Γ'   28 Feb 1714 – 23 Mar 1716   d. 1736
(ex former p.Alexandria) resigned (to former, to p.Alexandria) 28 Nov 1736+

217. Jeremias III   Ιερεμίας Γ'   (1ˢᵗ time)   23/25 Mar 1716 – 19 Nov 1726   d. 1735
(ex m.Kaisaria) deposed and exiled to Sinai (to former, to p.Constantinople) see note 41

218. Callinicus III   Καλλίνικος Γ'   19 Nov 1726 – 20 Nov 1726+   d. 1726
(ex m.Iraklia) see note 42

219. Païsius II   Παΐσιος Β'   (1ˢᵗ time)   20 Nov 1726 – m.Sep 1732   d. 1756
Kiomourtzoglous (ex m.Nikomidia) deposed and exiled to Cyprus (to former, to p.Const)

-----. Jeremias III   Ιερεμίας Γ'   (2ⁿᵈ time)   15 Sep 1732 – m.Mar 1733   d. 1735
(ex former p.Constantinople) deposed and exiled to Athos, Oct 1735+

220. Seraphim I   Σεραφείμ Α'   m.Mar 1733 – e.Sep 1734   d. ?
(ex m.Nikomidia) deposed and exiled to Limnos

221. Neophytus VI   Νεόφυτος ΣΤ'   (1ˢᵗ time)   27 Sep 1734 – Aug 1740   d. 1747
(ex m.Kaisaria) deposed (to former, to p.Constantinople)

-----. Païsius II   Παΐσιος Β'   (2ⁿᵈ time)   Aug 1740 – m.May 1743   d. 1756
Kiomourtzoglous (ex former p.Constantinople) deposed (to former, to p.Constantinople)

-----. Neophytus VI   Νεόφυτος ΣΤ'   (2ⁿᵈ time)   m.May 1743 – Mar 1744   d. 1747
(ex former p.Constantinople) deposed and exiled to Patmos, Feb/Mar 1747+

-----. Païsius II   Παΐσιος Β'   (3ʳᵈ time)   Mar 1744 – 28 Sep 1748   d. 1756
Kiomourtzoglous (ex former p.Constantinople) resigned (to former, to p.Constantinople)

222. Cyril V   Κύριλλος Ε'   (1ˢᵗ time)   28 Sep 1748 – e.May 1751   d. 1775
Karakallos (ex m.Nikomidia) deposed (to former, to p.Constantinople)

-----. Païsius II   Παΐσιος Β'   (4ᵗʰ time)   e.May 1751 – b.Sep 1752   d. 1756
Kiomourtzoglous (ex former p.Constantinople) deposed, Oct/Dec 1756+

-----. Cyril V   Κύριλλος Ε'   (2ⁿᵈ time)   7 Sep 1752 – 16 Jan 1757   d. 1775
Karakallos (ex former p.Constantinople) deposed and exiled to Sinai, 27 Jul 1775+

223. Callinicus IV   Καλλίνικος Δ'   16 Jan 1757 – 22 Jul 1757   1713-1791
Constantine Mavrikios (ex former m.Proilavos), deposed and exiled to Limnos

224. Seraphim II   Σεραφείμ Β'   22 Jul 1757 – 26 Mar 1761   d. 1781/2
(ex m.Philippoupolis) deposed and exiled to Athos

225. Johnnicius III   Ιωαννίκιος Γ'   26 Mar 1761 – 21 May 1763   d. 1793
Karatzas (ex m.Chalkidon) deposed and exiled to Athos

226. Samuel   Σαμουήλ   (1ˢᵗ time)   24 May 1763 – 5 Nov 1768   d. 1775
Scarlatus Giannakis (ex m.Derki) deposed and exiled to Athos (to former, to p.Constantinople)

227. Meletius II   Μελέτιος Β'   5 Nov 1768 – 11 Apr 1769   d≥1777
Kalvokoresis (ex m.Larissa) imprisoned 8 Apr 1769, deposed and exiled to Lesvos

228. Theodosius II   Θεοδόσιος Β'   11 Apr 1769 – 16 Nov 1773   d. 1785
Christianopoulos/Maridakis (ex m.Thessaloniki) deposed

-----. Samuel   Σαμουήλ   (2ⁿᵈ time)   17 Nov 1773 – 24 Dec 1774   d. 1775
Scarlatus Giannakis, byname Chantzeris (ex former p.Constantinople) deposed, 10 May 1775+

229. Sophronius II   Σωφρόνιος Β'   24 Dec 1774 – 8 Oct 1780+   d. 1780
(ex p.Jerusalem)

230. Gabriel IV	Γαβριήλ Δ´		8 Oct 1780 – 29 Jun 1785+	d. 1785
(ex m.Old Patra)				
231. Procopius	Προκόπιος		29 Jun/1 Jul 1785 – 30 Apr 1789	1730-1812
Pelekasis (ex m.Smyrni) deposed and exiled to Athos, 13 Mar 1812+				
232. Neophytus VII	Νεόφυτος Ζ´	(1st time)	1 May 1789 – 1 Mar 1794	d≥1804
(ex m.Maronia) deposed and exiled to Rhodos (to former, to p.Constantinople)				
233. Gerasimus III	Γεράσιμος Γ´		3 Mar 1794 – 19 Apr 1797	d≥1799
(ex m.Derki) resigned				
234. Gregory V	Γρηγόριος Ε´	(1st time)	19 Apr 1797 – 18 Dec 1798	1746-1821
George Angelopoulos (ex m.Smyrni) deposed and exiled to Zichna (to former, to p.Const)				
-----. Neophytus VII	Νεόφυτος Ζ´	(2nd time)	19 Dec 1798 – 17 Jun 1801	d≥1804
(ex former p.Constantinople) deposed and exiled to Athos				
235. Callinicus V	Καλλίνικος Ε´	(1st time)	17 Jun 1801 – 22 Sep 1806	d≥1809
(ex m.Nikaia) resigned (to former, to p.Constantinople)				
-----. Gregory V	Γρηγόριος Ε´	(2nd time)	23 Sep 1806 – 10 Sep 1808	1746-1821
George Angelopoulos (ex former p.Constantinople) resigned (to former, to p.Constantinople)				
-----. Callinicus V	Καλλίνικος Ε´	(2nd time)	10 Sep 1808 – 23 Apr 1809	d. ?
(ex former p.Constantinople) deposed				
236. Jeremias IV	Ιερεμίας Δ´		23 Apr 1809 – 4 Mar 1813	d. 1824
(ex m.Mytilini) resigned, 5 Mar 1824+				
237. Cyril VI	Κύριλλος ΣΤ´		4 Mar 1813 – 13 Dec 1818	1775-1821
Constantine Sermpetzoglous (ex m.Adrianoupolis) resigned, 18 Apr 1821++ see note 43				
-----. Gregory V	Γρηγόριος Ε´	(3rd time)	14 Dec 1818 – 10 Apr 1821++	1746-1821
George Angelopoulos (ex former p.Constantinople) deposed and executed, see note 44				
238. Eugene II	Ευγένιος Β´		10 Apr 1821 – 27 Jul 1822+	1780-1822
(ex m.Pisidia)				
239. Anthimus III	Άνθιμος Γ´		28 Jul 1822 – 9 Jul 1824	d. 1842
(ex m.Chalkidon) deposed and exiled to Caesaria, 13 Aug 1842+				
240. Chrysanthus	Χρύσανθος		9 Jul 1824 – 26 Sep 1826	1768-1834
(ex m.Serres) deposed and exiled to Caesaria, 10 Sep 1834+				
241. Agathangelus	Αγαθάγγελος		26 Sep 1826 – 5 Jul 1830	d.1831
(ex m.Chalkidon) deposed and exiled to Caesaria, 30 Nov 1831+				
242. Constantius I	Κωνστάντιος Α´		6 Jul 1830 – 18 Aug 1834	1770-1859
(fm a.Sinai) resigned (to a.Sinai) 5 Jan 1859+				
243. Constantius II	Κωνστάντιος Β´		18 Aug 1834 – 26 Sep 1835	1760-1859
(ex former m.Tornovo) deposed, 17 Jun 1859+				
244. Gregory VI	Γρηγόριος ΣΤ´	(1st time)	27 Sep 1835 – 20 Feb 1840	1798-1881
George Fourtouniadis (ex m.Serres) deposed (to former, to p.Constantinople)				
245. Anthimus IV	Άνθιμος Δ´	(1st time)	20 Feb 1840 – 6 May 1841	1788-1878
Vamvakis (fm m.Nikomidia) deposed (to former, to p.Constantinople)				
246. Anthimus V	Άνθιμος Ε´		6 May 1841 – 12 Jun 1842+	d. 1842
Chrysafidis (fm m.Kyzikos)				
247. Germanus IV	Γερμανός Δ´	(1st time)	14 Jun 1842 – 18 Apr 1845	1788-1853
(ex m.Derki) deposed (to former, to p.Constantinople)				
248. Meletius III	Μελέτιος Γ´		18 Apr 1845 – 28 Nov 1845+	1772-1845
Pangalos (fm m.Kyzikos)				
249. Anthimus VI	Άνθιμος ΣΤ´	(1st time)	4 Dec 1845 – 18 Oct 1848	1782-1878
Ioannidis (ex m.Ephesos) deposed (to former, to p.Constantinople)				
----. Anthimus IV	Άνθιμος Δ´	(2nd time)	18 Oct 1848 – 30 Oct 1852	1788-1878
Vamvakis (ex former p.Constantinople) deposed, 1878+				

----. Germanus IV   Γερμανός Δ´   (2nd time)   1 Nov 1852 – 16 Sep 1853+   1788-1853
(ex former p.Constantinople)

----. Anthimus VI   Ανθιμος ΣΤ´   (2nd time)   24 Sep 1853 – 21 Sep 1855   1782-1878
Ioannidis (ex former p.Constantinople) deposed (to former, to p.Constantinople)

250. Cyril VII   Κύριλλος Ζ´   21 Sep 1855 – 1 Jul 1860   1800-1872
(ex m.Amasia) deposed, 13 Mar 1872+

251. Joachim II   Ιωακείμ Β´   (1st time)   4 Oct 1860 – 9 Jul 1863   1802-1878
John Kokkodis (ex m.Kyzikos) deposed (to former, to p.Constantinople)

252. Sophronius III   Σωφρόνιος Γ´   20 Sep 1863 – 4 Dec 1866   1802-1899
Stavrus Meidantzoglous (ex m.Amasia) resigned (to former, to p.Alexandria) 22 Aug 1899+

----. Gregory VI   Γρηγόριος ΣΤ´   (2nd time)   10 Feb 1867 – 10 Jun 1871   1798-1881
George Fourtouniadis (ex former p.Constaninople) resigned, 8 Jun 1881+

----. Anthimus VI   Άνθιμος ΣΤ´   (3rd time)   5 Sep 1871 – 30 Sep 1873   1790-1878
Ioannidis (ex former p.Constantinople) resigned, 7 Dec 1878+

----. Joachim II   Ιωακείμ Β´   (2nd time)   23 Nov 1873 – 4 Aug 1878+   1802-1878
John Kokkodis (ex former p.Constantinople)

253. Joachim III   Ιωακείμ Γ´   (1st time)   4 Oct 1878 – 30 Mar 1884   1834-1912
Christus Devetzis (ex m.Thessaloniki) resigned (to former, to p.Constantinople)

254. Joachim IV   Ιωακείμ Δ´   1 Oct 1884 – 14 Nov 1886   1837-1887
Nicholas Krousouloudis (ex m.Derki) resigned, 15 Feb 1887+

255. Dionysios V   Διονύσιος Ε´   23 Jan 1887 – 13 Aug 1891+   1820-1891
Dionysius Charitonidis (ex m.Adrianoupolis)

256. Neophytus VIII   Νεόφυτος Η´   27 Oct 1891 – 25 Oct 1894   1832-1909
Joachim Papakonstantinou (ex m.Nikopolis) resigned, 4 Jul 1909+

257. Anthimus VII   Άνθιμος Ζ´   20 Jan 1895 – 29 Jan 1897   1832-1913
Angelus Tsatsos (ex m.Leros) resigned, 5 Dec 1913+

258. Constantine V   Κωνσταντίνος Ε´   2 Apr 1897 – 27 Mar 1901   1833-1914
Constantine Valiadis (ex m.Ephesos) deposed, 27 Feb 1914+

----. Joachim III   Ιωακείμ Γ´   (2nd time)   25 May 1901 – 13 Nov 1912+   1834-1912
Christus Devetzis (ex former p.Constantinople)

259. Germanus V   Γερμανός Ε´   28 Jan 1913 – 12 Oct 1918   1835-1920
George Kavvakopoulos (ex m.Chalkidon) resigned, 19 Dec 1920+ see note 45

260. Meletius IV   Μελέτιος Δ´   25 Nov 1921 – 20 Sep 1923   1871-1935
Emmanuel Metaxakis (ex former m.Athina) (to former, to p.Alexandria) 28 Jul 1935+ see note 46

261. Gregory VII   Γρηγόριος Ζ´   6 Dec 1923 – 17 Nov 1924+   1855-1924
Gregory Zervoudakis (ex m.Chalkidon)

262. Constantine VI   Κωνσταντίνος ΣΤ´   17 Dec 1924 – 22 May 1925   1859-1930
Constantine Arampoglous (ex m.Derki) resigned, 28 Nov 1930+ see note 47

263. Basil III   Βασίλειος Γ´   13 Jul 1925 – 29 Sep 1929+   1846-1929
Basil Georgiadis (ex m.Nikaia)

264. Photius II   Φώτιος Β´   7 Oct 1929 – 29 Dec 1935+   1874-1935
Demetrius Maniatis (ex m.Derki)

265. Benjamin   Βενιαμίν   18 Jan 1936 – 17 Feb 1946+   1871-1946
Benjamin Kyriakou (ex m.Iraklia)

266. Maximus V   Μάξιμος Ε´   20 Feb 1946 – 18 Oct 1948   1897-1972
Maximus Vaportzis (ex m.Chalkidon) resigned (to president m.Ephesos) 1 Jan 1972+ see note 48

267. Athenagoras   Αθηναγόρας   1 Nov 1948 – 7 Jul 1972+   1886-1972
Aristocles Spyrou (ex a.America)

268. Demetrius   Δημήτριος   16 Jul 1972 – 2 Oct 1991+   1914-1991
Demetrius Papadopoulos (ex m.Imvros)

269. Bartholomew   Βαρθολομαῖος   22 Oct 1991 –   b. 1940
      Demetrius Archontonis (ex m.Chalkidon) see note

NOTES

1. For the dates before 1453 we follow Venance Grumel, *La Chronologie*, Paris 1958, p. 434-440, with any deviations explained by notes. As Bishops of Byzantium, Grumel lists only Philadelphus (211-17), Eugene (240-65), Rufinus (284-93), and Metrophanes (306/7-14), as mentioned by Byzantine historians Kedrinos and Logothetes Symeon. The rest of the Bishops are mentioned in the catalog written by Dorotheus of Tyre, which is not accepted as historic by some scholars. Manuel Gedeon, in his work Πατριαρχικοί Πίνακες, tried to organize the dates of Dorotheus into a realistic listing, and this listing has been followed here, adjusted to keep the dates given by Grumel for the aforementioned four Bishops.
2. Paul I was strangled by Arian heretics after his arrival to Armenia.
3. Maximus the Cynic was secretly consecrated Archbishop of Constantinople at the end of 379 or beginning of 380, before the death of the Patriarch of Alexandria, Peter II (February 15, 380), but was immediately exposed and forced to leave the city. His consecration was officially annulled by the Second Ecumenical Council in May 381. Although some scholars, including Grumel, give February 15, 380 as Peter's death date, other scholars show February 15, 381. If we accept this later case, Maximus's consecration may have occurred late in 380. After being expelled from Constantinople, Maximus went to Thessalonica to see Emperor Theodosius, but failed to get his support; he returned to Alexandria and tried unsuccessfully to be named Peter's successor.
4. Gregory arrived to Constantinople before Pentecost of 379, acting as Bishop of the Orthodox until his official election to the See of Constantinople by the Second Ecumenical Council in May 381.
5. Flavian was maltreated during the "Robber" Council of Ephesus, which deposed him on August 8, 449. He died on his way to exile three days later.
6. When Emperor Justinian II regained his throne in August 705, he arrested Patriarch Callinicus I, blinded him, and exiled him to Rome, where he died in Nov 711, four days after his release from prison following Justinian's death.
7. Two years following his deposition he was accused of conspiring against the Emperor Constantine V (741-75), former Patriarch Constantine II was thrown into Constantinople's Hippodrome, where he was ridiculed, maltreated, and finally beheaded.
8. There was a vacancy of four and a half years during this period. Most scholars, including Grumel, whose dates have been followed in this list, place the vacancy after Patriarch Nicholas II; however, some writers, among them Gregoire, place the vacancy before Nicholas, listing 984 as the year of his election and 996 as the year of his death. For the difference in the dates listed here for Basil I, Anthony III, and Nicholas II from the dates given by Grumel, see *REB* XLVI (1988), p. 55-60.
9. The first attempt to elect the Patriarch of Jerusalem, Dositheus, as Ecumenical Patriarch occurred in February 1189, however after nine days his election was cancelled.
10. John XI stayed in Didymotichon after the fall of Constantinople to the Crusaders, and he finally sent his resignation to the Emperor at Nicaea in April/May 1206.
11. For the dates given for Germanus II, see V. Laurent, in *Revue des Études Byzantines* 27, Paris 1969, p. 136.
12. Manuel II remained Patriarch for eleven years, and died before November 3, 1254 (the date of Emperor's John III death), but close to that date.
13. The See of the Patriarchate returned to Constantinople in August 1261. Arsenius was allowed to return to his position a few months earlier.
14. Isaiah was deposed by Emperor Andronicus II (1282-1328) in December 1327, but was reinstated by the new Emperor Andronicus III (1328-41) on May 24, 1328.
15. Regarding the dates given for the deposition of Callistus I, see A. Failler, "La Deposition du Patriarche Calliste Ier", *Revue des Études Byzantines*, 31, Paris 1973, p. 5-163.
16. Philotheus was deposed after August 12, 1376 (the date that Emperor Andronicus IV deposed his father, John V). See J. Darruzes, *Les Régestes des Actes du Patriarcat de Constantinople Fasc. V*, p. 564.
17. Macarius was deposed after July 1, 1379 (the date that Emperor John V was restored to the throne). See J. Darruzes, *Les Régestes des Actes du Patriarcat de Constantinople Fasc. IV*, p. 4. He was most probably deposed again after September 17, 1390 (the date on which Emperor Manuel II re-entered Constantinople), and Anthony IV was restored shortly thereafter, if not instantly. See J. Darruzes, *Les Régestes des Actes du Patriarcat de Constantinople Fasc. VI*, p. 174.

18. Matthew was deposed by a Synod composed of four Metropolitans in Summer 1402, while Emperor Manuel II (1391-1425) was visiting western Europe, but he was reinstated by Manuel on his return to Constantinople in June 1403.

19. For the election of Gregory III in Summer 1445 see J. Darruzes, *Les Régestes des Actes du Patriarcat de Constantinople Fasc. VII.* According to the records published in Rome by Leo Allatius (1588-1669), a Synod of the Orthodox Patriarchs convened during 1450 in Hagia Sophia, Constantinople, expelled Patriarch Gregory III, and elected and consecrated the Abbot of Perivleptos Monastery, Athanasius, as Patriarch. Some scholars believe the Synod and its records to be false, others believe the Synod to have taken place but its records to be false, and some accept both the Synod and its records. In any case, the uniate Patriarch Gregory III was forced to depart from Constantinople probably during the Summer of 1450, and remained in the Peloponnese for about one year (his presence there is reported on October 12, 1450), before arriving in Rome in August 1451. If Athanasius was indeed elected, he remained Patriarch only for a few months.

20. Most documentation for the dates after 1453 can be found in Σάρδεων Γερμανός (Sardeon Germanos), "Συμβολή εις τους Πατριαρχικούς Καταλόγους Κωνσταντινουπόλεως από της Αλώσεως και εξής", *Ορθοδοξία*, 8-13, 1933-38. A listing based on the works of Germanos is included by Βασίλειος Σταυρίδης (Vasilios Stavridis) in *Θρησκευτική και Ηθική Εγκυκλοπαιδεία (ΘΗΕ)*, Athens 1966, Vol.9 p. 831-34; this listing is reproduced in the Patriarchate's official annual publication, *Ημερολόγιον του Οικουμενικού Πατριαρχείου*. Venance Grumel in *La Chronologie*, Paris 1958, p. 434-40, alters the dates given for the first few Patriarchs after 1453, as does Χ. Γ. Πατρινελης (Ch. G. Patrinelis), whose research in the era is reflected in his catalog, "Χρονολογικός κατάλογος των Πατριαρχών Κωνσταντινουπόλεως κατά την περίοδο 1453-1669", *Ιστορία του Ελληνικού Έθνους*, Ekdotiki Athinon, Athina 1974, Vol.10 p.102. Gerhard Podskalsky in "Griechische Theologie in der Zeit der Turkenherrschaft 1453-1821", C. H. Beck'sche Verlagsbuchhandlung, Munchen 1988, alters these dates even further, based on Vitalien Laurent's "Les Premiers Patriarches de Constantinople sous la Domination Turque (1454-1476)," *Revue des Études Byzantines*, 26, Paris 1968, p. 229-63 and other works listed in his notes. Most of the differences are noted below, with the dates adopted in this listing highlighted in bold lettering. All dates are presented in the Julian calendar until February 15, 1923 and in the Gregorian calendar from March 1, 1923 onwards.

21.1 Dates given for Gennadius II (1st time) by Germanos are "Spring 1454-1456." Grumel and Podskalsky agree in "**6 Jan 1454-6 Jan 1456**," while Patrinelis gives "6 Jan 1454-Apr 1456."

21.2 Dates given for Isidore II by Germanos and Grumel are "beg 1456 (before May)-Spring 1462." Πατρινελης gives "May 1456-**31 Mar 1462**" and Podskalsky "c.15 Jan 1456-31 Mar 1462."

21.3 Dates given for Joasaph I by Germanos are "Dec 1464/beg 1465-first months of 1466." Grumel gives "Jul 1465-c.mid 1466," Patrinelis "**1 Apr 1462**-summer 1463" and Podskalsky "**1 Apr 1462-10 Apr 1463**." Germanos and Grumel put Joasaph's Patriarchy after Gennadius' 3rd time, while Patrinelis and Podskalsky agree that Joasaph was Isidore's successor.

21.4 Dates given for Gennadius II (2nd time) by Germanos and Grumel are "c.summer 1462-summer 1463." Patrinelis gives "**summer 1463-end 1463**," and Podskalsky "e.**Apr 1463**-May(?) 1463." Patrinelis and Podskalsky shorten Gennadius second term to accommodate the insertion of Joasaph's Patriarchy in 1462-1463.

21.5 Dates given for Sophronius I by Germanos and Grumel are "c.Aug 1463-**b.Aug 1464**." Patrinelis gives "end 1463-**Aug 1464**," and Podskalsky "**Jun 1463**-c.Jul 1464."

21.6 Dates given for Gennadius II (3rd time) by Germanos are "Aug 1464-end 1464." Grumel gives "Aug 1464-Jul 1465." Patrinelis gives "**Aug 1464-autumn 1465**," and Podskalsky "b.**Aug 1464-autumn 1465**." Germanos and Grumel place Joasaph's Patriarchy in 1465-1466.

21.7 Dates given for Mark II by Germanos are "first months of 1466-c.mid 1466." Grumel gives "c.mid 1466-Nov/Dec 1466." Patrinelis gives "beg 1466-mid 1466," and Podskalsky "beg 1466-**autumn 1466**." Grumel cites L. Petit "Deposition du Patriarche Marc Xylokaravi," *Revue de l'Orient Chretien*, 8, Paris 1903, p. 114-149, as a source unknown by Germanos, which places the end of Mark's Patriarchy in autumn 1466. Chroniclers mention that he remained Patriarch for almost one year.

21.8 Dates given for Symeon (1st time) by Germanos and Patrinelis are "c.mid 1466-**end 1466.**" Grumel gives "Nov/Dec 1466-end 1467," and Podskalsky "autumn 1465-beg 1466." Germanos, Patrinelis, and Grumel place Symeon's 1st Patriarchy after the Patriarchy of Mark II, while Podskalsky places it before, in the place where Germanos and Grumel place Joasaph's Patriarchy. Chronicler Dorotheos of Monemvasia mentions explicitly that Symeon deposed and succeeded Mark Xylokaravis.

21.9 Dates given for Dionysius I (1st time) by Germanos are "e.Dec 1466/b.Jan 1467-c.**end 1471**." Grumel gives "e.Dec 1467-c.**end 1471**." Patrinelis and Podskalsky give "autumn 1466-**end 1471**" (but Patrinelis lists "**-end 1466**" for Symeon and "autumn 1466-" for Dionysius I, which should also be "**end 1466**-"). Germanos, Grumel, and Patrinelis place Symeon's 1st Patriarchy between the Patriarchies of Mark II and Dionysius I. Podskalsky places Symeon's Patriarchy before Mark. A synodic document signed by Dionysius I on January 15, 1467 makes it difficult to accept Grumel's date of Dec 1467 for the election of Dionysius.

22. Manouil was Megas Ekklesiarchis (a high ranking officer) of the Patriarchate. On his election he became a monk, changing his name to Maximus, and the next day he was consecrated Patriarch. Manouil's nose was cut by order of the Sultan during the events leading to the deposition of Joasaph I. Dates given for Maximus III by Germanos and Grumel are "**spring 1476**-end 1481/beg 1482," and for Symeon (3rd time) "beg 1482-**autumn 1486**." Patrinelis and Podskalsky give the correct "**spring 1476-3 Apr 1482**" for Maximus and "**Apr 1482-autumn 1486**" for Symeon. Maximus' date of death (3 Apr 1482) is inscribed on the British Museum manuscript Add.22492, 192V.

23. His name as Metropolitan of Serres was Manasses, but he changed it to Maximus on his election to the Ecumenical See, a unique instance in the history of the Ecumenical Patriarchate.

24. Dates given for Jeremias I by Germanos and Grumel are "**31 Dec 1522**-end 1545," and for the intruder Johnnicius I "c.spring 1526/few months." Patrinelis and Podskalsky give the correct "**31 Dec 1522-13 Jan 1546**" for Jeremias I and "spring 1524-autumn 1525" for Johnnicius's intrusion. Μιχαήλ Στρουμπακης (Michail Stroubakis), in *Ιερεμίας Α΄ Πατριάρχης Κωνσταντινουπόλεως*, Athens 2004, gives the final dates for Ioannicius as "**Apr/May 1524-24 Sep 1525**." Patrinelis gives details for Jeremias's restoration to the Patriarchy and his death (13 Jan 1546) in his relevant article in *ΘHE* Vol.6, p. 779-80.

25. Dates given for Dionysius II by Germanos are "**17 Apr 1546**-Aug 1555." Grumel gives "**17 Apr 1546**-after Aug 1554," while Patrinelis and Podskalsky give "**17 Apr 1546-Jul 1556**." Patrinelis gives details for Jeremias's restoration to the Patriarchy and his death (13 Jan 1546) in his article for Jeremias in *ΘHE* Vol.6, p. 779-80.

26. Dates given for Joasaph II by Germanos are "after Aug 1555-Jan 1565." Grumel gives "after Aug 1554-Jan 1565," while Patrinelis and Podskalsky give "**Jul/Aug 1556-Jan 1565.**"

27. The date given for Jeremias II's first deposition and the election of Metrophanes III (2nd time) by Germanos and Grumel is "29 Nov 1579." Patrinelis gives "mid Nov 1579" and Podskalsky "**23 Nov 1579.**" For the date given, Podskalsky cites Otto Kresten, *Das Patriarchat von Konstantinopel im ausgehenden 16. Jahrhundert*, Vienna 1970, who in turn cites Κωνσταντίνος Μερτζιος (Konstantinos Mertzios), *Πατριαρχικά ήτοι ανέκδοτοι πληροφορίαι σχετικαί προς τους Πατριάρχας Κωνσταντινουπόλεως από του 1556-1702*, Πραγματείαι της Ακαδημίας Αθηνών 15 (1951), Nr.4.

28. The date given for Jeremias II's second deposition by Germanos and Grumel is "e.Feb/b.Mar 1584," and for the intrusion of Pachomius II "**22 Feb 1584.**" Patrinelis gives "e.Feb 1584" for both incidents ,and Podskalsky gives "22 Feb 1584" for both. For the date given, Podskalsky cites Kresten (see note 27), who in turn cites Παπαδοπουλος-Κεραμευς (Papadapoulos-Kerameus), *Πατριαρχικοί κατάλογοι (1453-1636)*, Byzantinische Zeitschrift 8 (1899) p. 392-401, listing γ': "αφπδ [1584] Μπατίστας Μιτυλινιός παντριάρχης δυνάμει του κρατούντος φευρουαρίου κβ' (22) στου σουλτάν Μουράτ" and Κωνσταντίνος ΣΑΘΑΣ, *Βιογραφικόν σχεδίασμα περί του Πατριάρχου Ιερεμίου Β'* (1572-1594), Athens 1870: "ο δηλωθείς Πατέστος...του πατριαρχείου εδράξατο...το εαυτού όνομα εκφωνείσθαι ηνάγκασε, το του γνησίου πατριάρχου αποκόψας μνημόσυνον...και εις τον επάνω πατριαρχικόν θρόνον εκαθέσθη, και εφίλουν οι όμοιοι αυτώ την χείρα αυτού...πρώτον μεν τον γνήσιον πατριάρχην εξορισθήνε εποίησεν...."

29. The date given for Pachomius II's deposition by Germanos and Grumel is "Feb 1585," and for the election of Theoleptus II "27 Feb 1585." Patrinelis and Podskalsky give "**m.Feb 1585**" for Pachomius, and "**16 Feb 1585**" for Theoleptus. Podskalsky cites Kresten (see note 27), who in turn cites the report of Konstantinos Astella and Emmanuel Muzikios in their essay, "Εχειροτονήθη πατριάρχης Κωνσταντινουπόλεως κύριος Θεόληπτος κς' (26) Φεβρουαρ 1585." Their Gregorian calendar date is converted to Julian as February 16. In the same work Kresten explains why 27 Feb is not the correct date.

30. The date given for Theoleptus II's deposition by Germanos and Grumel is "Apr/May 1586," and for the restoration of Jeremias II "beg/mid 1587." Patrinelis gives "**May 1586**" for Theoleptus, and "**Apr 1587**" for Jeremias II. Podskalsky gives "m.Apr 1587" for both Theoleptus and Jeremias II. In May 1586 Theoleptus was deposed *in absentia*, and the deacon Nicephorus (1596+) served as *Locum Tenens* until Jeremias II was reinstalled as Patriarch in Apr 1587 (19 Apr 1587, according to Kresten). Deacon Dionysius (1611++) briefly interupted the term of Nicephorus, becoming *Locum Tenens* for 10 days; he later was elected Metropolitan of Larissa (1593-1601) and was horribly executed in 1611 (skinned alive) for instigating a rebellion.

31. The death date of Jeremias II given by Germanos, Grumel, and Patrinelis is "**end 1595.**" Podskalsky gives "Sep 1595," citing Kresten (see note 27) for this date; however, although Kresten lists "Sep 1595" in his chronological appendix, he gives "end 1595" in the body of his work (p.31). Sep 1595 is only the date of the last known document signed by Jeremias II.

32. Metropolitan Theophanes of Athens served as *Locum Tenens* from Aug 1596-Dec 1596, and the Patriarch of Alexandria, Meletius I (1590-1601), served as *Locum Tenens* from Dec 1596-Feb 1597.

33. In May 1630 Patriarch Cyril I thwarted a deposition attempt by the Metropolitan of Chalkidon, Isaacius (d. 1637?), who was defrocked on May 13, 1630, but pardoned and elected Metropolitan of Kaisaria on June 8, 1630.
34. Patriarch Cyril I was accused of corresponding with Russia to instigate a rebellion. He was deposed, and on June 27, 1638 janissary soldiers arrested him, put him on a ship, and, after the ship had sailed, strangled him and threw his body to the sea.
35. Patriarch Cyril II was hanged by the Ottoman authorities of Tunis on June 24, 1640, after refusing to save his life by converting to Islam.
36. Patriarch Parthenius II was accused of corresponding with Russia to instigate a rebellion. On May 16, 1651, janissary soldiers arrested him, put him on a ship, and, after the ship had sailed, strangled him and threw his body to the sea.
37. Patriarch Parthenius III was accused of conspiring with foreign powers against the Sultan. Although in his subsequent trial the accusation was proven false, the Sultan ordered his execution in order "to set an example for those who may try that in the future." He was hanged by the Turkish authorities on March 24, 1657.
38. Former Ecumenical Patriarch and president of the Metropolitanate of Prousa Gabriel was accused of converting a Muslim to Christianity. He was hanged by the Ottoman authorities on December 3, 1659, after refusing to save his life by converting to Islam.
39. Patriarch Parthenius IV was deposed in April 1659 by Theophanes, the former Metropolitan of Melenikon; however, three days later Parthenius managed to annul the decision.
40. Clement bought the position of Patriarch from the Ottoman authorities on September 9, 1667, but the other Hierarchs did not accept him and collectively defrocked him on September 13, 1667. Clement could not remain in Constantinople, so he moved to Adrianople, staying close to the Ottoman Sultan who was also residing there at the time. With the help of the Ottoman authorities he remained Patriarch until January 5, 1668, when permission to elect his successor was given to the Synod.
41. Patriarch Jeremias III managed to thwart two serious attempts at his deposition: On January 1, 1718 Cyril, the Metropolitan of Prousa (d. 1724?), was elected in his place; however, on January 17, 1718 Jeremias managed to annul that decision and remained Patriarch. On January 10, 1720 Jeremias was imprisoned and former Ecumenical Patriarch Cyril IV was elected in his place; however, on January 22, 1720 Jeremias managed to annul that decision and remained Patriarch.
42. After the Hierarchs who opposed Jeremias III secured permission from the Ottoman authorities to remove the Patriarch, they convened and elected Callinicus III on the evening of November 19, 1726. However, when they visited him the next morning in order to accompany him to his enthronement, they found him dead inside his house. Fearing that Jeremias III could use the confusion to remain on the throne, they announced to the Turkish authorities that they had elected Païsius II as the new Patriarch.
43. Former Patriarch Cyril VI was hanged in Adrianople by the Ottoman authorities on April 18, 1821, a few days after the beginning of the Greek revolution.
44. Patriarch Gregory V was deposed on April 10, Easter Sunday, 1821, right after the Resurrection Mass, being accused of treason against the Sultan as a supposed instigator of the Greek Revolution. While his successor was enthroned at 14:00 hours of the same day, Gregory was maltreated by the masses, and after refusing to save his life by converting to Islam, he was hanged on the central entrance of the Patriarchate. The door of the Patriarchate's central entrance never reopened after that incident; it remains permanently closed to this day.
45. In 1860 the Holy Synod created the position of *Locum Tenens* (grk Τοποτηρητής), the Caretaker of the Throne who was elected after a Patriarchal vacancy, making it mandatory for the first time (Caretakers had been elected on an *ad hoc* basis prior to this date). His main duty was to prepare for the election of the next Patriarch; he could not, however, appoint new Hierarchs. After the resignation of Germanus V in 1918, the political turmoil in the final years of the Ottoman Empire (1918-23) resulted in several periods when no Patriarch could be elected, and the *Locum Tenens* of the time assumed some additional duties as a result. In 1923 the title of the Caretaker was changed to Provisional Head of the Synod. The following Metropolitans held these positions: Joannicius of Nikaia (7 Jul-4 Oct 1860), Meletius of Raskopresreni (11 Jul-20 Sep 1863), Neophytus of Koritsa (5 Dec 1866-10 Feb 1867), Dionysius of Didymotichon (10 Jun-5 Sep 1871), Seraphim of Arta (30 Sep-23 Nov 1873), Agathangelus of Ephesos (7 Aug-4 Oct 1878 & 30 Mar-1 Oct 1884), John of Kaisaria (16 Nov 1886-23 Jan 1887), Dorotheus of Velegrades (16 Aug-27 Oct 1891), Nathanael of Prousa (26 Oct 1894-20 Jan 1895 & 30 Mar-25 May 1901), Constantine of Ephesos (29 Jan-2 Apr 1897), Germanus of Amasia (20 Nov 1912-28 Jan 1913), Dorotheus of Prousa (12 Oct 1918-6 Mar 1921+), Nicholas of Kaisaria (6 Mar-25 Nov 1921, 10 Jul-2 Oct 1923, & 22 May-13 Jul 1925), Callinicus of Kyzikos (2 Oct-6 Dec 1923, 17-24 Nov 1924, & 29 Sep-7 Oct 1929), Basil of Nikaia (24 Nov-17 Dec 1924), Benjamin of Iraklia (29 Dec 1935-18 Jan 1936), Maximus of Chalkidon (17-20 Feb 1946), Thomas of Chalkidon (18 Oct-1 Nov 1948), Meliton of Chalkidon (7-16 Jul 1972), and Bartholomew of Chalkidon (2-22 Oct 1991)

46. Patriarch Meletius IV was forced to leave Turkey on July 10, 1923. He resigned a couple of months later, and on May 20, 1926 was elected Meletius II, Patriarch of Alexandria (1926-35).
47. Patriarch Constantine VI was deported to Greece by the Turkish authorities on January 30, 1925. He resigned a few months later, after all efforts to secure his return to Turkey failed.
48. Patriarch Maximus V was named president of the Metropolitanate of Ephesus on March 27, 1948, a few months before his resignation; this was finally accepted by the Synod.

PART II

METROPOLITANATES OF THE ECUMENICAL PATRIARCHATE

History of Eparchies and Catalog of Hierarchs

This section examines the individual Metropolitanates that today remain under the control of the Ecumenical Patriarchate. Each article devoted to a specific Metropolitanate contains its epigrammatic history, followed by an annotated catalog of its Hierarchs after the year 1800.

The main cities inside the area of each Metropolitanate are mentioned, along with their Turkish names, in order for the reader to be able to visualize the approximate area and location of each Metropolitanate on a map of modern Turkey. A map of each Metropolitanate will be included in a future edition of this work.[1]

The catalogs themselves are not simply lists of dates, but are enhanced with biographical information on the Hierarchs, such as their family surnames, dates of birth and death, previous position if they came to the current Metropolitanate by transfer (*e.g.*, "ex m.Nikaia"), and their subsequent position if they afterwards were transferred to another Metropolitanate (*e.g.*, "to m.Nikomidia"). Since many Eparchies have been transferred to the jurisdiction of other Orthodox Churches or abolished, a detailed list of all the Eparchies under the jurisdiction of the Ecumenical Patriarchate after the year 1800 is given in Appendix B.

The Hierarch names are listed in two forms: the English-language version and the original Greek name as written in the Greek alphabet. The exact transliteration of all Greek names in the Latin alphabet can be found in Appendix C, along with a guide on how to pronounce the Greek names.

Since the catalogs of the Eparchies' Hierarchs before the year 1800 are incomplete, they are included in Appendix A. Note that the numbering of the Hierarchs does not reflect the actual number of an Eparchy's Hierarchs, but rather the number of an Eparchy's known Hierarchs. Further names may be added by research in the future.

Abbreviations used in the catalogs are: b. (born, if appearing before a date; Bishop if appearing before an Eparchy name), d. (died, if appearing before a date; Diocese, if appearing before an Eparchy name), a. (Archbishop), m. (Metropolitan), p. (Patriarch), t.b. (Titular Bishop), t.m. (Titular Metropolitan).

A new Hierarch's tenure is regarded to have begun on the date of his Episcopal consecration. Whenever that date was not available, the date of his election, in Italic font, is noted instead.[3] Of course, when a Hierarch is transferred from one Eparchy to another, the date of his election also marks the beginning of his tenure there.

A Hierarch-elect whose tenure ended before he was actually consecrated is not listed here, since in essence he never legally became a Hierarch of the Eparchy. His case may be mentioned in a note.

In cases where a Titular Hierarch has been elected to an Eparchy, the date of his consecration (or election in italics) to the Titular See is noted next to his former title (*e.g.*, "ex t.b.Myra 3 Jul 1893"). Where the Hierarch previously held more than one titular title, all of his titles will be noted (*e.g.*, "ex t.b.Meloi 25 Sep 1960, t.m.Kalavria 30 Mar 1965," meaning that the Hierarch was first consecrated Titular Bishop of Meloi, and five years later was promoted to the Titular Metropolitanate of Calabria).

A Hierarch's tenure can end in various ways, and all are noted in the catalogs. A plus sign '+' after a date means that the Hierarch died on that date. Two plus signs '++' after the date means that the Hierarch suffered a martyr's death, and there will be a note explaining the circumstances. If the Hierarch was transferred to another See,[2] the name of that See is noted in brackets under his name (*e.g.*, "to Nikaia"). Also noted are cases where a Hierarch resigned,[4] was suspended, was deposed,[5] or was defrocked by the Synod of the Patriarchate, or if he did not accept his new position.[6]

In cases of resignation, suspension, or deposition, the Hierarch then held the title of former Hierarch of the Eparchy (*e.g.*, "Former Metropolitan of Kyzikos") until his election to another Eparchy. These cases are specifically noted; *e.g.*, "to former, to m.Nikaia" means that the Hierarch was titled "former Metropolitan" of the current Eparchy for a particular period of time, and then was elected to the Metropolitanate of Nikaia. Also, "ex former m.Kyzikos" means that the newly elected Metropolitan was previously a Metropolitan of Kyzikos who either resigned, was suspended, or was deposed before his current election.

There are cases where two Hierarchs were simultaneously transferred to each other's Eparchy. For these cases to be registered canonically, one Hierarch had to have resigned, while the other Hierarch was transferred to the resigned Hierarch's Eparchy, and then the resigned Hierarch was transferred to the transferred Hierarch's Eparchy (with all these acts being registered the same day). These iconic resignations are not noted as resignations here; both Hierarchs are listed as having been transferred. Sometimes these simultaneous transfers involve three or more Hierarchs; the same approach is taken in these cases.

Another case is when a Metropolitan is transferred to a Diocese. Of course the Metropolitan is not demoted to Bishop in this case, nor is the Diocese promoted to a Metropolitanate, but the Metropolitan is registered as presiding over the Diocese. These cases of transfer are so noted (*e.g.*, "to president d.Kitros"), and the Metropolitan is listed among the Diocese's Bishops with his special status noted.

All dates are presented in the Julian calendar until February 15, 1923, and in the Gregorian calendar from March 1, 1923 on.[7]

The Ecumenical Patriarchate used the system of Metropolitanates that had Dioceses under their jurisdiction, as established in 325 AD by the first Ecumenical Council. Each Metropolitanate had its own local synod, comprised of the Bishops of its Dioceses. The Metropolitan was responsible for the election of his Bishops locally, although sometimes the Ecumenical Patriarchate intervened and directly elected a Bishop, usually at the request of the Metropolitan.

Sometimes a Diocese was promoted to Archdiocese by the Patriarch; that is, its Hierarch ceased being under the local Metropolitan, and was thereafter elected directly by the Patriarch.

A tendency to elevate all Dioceses and Archdioceses to the status of Metropolitanate appeared after the massive loss of Metropolitanates by the Patriarchate in the eighteenth century. The last Archdiocese of the Ecumenical Patriarchate (Archdiocese of

Nevrokopion) was promoted to a Metropolitanate in 1887. The last Metropolitanate with a Synod of Bishops[8] (the Metropolitanate of Thessaloniki) lost its four remaining Dioceses when they were promoted to Metropolitanates on October 7, 1924.

Since I intend to publish similar works covering the Eparchies of the other Orthodox Churches, including the periods where their Metropolitanates were under the jurisdiction of the Ecumenical Patriarchate, one will eventually be able to follow a Hierarch's transfer history from the day of his consecration to the day of his death.

NOTES

1. As this work deals with ecclesiastic terms and not political terms, the cities are mentioned with their ancient Roman names, and modern Turkish names are mentioned only once, inside parentheses. Ecclesiastic terms keep the names of cities, etc. as used in the Roman era. It is characteristic that in the Patriarchate's ecclesiastic documents of the Ottoman era, the Sultan is commonly referred as "Emperor."
2. Under normal circumstances, consecration occurred a few days after the election of a Hierarch, usually on the following Saturday or Sunday. However, there have been cases where due to various problems the consecration occurred much later—months, even years after the election.
3. The policy of systematically transferring the Hierarchs of the Ecumenical Patriarchate to other Metropolitanates started during the Ottoman period. It was not uncommon for Hierarchs to be successively transferred five times, or even more, during their lifetime.
4. In cases of resignation, the date noted is not the date that the Hierarch submitted his resignation to the Synod, but the date that the Synod accepted the resignation. This date is assumed to be the date the Synod elected the Hierarch's successor, except when known otherwise. (If a Hierarch submits his resignation but the Synod does not accept it, the resignation is annulled.)
5. Some of the suspensions or depositions were forced on the Patriarchate by the Ottoman Authorities.
6. When a Hierarch did not accept his transfer, the Patriarchate could restore him to his former See, transfer him to another See, suspend him, or depose him. In some cases, however, the election itself was cancelled. Cancelled elections are not listed in the catalogs.
7. Dates in the Julian calendar from March 1900 to February 1923 can be converted to the Gregorian calendar by adding 13 days to them. Dates in the Julian calendar from March 1800 to February 1900 can be converted to the Gregorian calendar by adding 12 days to them. Dates in the Julian calendar from March 1700 to February 1800 can be converted to the Gregorian calendar by adding 11 days to them. Dates in the Julian calendar from October 1582 to February 1700 can be converted to the Gregorian calendar by adding 10 days to them.
8. There is, of course, the special case of the Metropolitanate of Crete, whose Synod survived due to the Metropolitanate's semi-autonomous status. Although the Dioceses in Crete were promoted to Metropolitanates on September 25, 1962, the local synod remains in operation under the Archbishop of Crete.

SECTION A:
METROPOLITANATES IN EASTERN THRACE

METROPOLITANATE OF ADRIANOUPOLIS
ΜΗΤΡΟΠΟΛΙΣ ΑΔΡΙΑΝΟΥΠΟΛΕΩΣ

Metropolitan of Adrianople, most honorable and Exarch of all Haemimontus

The city of Adrianoupolis (Adrianople, Grk Αδριανούπολις, Trk Edirne, derived by the popular abbreviation of its name to Adrianou, Grk Αδριανού) was found by Emperor Hadrian (117-38) in the year 127 AD in place of the Thracian city Uscudama, called Gonis (Γονείς) by the Greeks, which came under direct Roman control in 46 AD. It is situated on the east bank of Evros river (called Meriç in Turkey, Maritsa in Bulgaria), 240 km northeast of Constantinople.

The Metropolitanate of Adrianople is bordered by the Metropolitanate of Sliven (Church of Bulgaria) on the north, the Metropolis of Saranta Ekklisies and the Metropolitanate of Vizyi on the east, the Metropolitanate of Heraclia on the south, and the Metropolitanate of Didymotichon (Church of Greece) on the west. Other large cities in the area of the Metropolitanate are Vourdizos (Grk Βούρδιζος, Trk Babaeski), 54 km southeast of Adrianoupolis, and Arkadioupolis (Grk Αρκαδιούπολις, Trk Lüleburgaz), 22 km east of Vourdizos.

Adrianople has been a Metropolitanate since 325 AD. It had five Dioceses under its jurisdiction in the seventh century, which increased to thirteen by the twelfth century. The city was occupied by the Ottoman Turks in 1362 and became their capital in 1413. The Ottoman capital was transferred to Constantinople in 1457. During this period the number of Dioceses decreased, with only Agathoupolis remaining by the sixteenth century, and none after 1760.

Adrianople was occupied by the Russian army in 1829 and again in 1878. It was occupied by the Bulgarian army from March 26-July 21, 1913, when it was recovered by the Ottomans. On July 12, 1920 it was occupied by the Greek army, and sixteen days later, on July 28, Greece officially annexed Western and Eastern Thrace, except for Constantinople and a small area adjoining it.

After the catastrophic defeat of the Greeks on the Asia Minor front, part of the peace treaty between Greece and Turkey, as mediated by the Western European powers, required the return of Eastern Thrace to Turkey. The Greek army completed the evacuation of the area on October 25, 1922 and it was delivered to Turkey on November 12. The Orthodox population living in the area followed the army into Greece.

In October 1924, the areas of the Metropolitanate that remained in Greek territory, being west of Evros river, were transferred to the new Metropolitanate of New Orestias. No Orthodox population remains inside the area of the Metropolitanate today.

Metropolitans of Adrianoupolis since 1800

63. Gabriel (ex m.Nikaia)	Γαβριήλ	Sep 1792 – 1810+	d. 1810
64. Cyril I Serbetzoglous (ex m.Ikonion) (to p.Constantinople)	Κύριλλος Α΄	Dec 1810 – 4 Mar 1813	1775-1821
65. Dorotheus Proios (ex m.Philadelphia) executed by the Ottomans	Δωρόθεος	Jun 1813 – 4 Jun 1821++	d. 1821
66. Nicephorus III Pilousiotis (ex a.Prikonnisos) (to m.Derki)	Νικηφόρος Γ΄	Jun 1821 – Sep 1824	d. 1835
67. Gerasimus IV Frydas (ex m.Prousa) resigned	Γεράσιμος Δ΄	Sep 1824 – May 1830	d. ?
68. Gregory II (ex m.Stromnitsa) resigned	Γρηγόριος Β΄	May 1830 – 24 Jun 1840	d. 1860
69. Gerasimus V Tzermias (ex m.Pelagonia) (to m.Chalkidon)	Γεράσιμος Ε΄	Jun 1840 – 15 Mar 1853	d. 1875
70. Cyril II Kyriakidis (ex m.Ganos) suspended (to former, to m.Silyvria)	Κύριλλος Β΄	15 Mar 1853 – 1 May 1873	d. 1881
71. Dionysius II Charitonidis (ex m.Didymotixon) (to m.Nikaia)	Διονύσιος Β΄ (1st time)	1 May 1873 – 14 Nov 1880	1820-1891
72. Neophytus II Papakonstantinou (ex m.Philippoupolis) resigned (to former, to m.Pelagonia)	Νεόφυτος Β΄	14 Nov 1880 – 23 Jan 1886	1832-1909
---. Dionysius II Charitonidis (ex m.Nikaia) (to p.Constantinople)	Διονύσιος Β΄ (2nd time)	23 Jan 1886 – 23 Jan 1887	1820-1891
73. Matthew III Petridis (ex m.Pelagonia) suspended	Ματθαίος Γ΄	28 Feb 1887 – 3 Jan 1890	d. ?
74. Cyril III Dimitriadis/Panagiotou (ex m.Limnos) resigned	Κύριλλος Γ΄	3 Jan 1890 – 26 Aug 1908	1845-1921
75. Callinicus II Georgiadis (to m.Kallipolis)	Καλλίνικος Β΄	26 Aug 1908 – 12 Aug 1910	d. 1912
76. Polycarp II Vardakis (ex m.Elasson) (to m.Chios) see note 1	Πολύκαρπος Β΄	12 Aug 1910 – 12 Feb 1931	1862-1945
77. Damascene Papandreou (ex m.Helvetia)	Δαμασκηνός	20 Jan 2003 –	b. 1936

1. Metropolitan Polycarp moved west of the Evros River to the areas of his Metropolitanate that remained inside the borders of Greece. On October 9, 1924 these areas formed the new temporal Metropolitanate of New Orestias, and he was given the title of "Metropolitan of New Orestias and Adrianople" until his transfer to the Metropolitanate of Chios.

METROPOLITANATE OF AINOS
ΜΗΤΡΟΠΟΛΙΣ ΑΙΝΟΥ

Metropolitan of Aenus, most honorable and Exarch of all Rhodope

The city of Ainos (Grk Αίνος, Trk Enez) was established as a colony of the Aeolian Greeks in the seventh century BC. It is situated on the shore of the Aegean Sea, near the estuary of Evros River, an area that came under Roman control in 148 BC.

The Metropolitanate of Ainos is bordered by the Metropolitanate of Heraclia on the north and east, the Aegean Sea on the south, and by the Metropolitanate of Alexandroupolis (Greece) on the west. Another city in the area of the Metropolitanate is Kypsela (Grk. Κύψελα, Trk. Ipsala), situated at its northern boundary, 35 km northeast of Ainos. Ainos was a Diocese of the Metropolitanate of Traïanoupolis. Between the years 527 and 565 it was promoted to an Archdiocese. Before 1032 it was promoted to a Metropolitanate. The city became a Genovese posession circa 1384, and was occupied by the Ottoman Turks in 1456.

In October 1885 the important city of Dedeagac (today Alexandroupolis, in Greek Western Thrace) was transferred from the neighboring Metropolitanate or Maronia to the Metropolitanate of Ainos, and soon thereafter the Metropolitanate See was transferred to Dedeagac.

The Metropolitanate became part of the Bulgarian state in between the Balkan wars, with Dedeagac being occupied by the Bulgarians from November 8, 1912-July 11, 1913, when the Greek army moved in. On July 28, 1913, it was returned to Bulgaria, until the western Allies occupied the city on October 18, 1919. Greek forces occupied the city a second time on May 14, 1920. On July 28 Greece officially annexed the area, changing the name of Dedeagac to Alexandroupolis (Αλεξανδρούπολις) in honor of King Alexander I (1917-20) of Greece.

In October 1922 all the Orthodox living in the lands of the Metropolitanate that were east of the Evros River, including the citizens of Ainos, moved west of the river (see Adrianople). All areas of Thrace situated on the east of Evros River were delivered to Turkey on November 12, 1922, and on November 17, 1922, all the areas of the Metropolitanate of Ainos that remained inside the borders of Greece became part of the new Metropolitanate of Alexandroupolis. No Orthodox population remains within the area of the Metropolitanate today.

Metropolitans of Ainos since 1800

33. Dionysius	Διονύσιος		Jul 1772 – 1807+	d. 1807
34. Matthew II Megalos (to m.Thessaloniki)	Ματθαίος Β΄		Feb 1807 – Jun 1821	d. 1831
35. Gregory (to former, to m.Drystra) suspended	Γρηγόριος		Jun 1821 – May 1831	d. 1840
36. Cyril (to m.Amasia)	Κύριλλος		May 1831 – Mar 1847	c.1800-1872
37. Sophronius (ex m.Anchialos) (to m.Kriti)	Σωφρόνιος	(1st time)	7 Mar 1847 – 24 Aug 1850	d. 1855
38. Ignatius (to m.Kassandria)	Ιγνάτιος		25 Aug 1850 – 8 Feb 1851	1814-1867
---. Sophronius (ex former m.Kriti)	Σωφρόνιος	(2nd time)	Feb 1851 – 1855+	d. 1855
39. Gabriel (ex m.Dimitrias)	Γαβριήλ		11 Jul 1855 – 17 Jul 1867+	d. 1867
40. Meletius II (ex former m.Loftsa) resigned	Μελέτιος Β΄		24 Aug 1867 – 3 Apr 1872	d. ?
41. Meletius III Kavasilas (ex m.Neokaisaria) (to president d.Kitros)	Μελέτιος Γ΄		3 Apr 1872 – 12 Mar 1873	d≥1874
42. Dorotheus II (ex b.Kitros)	Δωρόθεος Β΄		12 Mar 1873 – 2 Sep 1877+	d. 1877
43. Anthimus Tsatsos (ex b.Paramythia) (to m.Anchialos)	Άνθιμος		11 Oct 1877 – 15 Oct 1888	1827-1913

44. Luke	Λουκάς	15 Oct 1888 – 22 May 1899	d. 1912
Petridis (ex m.Serres) (to m.Dryinoupolis)			
45. Germanus I	Γερμανός Α΄	22 May 1899 – 8 Aug 1903	1845-1918
Theotokas (ex t.b.Myra 3 Jul 1893) (to m.Leros)			
46. Leontius	Λεόντιος	8 Aug 1903 – 27 Jan 1907	d. ?
Eleftheriadis (ex m.Kassandria) suspended			
47. Joachim II	Ιωακείμ Β΄	27 Jan 1907 – 20 Dec 1923	1875-1927
Georgiadis (ex t.b.Christoupolis 1 Dec 1902) (to m.Chalkidon)			
48. Germanus II	Γερμανός Β΄	3 Sep 1936 – 22 Jan 1962+	1893-1962
Garofallidis (ex t.b.Avydos 25 Mar 1931)			
49. Apostolus	Απόστολος	13 Feb 1975 – 28 Nov 1977+	1915-1977
Papaïoannou (ex m.Karpathos)			
50. Maximus	Μάξιμος	24 Nov 1997 – 20 Dec 2002	b. 1935
Agiorgousis (ex b.Pittsburgh) (to m.Pittsburgh)			

METROPOLITANATE OF DERKI
ΜΗΤΡΟΠΟΛΙΣ ΔΕΡΚΩΝ

Metropolitan of Derki, most honorable and Exarch of Bosporus, Thracian and Cyanea

The city of Derki (Grk. Δέρκοι, Trk. Durusu) was built by Emperor Anastasius I (491-518) in 507. It is situated next to the lake of the same name, 45 km northeast of Constantinople.

The Metropolitanate of Derki is bordered by the Black Sea on the north; the Bosporus Strait and the Archdiocese of Constantinople on the east; the Sea of Marmara, the Metropolitanate of Metres, and the Metropolitanate of Silyvria on the south; and the Metropolitanate of Tyroloi on the west.

Derki was a Diocese of the Metropolitanate of Heraclea before the eighth century. At the beginning of that century it was promoted to an Archdiocese. About 1380 it was promoted to a Metropolitanate. The area of the Metropolitanate was occupied by the Ottoman Turks in early 1453. Around that time it was abolished due to depopulation.

In June 1655 the Metropolitanate of Derki was re-established, and its See was transferred to Therapia (Grk. Θεραπειά, Trk Tarabya), then a city on the Bosporus Strait, 15 km north of Constantinople, today a suburb of modern Istanbul. After the population exchange of 1923 between Greece and Turkey, an Orthodox population remains only in the parts of the Metropolitanate that are suburbs of Istanbul.

Metropolitans of Derki since 1800

27. Macarius III	Μακάριος Γ΄	4 Mar 1794 – Jun 1801	d. 1803
Balasakis (ex m.Nafpaktos) (to m.Ephesos)			
28. Gregory III	Γρηγόριος Γ΄	Jun 1801 – 4 Jun 1821++	c.1747-1821
(ex Vidyni) executed by the Ottomans			
29. Jeremias	Ιερεμίας	9 Jun 1821 – 9 Jun 1824	d. 1824
(ex m.Vizyi) defrocked			
30. Nicephorus	Νικηφόρος	Sep 1824 – 1835+	d. 1835
Pilousiotis (ex m.Adrianoupolis)			
31. Germanus	Γερμανός	Nov 1835 – 14 Jun 1842	1788-1853
(ex m.Drama) (to p.Constantinople)			

32. Neophytus III Vegleris/Psaroudis (ex m.Philippi)	Νεόφυτος Γ'	Jun 1842 – 13 Mar 1853+	d. 1853
33. Gerasimus II Pournaras/Lachovaris (ex m.Pelagonia)	Γεράσιμος Β'	15 Mar 1853 – 12 Mar 1865+	d. 1865
34. Neophytus IV Drymadis (ex m.Kassandria)	Νεόφυτος Δ'	14 Mar 1865 – 5 Aug 1875+	1820-1875
35. Joachim I Krousouloudis (ex m.Larissa) (to p.Constantinople)	Ιωακείμ Α'	7 Aug 1875 – 1 Oct 1884	1837-1887
36. Callinicus Photiadis (ex m.Thessaloniki) (to m.Ephesos)	Καλλίνικος	20 Dec 1884 – 8 May 1924	1841-1926
37. Constantine II Arampoglous (ex m.Prousa) (to p.Constantinople)	Κωνσταντίνος Β'	8 May 1924 – 17 Dec 1924	1859-1930
38. Photius Maniatis (ex m.Philadelphia) (to p.Constantinople)	Φώτιος	17 Jan 1925 – 7 Oct 1929	1874-1935
39. Ambrose Stavrinos (ex m.Neokaisaria)	Αμβρόσιος	24 Oct 1929 – 9 Dec 1931+	1854-1931
40. Joachim II Pelekanos (ex t.m.Stavroupolis 24 Jun 1926)	Ιωακείμ Β'	12 Dec 1931 – 23 Jan 1950+	1892-1950
41. Jacob Papapaïsiou (ex m.Imvros) resigned, 5 Mar 1980+	Ιάκωβος	27 May 1950 – 1 Mar 1977	1885-1980
42. Constantine III Charisiadis (ex m.Pringiponnisa)	Κωνσταντίνος Γ'	15 Mar 1977 –	b. 1929

METROPOLITANATE OF GANOS AND CHORA
ΜΗΤΡΟΠΟΛΙΣ ΓΑΝΟΥ ΚΑΙ ΧΩΡΑΣ

Metropolitan of Ganus and Chora, most honorable and Exarch of Thrace Coast

The city of Ganos (Grk. Γάνος, Trk. Gazikoy) was established as a colony of Greeks from Megara in the fifth century BC. It is situated on the shore of the Marmara Sea, 165 km southwest of Constantinople, in area under Roman control since 148 BC. Chora (Grk. Χώρα, Trk. Hoskoy), the current See of the Metropolitanate, was built c.1235 by Emperor John III (1222-54), on the shore of the Marmara Sea, 5 km southwest of Ganos. The transfer of the Metropolitanate's See to Chora occurred in 1912, after a strong earthquake destroyed the Metropolitan's residence in Ganos.

The Metropolitanate of Ganos and Chora is bordered by the Metropolitanate of Heraclia on the north and west, the Marmara Sea on the southeast, and by the Metropolitanate of Myriophyton on the southwest.

Before the thirteenth century, Ganos was part of the Diocese of Peristasis under the Metropolitanate of Heraclia. It became an Archdiocese before 1324, and was promoted to a Metropolitanate before 1347. The area was occupied by the Ottomans circa 1360.

On July 28, 1920 Greece officially annexed the area, but in October 1922 all the Orthodox within the Metropolitanate were evacuated (see Adrianople), and the area was delivered to Turkey on November 12, 1922. No Orthodox population remains inside the area of the Metropolitanate today.

Metropolitans of Ganos and Chora since 1800

36. Gerasimus executed by the Ottomans	Γεράσιμος	Sep 1798 – 28 May 1821++	d. 1821

37. Leontius II (to m.Sisanion)	Λεόντιος Β'	mid 1821 – May 1835	d. 1852
38. Macarius II (ex b.Krini)	Μακάριος Β'	May 1835 – 15 Apr 1837+	d. 1837
39. Meletius (ex t.b.Elaia) (to m.Dimitrias)	Μελέτιος	27 Apr 1837 – May 1841	d. 1849
40. Matthew III Aristarchis (ex m.Dimitrias) resigned (to former, to m.Samakovion)	Ματθαίος Γ'	May 1841 – Dec 1845	d. 1862
41. Cyril II (ex m.Korytsa)	Κύριλλος Β'	Dec 1845 – Aug 1848+	d. 1848
42. Cyril III Kyriakidis (ex m.Svornikion) (to m.Adrianoupolis)	Κύριλλος Γ'	20 Aug 1848 – 15 Mar 1853	d. 1881
43. Chrysanthus Tzounis, resigned, 21 Nov 1873+	Χρύσανθος	*15 Mar* 1853 – 17 Apr 1873	d. 1873
44. Gregory III Mislianos (ex m.Kassandria)	Γρηγόριος Γ'	17 Apr 1873 – Jul 1873+	d. 1873
45. Timothy I Lampridis (ex m.Halepion) murdered during a period of civil unrest	Τιμόθεος Α'	14 Jul 1873 – 12 May 1875++	d. 1875
46. Parthenius Papafotinos (to m.Sozoagathoupolis)	Παρθένιος	22 May 1875 – 11 Feb 1881	d. 1900
47. Benedict Adamantidis (ex m.Anchialos) (to m.Pisidia)	Βενέδικτος	11 Feb 1881 – Feb 1886	d. 1906
48. Polycarp Konstantinidis (to m.Varna)	Πολύκαρπος	9 Mar 1886 – 1 Aug 1891	d. 1906
49. Dionysius II (ex m.Xanthi)	Διονύσιος Β'	1 Aug 1891 – 10 Sep 1897+	d. 1897
50. Constantine II Mikroulis (ex m.Paramythia) (to m.Sozoagathoupolis)	Κωνσταντίνος Β'	27 Sep 1897 – 23 May 1900	d. 1939
51. Constantine III Apostolou/Vallioulis (ex former b.Myriophyton) (to m.Pisidia)	Κωνσταντίνος Γ'	3 Jun 1900 – 3 Jun 1906	d. 1912
52. Constantius II Isaakidis (ex m.Veria) resigned, 26 Aug 1908+	Κωνστάντιος Β'	3 Jun 1906 – 21 Aug 1906	1835-1908
53. Constantine IV Chatziapostolou (ex former m.Melenikon) (to m.Anchialos)	Κωνσταντίνος Δ'	22 Aug 1906 – 12 May 1909	d. 1922
54. Seraphim Skaroulis (ex m.Sisanion) see note 1	Σεραφείμ	14 May 1909 – 29 Jul 1913+	1852-1913
55. Timothy II Lamnis (ex m.Philippoupolis) (to m.Metsovon)	Τιμόθεος Β'	10 Sep 1913 – 7 Oct 1924	1872-1928
56. Pangratius Vatopedinos (ex t.b.Lefki 6 Nov 1926)	Παγκράτιος	5 Oct 1943 – 30 May 1952+	1870-1952
57. Nectarius Chatzimichalis (ex former m.Leros)	Νεκτάριος	29 Aug 2007 –	b. 1932

1. On July 1, 1910 Metropolitan Seraphim was transferred to the Metropolitanate of Servia and Kozani, but he did not accept the transfer, and on August 5 another Hierarch was transferred to Servia in his place.

METROPOLITANATE OF IRAKLIA
ΜΗΤΡΟΠΟΛΙΣ ΗΡΑΚΛΕΙΑΣ

Metropolitan of Heraclia, president of most honorables and Exarch of all Thrace and Macedonia

The city of Perinthos (Grk. Πέρινθος), situated on the shore of the Marmara Sea, 95 km west of Constantinople, was established as a colony of Greeks from Samos in the fifth century BC. When the Romans annexed Thrace in 46 AD, Perinthos became the capital of the new Roman province. By the second century AD Perinthos was already a Christian Diocese. In the third century AD Perinthos was renamed Iraklia (Heraclia, Grk Ηράκλεια, Trk Marmaraereglisi) and became a Metropolitanate. The city was occupied by the Ottoman Turks in 1394, but returned to the Romans in January/February 1403, remaining in Byzantine hands with brief interruptions until 1452.

The Metropolitanate of Heraclia is bordered by the Metropolitanate of Adrianoupolis and the Metropolitanate of Vizyi on the north; the Metropolitanate of Tyroloi and the Metropolitanate of Silyvria on the east; the Marmara Sea, the Metropolitanate of Ganos, the Metropolitanate of Myriophyton, the Metropolitanate of Kallipolis, and the Aegean Sea on the south; and by the Metropolitanate of Ainos and the Metropolitanate of Alexandroupolis (Church of Greece) on the west.

Iraklia became a Metropolitanate in 325 AD, exercising honorary primacy over the other Metropolitanates of the Thracian Division: Adrianoupolis, Traïanoupolis, Philippoupolis, Markianoupolis, Tomis, and Pantikapaion in the Tavriki Peninsula (Grk Ταυρική Χερσόνησος, now the Crimea Peninsula). After the Second Ecumenical Council of 381, the Patriarchate of Constantinople officially assumed jurisdiction over the Metropolitanates in the area, including Iraklia.

Iraklia had five Dioceses under its jurisdiction in the seventh century, which increased to seventeen by the tenth century. In the twelfth century it still had sixteen Dioceses; however, after the Ottoman occupation the number steadily decreased, with six remaining in the sixteenth century, four after 1694, three after 1840, two after 1901, and none after 1909.

In 1694 the Metropolitanate's Diocese of Raidestos was promoted to an Archdiocese. In 1702 this Archdiocese was integrated in the Metropolitanate of Heraclia, which thereafter was known as Metropolitanate of Heraclia and Raidestos until well into the nineteenth century. In 1726 the See of the Metropolitanate was transferred to Raidestos, where it remains up to this date. Raidestos (Grk. Ραιδεστός, Trk. Tekirdag) is situated on the shore of the Marmara Sea, 40 km west of Heraclia.

The Metropolitanate of Heraclia remains the largest Metropolitanate in Eastern Thrace. Other important cities within it are Malgara (Grk. Μαλγαρά, Trk. Malkara), 54 km west of Raidestos; Kessani (Grk. Κεσσάνη, Trk. Kesan), 25 km west of Malgara; Charioupolis (Grk. Χαριούπολις, Trk. Hayrabolu), 52 km northwest of Raidestos; Makra Gefyra (Grk. Μακρά Γέφυρα, Trk. Uzunkorpu), 37 km west of Charioupolis.

On July 28, 1920 Greece officially annexed the area, but in October 1922 all the Orthodox living in the Metropolitanate were evacuated (see Adrianople), and it was delivered to Turkey on November 12, 1922. No Orthodox population remains inside the area of the Metropolitanate today.

Metropolitans of Iraklia since 1800

69. Meletius	Μελέτιος	Nov 1794 – 19 Sep 1821	d. ?
(ex b.Myriophyton) resigned			

70. Ignatius Staraveros	Ιγνάτιος	*Sep* 1821 – Jul 1830+	1765/8-1830
71. Dionysius II (ex b.Tyroloi)	Διονύσιος Β'	Jul 1830 – Jul 1848+	d. 1848
72. Panaretus (ex former m.Tornovo)	Πανάρετος	30 Jul 1848 – 9 May 1878+	1785-1878
73. Johnnicius II (ex m.Nikaia)	Ιωαννίκιος Β'	12 May 1878 – 25 Jan 1879+	d. 1879
74. Gregory II Pavlidis (ex m.Serres)	Γρηγόριος Β'	27 Jan 1879 – 6 Feb 1888+	1825-1888
75. Germanus III Kavvakopoulos (ex m.Rhodes) (to m.Chalkidon)	Γερμανός Γ'	8 Feb 1888 – 10 May 1897	1835-1920
76. Hieronymus Gorgias (ex m.Nikaia) (to m.Nikaia)	Ιερώνυμος	13 May 1897 – 22 May 1902	1837-1910
77. Gregory III Kalliadis (ex m.Ioannina)	Γρηγόριος Γ'	22 May 1902 – 25 Jul 1925+	1844-1925
78. Philaretus Vafidis (ex m.Didymotichon)	Φιλάρετος	21 Feb 1928 – 11 Oct 1933+	1848-1933
79. Benjamin Kyriakou (ex m.Nikaia) (to p.Constantinople)	Βενιαμίν	21 Oct 1933 – 18 Jan 1936	1871-1946
80. Photius Savvaïdis (ex m.Imvros)	Φώτιος	5 Sep 2002 – 24 Jun 2007+	1924-2007

METROPOLITANATE OF KALLIPOLIS AND MADYTOS
ΜΗΤΡΟΠΟΛΙΣ ΚΑΛΛΙΟΥΠΟΛΕΩΣ ΚΑΙ ΜΑΔΥΤΟΥ

Metropolitan of Callipolis and Madytus, most honorable and Exarch of Thracian Peninsula

The city of Kallipolis (Grk Καλλίπολις, Trk Gelibolu) was established as a colony of the Macedonian Greeks in the fifth century BC, coming under Roman control in 146 BC. It is situated in the Dardanelles Strait at the strait's exit into the Marmara Sea, 240 km southwest of Constantinople. In the fourth century AD Kallipolis was a Diocese under the Metropolitanate of Heraclia. Madytos (Grk Μάδυτος, Trk Eceabat), another city inside the Dardanelles strait, 40 km southwest of Kallipolis, became a Diocese under Heraclia in the tenth century.

Kallipolis was occupied by the Latins of Constantinople in 1205, but the Romans retook it in 1234. The Ottoman Turks took Kallipolis in March 1354, but a Crusading army expelled them in 1366, and the city returned to the Romans in June 1367, who returned it to the Ottomans in September 3, 1376.

Both Dioceses were promoted to Metropolitanates in the thirteenth century; however, after the area was occupied by the Ottoman Turks, both Metropolitanates were abolished due to depopulation. During that time Kallipolis became again a Diocese under Heraclia, until in December 1901 it was promoted to a Metropolitanate.

The Metropolitanate of Kallipolis and Madytos occupies the Kallipolis Peninsula, and is bordered by the Metropolitanate of Heraclia and the Aegean Sea on the north, the Dardanelles Strait and the Sea of Marmara on the south and east, and the Aegean Sea on the west. Another town in the area of the Metropolitanate is Kynos Sima (Grk Κυνός Σήμα, Trk Kilitbahir), inside the Dardanelles strait, 5 km southwest of Madytos.

On July 28, 1920 Greece officially annexed the area, but in October 1922 all the Orthodox living in the Metropolitanate were evacuated (see Adrianople), and it was delivered to Turkey on November 12, 1922. No Orthodox population remains inside the area of the Metropolitanate today.

Hierarchs of Kallipolis and Madytos since 1800
(Bishops until Dec 1901, Metropolitans afterwards)

11. Joachim	Ιωακείμ	1795 – Dec 1834+	d. 1834
12. Gregory II	Γρηγόριος Β´	Jan 1835 – 1880/81	d. 1881
Poumpouras (ex b.Tyroloi) resigned			
13. Abercius	Αβέρκιος	Jan 1881 – 5 Feb 1891	d. 1900
(ex t.b.Lefki 26 Oct 1874) (to m.Moglena)			
14. Photius	Φώτιος	16 Feb 1891 – Jan 1892+	d. 1892
Vougioukas			
15. Dorotheus	Δωρόθεος	10 Mar 1892 – 7 Dec 1896	1861-1921
Mammelis (to m.Grevena)			
16. Hieronymus	Ιερώνυμος	31 May 1897 – 9 Jul 1909	1860-1931
Gorgias (ex t.b.Irinoupolis 2 Apr 1892) (to m.Chios) promoted to Metropolitan in Dec 1901			
17. Panaretus	Πανάρετος	14 Jul 1909 – 12 Aug 1910	d. 1922
Petridis (ex m.Eleftheroupolis) (to m.Ilioupolis)			
18. Callinicus	Καλλίνικος	12 Aug 1910 – 29 Feb 1912+	d. 1912
Georgiadis (ex m.Adrianoupolis)			
19. Constantine	Κωνσταντίνος	8 Mar 1912 – 7 Oct 1924	1876-1954
Koïdakis (ex t.b.Dafnousia 14 Sep 1908) (to m.Plomarion)			

METROPOLITANATE OF METRES AND ATHYRA
ΜΗΤΡΟΠΟΛΙΣ ΜΕΤΡΩΝ ΚΑΙ ΑΘΥΡΩΝ

Metropolitan of Metres and Athyra, most honorable and Exarch of Thrace Coast

The city of Metres (Grk Μέτρες, Trk Çatalca), situated 50 km west of Constantinople, became in the ninth century a Diocese of the Metropolitanate of Heraclia. The city of Athyra (Grk. Άθυρα, Trk. Buyukcekmece) is situated on the shore of the Marmara Sea, 35 km west of Constantinople. It too became a Diocese of the Metropolitanate of Heraclia in the twelfth century.

The Metropolitanate of Metres and Athyra is bordered by the Metropolitanate of Derki on the north and the east, the Sea of Marmara on the south, the Metropolitanate of Tyroloi and the Metropolitanate of Heraclia on the west.

The general area where both cities are located came under Roman control in 46 AD. Metres were taken by the Ottoman Turks in 1371, while the area of Athyra was taken in 1453. A common Diocese of Metres and Athyra under the Metropolitanate of Heraclia is first mentioned in the sixteenth century. The Diocese was promoted to a Metropolitanate in October 1909.

After the population exchange of 1923 between Greece and Turkey, no Orthodox population today remains inside the area of the Metropolitanate.

Hierarchs of Metres and Athyra since 1800
(Bishops until Oct 1909, Metropolitans afterwards)

28. Sophronius	Σωφρόνιος	21 Sep 1783 – 1816	d. 1816?

29. Meletius	Μελέτιος	1816 – 4 Jun 1822	d. 1840
resigned (to former, to b.Achaïa of Greek Church)			
30. Gabriel	Γαβριήλ	*Sep* 1822 – Jul 1832	d≥1844
(to m.Skopia)			
31. Theocletus I	Θεόκλητος Α' (1st time)	1832 – Feb 1853	d. 1865
(to former) deposed by order of the Turkish Authorities			
32. Zacharias	Ζαχαρίας	Feb 1853 – 12 Jun 1861	d. 1877
(ex t.b.Erythres) (to m.Silyvria)			
---. Theocletus I	Θεόκλητος Α' (2nd time)	22 Jun 1861 – Oct 1865+	d. 1865
(ex former m.Metres)			
33. Anthimus II	Ἄνθιμος Β'	*7 Oct* 1865 – 10 Jun 1874+	d. 1874
34. Dositheus	Δοσίθεος	15 Jun 1874 – 17 Nov 1879	d. 1915
(ex t.b.Synnada *8 Mar* 1872) resigned, 8 Sep 1915+			
35. Athanasius	Ἀθανάσιος	17 Nov 1879 – Jun 1888	d. 1900
Nikolaïdis (ex t.b.Argyroupolis *14 Oct* 1867) (to m.Kos)			
36. Neophytus III	Νεόφυτος Γ'	18 Aug 1888 – Mar 1890	d. 1898
Kalogeridis (ex former b.Ierositia) resigned			
37. Anthimus III	Ἄνθιμος Γ'	14 Apr 1890 – 18 Mar 1899	d. 1922
Anastasiadis (ex t.b.Erythres *30 Oct* 1886) (to m.Prespes)			
38. Joachim I	Ἰωακείμ Α'	20 Mar 1899 – 22 Sep 1909	d. ?
Epasoglou (ex b.Polyani) suspended			
39. Gregory	Γρηγόριος	*22 Sep* 1909 – 26 Apr 1914	d. 1936
Papadopoulos/Papathanasiou, suspended, 1 Dec 1936+			
40. Joachim II	Ἰωακείμ Β'	4 May 1914 – 27 Mar 1923	1883-1962
Apostolidis (to m.Servia)			
41. Theocletus II	Θεόκλητος Β'	8 Jun 1993 – 22 Apr 2004+	1939-2004
Rokas (ex t.b.Sevastia 22 May 1977, t.m.Amfipolis 5 Feb 1987)			

METROPOLITANATE OF MYRIOPHYTON AND PERISTASIS
ΜΗΤΡΟΠΟΛΙΣ ΜΥΡΙΟΦΥΤΟΥ ΚΑΙ ΠΕΡΙΣΤΑΣΕΩΣ

Metropolitan of Myriophyton and Peristasis, most honorable and Exarch of Propontis

The city of Peristasis (Grk Περίστασις, Trk Sarkoy) was established as a colony of Greeks from Samos in the seventh century BC. It is situated on the shore of the Marmara Sea, 190 km southwest of Constantinople, in an area under Roman control since 146 BC. The city of Myriophyton (Grk Μυριόφυτον, Trk Murefte), also situated on the shore of the Marmara Sea, 10 km northeast of Peristasis, is first mentioned in 1063.

The Metropolitanate of Myriophyton and Peristasis is bordered by the Metropolitanate of Heraclia on the north and west, the Metropolitanate of Ganos on the northeast, and the Sea of Marmara on the southeast.

A Diocese of Peristasis under the Metropolitanate of Heraclia was established in the twelfth century. The area was occupied by the Ottoman Turks circa 1360. Later the Diocese's See was transferred to Myriophyton, and in the sixteenth century it was called Diocese of Peristasis and Myriophyton, while in the seventeenth century the name changed to Diocese of Myriophyton and Peristasis. The Diocese was promoted to a Metropolitanate in January 1909.

On July 28, 1920 Greece officially annexed the area, but in October 1922 all the Orthodox living in the Metropolitanate were evacuated (see Adrianople), and it was delivered to Turkey on November 12, 1922. No Orthodox population remains inside the area of the Metropolitanate today.

Hierarchs of Myriophyton and Peristasis since 1800
(Bishops until Jan 1909, Metropolitans afterwards)

13. Neophytus II	Νεόφυτος Β΄		1795 – May 1821++	d. 1821
beheaded by the Ottomans				
14. Seraphim	Σεραφείμ		1821/2 – 16 Dec 1834+	d. 1834
15. Neophytus III	Νεόφυτος Γ΄		before 1838 – 1864+	d. 1864
16. Gregory I	Γρηγόριος Α΄		*17 Feb* 1864 – 3 Nov 1881+	d. 1881
Leontopoulos				
17. Gregory II	Γρηγόριος Β΄		17 Jan 1882 – 28 Feb 1891	1811-1900
Fotinos (ex t.b.Sion *23 Mar* 1881) resigned, 6 Feb 1900+				
18. Nicodemus II	Νικόδημος Β΄		17 Mar 1891 – Apr 1894	1857-1935
Komninos Andreou, resigned (to former, to m.Vodena)				
19. Constantine	Κωνσταντίνος		*15 Jul* 1895 – 2 Dec 1899	d. 1912
Apostolou/Valioulis, suspended (to former, to m.Ganos)				
20. Smaragdus	Σμάραγδος		*22 Feb* 1900 – 21 Feb 1908	1871-1928
Chatziefstathiou (to m.Moglena)				
21. Philotheus	Φιλόθεος		11 Mar 1908 – 15 Feb 1916+	d. 1916
Michaïlidis (ex t.b.Charioupolis *13 Feb* 1903) promoted to Metropolitan in Jan 1909				
22. Sophronius	Σωφρόνιος	(1st time)	5 Mar 1917 – 22 May 1923	1875-1960
Stamoulis (to former) suspended				
23. Callinicus II	Καλλίνικος Β΄		22 May 1923 – 15 Apr 1924	1881-1957
Lamprinidis (ex m.Krini) (to m.Krini)				
---. Sophronius	Σωφρόνιος	(2nd time)	15 Apr 1924 – 7 Oct 1924	1875-1960
Stamoulis (ex former m.Myriophyton) (to m.Veria)				
24. Irenaeus	Ειρηναίος		4 Sep 2000 –	b. 1951
Ioannidis (ex t.m.Evdokias 21 Nov 1995)				

METROPOLITANATE OF SARANTA EKKLISIES
ΜΗΤΡΟΠΟΛΙΣ ΣΑΡΑΝΤΑ ΕΚΚΛΗΣΙΩΝ

Metropolitan of Saranta Ecclesies, most honorable and Exarch of all Thrace

The city of Saranta Ekklisies, or "Forty Churches" (Grk Σαράντα Εκκλησίες, Trk Kirklareli) is first mentioned in the fifteenth century. The Metropolitanate of Saranta Ekklisies was established in May 1906 from part of the Metropolitanate of Adrianople.

The Metropolitanate of Saranta Ekklisies is bordered by the Metropolitanate of Sliven (Bulgaria) on the north (and by the Metropolitanate of Sozoagathoupolis prior to 1913), the Metropolitanate of Vizyi on the east, and the Metropolitanate of Adrianople on the south and west. Other noteworthy towns and settlements in the area are Vrysi (Grk Βρύση, Trk Pinarhisar), 30 km southeast of Saranta Ekklisies; Genna (Grk Γέννα, Trk Kaynarca), 25 km southeast of Saranta Ekklisies; Skopos (Grk Σκοπός, Trk Uskup), 15 km east of Saranta Ekklisies; Skopelos (Grk Σκόπελος, Trk Yoguntas), 15 km northwest of Saranta Ekklisies.

The Diocese of Skopelos under the Metropolitanate of Adrianople existed as early as the tenth century. However, the area was occupied by the Ottoman Turks circa 1365, and the Diocese was abolished shortly afterwards due to depopulation.

In March 1913 the Bulgarian army occupied the area, remaining until July 1913, when the Ottomans recovered it. The Greek army occupied the city of Saranta Ekklisies on July 14, 1920. On July 28, 1920 Greece officially annexed the area, but in October 1922 all the Orthodox living in the Metropolitanate were evacuated (see Adrianople), and it was delivered to Turkey on November 12, 1922. No Orthodox population remains inside the area of the Metropolitanate today.

Metropolitans of Saranta Ekklisies

1. Anthimus	Άνθιμος	3 May 1906 – 25 Nov 1910	d. 1922	
Anastasiadis (ex m.Prespes) (to m.Xanthi)				
2. Agathangelus	Αγαθάγγελος	25 Nov 1910 – 20 Oct 1922	d. 1929	
Papanastasiadis (ex t.b.Elaia *12 May* 1903) (to m.Edessa)				
3. Silas	Σίλας	15 Oct 1996 – 12 Dec 2000+	1919-2000	
Koskinas (ex m.New Jersey)				

METROPOLITANATE OF SILYVRIA
ΜΗΤΡΟΠΟΛΙΣ ΣΗΛΥΒΡΙΑΣ

Metropolitan of Silyvria, most honorable and Exarch of Europe

The city of Silyvria (Grk Σηλυβρία, Trk Silivri) was established as a colony of Greeks from Megara in the eighth century BC. It is situated on the shore of Marmara Sea, 65 km west of Constantinople.

The Metropolitanate of Silyvria is bordered by the Metropolitanate of Derki on the north, the Metropolitanate of Metres on the east, the Sea of Marmara on the south, and the Metropolitanate of Heraclia and the Metropolitanate of Tiroloi on the west. Another city in the area is Epivates (Grk Επιβάτες, Trk Selimpasa), 10 km east of Silyvria.

The Diocese of Silyvria under the Metropolitanate of Heraclia was promoted to an Archdiocese in the sixth century and to a Metropolitanate between the years 1143 and 1180. The city was occupied by the Ottoman Turks in 1453, shortly after the fall of Constantinople.

On July 28, 1920 Greece officially annexed the area, but in October 1922 all the Orthodox living in the Metropolitanate were evacuated (see Adrianople), and it was delivered to Turkey on November 12, 1922. No Orthodox population remains inside the area of the Metropolitanate today.

Metropolitans of Silyvria since 1800

48. Callinicus	Καλλίνικος	Dec 1790 – Aug 1816	d. ?	
resigned				
49. Païsius	Παΐσιος	Aug 1816 – Mar 1818	d. 1822	
(ex former b.Stagi) (to m.Philippoupolis)				
50. Johnnicius I	Ιωαννίκιος Α'	Mar 1818 – 3 Feb 1819+	d. 1819	
(ex m.Philippoupolis)				
51. Macarius V	Μακάριος Ε'	*Feb* 1819 – Oct 1821	d≥1852	
Soutsos, resigned (to former, to b.Methoni of Greek Church)				
52. Dionysius I	Διονύσιος Α'	*Oct* 1821 – Jul 1826	d. 1877	
Kotatis (to m.Amasia)				

53. Hierotheus (ex m.Samakovion) (to m.Chalkidon)	Ιερόθεος		Jul 1826 – May 1834	d. 1853
54. Matthew Aristarchis (to m.Dimitrias)	Ματθαίος		*May* 1834 – 10 Nov 1838	d. 1862
55. Sophronius II (ex t.b.Sotirioupolis Jun 1827)	Σωφρόνιος Β'		Nov 1838 – 11 Oct 1849+	d. 1849
56. Johnnicius II (ex m.Grevena) resigned	Ιωαννίκιος Β'		12 Oct 1849 – 23 Jun 1853	d. ?
57. Meletius II (to m.Serres)	Μελέτιος Β'		*23 Jun* 1853 – May 1861	d. 1867
58. Zacharias (ex b.Metres)	Ζαχαρίας		12 Jun 1861 – 1 Feb 1877+	d. 1877
59. Cyril Votosiadis/Kyriakidis (ex former m.Adrianoupolis)	Κύριλλος		9 Feb 1877 – 27 Oct 1881+	d. 1881
60. Germanus Apostolidis (ex m.Moglena)	Γερμανός		31 Oct 1881 – 8 Apr 1892+	1836-1892
61. Constantius Gazis (ex m.Cassandria) (to m.Maronia)	Κωνστάντιος		14 Apr 1892 – 7 Sep 1900	d. 1908
62. Dionysius II Stavridis (ex m.Eleftheroupolis)	Διονύσιος Β'		3 Oct 1900 – 29 Mar 1913+	d. 1913
63. Benjamin Kyriakou (ex m.Rhodes) (to m.Philippoupolis)	Βενιαμίν		11 Jun 1913 – 10 Sep 1913	1871-1946
64. Eugene Papathomas (ex t.b.Amfipolis *27 Apr* 1906) (to m.Servia)	Ευγένιος	(1st time)	10 Sep 1913 – 20 May 1926	1855-1934
---. Eugene Papathomas (ex former m.Servia)	Ευγένιος	(2nd time)	26 Mar 1927 – 22 Jun 1934+	1855-1934
65. Aemilian Timiadis (ex t.b.Meloi 25 Sep 1960, t.m.Kalavria 30 Mar 1965)	Αιμιλιανός		15 Nov 1977 – 21 Feb 2008+	1916-2008

METROPOLITANATE OF TYROLOI AND SERENTION
ΜΗΤΡΟΠΟΛΙΣ ΤΥΡΟΛΟΗΣ ΚΑΙ ΣΕΡΕΝΤΙΟΥ

Metropolitan of Tyroloe and Serention, most honorable and Exarch of Thrace

The city of Tyroloi (Grk Τυρολόη, Trk Çorlu), located 105 km west of Constantinople, became a Diocese under the Metropolitanate of Heraclia in the eighth century, then called Tzouroulos (Grk Τζουρουλός). The city of Serention (Grk Σερέντιον, Trk Binkilic), located 45 km northeast of Tyroloi, became a Diocese under the Metropolitanate of Heraclia in the tenth century.

The Metropolitanate of Tyroloi and Serention is bordered by the Metropolitanate of Vizyi and the Black Sea on the north, the Metropolitanate of Derki and the Metropolitanate of Silyvria on the east, and the Metropolitanate of Heraclia on the south and west. The Diocese of Tyroloi was promoted to an Archdiocese before 1328 and to a Metropolitanate before 1347. Tyroloi was occupied by the Ottoman Turks in 1359, and afterwards the Metropolitanate of Tyroloi again became a Diocese under Heraclia, and was united with the Diocese of Serention.

On December 9, 1840, the Diocese of Tyroloi and Serention was promoted to a Metropolitanate; however, in June 1848 the Metropolitanate was abolished and its area was given to the Metropolitanate of Heraclia. On February 8, 1907, the Metropolitanate was re-established.

On July 28, 1920 Greece officially annexed the area, but in October 1922 all the Orthodox living in the Metropolitanate were evacuated (see Adrianople), and it was delivered to Turkey on November 12, 1922. No Orthodox population remains inside the area of the Metropolitanate today.

Hierarchs of Tyroloi and Serention since 1800
(Bishops until 9 Dec 1840, Metropolitans afterwards)

7. Neophytus II	Νεόφυτος Β'	1781 – 1808	d. 1808?
8. Seraphim	Σεραφείμ	1808 – ...	d. ?
9. Dionysius (to m.Iraklia)	Διονύσιος	1821 – July 1830	d. 1848
10. Gregory Poumpouras (to b.Kallipolis)	Γρηγόριος	*Aug* 1830 – Jan 1835	d. ?
11. Nicodemus Akris (to former, to m.Dryinoupolis) deposed	Νικόδημος	*Jan* 1835 – 1840?	d≥1847
12. Meletius (to m.Pogoniani)	Μελέτιος	*9 Dec* 1840 – Jun 1848	d. 1872
13. Nicephorus Leventiadis (ex m.Lititza) (to m.Mesimvria)	Νικηφόρος	8 Feb 1907 – 15 Feb 1911	d. 1931
14. Chrysostom Papachristou (ex t.b.Photiki *22 Dec* 1907)	Χρυσόστομος	15 Feb 1911 – 8 Oct 1958+	1868-1958
15. Panteleimon Rodopoulos (ex t.m.Tyana 9 Jun 1974)	Παντελεήμων	15 Nov 1977 –	b. 1929

METROPOLITANATE OF VIZYI AND MIDIA
ΜΗΤΡΟΠΟΛΙΣ ΒΙΖΥΗΣ ΚΑΙ ΜΗΔΕΙΑΣ

Metropolitan of Vizye and Media, most honorable and Exarch of Black Sea

The city of Vizyi (Grk Βιζύη, Trk Vize), located 140 km northwest of Constantinople, was a Diocese under the Metropolitanate of Heraclia until the sixth century, when it was promoted to an Archdiocese. The city of Midia (Grk Μήδεια, Trk Kiyikoy), situated on the shore of the Black Sea, 30 km east of Vizyi, became a Diocese under the Metropolitanate of Heraclia in the ninth century. Both cities had been part of the Roman Empire since 46 AD.

The Metropolitanate of Vizyi and Midia is bordered by the Metropolitanate of Sliven (Bulgaria) on the north (by the Metropolitanate of Sozoagathoupolis prior to 1913), the Black Sea on the east, the Metropolitanate of Iraklia and the Metropolitanate of Tyroloi on the south, and the Metropolitanate of Saranta Ekklisies and the Metropolitanate of Adrianople on the west. At some point the Metropolitanate See was moved 30 km north to Samakovion (Grk. Σαμακόβιον, Trk Demirkoy), but in 1839 it returned to Vizyi. Other noteworthy cities in the area are Iniada (Grk Ίνιάδα, Trk Igneada), on the Black Sea, 65 km northeast of Vizyi; and Anaktorion (Grk Ανακτόριον, Trk Saray), 20 km southeast of Vizyi.

The Archdiocese of Vizyi was promoted to a Metropolitanate circa 1350. The Diocese of Midia was also promoted to a Metropolitanate around that time. Vizyi was occupied by the Ottoman Turks in March 1453, and soon afterwards both Metropolitanates was abolished due to depopulation. By the year 1565, the Metropolitanate of Vizyi had been re-established, and so was the Metropolitanate of Midia by the year 1623. On

August 1623 the Metropolitanate of Midia was united with the northerly-located Metropolitanate of Sozopolis into the Metropolitanate of Midia and Sozopolis. This arrangement was short-lived, however, since the Metropolitanate of Midia and Sozopolis split into two in 1628. By 1682 the Metropolitanate of Vizyi had been united with the Metropolitanate of Midia into a Metropolitanate of Vizyi and Midia. This was split into the Metropolitanate of Vizyi and Metropolitanate of Midia before the year 1715, but again restored before the year 1725. The area was occupied by the Bulgarian army between March-July 1913.

On July 28, 1920 Greece officially annexed the area, but in October 1922 all the Orthodox living in the Metropolitanate were evacuated (see Adrianople), and it was delivered to Turkey on November 12, 1922. No Orthodox population remains inside the area of the Metropolitanate today.

Metropolitans of Vizyi and Midia since 1800

42. Daniel II (ex t.b.Sevastia 5/1784)	Δανιήλ Β΄		Jun 1792 – Aug 1813+	d. 1813
43. Neophytus II	Νεόφυτος Β΄		*Aug* 1813 – 1816+	d. 1816
44. Jeremias II (to m.Derki)	Ιερεμίας Β΄		*Aug* 1816 – 9 Jun 1821	d. 1824
45. Joasaph Marmaras (to m.Nyssa)	Ιωάσαφ	(1st time)	*Jun* 1821 – Aug 1826	d≥1837
46. Joseph (ex b.Eleftheroupolis) (to m.Nyssa)	Ιωσήφ		Aug 1826 – Oct 1826	1774-1850
---. Joasaph Marmaras (ex m.Nyssa) resigned	Ιωάσαφ	(2nd time)	Oct 1826 – Sep 1830	d≥1837
47. Cosmas II (ex m.Prikonnisos) (to m.Chios)	Κοσμάς Β΄		Sep 1830 – Aug 1837	d. 1839
48. Gregory II Konstantinidis (ex m.Chios) (to m.Chios)	Γρηγόριος Β΄		Aug 1837 – 27 Sep 1855	1795-1856
49. Matthew suspended	Ματθαίος		*28 Sep* 1855 – 27 Feb 1863	d. ?
50. Plato Skoulikidis	Πλάτων		2 Mar 1863 – 27 Jul 1877+	1806-1877
51. Constantius Stavridis (ex t.b.Elenoupolis *13 Mar* 1869)	Κωνστάντιος		1 Aug 1877 – Jul 1889+	d. 1889
52. Hierotheus Dimitriadis (to m.Rhodes)	Ιερόθεος		*12 Aug* 1889 – 3 Feb 1900	d. 1900
53. Dorotheus II Christidis (ex m.Velegrades) (to m.Sozoagathoupolis)	Δωρόθεος Β΄		5 Feb 1900 – 29 Jan 1904	d. 1924
54. Nicodemus Komninos Andreou (ex m.Vodena) (to m.Kos)	Νικόδημος		29 Jan 1904 – 19 Feb 1908	1857-1935
55. Anthimus II Sarridis (ex m.Moglena) (to m.Maronia)	Άνθιμος Β΄		19 Feb 1908 – 17 Nov 1922	1870-1938
56. Christopher Knitis (ex.a.Australia)	Χριστόφορος		4 Feb 1928 – 7 Aug 1958+	1872-1958

SECTION B:
METROPOLITANATES IN THE ISLANDS

METROPOLITANATE OF IMVROS AND TENEDOS
ΜΗΤΡΟΠΟΛΙΣ ΙΜΒΡΟΥ ΚΑΙ ΤΕΝΕΔΟΥ

Metropolitan of Imbros and Tenedos, most honorable and Exarch of Aegean Sea

The island of Imvros (Grk Ἴμβρος, Trk Gokceada), located 20 km northwest of the Dardanelles Strait, has an area of 279 km.² Notable towns on the island are Panagia (Grk Παναγία, Trk Imroz) in its center, and Kastro (Grk Κάστρο, Trk Kalekoy) on its northern shore. The See of the Metropolitanate is in Panagia.

The island of Tenedos (Grk Τένεδος, Trk Bocsaada), located 20 km south of the Dardanelles Strait, has an area of 37 km.² Tenedos city (Trk Bocsaada) is situated on its northeastern shore. In ancient times it was settled by Aeolian Greeks from nearby Lesvos Island.

Imvros Island came under the control of Athens in the fifth century BC. It passed under Roman control in 146 BC. In 1204 the island passed to the Venetians, but the Romans recovered it in 1262. The island was given to the Genovese of Ainos circa 1450. The Ottoman Turks occupied it in 1458, the Venetians in 1463, and the Ottomans returned in June 1470.

In the fifth century AD Imvros was part of the "Diocese of Limnos and Imvros" under the Metropolitanate of Corinth, as per the political division of the Roman provinces. By the ninth century it became an Archdiocese, and around the year 1010 an exarchate, directly accountable to the Patriarch. In 1397 the Exarchate was abolished, and Imvros island became an Archdiocese, which was promoted to a Metropolitanate during the fifteenth century (before the fall of Constantinople).

Initially the northernmost island under the Metropolitanate of Rhodes, Tenedos became a Diocese under the new Metropolitanate of Mytilini during the ninth century, and was promoted to a Metropolitanate in the early fourteenth century (Metropolitan Joseph of Tenedos is mentioned in 1354). In 1368 the Metropolitanate of Tenedos was attached to the Metropolitanate of Peritheorion in Thrace, but in 1383 the Venetians relocated all 4,000 inhabitants of Tenedos to Crete, Kythira, and Karystos. The island remained uninhabited until the Ottomans occupied it in 1456. Thereafter Tenedos was part of the Metropolitanate of Mytilini (the main city of Lesvos island), until it was attached to the Metropolitanate of Imvros on January 22, 1925 (after Lesvos had been ceded to Greece).

The Metropolitanate of Imvros and Tenedos is bordered by the Metropolitanate of Alexandroupolis (Samothrace Island, Greece) on the north, the Metropolitanate of Kallioupolis (Eastern Thrace) and the Metropolitanate of Dardanellia (Asia Minor) on the east, and the Metropolitanate of Lesvos (Greece) on the south and the Metropolitanate of Limnos (Greece) on the west.

The Greek navy occupied Imvros on October 18, 1912 and Tenedos on October 24, 1912. The islands remained a Greek possession until they were returned to Turkey on November 12, 1922, due to the treaty signed after the defeat of the Greek army in Asia Minor. The Greek population of the islands was permitted to remain, but the Turkish government soon afterwards encouraged Muslim settlement and Greek emigration, making the Greek Orthodox a minority on the islands today.

Metropolitans of Imvros and Tenedos since 1800
(Metropolitans of Imvros before 22 Jan 1925)

32. Nicephorus II Tsepelis	Νικηφόρος Β'		*Jan* 1793 – Feb 1825+	d. 1825
33. Joseph II (to m.Varna)	Ιωσήφ Β'		*Oct* 1825 – Feb 1835	d≥1860
34. Neophytus II (ex m.Kastoria)	Νεόφυτος Β'		Feb 1835 – 1836+	d. 1836
35. Neophytus III (to m.Stromnitsa)	Νεόφυτος Γ'		*2 Nov* 1836 – 10 Jan 1853	d. 1861
36. Johnnicius I (ex a.Lititza) suspended	Ιωαννίκιος Α'		10 Jan 1853 – 20 Dec 1863	d. ?
37. Païsius II Kourentis (to m.Mithymna)	Παΐσιος Β'	(1st time)	*Dec* 1863 – 1 May 1873	d. 1904
38. Nicephorus III Glykas (to m.Mithymna)	Νικηφόρος Γ'		*2 May* 1873 – 23 Mar 1881	1819-1896
---. Païsius II Kourentis (ex m.Mithymna) suspended, 19/12/1904+	Παΐσιος Β'	(2nd time)	23 Mar 1881 – 16 May 1902	d. 1904
39. Philotheus Konstantinidis (ex m.Philippi)	Φιλόθεος		18 May 1902 – 27 Nov 1904+	d. 1904
40. Johnnicius II Margaritiadis (ex m.Moglena)	Ιωαννίκιος Β'		31 Mar 1905 – Jan 1908+	d. 1908
41. Chrysostom Kavouridis (to m.Pelagonia)	Χρυσόστομος		*31 Jul* 1908 – 14 Jun 1912	1870-1955
42. Panaretus Petridis (ex m.Ilioupolis)	Πανάρετος		21 Jun 1912 – Feb 1922+	d. 1922
43. Joachim IV Kavyris (ex t.b.Amphipolis 5 Nov 1917) (to m.Ikaria)	Ιωακείμ Δ'		24 Feb 1922 – 9 Oct 1924	1880-1974
44. John Vasilikos (ex t.b.Konstantia 24 Nov 1909) (to m.Vella)	Ιωάννης		16 Oct 1924 – 23 Mar 1926	d. 1941
45. Jacob II Papapaïsiou (to m.Derki)	Ιάκωβος Β'		4 Apr 1926 – 27 May 1950	1885-1980
46. Meliton Chatzis (to m.Ilioupolis)	Μελίτων		30 Nov 1950 – 19 Feb 1963	1913-1989
47. Nicholas Koutroumpis (to m.Anea)	Νικόλαος		*4 Apr* 1964 – 15 Feb 1972	1903-1972
48. Demetrius Papadopoulos (ex t.b.Elaia 9 Aug 1964) (to p.Constantinople)	Δημήτριος		15 Feb 1972 – 16 Jul 1972	1914-1991
49. Photius Savvaïdis (ex t.b.Trallis 28 Jun 1959) (to m.Iraklia)	Φώτιος		12 Sep 1972 – 5 Sep 2002	1924-2007
50. Cyril Dragounis (ex t.m.Selefkia 27 Oct 1985)	Κύριλλος		5 Sep 2002 –	b. 1942

METROPOLITANATE OF MOSCHONISIA
ΜΗΤΡΟΠΟΛΙΣ ΜΟΣΧΟΝΗΣΙΩΝ

Metropolitan of Moschonesia, most honorable and Exarch of Ide and Seashores

The island of Moschonisos (Grk Μοσχόνησος, Trk Alibey Adasi), located in the north Aegean Sea adjacent to the Asia Minor coast opposite the Greek island of Lesvos, is the main island of the island group of Moschonesia. The only town on the island is Moschos (Grk Μόσχος, Trk Alibey) on the south shore of the island. The island is connected by bridge to the city of Kydonies (Ayvalik) in Asia Minor.

Other notable islands of the group are Pyrgonisi (Grk Πυργονήσι, Trk Maden Ad.), Moschopoulo (Grk Μοσχόπουλο, Trk Pinar Ad.), Lipsos (Grk Λειψός Trk Yellice Ad.), Eleousa (Grk Ελεούσα Trk Gunes Ad.), Gymno (Grk Γυμνό Trk Ciplak Ad.), Psariano (Grk Ψαριανό Trk Balik Ad.), Angistri (Grk Αγκίστρι Trk Cicek Ad.), Kalamos (Grk Κάλαμος, Trk Kamis Ad.), Daskalio (Grk Δασκαλιό, Trk Ikiz Kayalar Ad.), Krommydonisi (Grk Κρομμυδονήσι, Trk Sogan Ad.), and many more smaller islands (the group is comprised of 22 islets).

The Metropolitanate of Moschonisia is bordered by the Metropolitanate of Dardanellia (Asia Minor) on the north, the Metropolitanate of Kydonies (Asia Minor) on the east and south, and the Metropolitanate of Lesvos (Greece) on the west.

Called Ekatonisi (Grk Εκατόνησοι) in antiquity, the island group was settled by the Aeolian Greeks in the ninth century BC. It passed under Roman control in 133 BC, and was occupied by the Seljuk Turks circa 1310 and the Ottoman Turks circa 1341.

The islands were initially under the jurisdiction of the Metropolitanate of Ephesos. They were transferred to the Metropolitanate of Mytilini in 1644, became a Patriarchal Exarchate before 1729, and were attached to the Metropolitanate of Smyrni in October 1742, to the Metropolitanate of Ephesos in Febrary 1750, and back to the Metropolitanate of Mytilini in December 1760. Shortly thereafter they reverted to Patriarchal Exarchate status, but were re-attached to the Metropolitanate of Smyrni in 1763. A Diocese of Moschonisia under the Metropolitanate of Smyrni was created on January 30, 1766, and was itself promoted to a Metropolitanate on February 19, 1922.

In May 1919 Greek forces occupied the islands; after their defeat in the Asian Minor front, they withdrew at the end of August 1922. Most of the Greek Orthodox inhabitants, however, did not follow the army. The Turkish army occupied the islands and evacuated the remaining inhabitants to Asia Minor, where on September 15, 1922 they were executed. No Orthodox population remains inside the area of the Metropolitanate today.

Hierarchs of Moschonisia
(Bishops until 19 Feb 1922, Metropolitans afterwards)

1. Gabriel	Γαβριήλ	4 Apr 1766 – Nov 1767	d. 1785
(to m.Ioannina)			
2. Cyril I	Κύριλλος Α'	Mar 1768 – 1794+	d. 1794
3. Païsius I	Παΐσιος Α'	Oct 1794 – 1800	d. 1821
Prikaios (to former, to m.Varna) see note 1			
4. Dionysius	Διονύσιος	Jul 1800 – after 1809	d. ?
5. Bartholomew	Βαρθολομαίος	1820 – Jun 1821	d. 1865
Pirounis (to former, to b.Kynaithi of Greek Church) resigned			

6. Callinicus	Καλλίνικος	Feb 1832 – 1842	d. 1842?
(ex t.b.Aurelioupolis *Jan* 1832)			
7. Meletius	Μελέτιος	1842 – Jun 1855	d. ?
suspended			
8. Cyril II	Κύριλλος Β'	*Jun* 1855 – 27 *Mar* 1872+	d. 1872
9. Païsius II	Παΐσιος Β'	*29 Mar* 1872 – 11 *Aug* 1882+	d. 1882
10. Jacob	Ιάκωβος	25 Aug 1882 – Aug 1897+	d. 1897
Leventinos (ex t.b.Amphipolis *12 Jun* 1875)			
11. Neophytus	Νεόφυτος	*11 Sep* 1897 – 27 Apr 1906	1862-1931
Kotzamanidis (to m.Varna)			
12. Nicodemus	Νικόδημος	23 May 1906 – 8 Dec 1911	d. 1920
Papadopoulos (ex t.b.Avydos *14 Apr* 1892) (to m.Prikonnisos)			
13. Diodorus	Διόδωρος	*26 Jan* 1912 – 30 Mar 1913	d. 1944
Karatzis (to b.Kampania)			
14. Photius	Φώτιος	30 Apr 1913 – 19 Feb 1922	1871-1930
Marinakis (ex former b.Kampania) resigned, Oct 1930+			
15. Ambrose	Αμβρόσιος	19 Feb 1922 – 15 Sep 1922++	1872-1922
Plianthidis (ex t.b.Xanthoupolis *6 Jul* 1913) executed by the Turkish army			
16. Apostolus	Απόστολος	4 Sep 2000 –	b. 1952
Daniilidis (ex t.m.Agathonikia 26 Nov 1995)			

1. Metropolitan Païsius of Sozopolis (transferred from Varna on October 1806) was executed by the Ottomans in May 1821, a few weeks after the beginning of the Greek revolution.

METROPOLITANATE OF PRINGIPONNISA
ΜΗΤΡΟΠΟΛΙΣ ΠΡΙΓΚΙΠΟΝΝΗΣΩΝ

Metropolitan of Principonnesa, most honorable and Exarch of Propontis

The island group of Pringiponnisa (Princes' Islands, Grk Πριγκιπόννησοι, Trk Kuzil Adalar), located in the Marmara Sea adjacent to the Asia Minor coast south of Bosporus strait, is composed of four islands and five islets, with a collective area of 11 km.^{2} The islands are (in order of closeness to Bosporus): Proti (Grk Πρώτη, Trk Kinali Ada, area 1.3 km^2), Antigoni (Grk Αντιγόνη, Trk Burgaz Ada, area 1.5 km^2), Chalki (Grk Χάλκη, Trk Heybeli Ada, area 2.4 km^2), and Pringipos (Grk Πρίγκιπος, Trk Buyuk Ada, area 5.36 km^2).

The See of the Metropolitanate is in Pringipos, the largest of the islands, and the Theological Seminary of the Patriarchate is located on Chalki, the second-largest island. The islets are: Oxia (Grk Οξεία, Trk Sivri Ada, area 0.05 km^2), Plati (Grk Πλάτη, Trk Yassi Ada, area 0.05 km^2), Pita (Grk Πίτα, Trk Kasik Ada, area 0.006 km^2), Niandros (Grk Νείανδρος, Trk Balikci Ada, formerly Tavsan Ada, area 0.004 km^2), and the newly inhabited Terevinthos (Grk Τερέβινθος, Trk Sedef Ada, area 0.157 km^2).

The Metropolitanate of Pringiponnisa is bordered by the Metropolitanate of Chalkidon (Asia Minor) on the north and east, the Metropolitanate of Nikomidia (Asia Minor) on the south, and the Metropolitanate of Prikonnisos on the west.

Named the Princes' Islands during Roman times (they often served as places of vacation or exile for members of the Emperors' families), they were occupied by the Ottoman Turks on April 17, 1453, a few weeks before the fall of Constantinople. The Greek Orthodox inhabitants of the islands were excluded from the 1923 population exchange between Greece and Turkey. The islands were part of the Metropolitanate of Chalkidon until January 1924, when the new Metropolitanate of the Princes' Islands was established.

Metropolitans of Pringiponnisa

1. Agathangelus Konstantinidis-Magnis (ex m.Neokaisaria) (to m.Chalkidon)	Αγαθάγγελος	20 Mar 1924 – 2 Apr 1927	1864-1935
2. Thomas Savvopoulos (ex m.Anea) (to m.Chalkidon)	Θωμάς	2 Apr 1927 – 12 Mar 1946	1889-1966
3. Dorotheus Georgiadis (ex t.m.Laodikia 1 Jan 1928)	Δωρόθεος	12 Mar 1946 – 21 Mar 1974+	1891-1974
4. Constantine Charisiadis (ex t.b.Apolloniada 16 Jan 1972) (to m.Derki)	Κωνσταντίνος	26 Mar 1974 – 15 Mar 1977	b. 1929
5. Agapius Ioannidis (ex t.m.Sozopolis 29 Nov 1970)	Αγάπιος	22 Mar 1977 – 29 Aug 1979+	1923-1979
6. Callinicus Alexandridis (ex t.m.Lystra 6 Dec 1970) (to t.m.Lystra)	Καλλίνικος	18 Sep 1979 – 5 Nov 1985	b. 1926
7. Symeon Amaryllios (ex t.m.Irinoupolis 26 Apr 1964) (to m.Nikomidia)	Συμεών	9 Jun 1987 – 9 Jul 2002	1916-2003
8. Jacob Sophroniadis (ex t.m.Laodikia 25 Dec 1987)	Ιάκωβος	9 Jul 2002 –	b. 1947

METROPOLITANATE OF PRIKONNISOS
ΜΗΤΡΟΠΟΛΙΣ ΠΡΟΙΚΟΝΝΗΣΟΥ

Metropolitan of Priconnesus, most honorable and Exarch of all Propontis

The island of Prikonnisos (Grk Προικόννησος, Trk Marmara Adasi), with an area of 120 km,[2] is the largest island in the Sea of Marmara. The main town on the island and See of the Metropolitanate is Marmaras (Grk Μαρμαράς, Trk Marmara), located on the southwest shore of the island.

The Metropolitanate also encompasses a group of four islands and five islets south of Prikonissos. The islands in west-to-east order are: Koutali (Grk Κούταλη, Trk Ekinlik Ad.), Ophiousa (Grk Οφιούσα, Trk Türkeli Ad, formerly Avşa Ad.), Akanthos (Grk Άκανθος, Trk Koyun Ad.), and Aloni (Grk Αλώνι, Trk Paşalimani Ad.). The five islets are: Porfyrioni, Polydori, Phivi, Skopelos, and Delphakia (Grk Πορφυριόνη, Πολυδώρη, Φοίβη, Σκόπελος, Δελφακία).

Prikonnisos is bordered by the Metropolitanate of Iraklia (Eastern Thrace) on the north, the Metropolitanate of Pringiponnisi on the east, the Metropolitanate of Kyzikos (Asia Minor) on the south, and the Metropolitanate of Kallipolis (East Thrace) on the west. The islands came under the protection of Athens in the fifth century BC and under Roman control in 133 BC. They were occupied by the Ottoman Turks circa 1360.

The Diocese of Prikonnisos under the Metropolitanate of Kyzikos was promoted to an Archdiocese during the ninth century AD and to a Metropolitanate in May 1823. Greek armed forces occupied the islands on July 4, 1920, but withdrew in September 1922, evacuating the Greek Orthodox population to Greece. No Orthodox population remains inside the area of the Metropolitanate today.

Hierarchs of Prikonnisos since 1800
(Archbishops until May 1823, Metropolitans afterwards)

31. Nicephorus II Pilousiotis (to m.Adrianoupolis)	Νικηφόρος Β΄		*Aug* 1795 – Jun 1821	d. 1835
32. Cosmas (to m.Vizyi) promoted to Metropolitan in May 1823	Κοσμάς		*Jun* 1821 – Sep 1830	d. 1839
33. Samouel (to m.Mesimvria)	Σαμουήλ		*Sep* 1830 – Jan 1835	d. 1855
34. Bessarion (ex m.Korytsa) (to m.Didymotichon)	Βησσαρίων		Jan 1835 – Aug 1841	d. 1847
35. Gideon (ex t.b.Lampsakos *Apr* 1839) (to m.Sophia)	Γεδεών	(1st time)	Aug 1841 – 14 Jul 1853	d. 1877
36. Sophronius I (ex t.b.Peristera *Sep* 1838) (to m.Nyssava)	Σωφρόνιος Α΄		14 Jul 1853 – 19 Apr 1861	d. 1895
---. Gideon (ex m.Sophia)	Γεδεών	(2nd time)	19 Apr 1861 – 12 Jan 1877+	d. 1877
37. Dionysius III Georgiadis (ex t.b.Pamphilos *11 Jan* 1862) suspended	Διονύσιος Γ΄		24 Jan 1877 – 12 Mar 1885	d. ?
38. Nicodemus I Angelidis/Amaxopoulos (to m.Elasson)	Νικόδημος Α΄		*12 Mar* 1885 – 14 Jan 1892	d. 1897
39. Ignatius (ex m.Lititza)	Ιγνάτιος		14 Jan 1892 – 4 Oct 1893+	d. 1893
40. Benedict Adamantidis (ex m.Pisidia) suspended, 16 Aug 1906+	Βενέδικτος		23 Oct 1893 – 9 Mar 1900	d. 1906
41. Parthenius Papafotinos (ex m.Sozoagathoupolis)	Παρθένιος		9 Mar 1900 – Dec 1900+	d. 1900
42. Sophronius II Argyropoulos/Voutsas (ex m.Stromnitsa)	Σωφρόνιος Β΄		16 Jan 1901 – 15 Nov 1911+	d. 1911
43. Nicodemus II Papadopoulos (ex b.Moschonisia)	Νικόδημος Β΄		8 Dec 1911 – 4 Aug 1920+	d. 1920
44. George Misaïlidis (to m.Thasos)	Γεώργιος		20 Feb 1922 – 9 Oct 1924	1882-1958
45. Philotheus Papakonstantinou/Stavridis (ex t.b.Nazianzos 29 Mar 1931)	Φιλόθεος		5 Oct 1943 – 13 Nov 1963+	1882-1963
46. Isaiah Chronopoulos (ex b.Denver) (to m.Denver)	Ησαΐας		24 Nov 1997 – 20 Dec 2002	b. 1931
47. Joseph Charkiolakis (ex former m.New Zealand)	Ιωσήφ		24 Jun 2008 –	b. 1955

SECTION C:
METROPOLITANATES IN NORTHWEST ASIA MINOR

METROPOLITANATE OF CHALKIDON
ΜΗΤΡΟΠΟΛΙΣ ΧΑΛΚΗΔΟΝΟΣ

Metropolitan of Chalcedon, most honorable and Exarch of all Bithynia

The city of Chalkidon (Grk Χαλκηδών, Trk Kadikoy), located on the Asian side of Bosporus Strait opposite Constantinople (today a suburb of modern Istanbul), was established in the 865 BC as colony of the Greeks from Megara. Passing under Roman control in 74 BC, it became a Diocese under the Metropolitanate of Nikomidia in 325, but was promoted to a Metropolitanate in 451, after the Fourth Ecumenical Council convened there. The Ottoman Turks occupied the city in 1353.

On the eastern area of the Metropolitanate, Pontoiraklia (Grk Ποντοηράκλεια, Trk Eregli), located 260 km northeast of Chalkidon, on the Black Sea shore, was taken by the Romans of Trapezous in 1205, by the Romans of Nikaia in 1214, sold to the Genovese in 1360, and taken by the Ottomans in 1454.

The Metropolitanate of Chalkidon is bordered by the Black Sea on the north; the Metropolitanate of Neokaisaria (Gangra section) on the east; the Marmara Sea, the Metropolitanate of Nikomidia, and the Metropolitanate of Ankyra on the south; and the Marmara Sea and the Bosporus Strait on the west.

Noteworthy cities in the area of the Metropolitanate include: Chrysoupolis (Grk Χρυσούπολις, Trk Uskudar), in the Asian side of Bosporus Strait opposite Constantinople, 4 km north of Chalkidon, also being today a suburb of Istanbul; Nymphaion (Grk Νύμφαιον, Trk Beykoz), in the Asian side of Bosporus strait, 15 km north of Chrysoupolis, again being today a suburb of Istanbul; Chartalimi (Grk Χαρταλιμή, Trk Kartal), on the Marmara Sea shore, 22 km southeast of Chalkidon; Pantichion (Grk Παντείχιον, Trk Pendik), on the Marmara Sea shore, 25 km southeast of Chalkidon; Daritsa (Grk Δάριτσα, Trk Darica), on the Marmara Sea shore, 15 km southeast of Pantichion; Dakivyza (Grk Δακίβυζα, Trk Gebze), on the Marmara Sea shore, 15 km southeast of Pantichion; Chili (Grk Χηλή, Trk Sile), on the Black Sea shore, 60 km northeast of Chalkidon; Kalpi (Grk Κάλπη, Trk Kandira), 50 km east of Chili; Prousias (Grk Προυσιάς, Trk Konuralp), 155 east of Chalkidon); Dia (Grk Δία, Trk Akcakoca), on the Black Sea shore, 45 km southwest of Pontoiraklia; Sandaraki (Grk Σανδάρακη, Trk Zonguldak), on the Black Sea shore, 37 km northeast of Pontoiraklia; and Klavdioupolis (Grk Κλαυδιούπολις, Trk Bolu), 87 km south of Pontoiraklia.

The area near the Bosporus Strait was occupied by Allied forces in November 1918, with Chalkidon returning to the Turks on October 5, 1923. Pontoiraklia and Sandaraki were occupied by French forces on March 5, 1919, returning to Turkish hands on May 26, 1920 and June 8, 1921 respectively. After the population exchange of 1923 between Greece and Turkey, Orthodox population remains only in the areas of the Metropolitanate that have become suburbs of Istanbul.

Metropolitans of Chalkidon since 1800

73. Jeremias III Mavrokordatos (ex m.Vidyni)	Ἰερεμίας Γ'	Nov 1790 – Nov 1810+	d. 1810
74. Gerasimus I (ex m.Thessaloniki)	Γεράσιμος Α'	Nov 1810 – Feb 1820+	d. 1820
75. Gregory II (ex m.Athina)	Γρηγόριος Β'	Feb 1820 – summer 1821+	d. 1821
76. Anthimus (ex m.Smyrna) (to p.Constantinople)	Ἄνθιμος	20 Oct 1821 – 28 Jul 1822	d. 1842
77. Callinicus II (ex t.b.Erythres)	Καλλίνικος Β'	Jul 1822 – Aug 1825+	d. 1825
78. Agathangelus I (ex m.Belgrade) (to p.Constantinople)	Ἀγαθάγγελος Α'	Aug 1825 – 26 Sep 1826	d. 1831
79. Zacharias II (ex former m.Kyzikos)	Ζαχαρίας Β'	Sep 1826 – May 1834+	d. 1834
80. Hierotheus (ex president b.Silyvria)	Ἰερόθεος	May 1834 – Mar 1853+	d. 1853
81. Gerasimus II Tzermias (ex m.Adrianoupolis)	Γεράσιμος Β'	15 Mar 1853 – 24 Feb 1875+	d. 1875
82. Callinicus III Thomaïdis (ex m.Xanthi)	Καλλίνικος Γ'	4 Mar 1875 – 14 Dec 1889+	d. 1889
83. Joachim I Efthyvoulis (ex m.Philippoupolis) (to m.Ephesos)	Ἰωακείμ Α'	17 Dec 1889 – 10 May 1897	1855-1920
84. Germanus Kavvakopoulos (ex m.Ieaklia) (to p.Constantinople)	Γερμανός	10 May 1897 – 28 Jan 1913	1835-1920
85. Gregory III Zervoudakis (ex m.Kyzikos) (to p.Constantinople)	Γρηγόριος Γ'	12 Feb 1913 – 6 Dec 1923	1855-1924
86. Joachim II Georgiadis (ex m.Ainos)	Ἰωακείμ Β'	20 Dec 1923 – 5 Feb 1927+	1875-1927
87. Nicholas II Sakkopoulos (ex m.Kaisaria)	Νικόλαος Β'	22 Feb 1927 – 17 Mar 1927+	1862-1927
88. Agathangelus II Konstantinidis-Magnis (ex m.Pringiponnisa) (to m.Ephesos)	Ἀγαθάγγελος Β'	2 Apr 1927 – 28 Jun 1932	1864-1935
89. Maximus Vaportzis (ex m.Philadelphia) (to p.Constantinople)	Μάξιμος	28 Jun 1932 – 20 Feb 1946	1897-1972
90. Thomas Savvopoulos (ex m.Pringiponnisa)	Θωμάς	12 Mar 1946 – 18 Oct 1966+	1889-1966
91. Meliton Chatzis (ex m.Ilioupolis)	Μελίτων	25 Oct 1966 – 27 Dec 1989+	1913-1989
92. Bartholomew Archontonis (ex m.Philadelphia) (to p.Constantinople)	Βαρθολομαίος	9 Jan 1990 – 22 Oct 1991	b. 1940
93. Joachim III Nerantzoulis (ex t.b.Melitini 23 Sep 1973, t.m.Melitini 27 Jun 1977)(to m.Nikomidia)	Ἰωακείμ Γ'	10 Dec 1991 – 21 Mar 2008	b. 1942
94. Athanasius Papas (ex m.Chalkidon)	Ἀθανάσιος	21 Mar 2008 –	b. 1936

METROPOLITANATE OF DARDANELLIA AND LAMPSAKOS
ΜΗΤΡΟΠΟΛΙΣ ΔΑΡΔΑΝΕΛΛΙΩΝ ΚΑΙ ΛΑΜΨΑΚΟΥ

Metropolitan of Dardanelles and Lampsacus, most honorable and Exarch of all Hellespond

The city of Dardanellia (Grk Δαρδανέλλια, Trk Çannakcale), located on the Asian side of the strait of the same name (also known as Hellespont, Grk Ελλήσποντος) was established in the fourth century BC as a colony of the Aeolian Greeks called Dardanos (Grk Δάρδανος), and came under Roman control in 133 BC.

Both Dardanellia and Lampsakos (Grk Λάμψακος, Trk Lapseki) became Dioceses under the Metropolitanate of Kyzikos before the seventh century. The Seljuk Turks occupied the area circa 1310, and the Ottomans circa 1360. Both Dioceses were dissolved due to depopulation before 1400, their lands coming directly under the Metropolitanate of Kyzikos.

A new Metropolitanate of Dardanellia and Lampsakos was established on March 5, 1913. It is bordered by the Sea of Marmara and the Dardanelles strait on the north, the Metropolitanate of Kyzikos on the east, the Metropolitanate of Pergamos on the south, and the Aegean Sea on the west. Lampsakos is also situated on the Asian side of Dardanelles strait, opposite Kallipolis, 35 km north of Dardanelles city. Other noteworthy cities include: Piges (Grk Πηγές, Trk Biga), 55 km east of Lampsakos; Neandria (Grk Νεάνδρια, Trk Ezine), 45 km south of Dardanelles city; and Lamponia (Grk Λαμπώνεια, Trk Ayvacik), 20 km south of Neandria.

The area was occupied by the British on October 26, 1918, returning to Turkish control on September 9, 1922. After the population exchange of 1923 between Greece and Turkey, no Orthodox population remains inside the area of the Metropolitanate.

Metropolitans of Dardanellia and Lampsakos

1. Irenaeus Papamichaïl (to m.Elasson)	Ειρηναίος	(1st time)	10 Mar 1913 – 10 Feb 1922	1878-1963
2. Cyril Afthentoulidis (to m.Nigrita)	Κύριλλος		22 Feb 1922 – 16 Oct 1924	d. 1942
–. Irenaeus Papamichaïl (ex former m.Elasson) (to m.Samos)	Ειρηναίος	(2nd time)	16 Oct 1924 – 10 Apr 1926	1878-1963
3. Anthony Gergiannakis (ex b.San Francisco) (to m.San Francisco)	Αντώνιος		24 Nov 1997 – 20 Dec 2002	1935-2004
4. Nicetas Loulias (ex m.Hong Kong)	Νικήτας		29 Aug 2007 –	b. 1955

METROPOLITANATE OF KYDONIES
ΜΗΤΡΟΠΟΛΙΣ ΚΥΔΩΝΙΩΝ

Metropolitan of Cydonies, most honorable and Exarch of Aeolis

The area of the Metropolitanate became Roman territory in 133 BC, and was occupied by the Seljuk Turks circa 1310 and the Ottomans circa 1341. The city of Kydonies (Grk Κυδωνιές, Trk Çannakcale), located on the shore of Aegean Sea, 140 km north of Smyrna, was established circa 1600 near the ruins of ancient Kisthini (Grk Κισθήνη) by the Greek Orthodox of the nearby lands.

The area was under the jurisdiction of the Metropolitanate of Ephesus until a Metropolitanate of Kydonies was established on July 22, 1908. It is bordered by the Aegean Sea on the north and west, and the Metropolitanate of Pergamos on the east and south. Other towns in the area are: Passandra (Grk Πάσσανδρα, Trk Armudova, formerly Gomec), situated 15 km northeast of Kydonies, and Agiasmation (Grk Αγιασμάτιον, Trk Altinova), situated 14 km southeast of Kydonies.

The area was occupied by Greek forces from May 19, 1919 to late August 1923, but the Greek Orthodox population decided not to evacuate the city along with the army. On August 29, 1923 the Turkish army entered and declared martial law. Most male citizens aged 18-45 years were arrested, removed from the city, and executed. The remaining people were permitted to flee to Greece by boat. No Orthodox population remains inside the area of the Metropolitanate today.

Metropolitans of Kydonies

1. Gregory	Γρηγόριος	22 Jul 1908 – 3 Oct 1922++	1864-1922
Orologas (ex m.Stromnitsa) executed by the Turkish army, see note 1			
2. Eugene	Ευγένιος	20 Mar 1924 – 28 Jun 1928	1885-1956
Theologou/Vakalis (ex m.Philadelphia) (to m.Nigrita)			
3. Agathangelus	Αγαθάγγελος	5 Oct 1943 – 23 Jul 1960+	1885-1960
Papatheodorou (ex t.b.Elaia 24 Apr 1926)			

1. Metropolitan Gregory was instrumental in arranging permission from the US Red Cross to secure boats (flying the USA flag) from Lesvos Island to evacuate the remaining people of Kydonies to Greece. However, on the last day of the evacuation, September 30, 1922, he was arrested along with the Orthodox priests who were waiting in the harbor to depart. On October 3, the prisoners were executed.

METROPOLITANATE OF KYZIKOS
ΜΗΤΡΟΠΟΛΙΣ ΚΥΖΙΚΟΥ

Metropolitan of Cyzicus, most honorable and Exarch of all Hellespond

The city of Kyzikos (Grk Κύζικος, Trk Balkiz), located on the Asian shore of the Sea of Marmara on the isthmus of Kyzikini Peninsula (Grk Κυζικηνή Χερσόνησος, Trk Kapidagi Yarimadasi), was established before the tenth century BC as a colony of the Pelasgi from Thessaly. In 133 BC it came under Roman control, was briefly occupied by the Seljuk Turks in 1090 and 1113, was occupied by the Crusaders of Constantinople in 1204, was retaken by the Romans of Nicaea in 1224, and was occupied by the Ottoman Turks circa 1336.

The Metropolitanate of Kyzikos was established in 325 AD. Initially under the honorary primacy of the Metropolitanate of Ephesos, it became a Metropolitanate of the Patriarchate of Constantinople in 451. It is bordered by the Sea of Marmara on the north; the Metropolitanate of Nicaea (Militopolis section) on the east; the Metropolitanate of Philadelphia and the Metropolitanate of Ephesus on the south; and by the Metropolitanate of Dardanellia and the Metropolitanate of Pergamos on the west.

Kyzikos was an important Metropolitanate of the Byzantine Empire, having twelve Dioceses under its jurisdiction in the seventh century, which increased to fourteen by the twelfth century. However after the Ottoman occupation of the area the number steadily decreased, with no Diocese remaining by the fifteenth century. Around that time the city of Kyzikos was deserted, and the Metropolitanate See was moved 8 km northeast to nearby Artaki (Grk Αρτάκη, Trk Erdek).

Other important cities inside the area are: Panormos (Grk. Πάνορμος, Trk. Bandirma), 15km southeast of Artaki; Zelia (Grk. Ζέλεια, Trk. Gonen), 45 km south of Artaki; Andrianouthyres (Handrian's Gates, Grk. Αδριανούθυρες, Trk. Balikesir), 93 km south of Panormos, and Avlokrini (Grk. Αυλοκρήνη, Trk. Bigadic), 35 km southeast of Adrianouthyres.

In June 1920 the area was occupied by the Greek army, with Adrianouthires being occupied on June 16, 1920, and Panormos, Kyzikos, and Artaki on June 19, 1920. The area was held until the Greek army's defeat in late August 1922, after which all Orthodox were evacuated to Greece or killed by the advancing Turkish army. The last units of the Greek army left Artaki on September 5, 1922. No Orthodox population remains inside the area of the Metropolitanate today.

Metropolitans of Kyzikos since 1800

64. Joachim I (ex m.Anchialos) resigned	Ιωακείμ Α'	Sep 1794 – 14 Mar 1806	d. ?
65. Macarius (ex m.Old Patra)	Μακάριος	Mar 1806 – Jul 1811+	d. 1811
66. Constantine I (ex m.Serres)	Κωνσταντίνος Α'	12 Jul 1811 – 1822+	d. 1822
67. Zacharias (ex m.Veria) (to former, to m.Chalkidon)	Ζαχαρίας	Jan 1823 – 1823	d. 1834
68. Matthew II Megalos (ex m.Thessaloniki)	Ματθαίος Β'	Aug 1823 – 1831+	d. 1831
69. Anthimus III Chrysafidis (ex m.Anchialos) (to p.Constantinople)	Άνθιμος Γ'	Jul 1831 – 6 May 1841	d. 1842
70. Meletius Pangalos (ex m.Thessaloniki) (to p.Constantinople)	Μελέτιος	May 1841 – 18 Apr 1845	1772-1845
71. Joachim II Kokkodis (ex m.Ioannina) (to p.Constantinople)	Ιωακείμ Β'	Apr 1845 – 4 Oct 1860	1802-1878
72. Jacob Pangostas (ex m.Serres) (to p.Alexandria)	Ιάκωβος	11 Oct 1860 – 24 May 1861	1803-1865
73. Nicodemus Konstantinidis (ex m.Serres)	Νικόδημος	24 May 1861 – Jan 1900+	d. 1900
74. Constantine II Chatzimarkou-Alexandridis (ex m.Rhodes)	Κωνσταντίνος Β'	18 Jan 1900 – Oct 1903+	d. 1903
75. Athanasius II Megaklis (ex m.Thessaliniki)	Αθανάσιος Β'	18 Oct 1903 – May 1909+	1848-1909
76. Gregory II Zervoudakis (ex m.Serres) (to m.Chalkidon)	Γρηγόριος Β'	12 May 1909 – 12 Feb 1913	1855-1924
77. Constantine III Arampoglous (ex m.Trapezous) (to m.Prousa)	Κωνσταντίνος Γ'	2 Apr 1913 – 10 Feb 1922	1859-1930
78. Callinicus Delikanis (ex m.Veria) (to m.Kaisaria)	Καλλίνικος	10 Feb 1922 – 26 Jul 1932	1855-1934

METROPOLITANATE OF NIKAIA
ΜΗΤΡΟΠΟΛΙΣ ΝΙΚΑΙΑΣ

Metropolitan of Nicaea, most honorable and Exarch of all Bithynia

The city of Nikaia (Nicaea, Grk Νίκαια, Trk Iznik), located in the eastern shore of Lake Askania (Grk Ασκανία Λίμνη, Trk Isnik Golu), was established by Macedonian-Greek King Antigonus I in 316 BC on the site of a previous settlement, and was named Antigonia (Grk Αντιγόνεια) in his honor. It was renamed Nikaia by the Macedonian-Greek King Lysimachus in 301 BC. In 74 BC it came under Roman control, was occupied by the Seljuk Turks in 1081, was retaken by the Romans and the Crusaders on June 19, 1097, served as the capital of the East Roman Empire during the period 1204-61, and was occupied by the Ottoman Turks on March 3, 1331 after a long siege.

Initially a Diocese under the Metropolitanate of Nicomedia, Nicaea was the site of the First (325) and Seventh (787) Ecumenical Councils, and was promoted to a Metropolitanate circa 370 by Emperor Valens. It had three Dioceses under its jurisdiction in the seventh century, which had increased to six by the tenth century; however, after the Ottoman occupation of the area, the number steadily declined, with none remaining by the year 1600, and the Metropolitanate itself comprising two disjoined sections. After the Ottoman occupation its See was moved 50 km west, to the city of Kios (Grk Κίος, Trk Gemlik), on the shore of the Marmara Sea, inside the gulf bearing the city's name.

The main section is bordered by the Metropolitanate of Nikomidia on the north, the Metropolitanate of Ankyra on the east, the Metropolitanate of Prousa on the south, and the Sea of Marmara on the west. Important cities are, besides Kios and Nikaia: Vasilinopolis (Grk Βασιλινόπολις, Trk Orhangazi), 40 km west of Nikaia, on the other side of the lake; Kyvala (Grk Κύβαλα, Trk Geyve), 55 km east of Nikaia; Lefkes (Grk Λεύκες, Trk Osmaneli), 30 km east of Nikaia; Angelokoma (Grk Αγγελόκωμα, Trk Inegol), 45 km south of Nikaia; and Thivazio (Grk Θηβάζιο, Τρκ Sogut), 80 km south of Nikaia.

The Militopolis section is bordered by the Sea of Marmara on the north; the Metropolitanate of Nikomidia (Apolloniada section) and the Metropolitanate of Prousa on the east; the Metropolitanate of Ankyra and the Metropolitanate of Kyzikos on the south; and the Metropolitanate of Kyzikos on the west. Important cities in this section are: Michalikion (Grk Μιχαλίκιον, Trk Karacabey), 85 km southwest of Kios; Kremasti (Grk Κρεμαστή, Trk Mustafakemalpasa), 20 km south of Michalitsi; Militopolis (Grk Μιλητόπολις, Trk Uluabat), 8 km east of Michalitsi, located on the west shore of Lake Apollonia (Grk Λίμνη Απολλωνία, Trk Uluabat Golu); and Adranos (Grk Αδρανός, Trk Orhaneli, ancient Handriani ad Olympum), 60 km southeast of Kremasti.

During 1920/21 most of the area was occupied by the Greek army, with Kios being occupied on July 3, 1920 and Lefkes on March 10, 1921 and again on June 27, 1921. The front line from Kios to the southern shore of Askania Lake and Nikaia was held until the Greek army's defeat in late August 1922, after which all Orthodox were evacuated to Greece or killed by the advanced Turkish army. No Orthodox population remains inside the area of the Metropolitanate today.

Metropolitans of Nikaia since 1800

66. Callinicus II	Καλλίνικος Β'	Sep 1792 – 17 Jun 1801	d≥1809
(ex m.Adrianoupolis) (to p.Constantinople)			
67. Daniel	Δανιήλ	Jun 1801 – 1809	d. ?
(ex m.Lakedaimonia) deposed			

68. Johnnicius II (ex m.Ankyra) (to m.Kaisaria)	Ιωαννίκιος Β'		Mar 1811 – Jun 1817	d. 1823
69. Macarius III (ex m.Tornovo) (to m.Ephesos)	Μακάριος Γ'		Jun 1817 – Apr 1821	d. 1830
70. Hierotheus (ex former m.Paronaxia) (to p.Alexandria)	Ιερόθεος		Apr 1821 – 29 Oct 1825	d. 1845
71. Joseph II (ex m.Pelagonia)	Ιωσήφ Β'		Oct 1825 – 1859+	d. 1859
72. Johnnicius III (ex m.Nyssa) (to m.Iraklia)	Ιωαννίκιος Γ'		20 Jun 1859 – 12 May 1878	d. 1879
73. Sophronius II Christidis (ex m.Didymotichon) (to former, to m.Nikaia) resigned	Σωφρόνιος Β'	(1st time)	12 May 1878 – 14 Nov 1880	d. 1890
74. Dionysius Charitonidis (ex m.Adrianoupolis) (to m.Adrianoupolis)	Διονύσιος		14 Nov 1880 – 23 Jan 1886	1820-1891
---. Sophronius II Christidis (ex former m.Nikaia)	Σωφρόνιος Β'	(2nd time)	23 Jan 1886 – 8 Jan 1890+	d. 1890
75. Hieronymus Gorgias (ex m.Nikopolis) (to m.Iraklia)	Ιερώνυμος	(1st time)	11 Jan 1890 – 13 May 1897	1837-1910
76. Sophronius III Christidis (ex m.Leros) (to m.Ioannina)	Σωφρόνιος Γ'		29 May 1897 – 22 May 1902	d. 1910
---. Hieronymus Γοργίας (ex m.Iraklia)	Ιερώνυμος		22 May 1902 – 30 Mar 1910+	1837-1910
77. Basil Georgiadis (ex m.Pelagonia) (to p.Constantinople)	Βασίλειος		13 May 1910 – 13 Jul 1925	1846-1929
78. Benjamin Kyriakou (ex m.Philippoupolis) (to m.Iraklia)	Βενιαμίν		21 Jul 1925 – 21 Oct 1933	1871-1946
79. John V Rinne (ex former a.Karelia and All Finland)	Ιωάννης Ε'		4 Oct 2001 –	b. 1923

METROPOLITANATE OF NIKOMIDIA
ΜΗΤΡΟΠΟΛΙΣ ΝΙΚΟΜΗΔΕΙΑΣ

Metropolitan of Nicomedia, most honorable and Exarch of all Bithynia

The city of Nikomidia (Nicomedia, Grk Νικομήδεια, Trk Izmit), located on the eastern shore of Marmara Sea, inside the gulf bearing the city's name, 90 km east of Chalkidon, was established by King of Bithynia, Nikomedes, in the second century BC on the site of a previous settlement. In 74 BC it came under Roman control, becoming the administrative center of East Roman Empire in 284 AD, and serving as such until the seat of government was transferred to Constantinople in 330. Taken by the Latins of Constantinople in 1206, it was retaken by the Romans circa 1240, and was occupied by the Ottoman Turks in 1337 after a long siege.

The Metropolitanate of Nicomedia was established in 325 AD. Initially under the honorary primacy of the Metropolitanate of Kaisaria, it became a Metropolitanate of the Patriarchate of Constantinople in 451. It had eight Dioceses under its jurisdiction in the seventh century, which had increased to twelve by the ninth century. Although by the twelfth century it still had twelve Dioceses, after the Ottoman occupation of the area, the number steadily decreased, with only the Diocese of Apollonias remaining by the year 1600, and soon afterwards none.

The Metropolitanate today is comprised of two disjoined sections, the main one bordered by the Metropolitanate of Chalkidon on the north and east, the Metropolitanate of Nikaia on the south, and the Sea of Marmara on the west. Besides Nikomidia, cities in this section are: Sangaria (Grk Σαγγάρια, Trk Sakarya, formerly Adapazari), 40 km east of Nikomidia; Chandakas (Grk Χάνδακας, Trk Hendek), 30 km east of Sangaria; Sophona (Grk Σοφώνα, Trk Sapanca), 30 km east of Nikomidia, located on the shore of Lake Voani (Grk Λίμνη Βοάνη, Trk Sapanca Golu); Prainetos (Grk Πραίνετος, Trk Karamursel), on the Marmara Sea shore, 35 km west of Nikomidia; and Elenopolis (Grk Ελενόπολις, Trk Yalova), on the Marmara Sea shore, 60 km west of Nikomidia.

Apollonias is bordered by the Sea of Marmara on the north; the Metropolitanate of Prousa on the east; and the Metropolitanate of Nikaia (Militopolis section) on the south and west. Settlements in this section include: Apollonias (Grk Απολλωνιάς, Trk Golyazi), 160 km west of Nikomidia, located on the north shore of Lake Apollonia (Grk Λίμνη Απολλωνία, Trk Uluabat Golu); Armoutlion (Grk Αρμουτλίον, Trk Armutlu), 110 km west of Nikomidia, on the shore of Marmara Sea; and Kalolimnos (Grk Καλόλιμνος, Trk Imrali), on the island of the same name. Kalolimnos was the first island in the Marmara Sea to be occupied by the Ottoman Turks, in 1308.

In June 1920 the area of the Apollonias section was occupied by the Greek army, which also occupied Nikomidia in July 1920 and Sangaria (Adapazari) on March 15, 1921. The Greek forces withdrew from Nikomedia on July 15, 1921, but remained in the Apollonias section until their defeat in late August 1922, after which all Orthodox were evacuated to Greece or killed by the advanced Turkish army. No Orthodox population remains inside the area of the Metropolitanate today.

Metropolitans of Nikomidia since 1800

68. Athanasius	Αθανάσιος	Nov 1791 – 10 Apr 1821++	1755-1821
Karydis (ex m.Libya, Patriarchate of Alexandria) executed by the Ottomans			
69. Panaretus	Πανάρετος	Apr 1821 – Apr 1837+	d. 1837
(ex m.Prousa)			
70. Anthimus II	Άνθιμος Β'	Aug 1837 – 20 Feb 1840	1788-1878
Vamvakis (ex m.Larissa) (to p.Constantinople)			
71. Dionysius II	Διονύσιος Β'	Feb 1840 – 22 Aug 1877+	d. 1877
Kotakis (ex former m.Amasia)			
72. Philotheus	Φιλόθεος	24 Aug 1877 – 25 Nov 1910	1833-1917
Vryennios (ex m.Serres) resigned			
73. Alexander	Αλέξανδρος	25 Nov 1910 – 27 Jun 1928+	1851-1928
Rigopoulos (ex m.Thessaloniki)			
74. Symeon	Συμεών	9 Jul 2002 – 18 Oct 2003+	1916-2003
Amaryllios (ex m.Pringiponnisa)			
75. Joachim	Ιωακείμ	21 Mar 2008 –	b. 1942
Nerantzoulis (ex m.Chalkidon)			

METROPOLITANATE OF PERGAMOS AND ADRAMYTTION
ΜΗΤΡΟΠΟΛΙΣ ΠΕΡΓΑΜΟΥ ΚΑΙ ΑΔΡΑΜΥΤΤΙΟΥ

Metropolitan of Pergamus and Adramyttion, most honorable and Exarch of Adramyttian Gulf

The city of Pergamos (Grk Πέργαμος, Trk Bergama), situated in the valley of Kaïkos River (Grk Κάικος Ποταμός, Trk Bakir Cayi), 100 km north of Smyrni, was established before the fourth century BC by Greek settlers from Epidaurus, Peloponnese. The city of Adramyttion (Grk Αδραμύττιον, Trk Edremit), situated 70 km north of Pergamos, was established by the Lydians and re-populated by Greeks from Delos Island in 422 BC. In 133 BC the area came under Roman control, and after 325 AD the Dioceses of Pergamos and Adramyttion came under the jurisdiction of the Metropolitanate of Ephesos. In 1197 Adramyttion was destroyed by Genovese pirates, and the city was moved to a safer location, 12 km to the northeast. In 1310 Pergamos was occupied by the Seljuk Turks and in 1341 by the Ottomans.

During the thirteenth century Pergamos was promoted to a Metropolitanate, but the army of Mongol Khan Tamerlane (real name Timur, reigned 1370-1405) destroyed the city in 1402, and soon afterwards the area of both former Dioceses came under the direct control of the Ephesus Metropolitanate. Pergamus was occupied by the Greek army on May 30, 1919 and Adramyttion on June 19, 1920.

The Metropolitanate of Pergamos and Adramyttion was re-established on February 19, 1922. It is bordered by the Metropolitanate of Dardanellia on the north, the Metropolitanate of Kyzikos and the Metropolitanate of Ephesos on the east, the Metropolitanate of Ephesos on the south, and the Aegean Sea on the west. Other notable cities in the area are: Kemerion (Grk Κεμέριον, Trk Burhaniye), located next to the initial site of Adramyttion; Dikeli (Grk Δικελή, Trk Dikili), 28 km west of Pergamos, on the Aegean Sea shore; and Kinikion (Grk Κινίκιον, Trk Kinik), 18 km east of Pergamos.

Greek forces withdrew from the area after their defeat in late August 1922, and all Orthodox were evacuated to Greece or killed by the advanced Turkish army. No Orthodox population remains inside the area of the Metropolitanate today.

Metropolitans of Pergamos and Adramyttion since 1800

16. Alexander Dilanas (ex m.Anea) (to m.Zichna)	Αλέξανδρος	19 Feb 1922 – 9 Oct 1924	1878-1958
17. Adamantius Kasapidis	Αδαμάντιος	9 Oct 1943 – 25 Nov 1958+	1909-1958
18. John II Zizioulas	Ιωάννης Β'	22 Jun 1986 –	b. 1931

METROPOLITANATE OF PROUSA
ΜΗΤΡΟΠΟΛΙΣ ΠΡΟΥΣΗΣ

Metropolitan of Prussa, most honorable and Exarch of Bithynia

The city of Prousa (Grk Προύσα, Trk Bursa), located 70 km southwest of Nicaea, was established circa 200 BC by King Prousias of Bithynia, and came under Roman control in 74 BC. The Diocese of Prousa came under the jurisdiction of the Metropolitanate of Nikomidia in 325 AD, and was promoted to a Metropolitanate circa 1190. Prousa was briefly renamed Theoupolis (God's City, Grk Θεούπολις) in the seventh century. After a long siege, Prousa was occupied by the Ottoman Turks on April 6, 1326 and became their capital, until they chose Adrianople as their capital in 1413. Meanwhile, in 1402 the city was sacked by the army of Tamerlane.

The Metropolitanate of Prousa is bordered by the Sea of Marmara and the Metropolitanate of Nikaia on the north, the Metropolitanate of Ankyra on the east, the Metropolitanate of Nikaia and the Metropolitanate of Ankyra on the south, and the Metropolitanate of Nikomidia (Apollonias section) on the west. Other notable cities in the area are: Apamia (Grk Απάμεια, Trk Mudanya), located on the Marmara Sea 25 km north of Prousa (itself a Metropolitanate until it was abolished in 1318); Triglia (Grk Τρίγλεια, Trk Zeytinbag), located on the Marmara Sea 30 km northwest of Prousa; Vilokoma (Grk Βηλόκωμα, Trk Bilecik), 90 km east of Prousa.

In 1920/21 the area was occupied by the Greek army, with Prousa being occupied on June 25, 1920 and Vilokoma on March 12, 1921 and again on June 30, 1921. The Greek forces withdrew from the area after their defeat in late August 1922 (Prousa itself was held until August 28, 1922), and all Orthodox were evacuated to Greece or killed by the advanced Turkish army. No Orthodox population remains there today.

Metropolitans of Prousa since 1800

40. Anthimus II	Άνθιμος Β'	*Jul* 1776 – 1807+	d. 1807
41. Johnnicius (to m.Tornovo) see note 1	Ιωαννίκιος	*Aug* 1807 – Jun 1817	d. 1821
42. Panaretus (ex m.Mithymna) (to m.Nikomidia)	Πανάρετος	Jun 1817 – Apr 1821	d. 1837
43. Gerasimus Frydas (to m.Adrianoupolis)	Γεράσιμος	*Apr* 1821 – Sep 1824	d≥1830
44. Nicodemus I (ex m.Philippi) deposed	Νικόδημος Α'	Sep 1824 – Jun 1833	d. ?
45. Anthimus III Ioannidis (ex m.Serres) (to m.Ephesos)	Άνθιμος Γ'	Jun 1833 – 1 Apr 1837	1782-1878
46. Chrysanthus II Karamalis (ex m.Smyrni)	Χρύσανθος Β'	1 Apr 1837 – 1846+	d. 1846
47. Constantius Kalogeras (ex m.Stromnitsa)	Κωνστάντιος	Jun 1846 – 21 Feb 1870+	d. 1870
48. Nicodemus II Konstantinidis (ex m.Vodena)	Νικόδημος Β'	2 Apr 1870 – Jan 1886+	d. 1886
49. Nathaniel Papanikas (ex m.Serres) (to m.Nikopolis)	Ναθαναήλ	Jan 1886 – 25 Oct 1908	d. 1910
50. Dorotheus Mammelis (ex m.Nikopolis)	Δωρόθεος	25 Oct 1908 – 6 Mar 1921+	1861-1921
51. Constantine Arampoglous (ex m.Kyzikos) (to m.Derki)	Κωνσταντίνος	10 Feb 1922 – 8 Μαΐου 1924	1859-1930
52. Nicodemus III Komninos Andreou (ex m.Varna)	Νικόδημος Γ'	24 May 1924 – 10 Apr 1935+	1857-1935
53. Polycarp Dimitriadis (ex t.m.Myra 25 Dec 1927)	Πολύκαρπος	28 Jan 1936 – 16 Aug 1953+	1892-1953
54. Dionysius II Psiachas (ex m.New Zealand)	Διονύσιος Β'	21 Jul 2003 – 6 Jan 2008+	1916-2008

1. Metropolitan Johnnicius was hanged in Constantinople by the Ottoman authorities on June 4, 1821, along with other Greek Hierarchs, a few months after the beginning of the Greek revolution.

SECTION D:
METROPOLITANATES IN SOUTHWEST ASIA MINOR

METROPOLITANATE OF ANEA
ΜΗΤΡΟΠΟΛΙΣ ΑΝΕΩΝ

Metropolitan of Anea, most honorable and Exarch of Ionia

The city of Anea (Grk Άνεα, Trk Sogucak), 9 km south of New Ephesos, was in ancient times located on the shore of the Aegean Sea. It came under Roman control in 133 BC, was taken by the Seljuk Turks circa 1085, retaken by the Romans in 1097, passed under Genovese control in 1261, retaken by the Seljuks in 1298, and taken by the Ottomans in 1390. In 1403 Tamerlane gave the area to the Emirate of Aydin, with the Ottomans returning in 1424. Afterwards the city became deserted, with the city of Sokia (Grk Σώκια, Trk Soke), located 10 km to the east, gaining importance in later years.

The Diocese of Anea came under the jurisdiction of the Metropolitanate of Ephesos in 325 AD, but was abolished after the Turkish occupation. A new Diocese of Krini and Anea was established in November 1806 under the Metropolitanate of Ephesos, which was split into the Diocese of Krini and the Diocese of Anea on May 9, 1883. The city of Sokia, which came to be known also as Anea, served as the See of the Diocese. The Diocese of Anea was promoted to a Metropolitanate on February 21, 1917.

The Metropolitanate of Anea is divided into two disjoined sections. The Anea section is bordered by the Metropolitanate of Ilioupolis and the Metropolitanate of Ephesos (New Ephesos section) on the north; the Metropolitanate of Ilioupolis on the east and south; and the Aegean Sea on the west. Notion section is bordered by the Metropolitanate of Krini (Mitropolis section) and the Metropolitanate of Ephesos on the north; the Metropolitanate of Ilioupolis on the east; the Metropolitanate of Ilioupolis and the Aegean Sea on the south; and the Metropolitanate of Vryoula on the west.

Other notable cities in the area are: Gerontas (Grk Γέροντας, Trk Yenihisar), located 45 km south of Anea (Sokia); Vagarasi (Grk Βαγάρασι, Trk Bagarasi), 15 km east of Anea (Sokia); and Notion (Grk Νότιον, Trk Ozdere), located 45 km northwest of Anea (Sokia), on the shore of the Aegean Sea.

In May 1919 the area was occupied by the Italian army; however the Italians withdrew from the area of Sokia in early April 1922, and the Greek army entered the city on April 8, 1922. The Greek forces withdrew from the area after their defeat in late August 1922, and all Orthodox were evacuated to Greece or killed by the advanced Turkish army. No Orthodox population remains inside the area of the Metropolitanate today.

Hierarchs of Anea since 1800
(Bishops until Mar 1917, Metropolitans afterwards)

12. Constantine   Κωνσταντίνος   9 May 1883 – 2 Nov 1902   1847-1912
    (ex t.b.Myrina Sep 1875) resigned

13. Anthimus	Ἄνθιμος	2 Nov 1902 – 1917+	d. 1917
Chimonios (ex t.b.Arkadioupolis *11 Jun* 1883)			
14. Alexander	Ἀλέξανδρος	21 Feb 1917 – 19 Feb 1922	1878-1958
Dilanas (ex t.b.Myra 18 Jul 1910) (to m.Pergamos) promoted to Metropolitan in March 1917			
15. Thomas	Θωμάς	26 Feb 1922 – 2 Apr 1927	1889-1966
Savvopoulos (to m.Pringiponnisa)			
16. Nicholas	Νικόλαος	15 Feb 1972 – 15 Oct 1972+	1903-1972
Koutroumpis (ex m.Imvros)			
17. Polyeuctus	Πολύευκτος	30 Apr 1974 – 2 Feb 1988+	1912-1988
Finfinis (ex m.Sweden)			
18. Methodius	Μεθόδιος	24 Nov 1997 – 20 Dec 2002	b. 1946
Tournas (ex b.Boston) (to m.Boston)			

METROPOLITANATE OF EPHESOS
ΜΗΤΡΟΠΟΛΙΣ ΕΦΕΣΟΥ

Metropolitan of Ephesus, most honorable and Exarch of all Asia

The city of Ephesos (Grk Ἔφεσος, Trk Selcuk), located 70 km south of Smyrni, was established in the thirteenth century BC, with Ionian Greeks settling there in the eleventh century BC. It came under Roman control in 133 BC, was taken by the Seljuk Turks circa 1085, retaken by the Romans in 1097 and by the Seljuk Turks in 1304, and was taken by the Ottoman Turks in 1390. The city was destroyed by the army of Tamerlane in 1402 and was subsequently abandoned, with the city of New Ephesos (Grk Νέα Ἔφεσος, Trk Kusadasi), located 10 km to the southwest, gaining importance in later years. Tamerlane gave the area to the resurrected Emirates of Aydin and Saruhan, with the Ottomans returning in 1424.

Ephesos became a Metropolitanate in 325 AD, exercising honorary primacy over the other Metropolitanates of the Asian Division: the Metropolitanates of Kyzikos, Sardis, Laodikia, Synnada, Antiochia of Pisidia, Aphrodisias, Pergi, and Rhodes. To these were later added the Metropolitanates of Myra (by division of Pergi), Sidi (by division of Pergi), and Ikonion (by division of Antiochia). The Third Ecumenical Council convened at Ephesos in 431. After the Fourth Ecumenical Council of 451, the Patriarchate of Constantinople officially placed under its jurisdiction all of the Metropolitanates in the area, including Ephesos. Ephesos had thirty-seven Dioceses under its jurisdiction in the seventh century, which increased to forty by the ninth century. In the twelfth century it still had thirty-three Dioceses; however, after the Ottoman occupation the number steadily decreased, with none remaining by the sixteenth century. During that time the See of the Metropolitanate was transferred 110 km north, to Magnisia (Grk Μαγνησία, Trk Manisa). After 1900 the Metropolitan also resided in Kordelio (Grk Κορδελιό, Trk Karsiyaka), a city 10 km north of Smyrni, which today is a suburb of modern Izmir.

A new Diocese of Ilioupolis under the Metropolitanate of Ephesos was created in 1774 and a Diocese of Krini and Anea in 1806, with the later splitting into two Dioceses in 1883. Ephesos thus had three Dioceses under its jurisdiction until the beginning of the twentieth century, when the Dioceses were incrementally promoted to Metropolitanates. Although the ruins of ancient Ephesos came to be in the area of the Metropolitanate of Ilioupolis, the city of New Ephesos remains part of the Metropolitanate of Ephesos.

The Metropolitanate of Ephesos is bordered by the Metropolitanate of Pergamos and the Metropolitanate of Kyzikos on the north; the Metropolitanate of Philadelphia on the east; the Metropolitanate of Ilioupolis, the Metropolitanate of Krini (Mitropolis section) and the Metropolitanate of Anea (Notion section) on the south; and the Metropolitanate of Vryoula, the Metropolitanate of Smyrni, the Metropolitanate of Pergamos and the Aegean Sea on the west. The city of New Ephesos is situated in a disjoined section which is bordered by the Metropolitanate of Ilioupolis on the north and east, the Metropolitanate of Anea on the south, and the Aegean Sea on the west.

Other notable cities in the area are: Nymphaion (Grk Νυμφαίον, Trk Kemalpasa), located 25 km east of Smyrni; Kasampas (Grk Κασαμπᾶς, Trk Turgutlu), 55 km east of Smyrni; Mainemeni (Grk Μαινεμένη, Trk Menemen), 30 km north of Smyrni; Phokaia (Grk Φώκαια, Trk Foca), on the shore of the Aegean Sea, 60 km north of Smyrni; New Phokaia (Grk Νέα Φώκαια, Trk Yenifoca), on the shore of the Aegean Sea, 70 km north of Smyrni; Thyatira (Grk Θυάτειρα, Trk Akhisar), 85 km northeast of Smyrni; Chliara (Grk Χλιαρά, Trk Kirkagac), 20 km northwest of Thyatira; and Soma (Grk Σώμα, Trk Soma), 10 km northwest of Chliara.

In May 1919 the Greek army occupied most of the area of the Metropolitanate, including Magnisia, and the remaining area was taken in the first major Greek offensive of June 1920, with Thyatira being occupied on June 9, 1920 and Soma on June 11, 1920. The isolated southern part of the Metropolitanate, New Ephesos, was occupied by Italian forces in May 5, 1919; however, the Italians withdrew from the city in April 1922, and the Greek army entered New Ephesos on April 18, 1922.

The Greek forces withdrew from the area after their defeat in late August 1922 (the Turkish army entered Magnisia on August 25, 1922), and all the Orthodox were evacuated to Greece or killed by the advanced Turkish army. No Orthodox population remains inside the area of the Metropolitanate today.

Metropolitans of Ephesos since 1800

110. Samuel (ex m.Philippoupolis)	Σαμουήλ	Feb 1780 – Jun 1801+	d. 1801
111. Macarius II Balasakis (ex m.Derki)	Μακάριος Β´	Jun 1801 – 1803+	d. 1803
112. Dionysius III Kalliarchis (ex m.Larissa) executed by the Ottomans	Διονύσιος Γ´	Sep 1803 – 10 Apr 1821++	d. 1821
113. Macarius III (ex m.Nikaia)	Μακάριος Γ´	Apr 1821 – Dec 1830+	d. 1830
114. Chrysanthus (ex m.Kaisaria)	Χρύσανθος	Dec 1830 – 1836+	d. 1836
115. Gerasimus Domninos (ex m.Ankyra)	Γεράσιμος	Sep 1836 – 1837+	d. 1837
116. Anthimus II Ioannidis (ex m.Prousa) (to p.Constantinople)	Ἄνθιμος Β´	1 Apr 1837 – 4 Dec 1845	1782-1878
117. Anthimus III Koutalianos (ex m.Maronia) resigned, 12 Apr 1879+	Ἄνθιμος Γ´	Dec 1845 – 14 Jul 1853	1804-1879
118. Païsius II (ex m.Sophia) suspended, 17 Jan 1877+	Παΐσιος Β´	14 Jul 1853 – 25 May 1872	d. 1877
119. Agathangelus I Gavriilidis (ex m.Filippi)	Αγαθάγγελος Α´	25 May 1872 – 26 Apr 1893+	1818-1893
120. Constantine III Valliadis (ex m.Mytilini) (to p.Constantinople)	Κωνσταντίνος Γ´	30 Apr 1893 – 2 Apr 1897	1833-1914
121. Joachim II Efthyvoulis (ex m.Chalkidon)	Ἰωακείμ Β´	10 May 1897 – 10 Jan 1920+	1885-1920

122. Chrysostom I	Χρυσόστομος Α΄	19 Feb 1922 – 5 Feb 1924	1880-1968
Chatzistavrou (ex m.Philadelphia) (to m.Rhodes)			
123. Callinicus	Καλλίνικος	8 May 1924 – 16 Jan 1926+	1841-1926
Fotiadis (ex m.Derki)			
124. Agathangelus II	Αγαθάγγελος Β΄	28 Jun 1932 – 16 Aug 1935+	1864-1935
Konstantinidis-Magnis (ex m.Chalkidon)			
125. Maximus II	Μάξιμος Β΄	27 Mar 1948 – 1 Jan 1972+	1897-1972
Vaportzis (ex p.Constantinople, as president) see note 1			
126. Chrysostom II	Χρυσόστομος Β΄	10 Dec 1991 – 13 Oct 2006+	1921-2006
Konstantinidis (ex t.m.Myra 5 Mar 1961)			

1. Patriarch Maximus V became president of the Metropolitanate of Ephesos on March 27, 1948. He resigned from the position of Patriarch on October 19, 1948, but retained the presidency of Ephesos.

METROPOLITANATE OF ILIOUPOLIS AND THIRA
ΜΗΤΡΟΠΟΛΙΣ ΗΛΙΟΥΠΟΛΕΩΣ ΚΑΙ ΘΕΙΡΩΝ

Metropolitan of Helioupolis and Thira, most honorable and Exarch of Lydia and all Caria

The city of Trallis (Grk Τράλλεις, Trk Aydin), located 105 km southeast of Smyrni, was established before the fourth century BC by the Trallians, came under Roman control in 133 BC, was occupied by the Seljuk Turks circa 1085, and retaken by the Romans in 1097. Emperor Andronicus II rebuilt the fortifications of the city in 1280, renaming it Andronikopolis (Grk Ανδρονικόπολις), but the city fell to the Seljuks in 1284 and the Ottoman Turks in 1390. In 1403 Tamerlane gave the area to the resurrected Emirate of Aydin, with the Ottomans returning in 1424. After the Seljuk occupation, the city came to be known as Ilioupolis (Grk Ηλιούπολις) by its Orthodox citizens, who popularly translated its Turkish name "Aydin" to Greek.

The Diocese of Trallis came under the jurisdiction of the Metropolitanate of Ephesos in 325 AD, but was abolished after the Turkish occupation. A new Diocese of Ilioupolis and Thyatira was established in July 1774 under the Metropolitanate of Ephesos. (But the city of Thyatira (Trk Akhisar) was actually located to the north, outside the area of the Diocese.) The Diocese was promoted to a Metropolitanate in December 1901, and soon thereafter its name was corrected to Metropolitanate of Ilioupolis and Thira, after the city of Thira (Grk Θείρα, Trk Tire), located 30 km north of Ilioupolis (Trallis).

The Metropolitanate of Ilioupolis and Thira is bordered by the Metropolitanate of Anea (Notion section), the Metropolitanate of Ephesos, the Metropolitanate of Philadelphia and the Metropolitanate of Sardis on the north; the Metropolitanate of Philadelphia on the east; the Metropolitanate of Pisidia on the south; and the Metropolitanate of Krini (Metropolis section), the Metropolitanate of Anea (both sections), the Metropolitanate of Ephesos (New Ephesos section) and the Aegean Sea on the west.

Other notable cities in the area are: Odemision (Grk Οδεμήσιον, Trk Odemis), located 55 km north of Ilioupolis; Kilvianon (Grk Κιλβιανόν, Trk Bayindir), 17 km north of Thira; Taves (Grk Τάβες, Trk Tavas), 125 km east of Ilioupolis; Mylasa (Grk Μύλασα, Trk Milas), 65 km south of Ilioupolis; Alikarnassos (Grk Αλίκαρνασσός, Trk Bodrum), on the shore of the Aegean Sea, 120 km south of Ilioupolis; and Movolla (Grk Μόβωλλα, Trk Mugla), 55 km east of Mylasa. The ruins of old Ephesos (Grk Έφεσος, Trk Selcuk) are also located inside the area of the Metropolitanate.

In May 1919 the area north of the Maiandros River (Grk Μαίανδρος, Trk Guyuk-menderes) was occupied by the Greek army (Ilioupolis itself was occupied on May 14, 1919), and the area south of the Maiandros was held by the Italian army (Alikarmasos was occupied on April 28, 1919); however, the Italians withdrew in April 1921, after reaching an agreement with the Turks. The Greek forces withdrew from the area after their defeat in late August 1922, and all Orthodox were evacuated to Greece or killed by the advanced Turkish army. No Orthodox population remains inside the area of the Metropolitanate today.

Hierarchs of Ilioupolis
(Bishops until Dec 1901, Metropolitans afterwards)

1. Gerasimus (ex t.b.Rysava)	Γεράσιμος	13 Jul 1774 – Jan 1777+	d. 1777
2. Leontius (ex t.b.Myrina)	Λεόντιος	Jan 1777 – 1803+	d. 1803
3. Callinicus (ex t.b.Myrina)	Καλλίνικος	Jul 1803 – 1811?	d. 1811?
4. Anthimus I Komninos (to former, to b.Kyklades of Greek Church) suspended	Άνθιμος Α΄	Feb 1811 – 30 Jul 1821	d. 1842
5. Theodosius (ex former m.Theodosioupolis, Patriarchate of Antioch) as president, resigned	Θεοδόσιος	30 Jul 1821 – Oct 1821	d. ?
6. Johnnicius (ex t.b.Arkadioupolis Aug 1821)	Ιωαννίκιος	Oct 1821 – 1841+	d. 1841
7. Anthimus II Lykaris (ex b.Krini) (to m.Smyrni)	Άνθιμος Β΄	Sep 1841 – 3 Jan 1851	d. 1853
8. Dionysius (ex t.b.Elaia Sep 1848) resigned, 6 Feb 1878+	Διονύσιος	3 Jan 1851 – 1877	d. 1878
9. Tarasius Vasiliou (ex t.b.Christoupolis *29 Jun* 1867) promoted to Metropolitan in Dec 1901	Ταράσιος	19 Feb 1877 – 12 Aug 1910	d. ?
10. Panaretus Petridis (ex m.Kallipolis) (to m.Imvros)	Πανάρετος	12 Aug 1910 – 21 Jun 1912	d. 1922
11. Smaragdus Chatziefstathiou (ex m.Philippoupolis) (to m.Goumenissa)	Σμάραγδος	21 Jun 1912 – 14 Oct 1924	1871-1928
12. Gennadius Arampatzoglous (ex t.b.Skopelos *4 Apr* 1913)	Γεννάδιος	29 Jan 1925 – 14 Mar 1956+	1883-1956
13. Meliton Chatzis (ex m.Imvros) (to m.Chalkidon)	Μελίτων	19 Feb 1963 – 25 Oct 1966	1913-1989
14. Polyeuctus Finfinis (ex m.Germany) (to m.Sweden)	Πολύευκτος	25 Jun 1968 – 12 Aug 1969	1912-1988
15. Apostolus Dimelis (ex t.b.Evmenia 25 Nov 1973) (to m.Rhodes)	Απόστολος	15 Nov 1977 – 5 May 1988	b. 1925
16. Athanasius Papas (ex t.b.Elenoupolis 24 Sep 1972, t.m.Elenoupolis 8 Nov 1976) (to m.Chalkidon)	Αθανάσιος	2 Oct 1990 – 21 Mar 2008	b. 1936

METROPOLITANATE OF KRINI
ΜΗΤΡΟΠΟΛΙΣ ΚΡΗΝΗΣ

Metropolitan of Crene, most honorable and Exarch of Ionia

The city of Erythres (Grk Ερυθρές, Trk Ildir), located on the shore of the Aegean Sea, 70 km west of Smyrni, was established before the ninth century BC by settlers from Crete, came under Roman control in 133 BC, was occupied by the Seljuk Turks circa

1085, retaken by the Romans in 1097, retaken by the Seljuks in 1304, and occupied by the Ottoman Turks in 1390. In 1403 Tamerlane gave the area to the resurrected Emirate of Aydin, with the Ottomans returning in 1424. After the Turkish occupation the city was mostly deserted, with the city of Krini (Grk Κρήνη, Trk Çesme), located 20 km to the southwest (also on the Aegean Sea shore), rising in prominence.

The Diocese of Erythres came under the jurisdiction of the Metropolitanate of Ephesos in 325 AD, but was abolished after the Turkish occupation. A new Diocese of Krini and Anea was established in November 1806 under the Metropolitanate of Ephesos, which was split into the Diocese of Krini and the Diocese of Anea on May 9, 1883. The Diocese of Krini was promoted to a Metropolitanate in March 1903.

The Metropolitanate of Krini is bordered by the Aegean Sea on the north, south and west, and the Metropolitanate of Vryoula on the east. The city of Mitropolis (Grk Μητρόπολις, Trk Torbali), located 45 km south of Smyrni, is situated in a disjoined section which is bordered by the Metropolitanate of Ephesos on the north; the Metropolitanate of Ilioupolis on the south; and the Metropolitanate of Anea (Notion section) on the south and west. Other notable cities in the area are: Alatsata (Grk Αλάτσατα, Trk Alacati), located 7 km east of Krini, and Melaina Akra (Grk Μέλαινα Άκρα, Trk Karaburun), located 55 km north of Krini, on the Aegean Sea shore. Notable islands are: Drymousa (Grk Δρυμούσα, popularly called Εγγλεζονήσι 'Island of the English', Trk Uzun Ada, having an area of 25 km²), located inside Ermaïkos Gulf (Grk Ερμαϊκός Κόλπος, Trk Izmir Korfezi), and the smaller islands of Gouni (Grk Γουνί, Trk Kara Ada) and Plakia (Grk Πλακιά, Trk Toprak Ada), both located in Erythres Gulf (Grk Κόλπος Ερυθρών, Trk Ildir Korfezi).

The area of the Metropolitanate was occupied by the Greek army on May 3, 1919. The Greek forces withdrew after their defeat in late August 1922, and all Orthodox were evacuated to Greece or killed by the advanced Turkish army. The last units of the Greek army departed from Krini on September 3, 1922. No Orthodox population remains inside the area of the Metropolitanate today.

Hierarchs of Krini
(Bishops until Mar 1903, Metropolitans afterwards)

1. Jacob I	Ιάκωβος Α'		*Nov* 1806 – 1812	d. 1812?
2. Ignatius	Ιγνάτιος		1812 – 1824++	d. 1824
imprisoned from 1821, died in prison				
3. Macarius	Μακάριος		1824 – May 1835	d. 1837
(to m.Ganos)				
4. Anthimus	Άνθιμος		*May* 1835 – Sep 1841	d. 1853
Lykaris (to b.Ilioupolis)				
5. Seraphim	Σεραφείμ		Sep 1841 – 1848+	d. 1848
(ex t.b.Arkadioupolis Jan 1840)				
6. Ambrose	Αμβρόσιος		Aug 1848 – 9 May 1883	d. 1884
Madytinos (ex t.b.Arkadioupolis Jan 1846) suspended, Aug 1884+				
7. Theocletus	Θεόκλητος		9 May 1883 – 10 Mar 1918+	d. 1918
Eleftheriou (ex t.b.Erythres *16 Nov* 1878) promoted to Metropolitan in Mar 1903				
8. Callinicus	Καλλίνικος	(1st time)	*9 Oct* 1918 – 22 May 1923	1881-1957
Lamprinidis (to m.Myriophyton)				
--. Callinicus	Καλλίνικος	(2nd time)	15 Apr 1924 – 14 Oct 1924	1881-1957
Lamprinidis (ex m.Myriophyton) (to m.Elasson)				
9. Jacob II	Ιάκωβος Β'		24 Nov 1997 – 20 Dec 2002	b. 1928
Gkarmatis (ex b.Chicago) (to m.Chicago)				

METROPOLITANATE OF PHILADELPHIA
ΜΗΤΡΟΠΟΛΙΣ ΦΙΛΑΔΕΛΦΕΙΑΣ

Metropolitan of Philadelphia, most honorable and Exarch of all Lydia

The city of Philadelphia (Grk Φιλαδέλφεια, Trk Alasehir), located 135 km east of Smyrni, was established circa 140 BC by the King of Pergamos, Attalos II Philadelphos. It came under Roman control in 133 BC, was occupied by the Seljuk Turks circa 1085, retaken by the Romans in 1097, and fell to the Ottoman Turks in 1390. Philadelphia was completely surrounded by Turkish territory from circa 1310, and later remained the last Roman city in Asia Minor. The army of Tamerlane sacked the city in 1402, giving the area to the resurrected Emirate of Germiyan, with the Ottomans taking control in 1429.

The Diocese of Philadelphia came under the jurisdiction of the Metropolitanate of Sardis in 325 AD, and was promoted to a Metropolitanate circa 1190. In July 1577 the See of the Metropolitanate was moved to the city of Venice in order to care for the Orthodox of Italy and Western Europe,[1] and in 1644 the Diocese of Kythira (one of the Ionian Islands which were then a Venetian possession) was transferred from the Metropolitanate of Monemvasia to the Metropolitanate of Philadelphia. However, in June 1712 the Patriarchate defrocked Metropolitan Meletius (1685-1712) of Philadelphia in Venice because he embraced Roman Catholic beliefs, and abolished the See. The Orthodox in Venice henceforth pressed for the re-establishment of the local Orthodox Metropolitanate, going so far as electing Hierarchs without the consent of the Patriarchate in 1762, 1768, and 1772. In 1780 the Venetian Orthodox managed to make the Patriarchate recognize the transfer of Metropolitan Sophronius of Cephallenia (another Ionian Island) to Venice, but after his death in 1790, the Patriarchate did not permit the election of a successor.

During the time that the See was in Venice, the area of the Metropolitanate in Asia Minor alternated between being attached to the Metropolitanate of Ephesos and being an Exarchate under the direct control of the Patriarch. Characteristically, in 1636 the Metropolitan of Ephesos was also president of the Metropolitanate of Philadelphia, but soon thereafter Philadelphia became an Exarchate, only to be officially annexed to the Metropolitanate of Ephesus in 1642/44. After the abolition of the Venetian See, Philadelphia of Asia Minor remained an Exarchate (mentioned as such in 1717), but by 1725 the Metropolitanate of Philadelphia in Asia Minor had been re-established.

The Metropolitanate of Philadelphia is bordered by the Metropolitanate of Kyzikos and the Metropolitanate of Ankyra on the north; the Metropolitanate of Ankyra, the Metropolitanate of Ikonion, and the Metropolitanate of Pisidia on the east; the Metropolitanate of Pisidia, the Metropolitanate of Ilioupolis, and the Metropolitanate of Sardis on the south; and the Metropolitanate of Ilioupolis and the Metropolitanate of Ephesos on the west.

Other notable cities are: Yrkanis (Grk Υρκανίς, Trk Salihli), 40 km west of Philadelphia; Tavala (Grk Τάβαλα, Trk Esme), 45 km east of Philadelphia; Opsikion Katakekavmenis (Grk Οψίκιον Κατεκεκαυμένης, Trk Kula), 25 km north of Philadelphia; Gordos (Grk Γόρδος, Trk Gordes), 90 km north of Philadelphia; Akmonia (Grk Ακμονία, Trk Demirci), 105 km north of Philadelphia; Synaos (Grk Συναός, Trk Simav), 140 km north of Philadelphia; Timenothyres (Grk Τημενοθύρες, Trk Usak), 95 km northeast of Philadelphia; Akroinos (Grk Ακροϊνός, Trk Afyon), 105 km east of Timenouthyres; Laodikia (Grk Λαοδίκεια, Trk Denizli), 110 km southeast of Philadelphia.

Most of the Metropolitanate's area was occupied by Greek forces in 1920/21, with Philadelphia being occupied on June 11, 1920, Timenothyres on August 16, 1920, and Akroinos from March 14-25, 1921 and again on June 30, 1921. The Greek forces withdrew after their defeat in late August 1922, and all Orthodox were evacuated to Greece or killed by the advanced Turkish army. No Orthodox population remains inside the area of the Metropolitanate today.

1. This happened at the initiative of Metropolitan of Philadelphia Gabriel II (1577-1616), who had moved to Venice instead of going to the See of his Metropolitanate. The Patriarchate initially requested his return to Philadelphia, and only in 1591 accepted the transfer of his See to Venice.

Metropolitans of Philadelphia since 1800

46. Jacob I resigned	Ἰάκωβος Α'	9 Jul 1765 – 1805	d. ?
47. Dorotheus Proios (to m.Adrianoupolis)	Δωρόθεος	*Dec* 1805 – Jun 1813	d. 1821
48. Gabriel III (ex m.Anchialos) suspended	Γαβριήλ Γ'	Jun 1813 – Sep 1824	d. ?
49. Panaretus (to m.Tornovo)	Πανάρετος	*Sep* 1824 – Feb 1838	1785-1878
50. Daniel (ex m.Maronia) (to m.Nyssa)	Δανιήλ	Feb 1838 – Mar 1845	d. ?
51. Sophronius III (to m.Arta)	Σωφρόνιος Γ'	*Mar* 1845 – Jan 1849	d. 1887
52. Johnnicius III	Ἰωαννίκιος Γ'	*Jan* 1849 – 1860+	d. 1860
53. Meletius III (ex m.Ankyra) (to m.Smyrni)	Μελέτιος Γ'	16 Oct 1860 – 25 Sep 1869	d. 1883
54. Dionysius II (ex former b.Paramythia) suspended	Διονύσιος Β'	2 Oct 1869 – 1 Oct 1887	d. ?
55. Stephen II Soulidis (to m.Mithymna)	Στέφανος Β'	*1 Oct* 1887 – 13 Feb 1896	d. 1915
56. Leontius II Eleftheriadis (ex m.Paramythia) (to m.Melenikon)	Λεόντιος Β'	13 Feb 1896 – 29 Apr 1899	d≥1907
57. Leontius III Choutouriotis (ex m.Kolonia) (to m.Rhodopolis)	Λεόντιος Γ'	29 Apr 1899 – 10 Oct 1906	1844-1926
58. Procopius Lazaridis (ex m.Dyrrachion) (to m.Ikonion)	Προκόπιος	10 Oct 1906 – 16 Jun 1911	d. 1923
59. Luke Petridis (ex m.Veria)	Λουκάς	23 Jun 1911 – Jul 1912+	d. 1912
60. Chrysostom Chatzistavrou (ex t.b.Trallis 26 Dec 1910) (to m.Ephesos)	Χρυσόστομος	16 Mar 1913 – 19 Feb 1922	1880-1968
61. Eugene Theologou/Vakalis (ex t.b.Amisos *17 May* 1911) (to m.Kydonies)	Εὐγένιος	19 Feb 1922 – 20 Mar 1924	1885-1956
62. Photius Maniatis (ex t.b.Irinoupolis *13 Jan* 1915) (to m.Derki)	Φώτιος	20 Mar 1924 – 17 Jan 1925	1874-1935
63. Cyril Moumtzis (ex m.Mytilini)	Κύριλλος	20 Jan 1925 – 1 Apr 1925+	1867-1925
64. Maximus Vaportzis (to m.Chalkidon)	Μάξιμος	9 Mar 1930 – 28 Jun 1932	1897-1972
65. Aemilian Papadimitriou (ex t.b.Militos 17 Aug 1928)	Αἰμιλιανός	3 Sep 1936 – 6 Dec 1946+	1892-1946
66. Athenagoras Kavvadas (ex t.b.Boston 5 Jun 1938) (to m.Thyatira/Great Britain)	Ἀθηναγόρας	7 Jun 1949 – 12 Apr 1951	1885-1962

67. Jacob II	Ἰάκωβος Β'	8 Aug 1954 – 12 Aug 1969	1920-1971
Tzanavaris/Papaïoannou (to m.Germany)			
68. Bartholomew	Βαρθολομαῖος	25 Dec 1973 – 9 Jan 1990	b. 1940
Archontonis (to m.Chalkidon)			
69. Meliton	Μελίτων	28 Oct 1990 –	b. 1951
Karras			

METROPOLITANATE OF PISIDIA
ΜΗΤΡΟΠΟΛΙΣ ΠΙΣΙΔΙΑΣ

Metropolitan of Pisidia, most honorable and Exarch of Side, Myra and Attalia

The city of Antioch in Pisidia (Grk Ἀντιόχεια Πισιδίας, Trk Yalvac), located 85 km southeast of Akroinos, was established by Macedonian-Greek King of Syria Seleucus I (reigned 321-281 BC) on the site of an existing settlement. It permanently came under Roman control in 25 BC, but lost its importance after it was razed by the Arabs in 717 AD, while nearby Sozopolis (Grk Σωζόπολις, Trk Uluborlu, 75 km southwest of Pisidian Antioch) rose to prominence. Sozopolis was occupied by the Seljuk Turks circa 1080, retaken by the Romans in 1120, remaining a Roman city until it fell to the Seljuk Turks circa 1180 and to the Ottoman Turks circa 1380. In 1403 Tamerlane gave the area to the resurrected Emirate of Karaman, with the Ottomans returning in 1414, Karaman retaking it in 1421, and the Ottomans again in 1435.

The Metropolitanate of Antioch of Pisidia was established in 325 AD. Initially under the honorary primacy of the Metropolitanate of Ephesos, it became a Metropolitanate of the Patriarchate of Constantinople in 451. It had eighteen Dioceses under its jurisdiction in the seventh century, which increased to twenty-one by the tenth century and remained so until the twelfth century. However, after the Seljuk occupation, the number steadily decreased, with none remaining by the fifteenth century. During the thirteenth century the Metropolitanate See was moved 105 km southwest to Varis (Grk Βάρις), a city that after the Ottoman occupation came to be known as Sparti (Grk Σπάρτη, Trk Isparta). During the period 1565-72 the three depopulated Metropolitanates of Sidi, Myra, and Attalia were attached to the Metropolitanate of Pisidia. The area first fell to the Seljuks circa 1085, was retaken by the Romans in 1097, the Seljuks in 1206 (Attalia coming under the rule of the Latins of Cyprus from 1362-72), and the Ottomans in 1390. In 1403 Tamerlane gave the area to the resurrected Emirates of Menteshe, Tekke, Germiyan and Karaman, with the Ottomans returning to Myra in 1429, and to Attalia and Sidi in 1435.

In January 1646 a Metropolitanate of Myra, including Sidi and Attalia, was reestablished, but in 1651 it was again annexed to Pisidia. After 1661 the Metropolitan resided in Attalia during the winter (Grk Ἀττάλεια, Trk Antalya), located 110 km south of Sparti, on the Mediterranean shore. An Archdiocese of Myra was established in March 1786, but was reintegrated into the Metropolitanate of Pisidia in July 1790.

The Metropolitanate of Pisidia is bordered by the Metropolitanate of Ilioupolis on the north; the Metropolitanate of Ikonion and the Metropolitanate of Adana (Patriarchate of Antioch) on the east (after the Metropolitanate of Selefkia was joined to the Metropolitanate of Adana in the early twentieth century); the Mediterranean Sea on the south; and the Metropolitanate of Philadelphia, the Metropolitanate of Ilioupolis, and the Aegean Sea on the west.

Other important cities are: Polydorion (Grk Πολυδώριον, Trk Burdur), 40 km west of Sparti; Myra (Grk Μύρα, Trk Kale), 125 km southwest of Attalia; Makri (Grk Μάκρη, Trk Fethiye), 175 km west of Attalia; Marmaris (Grk Μαρμαρίς, Trk Marmaris), 210 km west of Attalia; Sidi (Grk Σίδη, Trk Manavgat), 75 km east of Attalia; Kalonoros (Grk Καλονόρος, Trk Alanya, called Korakision, Grk Κορακήσιον, before the second century AD), 125 km east of Attalia; and Traïanoupolis (Grk Τραϊανούπολις, Trk Gazipasa, called Selinous, Grk Σελινούς, before 117 AD). The last six of these cities are located on the shore of the Mediterranean Sea.

In 1919 the area was occupied by the Italian army (Attalia on April 16, 1919, Makri and Marmaris on April 28, 1919); however, the Italians signed an agreement with the Turks on February 28, 1921 and evacuated their army in early April. After the population exchange of 1923 between Greece and Turkey, no Orthodox population remains inside the area of the Metropolitanate.

Metropolitans of Pisidia since 1800

42. Cyril II	Κύριλλος Β'	Aug 1781 – Jan 1814+	d. 1814
43. Dionysius (ex m.Vidyni)	Διονύσιος	Jan 1814 – Jul 1814+	d. 1814
44. Eugene (to p.Constantinople)	Ευγένιος	*Jul* 1814 – 10 Apr 1821	1780-1822
45. Gerasimus I resigned (to former, to m.Pisidia)	Γεράσιμος Α' (1ˢᵗ time)	*Aug* 1821 – Sep 1827	d≥1848
46. Samuel (ex former m.Philippoupolis) resigned (to former, to m.Ikonion)	Σαμουήλ	Sep 1827 – Nov 1830	d≥1840
---. Gerasimus I (ex former m.Pisidia) deposed	Γεράσιμος Α' (2ⁿᵈ time)	Nov 1830 – Mar 1848	d. ?
47. Meletius (ex m.Vodena) resigned	Μελέτιος	Mar 1848 – 2 Jun 1861	d. ?
48. Caesarius (ex t.b.Xanthoupolis 1852) suspended, 18 Sep 1884+	Καισάριος	2 Jun 1861 – Jun 1880	1812-1884
49. Parthenius Prodromidis (ex t.b.Laodikia *1 Feb* 1871)	Παρθένιος	Jun 1880 – 1886+	d. 1886
50. Benedict II Adamantidis (ex m.Ganos) (to m.Prikonnisos)	Βενέδικτος Β'	Feb 1886 – 23 Oct 1893	d. 1906
51. Gerasimus II Tantalidis (ex m.Servia) (to m.Ioannina)	Γεράσιμος Β' (1ˢᵗ time)	23 Oct 1893 – 1 Jun 1906	1854-1928
52. Constantine Apostolou (ex m.Ganos)	Κωνσταντίνος	3 Jun 1906 – 17 Jan 1912+	d. 1912
---. Gerasimus II Tantalidis (ex m.Rhodes) resigned, 23 Aug 1928+	Γεράσιμος Β' (2ⁿᵈ time)	26 Jan 1912 – Mar 1923	1854-1928
53. Germanus Athanasiadis (as Metropolitan of Sardis and Pisidia, see note 1)	Γερμανός	18 Mar 1924 – 9 Nov 1943	1885-1945
54. Ezekiel Tsoukalas (ex a.Australia) (to m.Kos)	Ιεζεκιήλ	5 Aug 1974 – 16 Sep 1979	1913-1987
55. Methodius II Fougias (ex former a.Thyatira/Great Britain)	Μεθόδιος Β'	12 Mar 1991 – 6 Jul 2006+	1925-2006
56. Soterius Trabas (ex m.Korea)	Σωτήριος	27 May 2008 –	b. 1929

1. Germanus was consecrated Metropolitan of Sardis on March 16, 1924, and two days later was also given the governance of the Metropolitanate of Pisidia, since the newly re-established Metropolitanate of Sardis occupied a very small area. On November 9, 1943, his governance over the Metropolitanate of Pisidia was terminated.

METROPOLITANATE OF SARDIS
ΜΗΤΡΟΠΟΛΙΣ ΣΑΡΔΕΩΝ

Metropolitan of Sardes, most honorable and Exarch of all Lydia

The city of Sardis (Grk Σάρδεις, Trk Sartmustafa), located 90 km west of Smyrni, was established circa 3000 BC. It came under Roman control in 133 BC, was occupied by the Seljuk Turks circa 1085, retaken by the Romans in 1097, retaken by the Seljuks circa 1315, taken by the Ottomans in 1390, razed by the army of Tamerlane in 1402, who gave the area to the ressurected Emirate of Saruhan, with the Ottomans returning in 1424.

The Metropolitanate of Sardis was established in 325 AD. Initially under the honorary primacy of the Metropolitanate of Ephesos, it became a Metropolitanate of the Patriarchate of Constantinople in 451. It had twenty-six Dioceses under its jurisdiction in the seventh century, which increased to twenty-seven by the tenth century. However, after the Seljuk occupation of the area, the number steadily decreased, with none remaining by the fourteenth century. Indeed, the Metropolitanate itself was abolished circa 1370, and all its area annexed to the Metropolitanate of Philadelphia, with the title of Metropolitan of Sardis given to titular Metropolitans thereafter.

In November 1919 the area was occupied by the Greek army. The Greek forces withdrew after their defeat in late August 1922, and all Orthodox were evacuated to Greece or killed by the advanced Turkish army, with no Orthodox population remaining in the area today. On March 13, 1924 the Metropolitanate of Sardis was reestablished, although encompassing only the city of Sardis and its immediate surrounding area. The Metropolitanate of Sardis is bordered by the Metropolitanate of Philadelphia on the north, east, and west, and the Metropolitanate of Ilioupolis on the south.

Metropolitans of Sardis since 1800

35. Nectarius Thomaïdis	Νεκτάριος	(titular)	1792 – 12 Jun 1831+	d. 1831
36. Meletius mentioned in sources dated 1836 and 1840	Μελέτιος	(titular)	1836, 1840	d. ?
37. Michael Kleovoulos	Μιχαήλ	(titular)	15 Jul 1901 – 23 Feb 1918+	1848-1918
38. Germanus Athanasiadis (see note under the Metropolitanate of Pisidia)	Γερμανός		16 Mar 1924 – 4 Mar 1945+	1885-1945
39. Maximus Christopoulos	Μάξιμος		16 Jun 1946 – 30 Dec 1986+	1914-1986

METROPOLITANATE OF SMYRNI
ΜΗΤΡΟΠΟΛΙΣ ΣΜΥΡΝΗΣ

Metropolitan of Smyrna, most honorable and Exarch of all Asia

The city of Smyrni (Grk Σμύρνη, Trk Izmir), located on the shore of the Aegean Sea, 300 km south of Artaki, was established in the third millennium BC. Taken by Aeolian Greeks in the eleventh century BC, it was destroyed by the Lydians circa 580 BC. The city was re-established circa 300 BC at the time of Macedonian-Greek King Alexander III the Great, and came under Roman control in 133 BC.

It was occupied by the Seljuk Turks circa 1085, retaken by the Romans in 1097, retaken by the Seljuks in 1317, taken by Knights of Rhodes on October 28, 1344, razed by the army of Tamerlane in December 1402, who gave it to the resurrected Emirate of Aydin, and finally occupied by the Ottoman Turks in 1424.

The Diocese of Smyrni came under the jurisdiction of the Metropolitanate of Ephesos in 325 AD, was promoted to an Archdiocese between 451 and 457, and promoted to a Metropolitanate during the ninth century, having three Dioceses under its jurisdiction. The Dioceses were returned to the Metropolitanate of Ephesus during the twelfth century, but were later reattached to the Metropolitanate of Smyrni. By the fourth century none remained. A Diocese of Moschonisia under the Metropolitanate of Smyrni was created in 1766, and was promoted to a Metropolitanate in 1922.

The Metropolitanate of Smyrni is bordered by the Metropolitanate of Ephesos on the north, east, and south, and by the Metropolitanate of Vryoula and the Aegean Sea on the west. Other notable cities are: Prinovaris (Grk Πρινόβαρις, Trk Bornova), 10 km north of Smyrni, today a suburb of modern Izmir; and Vouzas (Grk Βουζάς, Trk Buca), 5 km south of Smyrni, today a suburb of modern Izmir.

On May 2, 1919 the city was occupied by the Greek army, but the Greek forces withdrew after their defeat in late August 1922, with the Turkish army entering the city on August 27, 1922 and setting it on fire. A large part of the Orthodox citizens of Smyrni and numerous Orthodox refugees from Asia Minor's interior were killed by the Turkish forces, while the remaining were evacuated to Greece. No Orthodox population remains inside the area of the Metropolitanate today.

Metropolitans of Smyrni since 1800

56. Anthimus I (to m.Chalkidon)	Άνθιμος Α'	*11 May* 1797 – 20 Oct 1821	d. 1842
57. Païsius I (ex t.b.Apamia) resigned (to m.Rhodes)	Παΐσιος Α'	Oct 1821 – Jun 1827	d≥1829
58. Hierotheus resigned (to former, to m.Vella)	Ιερόθεος	*Jun* 1827 – Oct 1831	d. 1848
59. Seraphim Drosos (ex m.Xanthi) deposed (to former, to b.Andros of Greek Church)	Σεραφείμ	Oct 1831 – Jul 1833	d. 1842
60. Chrysanthus I Karamalis (ex m.Dyrrachion) (to m.Prousa)	Χρύσανθος Α'	Jul 1833 – 1 Apr 1837	d. 1846
61. Païsius II (ex m.Sophia) deposed (to former, to m.Sophia)	Παΐσιος Β'	1 Apr 1837 – Mar 1840	d. 1877
62. Chrysanthus II (ex t.b.Myra Apr 1834) deposed (to former, to m.Kriti)	Χρύσανθος Β' (1st time)	Jun 1840 – Dec 1840	d. 1869
63. Athanasius II Chatzivasiliou (ex m.Kastoria)	Αθανάσιος Β'	Jan 1841 – 27 Dec 1850+	d. 1850
64. Anthimus II Lykaris (ex b.Ilioupolis)	Άνθιμος Β'	3 Jan 1851 – 1853+	d. 1853
65. Païsius III Klinovios (to m.Philippoupolis)	Παΐσιος Γ'	*15 Feb* 1853 – 15 Nov 1857	d. 1872
---. Chrysanthus II (ex m.Philippoupolis)	Χρύσανθος Β' (2nd time)	15 Nov 1857 – 4 Sep 1869+	d. 1869
66. Meletius (ex m.Philadelphia)	Μελέτιος	25 Sep 1869 – 30 Dec 1883+	d. 1883
67. Basil Asteriadis (ex m.Anchialos)	Βασίλειος	22 Dec 1884 – 23 Jan 1910+	d. 1910

68. Chrysostom   Χρυσόστομος   11 Mar 1910 – 27 Aug 1922++   1868-1922
Kalafatsi (ex m.Philippi) tortured to death by a Turkish mob

METROPOLITANATE OF VRYOULA
ΜΗΤΡΟΠΟΛΙΣ ΒΡΥΟΥΛΩΝ

Metropolitan of Briula, most honorable and Exarch of Erythraia

The city of Klazomenes (Grk Κλαζομενές, Trk Klazumen), located on the shore of the Aegean Sea 70 km west of Smyrni, was first settled in the Neolithic age and came under Roman control circa 133 BC. During Roman times the new city of Vryoula (Grk Βρύουλα, Trk Urla), located 5 km to the south, appeared. The area was occupied by the Seljuk Turks circa 1085, retaken by the Romans in 1097, retaken by the Seljuks in 1304, and occupied by the Ottoman Turks in 1390. In 1403 Tamerlane gave the area to the resurrected Emirate of Aydin, with the Ottomans returning in 1424. After the Turkish occupation, the city of Klazomenes was deserted, with nearby Vryoula rising in prominence. The Diocese of Klazomenes came under the jurisdiction of the Metropolitanate of Ephesos in 325 AD. A Diocese of Vryoula also appeared by the seventh century under Ephesos. In the ninth century the Diocese of Klazomenes was transferred to the jurisdiction of the new Metropolitanate of Smyrna, although it returned to Ephesus for a time during the twelfth century. After the Turkish occupation of the area, both Dioceses were abolished, their areas annexed by the Metropolitanate of Ephesos. A new Metropolitanate of Vryoula was established on February 22, 1922.

The Metropolitanate of Vryoula is bordered by the Aegean Sea on the north and south; the Metropolitanate of Smyrna, the Metropolitanate of Ephesos, and the Metropolitanate of Anea (Notion section) on the east; and the Metropolitanate of Krini on the west. Other notable cities are: Teos (Grk Τέως, Trk Seferihisar), 17 km south of Vryoula, and Ypsili (Grk Υψηλή, Trk Doganbey), 30 km south of Vryoula. Also inside the area of the Metropolitanate is Iatrou island (Grk Νήσος Ιατρού, Trk Hakim Ada), located inside Ermaïkos Gulf (Grk Ερμαϊκός Κόλπος, Trk Izmir Korfezi). The area of the Metropolitanate was occupied by the Greek army on May 3, 1919. Greek forces withdrew after their defeat in late August 1922, with the Turks entering Vryoula on August 30, 1922. Most of the inhabitants refused to evacuate the city and were killed by the Turkish forces. No Orthodox population remains inside the area of the Metropolitanate today.

Metropolitans of Vryoula

1. Dionysius   Διονύσιος   6 Mar 1922 – 25 Oct 1922   1879-1951
Minas (to m.Mithymna)
2. Epiphanius   Επιφάνιος   30 Apr 2007 –   b. 1935
Perialas (ex m.Spain)

SECTION E:
METROPOLITANATES IN CENTRAL ASIA MINOR

METROPOLITANATE OF AMASIA
ΜΗΤΡΟΠΟΛΙΣ ΑΜΑΣΕΙΑΣ

Metropolitan of Amasia, most honorable and Exarch of all Euxenus Pontus

The city of Amasia (Grk Αμάσεια, Trk Amasya), located 334 km northeast of Ankyra, was established by Pontus King Mithridates I circa 300 BC on the site of an existing settlement. It served as the capital of the Kingdom until 183 BC, and came under Roman control in 3 BC. It was occupied by the Seljuk Turks circa 1075, retaken by the Romans circa 1106, taken by the Turks circa 1120, and the Ottoman Turks in 1392.

The Metropolitanate of Amasia was established in 325 AD. Initially under the honorary primacy of the Metropolitanate of Kaisaria, it became a Metropolitanate of the Patriarchate of Constantinople in 451. It had six Dioceses under its jurisdiction in the seventh century, which increased to seven by the twelfth century; however, after the Seljuk occupation of the area the number steadily decreased, with none remaining by the fourteenth century. During that time the Metropolitanate See was moved 110 km north to Amisos (Grk Αμισός, Trk Samsun), where it still remains.

Amisos, located on the shore of the Black Sea, was established in the seventh century BC by Greeks from Miletus (Grk Μίλητος, called Palation in Roman times, Grk Παλάτιον, Trk Balat, located in the Metropolitanate of Anea), and was taken by the Romans in 71 BC. After the Seljuk Turks occupied the city (circa 1080), a Turkish settlement called Samsun was established next to the Roman city's walls. The Byzantines took the city again circa 1107, the Seljuks occupied it in 1214, and the Ottomans in 1392. After the Mongol warlord Tamerlane razed the city in 1402, he gave it to the resurrected Emirate of Candar, which the Ottomans annexed in 1461.

The Metropolitanate of Amasia is bordered by the Black Sea on the north; the Metropolitanate of Neokaisaria on the east; the Metropolitanate of Neokaisaria and the Metropolitanate of Kaisaria on the south; and the Metropolitanate of Kaisaria and the Metropolitanate of Neokaisaria (Gangra section) on the west. Other important cities are: Sinopi (Grk Σινώπη, Trk Sinop), on the Black Sea, 145 km northwest of Amisos; Aigialos (Grk Αιγιαλός, Trk Ayancik), on the Black Sea, 185 km northwest of Amisos; Themiskyra (Grk Θεμίσκυρα, Trk Carsamba), 40 km east of Amisos; Thermodon (Grk Θερμόδων, Trk Terme), on the Black Sea, 55 km east of Amisos; Paphra (Grk Πάφρα, Trk Bafra), 48 km northwest of Amisos; Neoklavdioupolis (Grk Νεοκλαυδιούπολις, Trk Vezirkorpu), 85 km southwest of Amisos; Vouvasion (Grk Βουβάσιον, Trk Boyabat), 170 km west of Amisos; Laodikia (Grk Λαοδίκεια, Trk Ladik), 60 km south of Amisos; Phazimon (Grk Φαζημών, Trk Merzifon), 90 km southwest of Amisos; and Iraklia (Grk Ηράκλεια, Trk Erbaa), 70 km east of Amasia.

During the period January-November 1920 the area was part of the ill-fated Greek-Armenian Republic of the Pontus (see m. Trapezous). After the population exchange of

1923 between Greece and Turkey, no Orthodox population remains inside the area of the Metropolitanate.

Metropolitans of Amasia since 1800

59. Païsius	Παΐσιος		*Sep 1780 – 1809+*	d. 1809
60. Neophytus resigned (to former, to m.Amasia)	Νεόφυτος	(1st time)	*Dec 1809 – Jul 1826*	d. ?
61. Dionysius III Kotakis (ex m.Silyvria) suspended (to former, to m.Amasia)	Διονύσιος Γ'		Jul 1826 – Jan 1827	d. 1877
---. Neophytus (ex former m.Amasia) resigned	Νεόφυτος	(2nd time)	Jan 1827 – Aug 1828	d. ?
62. Meletius IV Pangalos (to m.Thessaloniki)	Μελέτιος Δ'		*Aug 1828 – Nov 1830*	1772-1845
---. Dionysius III Kotakis (ex former m.Amasia) deposed (to former, to m.Nikomidia)	Διονύσιος Γ'	(2nd time)	Nov 1830 – Sep 1835	d. 1877
63. Callinicus II (ex m.Didymotichon)	Καλλίνικος Β'		Sep 1835 – Mar 1847+	d. 1847
64. Cyril (ex m.Ainos) (to p.Constantinople)	Κύριλλος		Mar 1847 – 21 Sep 1855	1800-1872
65. Sophronius I Meïdantzoglous (ex m.Chios) (to p.Constantinople)	Σωφρόνιος Α'		27 Sep 1855 – 20 Sep 1863	1798-1899
66. Sophronius II (ex m.Arta)	Σωφρόνιος Β'		17 Jan 1864 – Jun 1887+	d. 1887
67. Anthimus II Alexoudis (ex m.Velegrades) suspended	Ἄνθιμος Β'		22 Jul 1887 – 5 Feb 1908	1824-1909
68. Germanus Karavangelis (ex m.Kastoria) (to m.Ioannina)	Γερμανός	(1st time)	5 Feb 1908 – 27 Oct 1922	1866-1935
69. Spyridon Vlachos (ex m.Ioannina) (to m.Ioannina)	Σπυρίδων		27 Oct 1922 – 15 Apr 1924	1873-1956
---. Germanus Karavangelis (ex m.Hungary) see note 1	Γερμανός	(2nd time)	12 Aug 1924 – 10 Feb 1935+	1866-1935
70. Apostolus Tryphonos (ex former m.Rhodes)	Ἀπόστολος		25 Oct 1951 – 29 Nov 1957+	1878-1957

1. Metropolitan Germanus was condemned to death *in absentia* by the Turkish authorities on June 7, 1921 and subsequently could not return to Turkey. He remained in Vienna as Exarch of Central Europe of the Ecumenical Patriarchate during the period 1924-35.

METROPOLITANATE OF ANKYRA
ΜΗΤΡΟΠΟΛΙΣ ΑΓΚΥΡΑΣ

Metropolitan of Ancyra, most honorable and Exarch of all Galatia

The city of Ankyra (Grk Ἄγκυρα, Trk Ankara), located 330 km southeast of Niko-midia, was established by the Phrygians in the tenth century BC. It became part of the Roman Empire in 25 BC, was occupied by the Seljuk Turks circa 1075, retaken briefly by the Romans in 1101, 1106, and 1134, and finally by the Ottoman Turks in 1356. The city was razed by Tamerlane in 1402.

The Metropolitanate of Ankyra was established in 325 AD. Initially under the honorary primacy of the Metropolitanate of Kaisaria, it became a Metropolitanate of the Patriarchate of Constantinople in 451. It had eight Dioceses under its jurisdiction in the seventh century, which decreased to six by the eleventh century; however, after the Seljuk occupation of the area the number decreased, with none remaining by the thirteenth century. The Metropolitanate of Ankyra is bordered by the Metropolitanate of Prousa, the Metropolitanate of Nikaia (Thivazion section), and the Metropolitanate of Neokaisaria (Gangra section) on the north; the Metropolitanate of Kaisaria on the east; the Metropolitanate of Ikonion and the Metropolitanate of Philadelphia on the south; and the Metropolitanate of Philadelphia, the Metropolitanate of Prousa, and the Metropolitanate of Nikaia (Thivazion section) on the west.

Other important cities are: Dorylaion (Grk Δορύλαιον, Trk Eskisehir), 228 km west of Ankyra; Kotyaion (Grk Κοτύαιον, Trk Kutahya), 65 km southeast of Dorylaion; Anastasioupolis (Grk Αναστασιούπολις, Trk Beypazari), 85 km northwest of Ankyra; Iouliopolis (Grk Ιουλιόπολις, Trk Nallihan), 135 km northwest of Ankyra; Ioustinianoupolis (Grk Ιουστινιανούπολις, Trk Sivrihisar), 135 km southwest of Ankyra; Gordion (Grk Γόρδιον, Trk Polatli), 70 km southwest of Ankyra; Kaloumni (Grk Καλούμνη, Trk Cubuk), 40 km north of Ankyra; Mizos (Grk Μείζος, Trk Ayas), 45 km west of Ankyra; and Koptolofos (Grk Κοπτόλοφος, Trk Kirikkale), 65 km east of Ankyra.

The eastern area of the Metropolitanate was occupied by Greek forces in 1921, with Kotyaion being occupied on July 7, 1921 and Dorylaion on July 6, 1921. The Greek forces withdrew after their defeat in August 1922, and all Orthodox were evacuated to Greece or killed by the advanced Turkish army. The Orthodox population in the remaining area of the Metropolitanate departed after the population exchange of 1923 between Greece and Turkey. No Orthodox population remains inside the area of the Metropolitanate today.

Metropolitans of Ankyra since 1800

57. Johnnicius II (to m.Nikaia)	Ιωαννίκιος Β΄	Jul 1779 – Mar 1811	d. 1823
58. Sophronius I	Σωφρόνιος Α΄	*Mar* 1811 – 1814+	d. 1814
59. Methodius (to p.Antioch)	Μεθόδιος	*Jun* 1814 – 13 May 1823	1771-1850
60. Agathangelus Myrianthousis (to m.Thiva)	Αγαθάγγελος	*May* 1823 – Sep 1827	1780-1852
61. Theodosius II (ex t.b.Zichna Mar 1821)	Θεοδόσιος Β΄	Oct 1827 – 1834+	d. 1834
62. Gerasimus III Domninos (ex former m.Kaisaria) (to m.Ephesos)	Γεράσιμος Γ΄	1834 – Sep 1836	d. 1837
63. Cyril (ex former m.Arta) resigned	Κύριλλος	Sep 1836 – Aug 1838	d. ?
64. Nicephorus (to m.Nyssa)	Νικηφόρος	*Aug* 1838 – Jun 1845	d. 1847
65. Hierotheus resigned, 4 Mar 1882+	Ιερόθεος	*Jun* 1845 – Dec 1852	d. 1882
66. Meletius II (ex t.b.Amisos) (to m.Philadelphia)	Μελέτιος Β΄	Dec 1852 – 16 Oct 1860	d. 1883
67. Johnnicius III Ikonomou (to m.Filippi)	Ιωαννίκιος Γ΄	*Oct* 1860 – 25 May 1872	d. 1879

68. Chrysanthus (ex former m.Kassandria)	Χρύσανθος	25 May 1872 – Aug 1877+	d. 1877
69. Gerasimus IV (ex m.Halepion)	Γεράσιμος Δ᾽	3 Sep 1877 – Jan 1899+	1820-1899
70. Nicholas II Sakkopoulos (ex m.Vodena) (to m.Maronia)	Νικόλαος Β᾽	1 May 1899 – 19 Oct 1902	1862-1927
71. Sophronius II Nistopoulos (ex m.Stromnitsa) (to m.Kaisaria)	Σωφρόνιος Β᾽	19 Oct 1902 – 27 Mar 1910	d. 1917
72. Gervase Sarasitis (ex m.Korytsa) (to m.Alexandroupolis)	Γερβάσιος	1 Apr 1910 – 17 Nov 1922	1867-1934

METROPOLITANATE OF IKONION
ΜΗΤΡΟΠΟΛΙΣ ΙΚΟΝΙΟΥ

Metropolitan of Iconium, most honorable and Exarch of all Lycaonia

The city of Ikonion (Grk Ικόνιον, Trk Konya), located 250 km south of Ankyra, was established by the Phrygians. It became part of the Roman Empire in 25 BC, was occupied by the Seljuk Turks circa 1075, taken by the Karaman Turkomans in 1308, the Ottoman Turks in 1390, given by Tamerlane to the resurrected Emirate of Karaman in 1403, and finally retaken by the Ottoman Turks in 1468.

Initially a Diocese under the Metropolitanate of Pisidian Antioch, Ikonion was promoted to a Metropolitanate in 372 AD. It had fifteen Dioceses under its jurisdiction in the seventh century; however, after the Seljuk occupation of the area the number steadily decreased, with none remaining by the thirteenth century. On September 15, 1655 the Metropolitanate of Ikonion was abolished and its area annexed to the Metropolitanate of Pisidia; it was re-established shorty thereafter, possibly in September 1661.

The Metropolitanate of Ikonion is bordered by the Metropolitanate of Ankyra on the north; the Metropolitanate of Kaisaria and the Metropolitanate of Adana (Patriarchate of Antioch) on the east; the Metropolitanate of Adana (Patriarchate of Antioch) on the south; and the Metropolitanate of Pisidia and the Metropolitanate of Philadelphia on the west. Other important cities are Nigdi: (Grk Νίγδη, Trk Nigde), 230 km east of Ikonion; Archelaïs (Grk Αρχελαΐς, Trk Aksaray), 150 km northeast of Ikonion; Karvali (Grk Καρβάλη, Trk Guzelyurt), 130 km northeast of Ikonion; Parnassos (Grk Παρνασσός, Trk Sereflikohisar), 200 km north of Ikonion, on the shore of lake Tatta (Grk Τάττα, Trk Tuz); Tyana (Grk Τύανα, Trk Kemerhisar), 210 km east of Ikonion; Vorissos (Grk Βορησσός, Trk Bor), 220 km east of Ikonion; Iraklia (Grk Ηράκλεια, Trk Eregli), 170 km east of Ikonion; Ydi (Grk Ύδη, Trk Karapinar), 120 km east of Ikonion; Laranda (Grk Λάρανδα, Trk Karaman), 110 km southeast of Ikonion; Dalisandos (Grk Δαλισανδός, Trk Şeydisehir), 85 km southwest of Ikonion; Korallia (Grk Κοραλλία, Trk Beysehir), 80 km west of Ikonion, on the shore of the homonymous lake; Tyriaion (Grk Τυριαίον, Trk Ilgin), 75 km northwest of Ikonion; and Philomilion (Grk Φιλομήλιον, Trk Aksehir), 120 km northwest of Ikonion, on the shore of the homonymous lake.

After the population exchange of 1923 between Greece and Turkey, no Orthodox population remains inside the area of the Metropolitanate.

Metropolitans of Ikonion since 1800

50. Raphael (to m.Larissa)	Ραφαήλ	*Jul* 1780 – Sep 1803	d≥1806

51. Cyril Sermpetzoglous (to m.Adrianoupolis)	Κύριλλος	*Sep* 1803 – Dec 1810	1775-1821
52. Neophytus I	Νεόφυτος Α´	*Dec* 1810 – 1825+	d. 1825
53. Anthimus III Vamvakis (to m.Larissa)	Ἄνθιμος Γ´	*Oct* 1825 – Sep 1835	1788-1878
54. Samuel (ex former m.Pisidia) resigned	Σαμουήλ	Sep 1835 – 8 Jan 1840	d. ?
55. Joachim II (ex m.Vodena) resigned	Ἰωακείμ Β´	Jan 1840 – Jun 1846	d. ?
56. Meletius II (ex m.Dimitrias)	Μελέτιος Β´	Jun 1846 – 1849+	d. 1849
57. Neophytus II (ex m.Elasson)	Νεόφυτος Β´	May 1849 – Jan 1865+	d. 1864
58. Sophronius Christidis (to m.Didymotichon)	Σωφρόνιος	*11 Jan* 1865 – 1 May 1873	d. 1890
59. Agathangelus (ex m.Mithymna)	Ἀγαθάγγελος	1 May 1873 – 17 Jul 1885+	d. 1885
60. Dorotheus Christidis (ex m.Korytsa) (to m.Velegrades)	Δωρόθεος	26 Aug 1885 – 22 Jul 1887	d. 1924
61. Ambrose Christidis (ex m.Chios)	Ἀμβρόσιος	22 Jul 1887 – 20 Mar 1889+	1832-1889
62. Athanasius III Iliadis	Ἀθανάσιος Γ´	*23 Mar* 1889 – 10 Jun 1911+	d. 1911
63. Procopius Lazaridis (ex m.Philadelphia) arrested by the Turkish authorities in 1922, died in prison	Προκόπιος	16 Jun 1911 – 12 Mar 1923++	d. 1923
64. Jacob Stephanidis	Ἰάκωβος	7 Jul 1950 – 16 Apr 1965+	1916-1965
65. Theoleptus Fenerlis	Θεόληπτος	10 Sep 2000 –	b. 1957

METROPOLITANATE OF KAISARIA
ΜΗΤΡΟΠΟΛΙΣ ΚΑΙΣΑΡΕΙΑΣ

Metropolitan of Caesaria, most honorable of most honorables and Exarch of all East

The city of Kaisaria (Caesaria, Grk Καισάρεια, Trk Kayseri), 290 km southeast of Ankyra, is located on a site inhabited since the fourth millennium BC. Initally called Mazaca, it was renamed Eusebia (Grk Εὐσέβεια) circa 150 BC in honor of the Cappadocian King Ariarathes V Eusebes, and Caesaria in 18 AD, one year after its annexation by the Roman Empire. The city was occupied by the Seljuk Turks circa 1075, taken by the Danishmend Turkomans in 1092, the Seljuks again in 1169, and the Ottoman Turks in 1397. Tamerlane gave it to the resurrected Emirate of Karaman in 1403, and the Ottoman Turks returned in 1468.

Kaisaria became a Metropolitanate in 325 AD, exercising honorary primacy over the other Metropolitanates of the Pontus Division: Nikomidia, Gangra, Ankyra, Amasia, Neokaisaria, and Sevastia. To these were later added the Metropolitanates of Klavdioupolis (by division of Gangra), Pessinous (by division of Ankyra), Tyana (by division of Kaisaria), and Melitini (by division of Kaisaria). After the Fourth Ecumenical Council of 451, the Patriarchate of Constantinople officially placed under its jurisdiction all of the Metropolitanates in the area, including the Metropolitanate of Kaisaria. Kaisaria had five Dioceses under its jurisdiction in the seventh century, which increased to fifteen by the tenth century. In the twelfth century it still had eight Dioceses; however, after the Seljuk occupation the number steadily decreased, with none remaining by the fourteenth century.

The Metropolitanate of Kaisaria is bordered by the Metropolitanate of Neokaisaria (Gangra section) and the Metropolitanate of Amasia on the north; the Metropolitanate of Neokaisaria on the east; the Metropolitanate of Adana (Patriarchate of Antioch) on the south; and the Metropolitanate of Ikonion and the Metropolitanate of Ankyra on the west. Other important cities are: Moutalaski (Grk Μουταλάσκη, Trk Talas), 10 km southeast of Kaisaria; Kamouliana (Grk Καμουλιανά, Trk Develi), 40 km south of Kaisaria; Neapolis (Grk Νεάπολις, Trk Nevsehir), 75 km west of Kaisaria; Prokopion (Grk Προκόπιον, Trk Urgup), 55 km west of Kaisaria; Mithridation (Grk Μιθριδάτιον, Trk Yozgat), 155 km north of Kaisaria; Mokissos (Grk Μωκισσός, Trk Kirsehir), 130 km northwest of Kaisaria; Kiskissos (Grk Κισκισσός, Trk Keskin), 205 km northwest of Kaisaria; Zila (Grk Ζήλα, Trk Zile), 250 km northeast of Kaisaria; Pterion (Grk Πτέριον, Trk Sungurlu), 245 km northwest of Kaisaria; Efchaïta (Grk Ευχάιτα, Trk Corum), 260 km north of Kaisaria; and Asklipiion (Grk Ασκληπιείον, Trk Iskilip), 310 km north of Kaisaria. After the population exchange of 1923 between Greece and Turkey, no Orthodox population remains inside the area of the Metropolitanate.

Metropolitans of Kaisaria since 1800

91. Leontius III (ex m.Melenikon) resigned	Λεόντιος Γ'	Jul 1796 – 1 Oct 1801	d. ?
92. Philotheus (ex former m.Tornovon)	Φιλόθεος	Oct 1801 – May 1816+	d. 1816
93. Meletius II (ex m.Neokaisaria)	Μελέτιος Β'	May 1816 – 1817+	d. 1817
94. Johnnicius (ex m.Nikaia) see note 1	Ιωαννίκιος	Jun 1817 – 15 Nov 1823++	d. 1823
95. Chrysanthus (to m.Ephesos)	Χρύσανθος	*Nov* 1823 – Dec 1830	d. 1836
96. Gerasimus Domninos (ex m.Ouzitsa) resigned (to former, to m.Ankyra)	Γεράσιμος	Dec 1830 – Mar 1832	d. 1837
97. Païsius II Kepoglous	Παΐσιος Β'	*Mar* 1832 – 30 Jan 1871+	1777-1871
98. Eustace Kleovoulos, see note 2	Ευστάθιος	3 Oct 1871 – 26 Jan 1876+	1824-1876
99. Methodius II Aronis (ex m.Mytilini) (to m.Didymotichon)	Μεθόδιος Β'	28 Jan 1876 – May 1878	d. 1897
100. John Anastasiadis	Ιωάννης	21 May 1878 – 28 Apr 1902+	1834-1902
101. Gervase Orologas (ex m.Korytsa) (to m.Ioannina)	Γερβάσιος	14 May 1902 – 16 Mar 1910	d. 1916
102. Sophronius Nistopoulos (ex m.Ankyra) suspended (to former, to m.Kolonia)	Σωφρόνιος	27 Mar 1910 – 25 Apr 1911	d. 1917
103. Ambrose Stavrinos (ex m.Neokaisaria) suspended (to former, to m.Neokaisaria)	Αμβρόσιος	25 Apr 1911 – 13 Feb 1914	1854-1931
104. Nicholas II Sakkopoulos (ex m.Maronia) (to m.Chalkidon)	Νικόλαος Β'	13 Feb 1914 – 22 Feb 1927	1862-1927

105. Callinicus   Καλλίνικος   26 Jul 1932 – 11 Jan 1934+   1855-1934
    Delikanis (ex m.Kyzikos)

1. Metropolitan Johnnicius was imprisoned by the Ottoman authorities in 1821 and died in prison.
2. On April 18, 1871 Metropolitan Basil (Asteriadis) of Anchialos was promoted to the Metropolitanate of Kaisaria, but he did not accept his promotion, and the election was cancelled.

METROPOLITANATE OF NEOKAISARIA
ΜΗΤΡΟΠΟΛΙΣ ΝΕΟΚΑΙΣΑΡΕΙΑΣ

Metropolitan of Neocaesaria, most honorable and Exarch of Pontus Polemoniacus

The city of Neokaisaria (Grk Νεοκαισάρεια, Trk Niksar), located 115 km east of Amasia, was initially called Cabira (Grk Κάβειρα), and served as the capital of the Kingdom of Pontus. Taken by the Romans in 73 BC and renamed Diospolis (Grk. Διόσπολις), it was returned to King Polemon I of Pontus in 37 BC, and was renamed Sebasti (Grk Σεβαστή). It finally passed to Roman control in 64 AD, and was renamed Neokaisaria. The city was occupied by the Seljuk Turks in 1075, retaken by the Romans circa 1086, taken by the Danishmend Turkomans circa 1090, retaken by the Seljuks circa 1175, and finally taken by the Ottomans in 1394.

Neokaisaria became a Metropolitanate in 325 AD. It had four Dioceses under its jurisdiction in the seventh century, which increased to ten by the twelfth century. However, after the Seljuk occupation the number steadily decreased, with none remaining by the fourteenth century. A new Diocese of Nikopolis under the Metropolitanate of Neokaisaria was established during the eighteenth century, but was promoted to a Metropolitanate (of Kolonia) in 1889. During the Ottoman occupation the See of the Metropolitanate was moved 50 km southwest to Evdokias (Grk Ευδοκιάς, Trk Tokat) from where, before 1903, it moved 120 km northeast to the city of Inoi (Grk Οινόη, Trk Unye), situated on the shore of the Black Sea.

The Metropolitanate is divided into two sections. The main part is bordered by the Black Sea on the north; the Metropolitanates of Chaldia, Kolonia, Theodosioupolis (Grk Θεοδοσιούπολις, Trk Erzerum, Patriarchate of Antioch), and Amida (Grk Άμιδα, Trk Diyarbakir, Patriarchate of Antioch) on the east; the Metropolitanate of Adana (Patriarchate of Antioch), the Metropolitanate of Veria (Grk Βέροια, now Halep in Syria, Patriarchate of Antioch), and the Metropolitanate of Adana (Grk Άδανα, Patriarchate of Antioch) on the south; and the Metropolitanate of Kaisaria and the Metropolitanate of Amasia on the west. The Gangra section is mainly comprised of the former Metropolitanate of Gangra, which was annexed to Neokaisaria on January 19, 1630. It is bordered by the Black Sea on the north; the Metropolitanate of Amasia on the east; the Metropolitanate of Kaisaria and the Metropolitanate of Ankyra on the south; and the Metropolitanate of Chalkidon on the west.

Other important cities inside the main section are: Phadissa (Grk Φάδισσα, Trk Fatsa), located on the Black Sea shore, 22 km east of Inoi; Polemonion (Grk Πολεμώνιον, Trk Bolaman), on the Black Sea shore, 33 km east of Inoi; Kotyora (Grk Κοτύωρα, Trk Ordu), on the Black Sea shore, 55 km east of Inoi; Gazioura (Grk Γαζίουρα, Trk Turhal), 50 km west of Evdokias; Sagylion (Grk Σαγύλιον, Trk Yildizeli), 55 km south of Evdokias; Sevastia (Grk Σεβάστεια, Trk Sivas), 100 km southeast of Evdokias; Garnaki (Grk Γαρνάκη, Trk Gurun), 125 km south of Sevastia; and Tephriki (Grk Τεφρική, Trk Divrigi), 130 km east of Sevastia. Important cities inside the Gangra section are: Kastamon (Grk Κασταμών, Trk Kastamonu), 350 km west of Inoi; Ionopolis (Grk Ιωνόπολις, Trk Inebolu), on the Black Sea shore, 65 km north of Kastamon; Kytoros (Grk Κύτωρος, Trk Cide), on the Black Sea shore, 95 km northeast of Kastamon; Pompeioupolis (Grk Πομπηιούπολις, Trk Taskopru), 45 km east of Kastamon; Dokia (Grk Δοκεία, Trk Tosya), 55 km south of Kastamon; Gangra (Grk Γάγγρα, Trk Cankiri), 90 km south of Kastamon; Antonioupolis (Grk Αντωνιούπολις, Trk Cerkes), 120 km southeast of Kastamon; Theodoroupolis (Grk Θεοδωρούπολις, Trk Safranbolu), 95 km west of Kastamon; Mavrogonion (Grk Μαυρογώνιον, Trk Karabuk), 105 km west of Kastamon; Parthenion (Grk Παρθένιον, Trk Bartin), 160 km northwest of Kastamon; Amastris (Grk Ἄμαστρις, Trk Amasra), on the Black Sea shore, 170 km northwest of Kastamon; Dadastana (Grk Δαδάστανα, Trk Devrek), 170 km west of Kastamon; and Kratia (Grk Κράτεια, Trk Gerede), 180 km southwest of Kastamon.

Gangra and Kastamon were occupied by the Danismendid Turkomans circa 1080, retaken by the Romans in 1132, retaken by the Danismendids the next year, and taken by the Seljuks circa 1174. The area was occupied by the Ottoman Turks in 1391, but was given by Tamerlane to the resurrected Emirate of Candar in 1403, from which it was taken by the Ottomans in 1417. From January-November 1920 the northern area of the main section (including Neokaisaria and Evdokias) was part of the ill-fated Greek-Armenian Republic of the Pontus (see m. Trapezous). After the population exchange of 1923 between Greece and Turkey, no Orthodox population remains inside the area of the Metropolitanate.

Metropolitans of Neokaisaria since 1800

43. Isaiah	Ησαΐας		May 1793 – 1801+	d. 1801
(ex m.Prespes) (to m.Kaisaria)				
44. Meletius I	Μελέτιος Α´		Mar 1801 – May 1816	d. 1817
(ex former m.Vodena) (to m.Kaisaria)				
45. Cyril III	Κύριλλος Γ´		*May* 1816 – 1850+	d. 1850
46. Leontius	Λεόντιος	(1st time)	4 May 1850 – 7 Nov 1864	d. 1868
(ex t.b.Nazianzos Sep 1848) suspended (to former, to m.Neokaisaria)				
47. Hierotheus	Ιερόθεος	(1st time)	7 Nov 1864 – 29 Aug 1868	d. 1883
Fintias (ex former m.Halepion) suspended (to former, to m.Neokaisaria)				
---. Leontius	Λεόντιος	(2nd time)	29 Aug 1868 – 1 Nov 1868+	d. 1868
(ex former m.Neokaisaria)				
48. Meletius II	Μελέτιος Β´		18 Nov 1868 – 3 Apr 1872	d≥1874
Kavasilas (ex b.Trikkis) (to m.Ainos)				
---. Hierotheus	Ιερόθεος	(2nd time)	3 Apr 1872 – 25 Aug 1883+	d. 1883
Fintias (ex former m.Neokaisaria)				
49. Constantius	Κωνστάντιος		3 Sep 1883 – 15 Jul 1895	1835-1908
Isaakidis (ex former m.Kastoria) (to m.Veria)				
50. Alexander	Αλέξανδρος		15 Jul 1895 – 18 Oct 1903	1851-1928
Rigopoulos (ex former m.Pelagonia) (to m.Thessaloniki)				
51. Ambrose	Αμβρόσιος	(1st time)	18 Oct 1903 – 25 Apr 1911	1854-1931
Stavrinos (ex m.Pelagonia) (to m.Kaisaria)				
52. Polycarp	Πολύκαρπος		28 Apr 1911 – 13 Oct 1922	1864-1936
Psomiadis (ex m.Kolonia) (to m.Xanthi)				
53. Agathangelus	Αγαθάγγελος		25 Oct 1922 – 20 Mar 1924	1864-1935
Konstantinidis/Magnis (ex m.Philippoi) (to m.Pringiponnisa)				
---. Ambrose	Αμβρόσιος	(2nd time)	22 Mar 1924 – 24 Oct 1929	1854-1931
Stavrinos (ex former m.Kaisaria) (to m.Derki)				
54. Chrysostom	Χρυσόστομος		7 May 1944 – 27 Nov 1976+	1894-1976
Koronaios, see note 1				

1. On July 22, 1950 Metropolitan Chrysostom was elected Metropolitan of Leros, but he did not accept the transfer, and the election was cancelled.

SECTION F:
METROPOLITANATES IN NORTHEAST ASIA MINOR

METROPOLITANATE OF CHALDIA, CHERIANA, AND KERASOUS
ΜΗΤΡΟΠΟΛΙΣ ΧΑΛΔΙΑΣ, ΧΕΡΟΙΑΝΩΝ ΚΑΙ ΚΕΡΑΣΟΥΝΤΟΣ

Metropolitan of Chaldia, Cheriana and Cerasus, most honorable and Exarch of Helenopontus

The city of Argyroupolis (Grk Αργυρούπολις, Trk Gümüşhane), located 80 km south of Trapezous, was established circa 700 BC as the settlement of Thyra (Grk Θύρα) by Ionian Greeks, who first discovered silver in the region. It came under Roman control in 63 BC, was given to King Polemon I of Pontus in 37 BC, and returned to the Romans in 64 AD. Many centuries later it was included in the new Roman (Byzantine) province of Chaldia (Grk Χαλδία) which was established circa 840. The name Argyroupolis (City of Silver) prevailed during the Roman times due to the nearby silver mines. Part of the Empire of Trebizond after 1204, it was protected by its mountainous terrain until it was occupied by the Ottoman Turks in 1479, eighteen years after the fall of Trebizond.

The area was initially part of the Metropolitanate of Neokaisaria until about 840, when the new Metropolitanate of Trapezous was established, with Cheriana as one of its subordinates. The Diocese of Cheriana was promoted to an Archdiocese between 1624-53, and to a Metropolitanate in July 1767 (the Metropolitanate of Chaldia and Cheriana, with its See at Argyroupolis).

The city of Kerasous (Grk Κερασούς, Trk Giresun), located on the Black Sea 120 km west of Trapezous, was attached to the Metropolitanate of Chaldia on December 12, 1913. Kerasous became a Diocese under the Metropolitanate of Neokaisaria before 431 AD, and was promoted to a Metropolitanate during 1085-1147. Still a Metropolitanate in 1621, it was made a Patriarchal Exarchate by 1644, until it was attached to the Metrpolitanate of Trapezous in October 1698. It thereafter reverted to Exarchate status and was again annexed to Trapezous in July 1774, remaining part of that Metropolitanate until 1913.

The Metropolitanate of Chaldia is bordered by the Black Sea, the Metropolitanate of Trapezous, and the Metropolitanate of Rhodopolis on the north; the Metropolitanate of Trapezous, the Metropolitanate of Rhodopolis, and the Metropolitanate of Theodosioupolis (Patriarchate of Antioch) on the east; the Metropolitanate of Theodosioupolis and the Metropolitanate of Kolonia on the south; and the Metropolitanate of Kolonia and the Metropolitanate of Neokaisaria on the west.

Other important cities are: Cheriana (Grk Χεροίανα, Trk Siran), 60 km southwest of Argyroupolis; Syissa (Grk Σύισσα, Trk Kelkit), 60 km south of Argyroupolis; Mesochaldion (Grk Μεσοχάλδιον, Trk Torul), 20 km northwest of Argyroupolis; and Thoania (Grk Θοανία, Trk Tonya), 65 km northwest of Argyroupolis.

Argyroupolis was occupied by the Russian army on July 20, 1916, but the Russians withdrew on February 15, 1918, after the fall of the Czar. During the period of January-November 1920 the area of the Metropolitanate was part of the ill-fated Greek-Armenian Republic of the Pontus (see m. Trapezous). After the population exchange of 1923 between Greece and Turkey, no Orthodox population remains inside the area of the Metropolitanate.

Metropolitans of Chaldia since 1800

15. Sophronius Lazaridis	Σωφρόνιος	*Nov* 1790 – 13 Nov 1818+	d. 1818
16. Sylvester II Lazaridis	Σίλβεστρος Β΄	*Jan* 1819 – 6 Aug 1830+	d. 1830
17. Theophilus Adysaios	Θεόφιλος	*Sep* 1830 – 17 Feb 1864+	d. 1864
18. Gervase Soumelidis, resigned, 8 Mar 1906+	Γερβάσιος	*14 Jul* 1864 – 1 May 1905	1820-1906
19. Laurentius Papadopoulos (to m.Filippi)	Λαυρέντιος	*1 May* 1905 – 25 Oct 1922	d. 1928
20. Basil (1st time) Komvopoulos (ex m.Mithymna) deposed (to former, to m.Chaldia), see note 1	Βασίλειος	25 Oct 1922 – 10 May 1924	1887-1941
---. Basil (2nd time) Komvopoulos (ex former m.Chaldia) (to m.Drama)	Βασίλειος	19 Jun 1930 – 2 Oct 1930	1887-1941
21. Cyril Axiotis	Κύριλλος	10 Oct 1943 – 1 May 1991+	1908-1991
21. Spyridon Papageorgiou (ex a.America) suspended	Σπυρίδων	19 Aug 1999 – 4 Sep 2000	b. 1940

1. Metropolitan Basil moved to the USA and styled himself "Metropolitan of America" between 1924-30. For this he was defrocked by the Ecumenical Patriarch on May 10, 1924. Six years later he expressed his repentance and was reinstated.

METROPOLITANATE OF KOLONIA
ΜΗΤΡΟΠΟΛΙΣ ΚΟΛΩΝΕΙΑΣ

Metropolitan of Colonia, most honorable and Exarch of Upper Pontus

The city of Nikopolis (Grk Νικόπολις, Trk Sebinkarahisar), located 180 km south-west of Trapezous, and the city of Kolonia (Grk Κολώνεια, Trk Koyulhisar), 65 km west of Nikopolis, were both established in 66 BC by the Roman General Pompey, who brought the area under Roman control. Both cities were given to King Polemon I of Pontus in 37 BC, and returned to Roman rule in 64 AD. The area was occupied by Seljuk Turks circa 1075, and was recovered by the Byzantine Empire circa 1108. After 1204 the area was alternating control between the Empire of Trebizond and the Seljuks or the Turkomans. It finally came under Ottoman control in 1473.

During the fourth century both Nikopolis and later Kolonia became Dioceses under the Metropolitanate of Sevastia. Kolonia was promoted to an Archdiocese in the ninth century (before 879) and to a Metropolitanate in the eleventh century (before 1067). In 1391 it was annexed to the Metropolitanate of Trapezous due to depopulation. The Diocese of Nikopolis was also abolished around the same time. The area was later attached to the Metropolitanate of Neokaisaria, and was organized into a new Diocese of Nikopolis under the Metropolitanate of Neokaisaria during the eighteenth century.

On January 10, 1889, the Diocese was promoted to a Metropolitanate; however, it was renamed the Metropolitanate of Kolonia to avoid having two Metropolitanates of Nikopolis under the Ecumenical Patriarchate (the other Metropolitanate of that name being situated in Epirus, Greece). Nevertheless, the See of the Metropolitanate of Kolonia remained in Nikopolis.

The Metropolitanate of Kolonia is bordered by the Metropolitanate of Neokaisaria and the Metropolitanate of Chaldia on the north; the Metropolitanate of Chaldia on the east; the Metropolitanate of Theodosioupolis (Patriarchate of Antioch) and the Metropolitanate of Neokaisaria on the south; and the Metropolitanate of Neokaisaria on the west. Other important cities are: Andira (Grk Ἄνδειρα, Trk Susehri), 35 km southwest of Nikopolis, and Kapsos (Grk Κάψος, Trk Alucra), 30 km east of Nikopolis.

During January-November 1920 the area of the Metropolitanate was part of the ill-fated Greek-Armenian Republic of the Pontus (see m. Trapezous). After the population exchange of 1923 between Greece and Turkey, no Orthodox population remains inside the area of the Metropolitanate.

Bishops of Nikopolis from 1800-89

11. Johnnicius	Ιωαννίκιος	. . . – 1832+	d. 1832
12. Christopher Fotianos, resigned	Χριστόφορος	*Oct* 1832 – 1860	d. 1863
13. Jeremias Georgiadis (ex t.b.Myra *13 Feb* 1860)	Ιερεμίας	27 Nov 1864 – Oct 1878+	d. 1878
14. Gennadius Vasiliadis (ex former a.Rhodopolis) suspended	Γεννάδιος	Aug 1879 – 10 Jan 1889	d. ?

Metropolitans of Kolonia since 1889

13. Dorotheus I (ex m.Halepion)	Δωρόθεος Α΄	12 Jan 1889 – 1894+	d. 1894
14. Leontius Choutouriotis (ex t.b.Lefki *Mar* 1886) (to m.Philadelphia)	Λεόντιος	15 Feb 1894 – 29 Apr 1899	1844-1926
15. Polycarp Psomiadis (to m.Neokaisaria)	Πολύκαρπος	16 May 1899 – 28 Apr 1911	1864-1935
16. Sophronius Nistopoulos (ex former m.Kaisaria)	Σωφρόνιος	28 Apr 1911 – 10 Feb 1917+	d. 1917
17. Dorotheus II Christidis (ex m.Sozoagathoupolis) resigned, 24 Oct 1924+	Δωρόθεος Β΄	11 Jul 1917 – 17 Jan 1919	d. 1924
18. Gabriel Premetidis	Γαβριήλ	9 Apr 1967 – 29 Dec 2003+	1919-2003

METROPOLITANATE OF RHODOPOLIS
ΜΗΤΡΟΠΟΛΙΣ ΡΟΔΟΠΟΛΕΩΣ

Metropolitan of Rhodopolis, most honorable and Exarch of Lazica

The city of Rhodopolis (Grk Ροδόπολις, today Kvatsikhe in Georgia) is situated 35 km east of Kutaisi, in the area of ancient Colchis. Later known as Lazika (Grk Λαζική), its inhabitants formed a Kingdom in the fourth century AD, which was occupied by Persia in 542 in order to neutralize the Roman influence. The Romans gained control of the area after fighting the Lazic war against the Persians during 549-56. Lazika remained under Roman control until the Arab occupation (circa 700). The Lazic population gradually moved southwestward as far as Trebizond, causing the area known as Lazika to shift towards the same direction.

Rhodopolis was a Diocese under the Metropolitanate of Phasis in the sixth century. The Metropolitanate of Phasis was abolished after the Arab conquest, its area being annexed to the new Metropolitanate of Trapezous in the ninth century.

In the mountainous area south of Trebizond are located three historic monasteries. Soumela (Grk Σουμελά), situated 20 km south of Dikaiosimon, was established in the year 386 according to tradition. Vazelon (formerly Zavoulon, Grk Βαζελών or Ζαβουλών), situated 10 km southwest of Dikaiosimon, was established in the year 270, according to tradition, and the monastery of Peristereota (Grk Περιστερεώτα) was established in the year 752. During the rule of the Empire of Trebizond all three monasteries enjoyed a great degree of ecclesiastic autonomy, which included their overlordship over the surrounding villages. This autonomy was maintained after the Ottoman occupation of the area in 1461, with the status of each monastery evolving to a Patriarchal Exarchate. In May 1863 the three Exarchates were abolished and their combined area constituted the new Archdiocese of Rhodopolis. The Archdiocese was short-lived however, as it was abolished on September 7, 1867, and the three Exarchates re-established. The Exarchates were again abolished in October 1902, and replaced by the new Metropolitanate of Rhodopolis.

The Metropolitanate of Rhodopolis is bordered by the Metropolitanate of Trapezous on the north and east, and the Metropolitanate of Chaldia on the south and west. The See of the Metropolitanate is in the city of Dikaiosimon (Grk Δικαιόσημον, Trk Macka), located 25 km south of Trapezous. The Turkish name is derived from the name of the overall area in Roman times, Matsouka (Grk Ματσούκα).

The Russian army occupied Dikaiosimon and the monasteries in 1916, but withdrew in 1918 after the fall of the Czar. During the period of January-November 1920 the area of the Metropolitanate was part of the ill-fated Greek-Armenian Republic of the Pontus (see m. Trapezous). After the population exchange of 1923 between Greece and Turkey, no Orthodox population remains inside the area of the Metropolitanate.

Hierarchs of Rhodopolis
(Archbishop 1863-1867, Metropolitans afterwards)

1. Gennadius	Γεννάδιος	*3 Jun* 1863 – 7 Sep 1867	d≥1889
Vasiliadis, suspended (to former, to b.Nikopolis)			
2. Gervase	Γερβάσιος	16 Nov 1902 – 10 Oct 1906	1867-1934
Sarasitis (ex t.b.Nazianzos *28 Jul* 1901) (to m.Korytsa)			
3. Leontius	Λεόντιος	10 Oct 1906 – 22 Sep 1909	1844-1926
Choutouriotis (ex m.Philadelphia) suspended, 2 Jun 1926+			
4. Cyril	Κύριλλος	*22 Sep* 1909 – 11 Jan 1944+	1872-1944
Chatzipapadimitriou			
5. Hieronymus	Ιερώνυμος	5 Aug 1954 – 17 Nov 2005+	1912-2005
Konstantinidis (ex t.b.Trallis 28 Jan 1951)			

METROPOLITANATE OF TRAPEZOUS
ΜΗΤΡΟΠΟΛΙΣ ΤΡΑΠΕΖΟΥΝΤΟΣ

Metropolitan of Trapezus, most honorable and Exarch of all Lazica

The city of Trapezous (Trebizond, Grk Τραπεζούς, Trk Trabzon), located 225 km east of Inoi on the Black Sea shore, was established in 756 BC by Ionian Greek settlers from Sinopi, and came under Roman control in 63 BC. The city was given to King Polemon I of Pontus in 37 BC, but returned to Roman control in 64 AD. Around the time Constantinople fell to the western Crusaders (April 1204), Trapezous declared its independence as the Roman Empire of Trebizond, until it fell to the Ottoman Turks on August 15, 1461.

Initially a Diocese under the Metropolitanate of Neokaisaria, Trapezous became an Archdiocese during the eighth century and a Metropolitanate circa 840. In the tenth century the Metropolitanate of Trapezous had seven Dioceses under its jurisdiction, which increased to eighteen by the twelfth century. Afterwards the number of Dioceses steadily decreased, with only two remaining by the fifteenth century—the Diocese of Chaldia or Kanin, which was promoted to an Archdiocese during the first half of the seventeenth century, and the Diocese of Ophis, which was abolished during the same period. No Dioceses remained by the eighteenth century.

The Metropolitanate of Trapezous is bordered by the Black Sea and the Diocese of Batumi (Georgian Patriarchate) on the north; the Metropolitanate of Theodosioupolis (Patriarchate of Antioch) on the east; the Metropolitanate of Chaldia, the Metropolitanate of Rhodopolis, and the Metropolitanate of Theodosioupolis on the south; and the Metropolitanate of Chaldia and the Metropolitanate of Rhodopolis on the west.

Other important cities, all situated on the Black Sea, are: Platana (Grk Πλάτανα, Trk Akcaabat), 15 km west of Trapezous; Philokalia (Grk Φιλοκάλεια, Trk Vakfikebir), 45 km west of Trapezous; Eleous (Grk Ελεούς, Trk Gorele derived from the Greek name of the area, Koralla, Grk Κόραλλα), 65 km west of Trapezous; Tripolis (Grk Τρίπολις, Trk Tirebolu), 85 km west of Trapezous; Thespias (Grk Θεσπιάς, Trk Espiye), 95 km west of Trapezous; Kassiopi (Grk Κασσιόπη, Trk Kesap), 115 km west of Trapezous; Gimora (Grk Γημωρά, Trk Yomra), 15 km east of Trapezous; Iraklia (Grk Ηράκλεια, Trk Arakli), 28 km east of Trapezous; Sourmena (Grk Σούρμενα, Trk Surmene), 35 km east of Trapezous; Ophis (Grk Όφις, Trk Of), 50 km east of Trapezous, Rizous (Grk Ριζούς, Trk Rize), 75 km east of Trapezous; Mapavri (Grk Μαπαύρη, Trk Cayeli), 95 km east of Trapezous; Athina (Grk Αθήνα, Trk Pazar), 115 km east of Trapezous; Armini (Grk Αρμήνη, Trk Ardesen), 125 km east of Trapezous, Archavis (Grk Άρχαβις, Trk Arhavi), 150 km east of Trapezous; and Apsaros (Grk Άψαρος, Trk Hopa), 165 km east of Trapezous.

Trebizond was occupied by the Russian army on April 18, 1916, but the Russians withdrew on February 24, 1918. Discussions ensued over the establishment of a Greek-Armenian state in the area, the Republic of the Pontus, with its capital in Trebizond. In January 1920 an agreement for the establishment of this state was signed by local Metropolitan Chrysanthos and Armenian Prime Minister Alexander Hatisyan. The treaty provided for the military cooperation of Greece and Armenia to protect the new state, and indeed, between January-November 1920 an embryonic government functioned in the Pontus (without, however, being officially proclaimed), due the to absence of the collapsing Ottoman authority in the region.

However, the Allies refused to allow the implementation of a local Armenian-Greek army, and by November 1920 the Turks under Mustafa Kemal reasserted their authority in the area. After the defeat of the Armenians by the Turkish Army in Erzerum and their capitulation in December 1920, the plan fell apart, with grave results for the Greek and Armenian population in the area. After the population exchange of 1923 between Greece and Turkey, no Orthodox population remains inside the area of the Metropolitanate.

Metropolitans of Trapezous since 1800

50. Parthenius	Παρθένιος	*Mar* 1798 – 1830+	d. 1830
51. Constantius I	Κωνστάντιος Α'	*Jul* 1830 – Apr 1879+	d. 1879
52. Gregory II	Γρηγόριος Β'	12 May 1879 – 22 Dec 1884	1844-1925
Kalliadis (ex t.b.Nazianzos Mar 1875) (to m.Thessaloniki)			
53. Gregory III	Γρηγόριος Γ'	29 Dec 1884 – 17 Mar 1888	d. 1902
Giannaros (ex m.Philippoupolis) (to m.Rhodes)			
54. Philaretus	Φιλάρετος	*14 May* 1888 – 10 Oct 1889	1848-1933
Vafidis (to m.Kastoria)			
55. Gabriel	Γαβριήλ	10 Oct 1889 – 23 Apr 1893	d. 1906
Iatroudakis (ex m.Varna) suspended (to former, to m.Maronia)			
56. Constantius II	Κωνστάντιος Β'	*29 Apr* 1893 – 18 Jun 1906+	d. 1906
Karatzopoulos			
57. Constantine II	Κωνσταντίνος Β'	29 Jun 1906 – 2 Apr 1913	1859-1930
Arampoglous (ex m.Vellas) (to m.Kyzikos)			
58. Chrysanthus	Χρύσανθος (1st time)	26 May 1913 – 10 Feb 1922	1881-1949
Filippidis (to m.Maronia) see note 1			
---. Chrysanthus	Χρύσανθος (2nd time)	27 Oct 1922 – 13 Dec 1938	1881-1949
Filippidis (ex m.Maronia) (to a.Athina/Head of Greek Church)			

1. Metropolitan Chrysanthus was sentenced to death *in absentia* by the Turkish authorities on September 7, 1921.

SECTION G:
METROPOLITANATES IN THE DODECANESE

METROPOLITANATE OF KARPATHOS AND KASOS
ΜΗΤΡΟΠΟΛΙΣ ΚΑΡΠΑΘΟΥ ΚΑΙ ΚΑΣΟΥ

Metropolitan of Carpathus and Casus, most honorable and Exarch of Cyclades Islands

The island of Karpathos (Grk Κάρπαθος, with an area of 301 km²), located 50 km southwest of Rhodes in the southwestern Aegean Sea, came under Roman control in 146 BC. It was occupied by Latins in 1204, reverted to Roman control in 1224 (under the Empire of Nicaea), was occupied by the Genovese in 1282, the Venetians in 1306, the Knights of Rhodes in 1311, and again by the Venetians in 1315. In 1537 the Ottoman Turks occupied Karpathos and the nearby island of Kasos (Grk Κάσος, located 6 km southeast of Karpathos, having an area of 66 km²), which shared the fate of Karpathos for most of its history.

After the Greek revolution, both islands expelled their Turkish officials, and in 1822 they became part of the new Greek state. However, Kasos was razed by the Turkish navy on May 29, 1824, and both islands returned to Turkish control on July 9, 1832. On April 30, 1912 the islands were occupied by Italy, in November 1943 by the Germans, on October 17, 1944 by the British, and on March 31, 1947 by Greece. They officially became part of Greece on March 7, 1948.

Karpathos became a Diocese under the jurisdiction of the Metropolitanate of Rhodes in the fourth century AD, and was promoted to an Archdiocese in the first half of the sixth century. During the Latin occupation of Karpathos, the Orthodox Archdiocese was abolished, but was re-established in 1562. On May 1, 1865 the Archdiocese of Karpathos and Kasos was promoted to a Metropolitanate.

The Metropolitanate of Karpathos and Kassos is bordered by the Metropolitanate of Symi on the north (Tilos and Chalki Islands), the Metropolitanate of Rhodes on the northeast, the Metropolitanate of Ierapytna of Kriti Island on the southwest, and the Metropolitanate of Leros on the northwest (Astypalaia Island).

Other islands of the Metropolitanate are: Saria (Grk Σαριά, adjoining the north coast of Karpathos, having an area of 21 km²), Syrna (Grk Σύρνα, located 72 km northwest of Karpathos, having an area of 6 km²), plus many islets. The See of the Metropolitanate is in the village of Aperion (Grk Απέριον), located on the south part of Karpathos Island. Other settlements on the islands are Karpathos city, located 5 km south of Aperion on the southeast coast of Karpathos Island, Olympos (Grk Όλυμπος), located 25 km north of Aperion, and Kassos city, located on the north coast of Kassos Island.

Hierarchs of Karpathos and Kasos since 1800
(Archbishops until 1 May 1865, Metropolitans afterwards)

24. Neophytus II   Νεόφυτος Β'   Jun 1793 – 1832   d. 1832?

25. Methodius	Μεθόδιος	autumn 1832 – 18 Nov 1864	d. 1868
Sapountzakis (ex former m.Rhodes) resigned			
26. Nicephorus III	Νικηφόρος Γ'	*17 Feb* 1865 – Jan 1869	d. ?
promoted to Metropolitan 1 May 1865, suspended			
27. Ignatius	Ιγνάτιος	16 Jan 1869 – 22 Feb 1875	d. ?
(ex t.b.Troas Aug 1862) resigned			
28. Gerasimus	Γεράσιμος	8 Mar 1875 – Nov 1885	1828-1888
Pigas (to president d.Polyani)			
29. Nilus	Νείλος	23 Jun 1886 – 5 Aug 1889	d≥1894
Smyrniotopoulos (ex t.b.Erythra *13 Aug* 1883) resigned			
30. Sophronius	Σωφρόνιος	5 Aug 1889 – 31 May 1897	d. 1911
Argyropoulos (ex m.Anchialos) (to m.Elasson)			
31. Agathangelus	Αγαθάγγελος	31 May 1897 – 31 Jul 1908	d. 1924
Archytas (ex t.b.Erythres *17 Apr* 1890) (to m.Kos)			
32. Eugene	Ευγένιος	31 Jul 1908 – 28 May 1912+	1843-1912
Mastorakis (ex t.b.Synnada *17 Jun* 1899)			
33. Germanus	Γερμανός	9 Jun 1912 – 27 Jan 1940+	1865-1940
Monodiadis (ex t.b.Militoupolis 13 Apr 1907) exiled to Kastellorizo 6 Jul 1922 to 1924			
34. Apostolus	Απόστολος	6 Aug 1950 – 13 Feb 1975	1915-1977
Papaïoannou (to m.Ainos)			
35. George	Γεώργιος	23 Feb 1975 – 16 Sep 1980	1918-1991
Orfanidis, resigned, 30 Oct 1991+			
36. Nectarius	Νεκτάριος	16 Sep 1980 – 24 May 1983	b. 1932
Chatzimichalis (ex m.Kissamos) (to m.Leros)			
37. Ambrose	Αμβρόσιος	19 Jun 1983 –	b. 1939
Panagiotidis			

METROPOLITANATE OF KOS AND NISYROS
ΜΗΤΡΟΠΟΛΙΣ ΚΩΟΥ ΚΑΙ ΝΙΣΥΡΟΥ

Metropolitan of Cos and Nisyrus, most honorable and Exarch of Cyclades Islands

The island of Kos (Grk Κως, with an area of 290 km²), located 80 km northwest of Rhodes in the southwestern Aegean Sea, came under Roman control in 146 BC. It was occupied by Venetians in 1204, the Knights of Rhodes in 1314, and the Ottoman Turks on January 5, 1523. That same year the Ottomans also occupied the nearby island of Nisyros (Grk Νίσυρος, located 15 km south of Kos, having an area of 41 km²), which shared the fate of Kos for most of its history.

On April 30, 1912 the islands were occupied by Italy, on October 1943 by the Germans (Kos being occupied on October 4), on May 9, 1945 by the British, and on March 31, 1947 by Greece. They officially became part of Greece on March 7, 1948.

Kos became a Diocese under the jurisdiction of the Metropolitanate of Rhodes in 325 AD, and was promoted to an Archdiocese circa 1300. During the Latin occupation the Orthodox Archdiocese was abolished, but was re-established in 1523. On April 11, 1838 the Archdiocese of Kos was promoted to a Metropolitanate. In 1937 the island of Kalymnos was attached to the Metropolitanate of Kos, but in 1947 it returned to the Metropolitanate of Leros. On April 20, 2004, the island of Nisyros was detached from the Metropolitanate of Rhodes and attached to the Metropolitanate of Kos.

The Metropolitanate of Kos and Nisyros is bordered by the Metropolitanate of Leros on the north (Kalymnos Island), the Metropolitanate of Pisidia (Asia Minor) on the east, the Metropolitanate of Symi (Tilos Island) on the south, and the Metropolitanate of Leros on the northwest (Astypalaia Island).

The island of Gyali (Grk Γυαλί), situated between Kos and Nisyros among many islets, has an area of 6 km². The See of the Metropolitanate is at the city of Kos, located on the northwest coast of the island. Mandrakion (Grk Μανδράκιον) is situated on the northwest coast of Nisyros.

Hierarchs of Kos and Nisyros since 1800
(Archbishops to 11 Apr 1828, Metropolitan of Kos 1828-1937, M. of Kos and Kalymnos 1937-1947, M. of Kos 1947-2004, M. of Kos and Nisyros since 20 April 2004)

28. Zacharias II	Ζαχαρίας Β΄	1790 – 1801+	d. 1801
29. Gerasimus II	Γεράσιμος Β΄	*Mar* 1801 – 1838+	d. 1838
30. Cyril II (to m.Vidyni)	Κύριλλος Β΄	*Mar* 1838 – Jul 1840	d≥1846
31. Synesius (ex t.b.Efchaïta Jul 1838)	Συνέσιος	Jul 1840 – 1842	d. ?
32. Cyril III (ex former b.Kitros) nine months	Κύριλλος Γ΄	1842 – 1843+	d. 1843
33. Pangratius resigned	Παγκράτιος	*Jul* 1843 – 23 Jul 1853	d. 1872/3
34. Cyril IV (to m.Elasson)	Κύριλλος Δ΄	*25 Jul* 1853 – Mar 1867	d. 1887
35. Germanus Kavvakopoulos (to m.Rhodes)	Γερμανός	*10 Mar* 1867 – 19 Feb 1876	1835-1920
36. Meletius III (ex m.Phanariofersala)	Μελέτιος Γ΄	19 Feb 1876 – Sep 1885+	d. 1885
37. Paul Symeonidis (ex t.b.Skopelos Sep 1880) suspended	Παύλος	14 Oct 1885 – Jun 1888	d≥1901
38. Athanasius II Nikolaïdis (ex b.Metres) (to m.Sisanion)	Αθανάσιος Β΄	Jun 1888 – 1 Jun 1893	d. 1900
39. Callinicus II Palaiokrasas (ex former m.Stromnitsa) (to m.Paramythia)	Καλλίνικος Β΄	1 Jun 1893 – 12 Feb 1900	d. 1906
40. Joachim II Vaxevanidis (ex t.b.Militoupolis *12 Dec* 1896) (to m.Kastoria)	Ιωακείμ Β΄	17 Feb 1900 – 14 Feb 1908	d. 1911
41. Nicodemus Komninos Andreou (ex m.Vizyi) resigned (to former, to m.Varna)	Νικόδημος	19 Feb 1908 – 31 Jul 1908	1857-1935
42. Agathangelus Archytas (ex m.Karpathos)	Αγαθάγγελος	31 Jul 1908 – 24 Jul 1924+	d. 1924
43. Emmanuel Karpathios (to t.m.Mesimvria) 5 Aug 1972+	Εμμανουήλ	1 Mar 1947 – 23 May 1967	1887-1972
44. Nathaniel I Dikaios (ex t.b.Militoupolis 7 May 1956, t.m.Militoupolis 1963)	Ναθαναήλ Α΄	23 May 1967 – 14 Aug 1979+	1919-1979
45. Ezekiel Tsoukalas (ex m.Pisidia) resigned, 22 Jul 1987+	Ιεζεκιήλ	16 Sep 1979 – 14 Dec 1982	1913-1987
46. Aemilian Zacharopoulos (ex m.Belgium) suspended	Αιμιλιανός	14 Dec 1982 – 23 Feb 2009	b. 1915
47. Nathaniel II Diakopanagiotis	Ναθαναήλ Β΄	8 Mar 2009 –	b. 1960

METROPOLITANATE OF LEROS, KALYMNOS, AND ASTYPALAIA
ΜΗΤΡΟΠΟΛΙΣ ΛΕΡΟΥ, ΚΑΛΥΜΝΟΥ ΚΑΙ ΑΣΤΥΠΑΛΑΙΑΣ

Metropolitan of Lerus, Calymnus and Astypalaia,
most honorable and Exarch of Sporades Islands

The island of Kalymnos (Grk Κάλυμνος), with an area of 111 km², is located 10 km north of Kos island in the southwestern Aegean Sea. The island of Leros (Grk Λέρος), with an area of 53 km², is located 2 km north of Kalymnos. The island of Astypalaia (Grk Αστυπάλαια), with an area of 97 km², is located 55 km southwest of Kalymnos, being the westerner of the Dodecanese Islands.

All three islands came under Roman control in 146 BC. They were occupied by Venetians in 1204, while the Knights of Rhodes took Kalymnos and Leros in 1314. The Ottoman Turks occupied the two islands in 1523, and Astypalaia in 1537.

After the Greek revolution both islands expelled the Turkish officials, and in May 1822 the islands became part of the new Greek state. However, they reverted to Turkish control on July 9, 1832. On April 14, 1912 Astypalaia was occupied by Italy, the first of the Dodecanese islands to pass under Italian control. Italy occupied Kalymnos and Leros on April 30, 1912. In November 1943 the islands were occupied by the Germans (Leros being occupied on November 16), on May 9, 1945 by the British, and on March 31, 1947 by Greece. They officially became part of Greece on March 7, 1948.

Leros became a Diocese under the jurisdiction of the Metropolitanate of Rhodes before 553 AD, as did Astypalaia during the tenth century. However, during the Latin occupation the Orthodox Dioceses were abolished, with only the Diocese of Lerni (sic) being re-established after the Ottoman occupation. Astypalaia was detached from the Diocese of Lerni, becoming a Patriarchal Exarchate, during the years c.1580-84, 1585-April 1610, and 1621-46. It was attached to the new Archdiocese of Siphnos in August 1646, and finally re-attached to the Diocese of Lerni in April 1838. Kalymnos was also detached from the Diocese of Lerni, becoming a Patriarchal Exarchate during the period 1598/1601-April 1610. The Diocese of Lerni was promoted to the Metropolitanate (of Leros and Kalymnos) in November 1888. In 1937 the island of Kalymnos was attached to the Metropolitanate of Kos at the request of the Italian authorities, but in 1947 it was re-attached to the Metropolitanate of Leros.

The Metropolitanate of Leros, Kalymnos, and Astypalaia is bordered by the Patriarchal Exarchate of Patmos on the north (Patmos and Lipsi Islands), the Metropolitanate of Ilioupolis (Asia Minor) on the east, the Metropolitanate of Kos on the south, the Metropolitanate of Thera (Church of Greece) on the northwest (Amorgos Island).

Other islands under the jurisdiction of the Metropolitanate are: Pserimos (Grk Ψέριμος, situated between Kalymnos and Kos, having an area of 14 km²), Telendos (Grk Τέλενδος, adjoining the west coast of Kalymnos, having an area of 5 km²), plus many islets, including Imia (Grk Ίμια), which are disputed by Turkey and were the site of a Greek-Turkish political incident in January 1996.

The See of the Metropolitanate is the town of Agia Marina (Grk Αγία Μαρίνα), located on the east coast of Leros island. Kalymnos city is situated on the south coast of Kalymnos. Astypalaia town is situated on the south coast of Astypalaia.

Hierarchs of Leros, Kalymnos and Astypalaia since 1800
(Bishops of Lerna until Nov 1888, M. of Leros and Kalymnos 1888-1937, M. of Leros and Astypalaia 1937-1947, M. of Leros, Kalymnos and Astypalaia since 1947)

12. Ignatius I	Ἰγνάτιος Α'	May 1756 – 1800+	d. 1800
13. Ignatius II Karlavas	Ἰγνάτιος Β'	1800 – 1818	d. ?
14. Jeremias	Ἰερεμίας	1818 – 1844+	d. 1844
15. Dionysius	Διονύσιος	*Jul* 1844 – 1863+	d. 1863
16. Ignatius III Ikonomidis	Ἰγνάτιος Γ'	*22 May* 1863 – 1870+	d. 1870
17. Macarius suspended (to former, to b.Eleftheroupolis)	Μακάριος	*2 Apr* 1870 – 7 Mar 1875	d≥1888
18. Daniel Kefalianos (ex t.b.Velitsa *14 Nov* 1870)	Δανιήλ	7 Mar 1875 – 3 Jul 1888+	d. 1888
19. Chrysanthus (ex m.Nevrokopion) resigned (to former, to m.Korytsa)	Χρύσανθος	20 Oct 1888 – 21 Jul 1894	d≥1895
20. Anthimus Tsatsos (ex m.Korytsa) (to p.Constantinople)	Ἄνθιμος	21 Jul 1894 – 20 Jan 1895	1827-1913
21. Sophronius Christidis (ex former m.Thessaloniki) (to m.Nikaia)	Σωφρόνιος	23 Feb 1895 – 29 May 1897	d. 1910
22. John II Chatziapostolou (ex former m.Diskati) (to m.Kassandria)	Ἰωάννης Β'	29 May 1897 – 8 Aug 1903	d. 1915
23. Germanus Theotokas (ex m.Ainos)	Γερμανός	8 Aug 1903 – 9 Jun 1918+	1845-1918
24. Apostolus Kavvakopoulos (ex t.b.Olympos *1 May* 1912) resigned, Nov 1947+	Ἀπόστολος	6 Sep 1918 – Jun 1946	d. 1947
25. Isidore Aïdonopoulos, see note 1	Ἰσίδωρος	2 Dec 1950 – 19 May 1983+	d. 1983
26. Nectarius Chatzimichalis (ex m.Karpathos) resigned (to former, to m.Ganos)	Νεκτάριος	24 May 1983 – 16 May 2005	b. 1932
27. Païsius Aravantinos	Παΐσιος	21 May 2005 –	b. 1944

1. On July 22, 1950 Metropolitan Chrysostom of Neokaisaria was transferred to the Metropolitanate of Leros, but he did not accept his transfer and his election was cancelled.

METROPOLITANATE OF RHODES
ΜΗΤΡΟΠΟΛΙΣ ΡΟΔΟΥ

Metropolitan of Rhodes, most honorable and Exarch of all Cyclades Islands

The island of Rhodes (Rhodes, Grk Ρόδος), with an area of 1,398 km², is located in the southwestern corner of the Aegean Sea. Rhodes signed a treaty of alliance with Rome in 164 BC and came under Roman control in 146 BC, although it remained free to run its internal affairs. After the fall of Constantinople to the Latins in 1204, the island declared its independence, but was recovered by the Romans of Nikaia in 1224, who gave it to their Genovese allies circa 1250. The Seljuk Turks occupied the island in 1283, but the Knights of St. John drove them out in 1309, after a three-year war (they thereafter were known as the Knights of Rhodes). The Ottoman Turks forced out the Knights on December 22, 1522, remaining on the island until Italy occupied it on April 23, 1912. Rhodes was occupied by Germany on September 11, 1943, by the British on May 9, 1945, and by Greece on March 31, 1947, officially becoming part of Greece on March 7, 1948.

The Metropolitanate of Rhodes was established in 325 AD. Initially under the honorary primacy of the Metropolitanate of Ephesos, it became a Metropolitanate of the Patriarchate of Constantinople in 451. It had eleven Dioceses under its jurisdiction in the seventh century; however, in later centuries the number decreased, with none remaining by the fourteenth century. After the Ottoman occupation of 1522 only the Diocese of Lerni was re-established, and that was promoted to a Metropolitanate in 1888.

The Metropolitanate of Rhodes is bordered by the Metropolitanate of Symi on the northwest (Symi and Chalki Islands), the Metropolitanate of Pisidia (Asia Minor) on the northeast, and the Metropolitanate of Karpathos on the southwest. Main cities on the island are: Rhodes city (See of the Metropolitanate), Ialysos (Grk Ιαλυσός), Kremasti (Grk Κρεμαστή), and Paradisio (Grk Παραδείσιο) on the north coast; Afantou (Grk Αφάντου) and Archangelos (Grk Αρχάγγελος) on the east coast.

The nearby islands of Symi, Tilos, Chalki, and Kastellorizo were under the jurisdiction of the Metropolitanate of Rhodes until they became the separate Metropolitanate of Symi on April 20, 2004. On the same date the island of Nisyros was given to the Metropolitanate of Kos.

Metropolitans of Rhodes since 1800

53. Agapius	Αγάπιος		1792 – 1827+	d. 1827
54. Païsius III	Παΐσιος Γ'		Jun 1827 – Apr 1829	d. ?
(ex former m.Smyrni) resigned				
55. Païsius IV	Παΐσιος Δ'	(1st time)	*Apr* 1829 – May 1831	d≥1838
Kampanis, deposed (to former, to m.Rhodes)				
56. Methodius	Μεθόδιος		May 1831 – May 1832	d. 1868
Sapountzakis (ex m.Verria) resigned (to former, to president a.Karpathos)				
---. Païsius IV	Παΐσιος Δ'	(2nd time)	May 1832 – Mar 1836	d≥1838
Kampanis (ex former m.Rhodes) (to m.Mesimvria)				
57. Callinicus II	Καλλίνικος Β'		Mar 1836 – Aug 1839	d. 1845
Kaloutzos (ex former m.Mesimbria) deposed (to former, to m.Kriti)				
58. Jacob	Ιάκωβος		*Aug* 1839 – 6 Feb 1856	d. 1876
resigned, 27 Jun 1876+				
59. Ignatius IV	Ιγνάτιος Δ'		*6 Feb* 1856 – Feb 1861	d≥1875
Vasiliadis (to m.Kestentilion)				
60. Cyril I	Κύριλλος Α'		*26 Feb* 1861 – 26 Oct 1861+	d. 1861
Pigas-Papadakis				
61. Dorotheus	Δωρόθεος		11 Jan 1862 – 3 Apr 1865+	d. 1865
Prasinos (ex t.b.Charioupolis *3 Dec* 1855)				
62. Synesius	Συνέσιος		15 Apr 1865 – Feb 1876	1799-1879
(ex b.Tzervenos) deposed, 6 Jan 1879+				
63. Germanus	Γερμανός		19 Feb 1876 – 8 Feb 1888	1835-1920
Kavvakopoulos (ex m.Kos) (to m.Iraklia)				
64. Gregory II	Γρηγόριος Β'		17 Mar 1888 – 1 Jun 1893	d. 1902
Giannaros (ex m.Trapezous) (to m.Korytsa)				
65. Constantine	Κωνσταντίνος		*1 Jun* 1893 – 18 Jan 1900	d. 1903
Chatzimarkou-Alexandridis (to m.Kyzikos)				
66. Hierotheus	Ιερόθεος		3 Feb 1900 – Aug 1900+	d. 1900
Dimitriadis (ex m.Vizyi)				

67. Joachim II Valasiadis (ex m.Maronia) (to m.Nikopolis)	Ἰωακείμ Β'		7 Sep 1900 – 13 Mar 1910	1860-1933
68. Gerasimus Tantalidis (ex m.Ioannina) (to m.Pisidia)	Γεράσιμος		13 Mar 1910 – 26 Jan 1912	1854-1928
69. Benjamin Kyriakou (to m.Silyvria)	Βενιαμίν		30 Jan 1912 – 11 Jun 1913	1871-1946
70. Apostolus I Tryfonos (to m.Veria) exiled to Patmos on 26 Sep 1921 and then to Constantinople on Nov 1921	Ἀπόστολος Α'	(1st time)	*11 Jun* 1913 – 5 Feb 1924	1878-1957
71. Chrysostom Chatzistavrou (ex m.Ephesos) (to m.Veria) Italian authorities refused permission for his arrival	Χρυσόστομος		5 Feb 1924 – 30 Apr 1924	1880-1968
---. Apostolus I Tryfonos (ex former m.Rhodes) resigned (to former, to m.Amasia) allowed to return on 5 Oct 1924	Ἀπόστολος Α'	(2nd time)	30 Apr 1924 – 6 Jun 1946	1878-1957
72. Timothy Evangelinidis (ex m.Australia) (to a.America)	Τιμόθεος	(1st time)	16 Jan 1947 – 7 Jun 1949	1880-1949
---. Timothy Evangelinidis (ex a.America)	Τιμόθεος	(2nd time)	20 Sep 1949 – 6 Oct 1949+	1880-1949
73. Spyridon Συνοδινός (ex t.b.Apamia 18 Nov 1945)	Σπυρίδων		25 Jan 1951 – 29 Apr 1988+	1907-1988
74. Apostolus II Dimelis (ex m.Ilioupolis) resigned	Ἀπόστολος Β'		5 May 1988 – 20 Apr 2004	b. 1925
75. Cyril II Kogerakis	Κύριλλος Β'		25 Apr 2004 –	b. 1964

METROPOLITANATE OF SYMI
ΜΗΤΡΟΠΟΛΙΣ ΣΥΜΗΣ

Metropolitan of Symi, most honorable and Exarch of South Aegean Sea

The island of Symi (Grk Σύμη), with an area of 58 km², is located 25 km north of Rhodes island in the southwestern Aegean Sea. The island of Tilos (Grk Τήλος), with an area of 63 km², is located 35 km west of Rhodes. The island of Chalki (Grk Χάλκη), with an area of 28 km², is located 10 km west of Rhodes. The island of Megisti (Grk Μεγίστη), more commonly known as Kastellorizo (Grk Καστελλόριζο), has an area of 9 km², and is located 125 km east of Rhodes.

All these islands came under Roman control in 146 BC. They were occupied by Francs in 1204, but were recovered by the Romans in 1224. The Knights of Rhodes took them in 1309, and the Ottoman Turks occupied them in 1523. Kastellorizo, being quite remote from the other islands, was occupied by the Knights of Rhodes in 1309, the Egyptian Turks in 1440, the Catalans in 1461, the Kingdom of Naples in 1470, the Ottomans in 1480, the Kingdom of Naples again in 1498, the Spanish in 1512, the Ottomans again in 1523, Venice in 1570, and yet again by the Ottomans in 1659.

After the Greek revolution the islands expelled their Turkish officials, and in 1822 became part of the new Greek state, until they reverted to Turkish control on July 9, 1832. Italy occupied Chalki on April 26, 1912, Tilos on April 30, 1912, and Symi on May 6, 1912. The inhabitants of Kastellorizo expelled the Turkish officials on March 1, 1913, requesting to be annexed by Greece. After insistent requests, Greece occupied the island on August 1, 1913; however, the Greek forces were replaced by the French on December 28, 1915, who surrendered the island to Italy on March 1, 1921. In November 1943 the islands were occupied by the Germans, on May 9, 1945 by the British (who had already gained control of Symi on December 25, 1944), and on March 31, 1947 by Greece. They officially became part of Greece on March 7, 1948.

The islands were under the jurisdiction of the Metropolitanate of Rhodes, except Kastellorizo, which was under the jurisdiction of the Metropolitanate of Pisidia. Kastellorizo became a Patriarchal Exarchate before 1640, and in January 1647 was included in the territory of the re-established Metropolitanate of Myra, which was annexed by the Metropolitanate of Pisidia in 1651. Kastelorizo became a Patriarchal Exarchate again before 1729, but was included in the territory of the new Archdiocese of Myra in 1786, which was annexed by the Metropolitanate of Pisidia in July 1790.

On February 5, 1924 a new Metropolitanate of Kyklades was established, with its See in Symi, created by separating the islands of Symi, Tilos, Chalki, and Nisyros from the Metropolitanate of Rhodes. On the same date Kastellorizo was attached to the Metropolitanate of Rhodes. The Italian authorities refused to accept the splitting of the Metropolitanate of Rhodes in two, so the Metropolitanate of Kyklades was annexed back to the Metropolitanate of Rhodes on October 9, 1924. A new Metropolitanate of Symi was established on April 20, 2004.

The Metropolitanate of Symi is bordered by the Metropolitanate of Kos (Nisyros Island) and the Metropolitanate of Pisidia (Asia Minor) on the north, the Metropolitanate of Rhodes on the east, and the Metropolitanate of Karpathos on the south (Saria Island) and west (Syrna Island).

Other islands under the jurisdiction of the Metropolitanate are: Alimia (Grk Αλιμιά, situated between Chalki and Rhodes, having an area of 7 km²), Nimos (Grk Νίμος, adjoining the north coast of Symi, having an area of 5 km²), plus many islets.

The See of the Metropolitanate is Symi town, located on the north coast of Symi Island. Chalki town is situated on the southeast coast of Chalki, Megalo Chorio (Grk Μεγάλο Χωριό) is situated on the northern part of Tilos, and Megisti is located on the north coast of Kastellorizo.

Metropolitans of Symi
(Metropolitan of Kyklades in 1924, Metropolitans of Symi since 2004)

1. Germanus	Γερμανός	5 Feb 1924 – 9 Oct 1924	1870-1941
Anastasiadis (ex m.Sisanion) (to m.Langada)			
2. Chrysostom	Χρυσόστομος	20 Apr 2004 –	b. 1944
Dimitriadis (ex t.b.Pamphilos 8 Nov 1980)			

A NOTE ON THE PATRIARCHAL EXARCHATE OF PATMOS
ΠΑΤΡΙΑΡΧΙΚΗ ΕΞΑΡΧΙΑ ΠΑΤΜΟΥ

The island of Patmos (Grk Πάτμος, with an area of 34 km²), located 20 km northwest of Leros in the southwestern Aegean Sea, is the location where St. John the Divine wrote the Book of Revelation (Grk Αποκάλυψις). Patmos came under Roman control in 146 BC, its area being under the jurisdiction of the Metropolitanate of Rhodes after 325 AD. However, by the eleventh century, Patmos was uninhabited. In April 1088 Emperor Alexius I Comnenus (1081-1118) issued an edict for the establishment of an autonomous monastery on Patmos, having under its jursidiction the nearby islands and islets.

Patmos was occupied by Venetians in 1207, the Knights of Rhodes in 1309, and the Ottoman Turks in 1537. In July 1715 the ecclesiastic self-government of Patmos and its nearby islands was secured by the declaration of a Patriarchal Exarchate in the area, the Patriarchal Exarch being always the Abbot of St. John Monastery.

In 1822 Patmos became part of the new Greek state, but reverted to Turkish control on July 9, 1832. On April 30, 1912 the island was occupied by Italy, in November 1943 by the Germans, on May 9, 1945 by the British, and on March 31, 1947 by Greece. Patmos officially became part of Greece on March 7, 1948.

The Patriarchal Exarchate of Patmos is bordered by the Metropolitanate of Samos on the north, the Metropolitanate of Anea (Asia Minor) on the east, the Metropolitanate of Leros on the south (Leros Island), and the Metropolitanate of Paronaxia (Church of Greece) on the west (Naxos Island).

The island of Lipsi (Grk Ληψοί), situated 10 km east of Patmos, has an area of 16 km². The island of Agathonisi (Grk Αγαθονήσι), situated 20 km northeast of Lipsi, has an area of 14 km². The island of Levitha (Grk Λεβίθα), situated 30 km south of Kalymnos has an area of 11 km². The island of Arki (Grk Αρκοί), situated 4 km north of Lipsi has an area of 7 km². The island of Kinaros (Grk Κίναρος), situated 10 km west of Levitha has an area of 5 km². The island of Pharmakonisi (Grk Φαρμακονήσι), situated 25 km east of Lipsi, has an area of 5 km². In 1918 the island group of Fourni (Grk Φούρνοι, situated 15 km north of Patmos), which was under Greek occupation, was transferred to the Metropolitanate of Samos.

Patmos is the only remaining Exarchate of the Ecumenical Patriarchate after the abolishment of Epirus's Metsovon Exarchate on October 7, 1924. A concise list of the Abbots/Exarchs is included in Appendix A.

SECTION H:
THE SEMI-AUTONOMOUS CHURCH OF CRETE

ARCHDIOCESE OF KRITI
ΑΡΧΙΕΠΙΣΚΟΠΗ ΚΡΗΤΗΣ

Archbishop of Crete, most honorable and Exarch of Europe

The island of Kriti (Crete, Grk Κρήτη), with an area of 8,261 km², is located 100 km southeast of the Peloponnese region and 150 km southwest of Rhodes Island. It came under Roman control in 69 BC, was occupied by the Arabs in 826, recovered by the Romans in 961 (Iraklion was occupied on March 7, 961), occupied by the Genovese in 1206, and the Venetians in 1211. The Ottoman Turks occupied the island after a twenty-four-year effort, starting with the occupation of Chania on August 22, 1645 and the occupation of Rethymnon on November 13, 1646, and ending with the occupation of Iraklion (Candia) on September 27, 1669. After the Greek revolution of 1821 spread to the island of Kriti, the Ottoman authorities executed its Orthodox hierarchy (June 1821). The Ecumenical Patriarchate elected new hierarchs, and after a new insurrection, the Sultan granted self-government under Ottoman suzerainty on December 9, 1898. The island was annexed by Greece on December 1, 1913. German forces occupied it on May 30, 1941, remaining there until May 8, 1945.

The Metropolitanate of Gortyna (Grk Γόρτυνα, the capital city of the Roman Province of Crete) was established in 325 AD. Initially under the honorary primacy of the Metropolitanate of Thessalonica, it became an Archdiocese of the Patriarchate of Rome in 535, and a Metropolitanate of the Patriarchate of Constantinople in 733. There were nine Dioceses under the Metropolitanate's jurisdiction in the third century, increasing to eleven by the eighth century,[1] but they were abolished after the Arab occupation, during which the Metropolitan could not live on the island. When the Byzantines recovered the island, the Dioceses were re-established and the Metropolitanate's See, although initially remaining in Gortyna, was soon moved to Iraklion (Grk Ηράκλειον), a city on the island's north coast, rebuilt by the Arabs to serve as their capital. During this time the title "Metropolitanate of Kriti" prevailed over the old style "Metropolitanate of Gortyna."

Gortyna, the island's primary city, served as the Romans' last stand during the Arab invasion and was devastated after its fall. It never recovered its former glory, and was finally abandoned during the Venetian period. Its ruins can be seen today near the town of Agïi Deka (Grk Άγιοι Δέκα), 35 km southwest of Iraklion, inside the area of the present Metropolitanate of Gortyna and Arkadia.

Iraklion, known as Iraklia (Grk Ηράκλεια) or Iraklioupolis (Grk Ηρακλειούπολις) during the first Roman period, probably became a Diocese under the jurisdiction of the Metropolitanate of Gortyna in 325 AD, but was abolished after the Arab occupation. During the Byzantine period the Romans used a Hellenized version of the Arab name for their capital city, Chandax (Grk Χάνδαξ), which became Candia (Grk Κάνδια) under the Venetians. The city was officially renamed Iraklion after the island became part of Greece.

During the Venetian occupation, all the Orthodox Dioceses were replaced by Roman Catholic ones, although at times an Orthodox Bishop was allowed to be installed in one of the island's Dioceses. The Ecumenical Patriarchate continued to elect Cretan Metropolitans, although they could not reside on the island. When the Ottomans occupied most of the island in 1646, eleven Orthodox Dioceses were re-established, their number being reduced to seven in 1831. On September 25, 1962 all seven Dioceses were promoted to Metropolitanates, to which an eighth Metropolitanate was added in 2001. On October 14, 1900 the government of the Cretan State reached an agreement with the Ecumenical Patriarchate, granting semi-autonomous status to the island's Orthodox Church, with its Metropolitan being elected by the Patriarch from a list of three candidates supplied by the island's political authorities. On February 28, 1967 the Metropolitanate of Kriti was promoted to an Archdiocese.

The Archdiocese's immediate area underwent many changes during the last two centuries. On November 24, 1831 the Diocese of Knossos was abolished, and its area integrated to the Metropolitanate of Kriti, and in July 1845 the same thing happened with the Diocese of Lampi. However, the Diocese of Lampi was re-established on May 22, 1863. In August 1900 the Diocese of Cherronisos was abolished, its area being integrated with that of the Metropolitanate of Kriti, and on December 20, 1900 the northern area of Gortyna was ceded to the Diocese of Arkadia (later the Diocese of Gortyna and Arkadia). Finally, on January 20, 2001, areas of the Archdiocese were ceded to the new Metropolitanate of Arkalochorion, and on March 15, 2001 additional areas were ceded to the neighboring Metropolitanates of Gortyna and Petra.

The area of the Archdiocese is bordered by the Sea of Crete on the north, the Metropolitanate of Petra and the Metropolitanate of Arkalochorion on the east, the Metropolitanate of Arkalochorion and the Metropolitanate of Gortyna on the south, and the Metropolitanate of Rethymnon on the west. The island of Dia (Grk Δία), located 12 km northeast of Iraklion, is also under the jurisdiction of the Archdiocese.

The western part of the Archdiocese's present area belonged during the fifth century to the Diocese of Apollonias (Grk Απολλωνιάς), a seaside city whose ruins are located near the village of Agia Pelagia (Grk Αγία Πελαγία), 15 km northwest of Iraklion.

1. Some scholars have been misled by the list of twenty-two Cretan cities in Hierocles' Synecdemus into assuming that there were twenty-two dioceses on the island. However, it has been demonstrated that Hierocles only documents the political divisions of the Roman Empire, not the ecclesiastic ones.

Hierarchs of Kriti since 1800
(Metropolitans until 28 Feb 1967, Archbishops afterwards)

59. Maximus Progiannakopoulos	Μάξιμος	*19 May* 1786 – 4 May 1800+	d. 1800
60. Gerasimus IV Pardalis, executed by the Ottomans	Γεράσιμος Δ'	*25 May* 1800 – 24 Jun 1821++	d. 1821
61. Callinicus III see note 1	Καλλίνικος Γ'	*Mar* 1823 – 24 Aug 1830+	d. 1830
62. Meletius I Nikoletakis (ex b.Sitia)	Μελέτιος Α'	28 Jan 1831 – 20 Jul 1839+	1801-1839
63. Porphyrius Fotiadis (ex m.Mytilini) resigned, 9 Feb 1852+	Πορφύριος	Aug 1839 – 9 Sep 1839	d. 1852
64. Callinicus IV Chougias (ex m.Mesimvria) resigned	Καλλίνικος Δ'	Sep 1839 – 12 Feb 1842	d≥1844

65. Callinicus V	Καλλίνικος Ε'		1 Mar 1842 – Dec 1843	d. 1845
Kaloutzos (ex former m.Rhodes) resigned, 7 Apr 1845+				
66. Chrysanthus	Χρύσανθος		Dec 1843 – 24 Aug 1850	d. 1869
(ex former m.Smyrni) (to m.Philippoupolis)				
67. Sophronius I	Σωφρόνιος Α'		24 Aug 1850 – 14 Dec 1850	d. 1855
(ex m.Ainos) resigned (to former, to m.Ainos)				
68. Dionysius I	Διονύσιος Α'		17 Dec 1850 – 28 Aug 1856	d. 1860
(ex m.Preslava) (to m.Vosna)				
69. Johnnicius	Ιωαννίκιος		28 Aug 1856 – 16 Jul 1858+	d. 1858
Zangos (ex former m.Ioannina)				
70. Dionysius II	Διονύσιος Β'		27 Jul 1858 – 16 Nov 1868	1820-1891
Charitonidis (to m.Didymotichon)				
71. Meletius II	Μελέτιος Β'	(1st time)	16 Nov 1868 – 23 Nov 1874	1817-1882
Kavasilas (ex m.Didymotichon) (to m.Didymotichon)				
72. Sophronius II	Σωφρόνιος Β'		23 Nov 1874 – 9 Jun 1877	d. 1890
Christidis (ex m.Didymotichon) (to m.Didymotichon)				
---. Meletius II	Μελέτιος Β'	(2nd time)	9 Jun 1877 – 13 Aug 1882+	1817-1882
Kavasilas (ex m.Didymotichon)				
73. Timothy I	Τιμόθεος Α'		19 Sep 1882 – 18 Feb 1897+	1841-1897
Kastrinogiannakis (ex b.Cherronisos)				
74. Eumenius II	Ευμένιος Β'		12 May 1898 – 1 Apr 1920+	1850-1920
Xiroudakis (ex b.Lampi)				
75. Titus II	Τίτος Β'		22 Feb 1922 – 25 Apr 1933+	1859-1933
Zografidis (ex b.Petra)				
76. Timothy II	Τιμόθεος Β'		22 Jul 1933 – 3 Jan 1941	1876-1941
Venieris (ex b.Rethymnon) suspended, Aug 1941+				
77. Basil V	Βασίλειος Ε'		8 Apr 1941 – Jan 1950+	1872-1950
Markakis (ex b.Arkadia) exiled to Athens 26 Mar 1942 to Feb 1945				
78. Eugene	Ευγένιος		23 May 1950 – 7 Feb 1978+	1912-1978
Psalidakis (ex b.Arkadia) promoted to Archbishop 28 Feb 1967				
79. Timothy III	Τιμόθεος Γ'		10 Mar 1978 – 26 Jul 2006+	1915-2006
Papoutsakis (ex m.Gortyna)				
80. Irenaeus	Ειρηναίος		30 Aug 2006 –	b. 1933
Athanasiadis (ex m.Kydonia)				

1. In 1823 Archimandrite Methodius Sapountzakis was elected Metropolitan, but he did not accept the position and his election was cancelled. Methodius was subsequently elected Metropolitan of Veria.

A NOTE ON THE FORMER DIOCESE OF KNOSSOS

The city of Knossos (Grk Κνωσσός), located 5 km southeast of Iraklion, was the second in importance on the island during the Roman times. It became a Diocese under the jurisdiction of the Metropolitan of Gortyna in 325 AD, and was re-established after the Roman reconquest of the island and after the Ottoman occupation of the island. The Diocese of Knossos was abolished unofficially in 1823 and officially on November 24, 1831, being annexed to the area of the Metropolitanate of Kriti. The See of the Diocese during the Ottoman times was in the town of Agios Myron (Grk Άγιος Μύρων), located 15 km southwest of Iraklion.

Bishops of Knossos since 1800

12. Gerasimus II	Γεράσιμος Β'	Dec 1782 – 5 Apr 1819+	d. 1819
13. Neophytus	Νεόφυτος	*1 May* 1819 – 24 June 1821++	d. 1821
Fyntikakis, executed by the Ottomans			

METROPOLITANATE OF ARKALOCHORION, KASTELION, AND VIANNOS
ΜΗΤΡΟΠΟΛΙΣ ΑΡΚΑΛΟΧΩΡΙΟΥ, ΚΑΣΤΕΛΛΙΟΥ ΚΑΙ ΒΙΑΝΝΟΥ

Metropolitan of Arcalochorion, Castelion and Biannus,
most honorable and Exarch of Pediada

The Metropolitanate of Arkalochorion was established on January 20, 2001, from areas separated from the Archdiocese of Kriti, the Metropolitanate of Gortyna, and the Metropolitanate of Petra. Its See is in the town of Arkalochorion (Grk Αρκαλοχώριον), located 25 km southeast of Iraklion. The town of Kastelion (Grk Καστέλιον) is located 12 km northeast of Arkalochorion, and the town of Viannos (Grk Βιάννος) is located 25 km southeast of Arkalochorion. The Metropolitanate of Arkalochorion, Kastelion and Viannos is bordered by the area of the Archdiocese of Kriti on the north, the Metropolitanate of Petra and the Metropolitanate of Ierapytna on the east, the Mediterranean Sea on the south, and the Metropolitanate of Gortyna and the Archdiocese of Kriti on the west.

Metropolitans of Arkalochorion, Kastelion and Viannos

1. Andrew	Ανδρέας	3 Nov 2001 –	b. 1957
Nanakis			

METROPOLITANATE OF GORTYNA AND ARKADIA
ΜΗΤΡΟΠΟΛΙΣ ΓΟΡΤΥΝΗΣ ΚΑΙ ΑΡΚΑΔΙΑΣ

Metropolitan of Gortyna and Arcadia, most honorable and Exarch of Central Crete

The city of Arkadia (Grk Αρκαδία) existed on the island of Crete during Roman times, near the present village of Afration (Grk Αφράτιον, located 40 km southeast of Iraklion), which is today inside the Metropolitanate of Arkalochorion. Arkadia became a Diocese under the jurisdiction of the Metropolitan of Gortyna, possibly during the sixth century (and certainly before 731 AD). Abolished twice by the Arabs and the Venetians, it was re-established after the Roman reconquest of the island, and again after the Ottoman occupation of the island.

On December 20, 1900, it gave the area of Viannos to the Diocese of Petra, and gained the northern region of Gortyna from the Metropolitanate of Kriti. On March 16, 1961, its name changed to the Diocese of Gortyna and Arkadia, and on September 25, 1962 it was promoted to a Metropolitanate (see also the section for the Archdiocese of Kriti). The See of the Metropolitanate was in the town of Agii Deka (Grk Άγιοι Δέκα), located 35 km southwest of Iraklion, until in March 1946 it moved to the town of Mires (Grk Μοίρες), located 50 km southwest of Iraklion, where it still remains.

The Metropolitanate of Gortyna and Arkadia is bordered by the Metropolitanate of Rethymnon and the area of the Archdiocese of Kriti on the north, the Metropolitanate of Arkalochorion on the east, the Mediterranean Sea on the south, and the Metropolitanate of Lampi on the west.

Hierarchs of Gortyna and Arkadia since 1800
(Bishops of Arkadia until 16 Mar 1961, Metropolitans after 25 Sep 1962)

10. Gerasimus resigned	Γεράσιμος	before 1793 – 20 Jun 1803	d. ?
11. Theophylactus (ex b.Sitia)	Θεοφύλακτος	20 Jun 1803 – 20 Aug 1809+	d. 1809
12. Neophytus *Locum Tenens* of the Metropolitanate from Jul 1821	Νεόφυτος	22 Aug 1809 – 6 May 1823+	d. 1823
13. Maximus Sivianos	Μάξιμος	1825 – 20 Oct 1844+	d. 1844
14. Joachim Skalaniotis	Ιωακείμ	15 Jan 1845 – 28 Dec 1854+	d. 1854
15. Gregory Smyrnios	Γρηγόριος	20 Mar 1855 – 25 Jun 1877+	d. 1877
16. Nicephorus Zachariadis (to b.Kydonia)	Νικηφόρος	4 Feb 1879 – Apr 1887	1835-1913
17. Nicodemus Katsarakis	Νικόδημος	26 Apr 1887 – 12 Dec 1900+	d. 1900
18. Basil Markakis (to m.Kriti)	Βασίλειος	30 Jun 1902 – 8 Apr 1941	1872-1950
19. Eugene Psalidakis (to m.Kriti)	Ευγένιος	20 Jan 1946 – 23 May 1950	1912-1978
20. Timothy Papoutsakis (to a.Kriti) promoted to Metropolitan 25 Sep 1962	Τιμόθεος	26 Aug 1956 – 10 Mar 1978	1915-2006
21. Cyril III Kypriotakis (ex m.Kissamos)	Κύριλλος Γ'	1979 – 24 Apr 2005+	1932-2005
22. Macarius Douloufakis (ex t.b.Knossos 8 Oct 2000)	Μακάριος	26 May 2005 –	b. 1961

METROPOLITANATE OF IERAPYTNA AND SITIA
ΜΗΤΡΟΠΟΛΙΣ ΙΕΡΑΠΥΤΝΗΣ ΚΑΙ ΣΗΤΕΙΑΣ

Metropolitan of Ierapytna and Setia, most honorable and Exarch of Eastern Crete

The city of Ierapetra (Grk Ιεράπετρα), situated on the south coast of Crete, 75 km southeast of Iraklion, was called Ierapytna (Grk Ιεράπυτνα) during Roman times. Ierapytna probably became a Diocese under the jurisdiction of the Metropolitan of Gortyna in 325 AD. Abolished by the Arabs, it was re-established after the Roman reconquest of the island as the Diocese of Iera Petra, suppressed by the Venetians, and then re-established again after the Ottoman occupation as the Diocese of Iera.

On November 24, 1831 it was united with the Diocese of Sitia, creating the Diocese of Iera and Sitia (alternatively called Diocese of Ierositia). In 1932 it was annexed to the Diocese of Petra, creating the Diocese of Neapolis, but on October 24, 1935 it was re-established. On March 16, 1961 its name changed to the Diocese of Ierapytna and Sitia, and on September 25, 1962 it was promoted to a Metropolitanate. The See of the Metropolitanate remains in the city of Ierapetra.

The Metropolitanate of Ierapytna and Sitia is bordered by Metropolitanate of Petra and the Sea of Crete on the north, the Mediterranean Sea on the east and south, and the Metropolitanate of Arkalochorion on the west.

Hierarchs of Ierapytna and Sitia since 1800
(Bishops of Iera until 24 Nov 1831, Bishops of Iera and Sitia until 16 Mar 1961, Metropolitans after 25 Sep 1962)

11. Gideon	Γεδεών	1790/93 – 8 Oct 1810+	d. 1810
12. Artemius	Αρτέμιος	16 Oct 1810 – Jun 1827	d. 1858
Pardalakis, in exile from 1821 (to m.Kestentilion)			
13. Gerasimus	Γεράσιμος	1831 – 1841+	d. 1841
14. Callinicus	Καλλίνικος	*Oct* 1841 – 1845+	d. 1845
15. Hilarion	Ιλαρίων	27 Jan 1846 – 10 May 1869	1808-1884
Katsoulis (to b.Rethymnon)			
16. Neophytus	Νεόφυτος	*10 May* 1869 – Feb 1878	d. 1898
Kalogeridis, suspended (to former to b.Metres)			
17. Misael	Μισαήλ	Jan 1879 – Oct 1879	d. 1900
Stratigakis (ex former b.Kissamos) suspended (to former, to b.Thavmakos)			
18. Gregory	Γρηγόριος	10 Feb 1880 – 9 Oct 1889+	1812-1889
Papadopetrakis			
19. Ambrose	Αμβρόσιος	28 Jan 1890 – 5 Jan 1929+	1856-1929
Sfakianakis			
20. Philotheus II	Φιλόθεος Β'	1 Jun 1936 – 6 Sep 1960+	1892-1960
Mazokopakis			
21. Philotheus III	Φιλόθεος Γ'	2 Jul 1961 – 15 Dec 1993+	1927-1993
Vouzounerakis, promoted to Metropolitan 25 Sep 1962			
22. Eugene	Ευγένιος	26 Jun 1994 –	b. 1952
Politis			

A NOTE ON THE FORMER DIOCESE OF SITIA

The city of Sitia (Grk Σητεία), situated on the north coast of Crete, 45 km northeast of Ierapetra, became a Diocese under the jurisdiction of the Metropolitan of Gortyna, possibly during the sixth century (and certainly before 731 AD). It was re-established after the Roman reconquest of the island and the Ottoman occupation of the island, and was abolished on November 24, 1831, being annexed to the Diocese of Iera, thereafter known as the Diocese of Iera and Sitia (or Ierositia).

Bishops of Sitia since 1800

9. Theophylactus	Θεοφύλακτος	1785?- 20 Jun 1803	d. 1809
(to b.Arkadia)			
10. Zacharias	Ζαχαρίας	21 Jun 1803 – 24 Jun 1821++	d. 1821
executed by the Ottomans			
11. Meletius	Μελέτιος	4 Jul 1826 – 28 Jan 1831	1801-1839
Nikoletakis (to m.Kriti)			

METROPOLITANATE OF KISSAMOS AND SELINON
ΜΗΤΡΟΠΟΛΙΣ ΚΙΣΑΜΟΥ ΚΑΙ ΣΕΛΙΝΟΥ

Metropolitan of Cissamus and Selinon, most honorable and Exarch of Western Crete

The city of Kissamos (Grk Κίσσαμος), situated on the north coast of Crete, 35 km west of Chania, probably became a Diocese under the jurisdiction of the Metropolitan of Gortyna in 325 AD. Abolished twice by the Arabs and the Venetians, it was re-established after the Roman reconquest of the island, and again after the Ottoman occupation.

On November 24, 1831 it was annexed to the Diocese of Kydonia, creating the Diocese of Kydonia and Kissamos. In February 1860 it was re-established as the Diocese of Kissamos and Selinon (Grk Σέλινον, the southern area of the Diocese), and on September 25, 1962 it was promoted to a Metropolitanate. The See of the Metropolitanate remains in the city of Kissamos (called Kastellion, Grk Καστέλλιον, until 1971). The island of Gavdos (Grk Γαύδος, located 35 km south of Crete, having an area of 30 km²) is also under the jurisdiction of the Metropolitanate.

In the area of Selinon is the city of Kantanos (Grk Κάντανος), located 30 km southeast of Kissamos, which became a Diocese under the Metropolitanate of Gortyna in the fourth centurury, and was abolished after the city was destroyed during the Arab occupation. Rebuild during the Ottoman occupation, Kantanos was razed to the ground by occupying Nazi forces on May 24, 1941, who also executed its entire population.

The Metropolitanate of Kissamos and Silinon is bordered by the Sea of Crete on the north, the Metropolitanate of Kydonia and the Metropolitanate of Lampi on the east, and the Mediterranean Sea on the south and west.

Hierarchs of Kissamos and Selinon since 1800
(Bishops of Kissamos until 24 Nov 1831, Metropolitans after 25 Sep 1962)

13. Joasaph resigned	Ιωάσαφ	1790/92 – 1808	d. ?
14. Seraphim	Σεραφείμ	1808 – 17 Nov 1817+	d. 1817
15. Melchisedek Despotakis, executed by the Ottomans	Μελχισεδέκ	*Jan* 1818 – 15 Jun 1821++	d. 1821
16. Gerasimus IV Stratigakis, suspended, 8 Jun 1886+	Γεράσιμος Δ'	*14 Apr* 1860 – 1868	d. 1886
17. Misael Stratigakis, suspended (to former, to b.Ierositia)	Μισαήλ	30 Jun 1869 – 1874	d. 1900
18. Panaretus (ex t.b.Rymni *14 Apr 1850*) see note 1	Πανάρετος	26 Jun 1875 – 1880+	d. 1880
19. Parthenius III Bitsakis (to b.Kampania)	Παρθένιος Γ'	22 Jan 1887 – 21 Jul 1892	d. 1911
20. Dorotheus Klonaris	Δωρόθεος	7 Mar 1893 – 12 Dec 1902+	1854-1902
20. Anthimus II Leledakis	Άνθιμος Β'	20 Jul 1903 – 17 Aug 1935+	1860-1935
21. Chrysostom Angelidakis	Χρυσόστομος	*28 Jan* 1936 – 13 Jun 1937+	1892-1937
22. Eudocimus Syngelakis, exiled to Athens 21 Nov 1941 to 10 Feb 1945	Ευδόκιμος	Mar 1938 – 8 Aug 1956+	1885-1956

23. Irenaeus	Ειρηναίος	(1st time)	8 Dec 1957 – 16 Dec 1971	b. 1911
Galanakis (to m.Germany)				
24. Cyril	Κύριλλος		16 Feb 1975 – 1979	1932-2005
Kypriotakis (to m.Gortyna)				
25. Nectarius	Νεκτάριος		3 Aug 1980 – 16 Sep 1980	b. 1932
Chatzimichalis (to m.Karpathos)				
---. Irenaeus	Ειρηναίος	(2nd time)	26 Jan 1981 – 24 Aug 2005	b. 1911
Galanakis (ex former m.Germany) resigned				
27. Amphilochius	Αμφιλόχιος		8 Oct 2005 –	b. 1964
Andronikakis				

1. In November 1880 archimandrite Parthenius Kelaïdis (1830-1905) was elected Bishop, but he resigned in December 1882 without ever being consecrated.

METROPOLITANATE OF KYDONIA AND APOKORONON
ΜΗΤΡΟΠΟΛΙΣ ΚΥΔΩΝΙΑΣ ΚΑΙ ΑΠΟΚΟΡΩΝΟΥ

Metropolitan of Cydonia and Apocoronum, most honorable
and Exarch of Cretan and Myrtoan Sea

The city of Chania (Grk Χανιά), situated on the north coast of Crete, 50 km northwest of Rethymnon, was called Kydonia (Grk Κυδωνία) during Roman times. Kydonia probably became a Diocese under the jurisdiction of the Metropolitan of Gortyna in 325 AD. Abolished by the Arabs after 826, it was re-established after the Roman reconquest of the island, with its See moved 10 km southwest to the town of Agia (Grk Αγιά). Having been renamed Diocese of Agia by the twelfth century, it was suppressed by the Venetians after 1211, and was re-established after the Ottoman occupation of 1645 as the Diocese of Kydonia, with its See returned to Chania.

On November 24, 1831 it annexed the Diocese of Kissamos, becoming the Diocese of Kydonia and Kissamos. In February 1860 the Diocese of Kissamos was re-established, the Diocese of Kydonia being renamed Diocese of Kydonia and Apokoronon (Grk Αποκόρωνον, the area to the east of Chania, taking its name from the ancient city of Ippokoronion, Grk Ιπποκορώνιον), and on September 25, 1962 it was promoted to a Metropolitanate. The See of the Metropolitanate remains in the city of Chania.

The Metropolitanate of Kydonia and Apokoronon is bordered by the Sea of Crete on the north, the Metropolitanate of Rethymnon on the east, the Metropolitanate of Lampi on the south, and the Metropolitanate of Kissamos on the west.

Hierarchs of Kydonia and Apokoronon since 1800
(Bishops of Kydonia until 24 Nov 1831, Metropolitans after 25 Sep 1962)

16. Gerasimus	Γεράσιμος	Mar 1780 – 30 Jan 1815+	d. 1815
17. Callinicus II	Καλλίνικος Β'	3 Apr 1815 – 1822++	d. 1822
Sarpakis, imprisoned from Jun 1821, died in prison after 10 Jul 1822			
18. Artemius	Αρτέμιος	8 Nov 1831 – 1846+	d. 1846
Bishop of Kydonia and Kissamos after 24 Nov 1831			
19. Callistus	Κάλλιστος	23 Jun 1846 – 15 May 1858++	d. 1858
Fyntakidis, Bishop of Kydonia and Kissamos, see note 1			
20. Misael	Μισαήλ	Jan 1859 – 18 Apr 1869+	d. 1869
Marmarakis/Ioannidis, Bishop of Kydonia and Kissamos until Feb 1860			

21. Gabriel Grigorakis	Γαβριήλ	29 Jun 1869 – 4 Sep 1880+	d. 1880
22. Hierotheus Praoudakis/Bragoudakis (to b.Rethymnon)	Ιερόθεος	25 Mar 1881 – 20 Dec 1882	1836-1896
23. Nicephorus I Zachariadis (ex b.Arkadia) resigned, 24 Jul 1913+	Νικηφόρος Α΄	Apr 1887 – Apr 1912	1835-1913
24. Agathangelus I Nikolakis	Αγαθάγγελος Α΄	23 May 1912 – 7 Jun 1935+	1871-1935
25. Agathangelus II Xirouchakis	Αγαθάγγελος Β΄	1 Mar 1936 – 24 Feb 1958+	1872-1958
26. Nicephorus II Sytzanakis, resigned, 18 Jul 1975+	Νικηφόρος Β΄	29 Mar 1959 – 1974	1894-1975
27. Irenaeus Athanasiadis (to a.Kriti)	Ειρηναίος	23 Feb 1975 – 30 Aug 2006	b. 1933
28. Damascenus Papagiannakis	Δαμασκηνός	18 Nov 2006 –	b. 1958

1. Bishop Callistus was pressured by the Ottoman authorities to sign a declaration condemning the Cretan insurrection of 1858, but he strongly refused to do so. When they attempted to make him sign the declaration by force, he collapsed and shortly thereafter expired.

METROPOLITANATE OF LAMPI, SYVRITOS, AND SPHAKIA
ΜΗΤΡΟΠΟΛΙΣ ΛΑΜΠΗΣ, ΣΥΒΡΙΤΟΥ ΚΑΙ ΣΦΑΚΙΩΝ

Metropolitan of Lambi, Sybritus and Sphacia, most honorable and Exarch of Southern Crete

The town of Argyroupolis (Grk Αργυρούπολις), located 20 km southwest of Rethymnon, was called Lampi (Grk Λάμπη) or Lappa (Grk Λάππα) during Roman times. Lampi became a Diocese under the jurisdiction of the Metropolitan of Gortyna in the fourth century. Abolished by the Arabs after 826, it was re-established after the Roman reconquest of the island, with its See moved 5 km north to the town of Kalamon (Grk Καλαμών, today called Episkopi, Grk Επισκοπή). Having been renamed Diocese of Kalamon before 1170, it was suppressed by the Venetians after 1211, but was re-established after the Ottoman occupation of 1646 as the Diocese of Lampi, with its See moved 28 km southeast to the village of Lampini (Grk Λαμπηνή).

In 1831 the territory of Sfakia (Grk Σφακιά) was attached to the Diocese of Lampi, which came informally to be called Diocese of Lampi and Sfakia. In the same year the Diocese's See was moved to the Monastery of Preveli (Grk Πρέβελη), located near the village Gianniou (Grk Γιαννιού), 15 km south of Lampini. However, the Diocese of Lampi was abolished on July 12, 1845, its area being annexed to the Metropolitanate of Kriti. On May 22, 1863 the Diocese of Lampi was re-established, again informally styled Diocese of Lampi and Sfakia (Bishop Païsios signing with both titles in 1870).

In 1886 the See of the Diocese was moved 18 km east to the Monastery of Agion Pnevma (Holy Ghost, Grk Άγιον Πνεύμα), located near the village Kissos (Grk Κισσός), and in 1900 it was moved again 22 km northeast to the Monastery of Asomaton (Grk Ασωμάτων), near the village of Monastirakion (Grk Μοναστηράκιον). The name of the Diocese officially changed to Lampi and Sfakia on December 20, 1900.

In 1932 the Diocese was abolished, its area being annexed to the Diocese of Rethymnon, but on October 24, 1935 it was re-established, with its See relocated 18 km west to the town of Spilion (Grk Σπήλιον), where it still remains (Spilion is just 2 km southeast of the village of Lampini). The Diocese was promoted to a Metropolitanate on

September 25, 1962 and its name changed to "Lampi, Syvritos, and Sfakia" on December 4, 2000.

The western part of the Diocese is the area of Sfakia, corresponding to the former Diocese of Phiniki (Grk Φοινίκη), a city on Crete's south coast near the present village of Loutra (Grk Λουτρά), 50 km west of Spilion. This Diocese existed during the eighth century. The eastern part of the Diocese corresponds to the area of the former Diocese of Syvritos (Grk Σύβριτος, today Thronos, Grk Θρόνος, a village 7 km north of Monastirakion), established before 451 AD and abolished after the Arab occupation of 826. Indeed, in 1646 the Diocese of Lampi was re-established in the area of the historic Diocese of Syvritos, while the area of the historic Diocese of Lampi became part of the Diocese of Agrion, later renamed Diocese of Rethymnon, under whose jurisdiction the aforementioned towns of Argyroupolis and Episkopi remain today.

The Metropolitanate of Lampi, Syvritos, and Sfakia is bordered by the Metropolitanate of Kydonia and the Metropolitanate of Rethymnon on the north, the Metropolitanate of Gortyna on the east, the Mediterranean Sea on the south, and the Metropolitanate of Kissamos on the west.

Hierarchs of Lampi, Syvritos, and Sfakia since 1800
(Bishops of Lampi until 1831, Bishops of Lampi and Sfakia afterwards,
Metropolitans after 25 Sep 1962)

11. Hierotheus executed by the Ottomans	Ιερόθεος	1793/5 – 24 Jun 1821++	d. 1821
12. Nicodemus Soumpasakis	Νικόδημος	2 Feb 1832 – 17 Jun 1845+	d. 1845
13. Païsius Pergaminos/Kirpas	Παΐσιος	22 May 1863 – 8 Feb 1883+	1808-1883
14. Eumenius I Xiroudakis (to m.Kriti)	Ευμένιος Α΄	28 Dec 1886 – 12 May 1898	1850-1920
15. Agathangelus Papadakis (ex b.Cherronisos)	Αγαθάγγελος	Aug 1900 – 11 Jun 1928+	1859-1928
16. Eumenius II Fanourakis	Ευμένιος Β΄	10 May 1936 – 2 Jan 1956+	1887-1956
17. Isidore Rousochatzakis	Ισίδωρος	25 Aug 1956 – 17 Oct 1968+	1905-1968
18. Theodore Tzedakis (to m.Rethymnon)	Θεόδωρος	17 Feb 1975 – 6 Oct 1987	1933-1996
19. Irenaeus Mesarchakis	Ειρηναίος	22 Feb 1990 –	b. 1944

METROPOLITANATE OF PETRA AND CHERRONISOS
ΜΗΤΡΟΠΟΛΙΣ ΠΕΤΡΑΣ ΚΑΙ ΧΕΡΡΟΝΗΣΟΥ

Metropolitan of Petra and Cherronesus, most honorable and Exarch of Carpathian Sea

The Diocese of Petra (Grk Πέτρα), situated on the north coast of Crete, 45 km northeast of Ierapetra, was established by division of the Diocese of Ierapetra after the Roman reconquest of 961. Abolished by the Venetians, it was re-established after the Ottoman occupation of the island. On December 20, 1900 the Viannos area of the Diocese of Arkadia was annexed to the Diocese of Petra, but on January 20, 2001, it became part of the newly established Metropolitanate of Arkalochorion.

During the Ottoman occupation, the See of the Diocese remained in the Monastery of Aretios (Grk Αρέτιος), located near the village of Karydion (Grk Καρύδιον), 55 km east of Iraklion, and for brief periods to the village of Epano Chorion (Grk Επάνω Χωριόν), located 5 km south of the Monastery. In 1866 it was moved 10 km southeast of Aretios to the city of Neapolis (Grk Νεάπολις), where it still remains. In 1932 the Diocese of Ierositia was annexed to the Diocese of Petra, whose name changed to Diocese of Neapolis, but on October 24, 1935 the Diocese of Ierositia was re-established, and the historic name of the Diocese of Petra was restored.

The Diocese of Petra was promoted to a Metropolitanate on September 25, 1962, its name being changed to Petra and Cherronisos on December 4, 2000. The eastern part of the former Diocese of Cherronisos (including the town of Chersonisos), until then part of the Archdiocese of Crete, was annexed to the Metropolitanate of Petra on March 15, 2001. The Metropolitanate of Petra and Cherronisos is bordered by the Sea of Crete on the north and east, the Metropolitanate of Ierapytna on the south, the Metropolitanate of Arkalochorion, and the area of the Archdiocese of Kriti on the west.

Hierarchs of Petra and Cherronisos since 1800
(Bishops of Petra until 4 Dec 2000, Bishop of Neapolis 1932-24 Oct 1935,
Metropolitans after 25 Sep 1962)

7. Joachim	Ιωακείμ	. . . – 25 Jun 1821++	d. 1821
Klontzas, executed by the Ottomans			
8. Dorotheus	Δωρόθεος	Jan 1825 – 25 Jul 1855	d. 1857
Diamantidis, resigned, 29 Nov 1857+			
9. Meletius II	Μελέτιος Β'	27 Jul 1855 – 2 Aug 1889+	1815-1889
Chlapoutakis			
10. Titus	Τίτος	22 Dec 1889 – 22 Feb 1922	1859-1933
Zografidis (to m.Kriti)			
11. Dionysius	Διονύσιος	Jun 1923 – 10 Feb 1953+	1872-1953
Marangoudakis			
12. Demetrius	Δημήτριος	19 Aug 1956 – 10 Jul 1990+	1921-1990
Bourlakis			
13. Nectarius	Νεκτάριος	6 Oct 1990 –	b. 1951
Papadakis			

A NOTE ON THE FORMER DIOCESE OF CHERRONISOS

The city of Cherronisos (Grk Χερρόνησος), called Limin Chersonisou today (Grk Λιμήν Χερσονήσου), is situated on the north coast of Crete, 25 km east of Iraklion and 22 km northwest of Neapolis. It became a Diocese under the jurisdiction of the Metropolitan of Gortyna before 431 AD. Abolished by the Arabs and the Venetians, it was re-established after the Roman reconquest of the island and the Ottoman occupation of the island, but was abolished on November 24, 1831, being annexed to the area of the Metropolitanate of Kriti.

The Diocese of Cherronisos was re-established on January 17, 1843, only to be abolished and annexed again to area of the Metropolitanate of Kriti in August 1900. Its See during the Ottoman occupation was moved 22 km southwest to the town of Episkopi Pediados (Grk Επισκοπή Πεδιάδος), and in the last part of the Ottoman period to the Monastery of Angarathos (Grk Αγκάραθος), 6 km south of Episkopi.

Bishops of Cherronisos since 1800

11. Gerasimus I Kalognomon (ex b.Sitia)	Γεράσιμος Α'	before 1777 – 29 Apr 1806+	d. 1806
12. Joachim (ex t.b.Dioupolis) executed by the Ottomans	Ιωακείμ	29 Apr 1806 – 24 Jun 1821++	d. 1821
13. Gerasimus II Lasithiotis	Γεράσιμος Β'	8 Jul 1825 – Sep 1829+	d. 1829
14. Meletius resigned, 24 Sep 1872+	Μελέτιος	May 1843 – 11 Jan 1870	d. 1872
15. Timotheus Kastrinogiannakis (to m.Kriti)	Τιμόθεος	20 Jan 1870 – 19 Sep 1882	1841-1897
16. Dionysius Kastrinogiannakis (ex b.Rethymnon) (to b.Rethymnon) brother of Timotheus	Διονύσιος	20 Dec 1882 – 11 Mar 1896	1856-1910
17. Agathangelus Papadakis (to b.Lampi)	Αγαθάγγελος	17 Mar 1896 – Aug 1900	1859-1928

METROPOLITANATE OF RETHYMNON AND AVLOPOTAMOS
ΜΗΤΡΟΠΟΛΙΣ ΡΕΘΥΜΝΗΣ ΚΑΙ ΑΥΛΟΠΟΤΑΜΟΥ

Metropolitan of Rethymnon and Aulopotamus,
most honorable and Exarch of Upper Crete and Cretan Sea

During Roman times the town of Rithymna (Grk Ρίθυμνα, today Rethymnon, Grk Ρέθυμνον, situated on the north coast of Crete, 67 km west of Iraklion) was not large enough to become the See of a Diocese. The western section of the present Metropolitanate of Rethymnon was part of the Diocese of Lampi (modern village of Argyroupolis, located 20 km southwest of Rethymnon); the eastern section was part of the Diocese of Eleftherna (Grk Ελεύθερνα, located 23 km southeast of Rethymnon), while the southern areas were part of the Diocese of Syvritos (Grk Σύβριτος, today Thronos, Grk Θρόνος, a village 24 km southeast of Rethymnon, inside the area of the present Metropolitanate of Lampi). Lampi, Eleftherna, and Syvritos became Dioceses under the jurisdiction of the Metropolitanate of Gortyna, probably in the fourth century, and certainly before 451 AD (Lampi before 431 AD), but were abolished after the Arab occupation of 826.

After the island's Roman reconquest of 961, the Diocese of Lampi was re-established (see the Metropolitanate of Lampi), but the former Diocese of Syvritos was replaced by the new Diocese of Arion (Grk Άριον) or Agrion (Grk Άγριον), today the village of Veran Episkopi (Grk Βεράν Επισκοπή), located 15 km north of Syvritos and 14 km east of Rethymnon; while the former Diocese of Eleftherna was replaced by the new Diocese of Avlopotamos (Grk Αυλοπόταμος) or Mylopotamos (Grk Μυλοπόταμος), today the village of Episkopi Mylopotamou (Grk Επισκοπή Μυλοποτάμου), located 11 km east of Eleftherna.

After 1211 the Venetians abolished the Orthodox Dioceses, although in the 1320s they permitted the establishment of the short-lived Orthodox Diocese of Kalliergipolis (Grk Καλλιεργήπολις) in place of the Diocese of Agrion. After the Ottoman Turks occupied the area in November 1646, the Diocese of Agrion was re-established, with its See moved 14 km westwards to the now important city of Rethymnon. The Diocese of Agrion now included the area formerly under the Diocese of Lampi, while the Diocese of Lampi was re-established in the southern areas, where the Diocese of Syvritos formerly existed.

During the period 1659-71 the name of the Diocese of Agrion changed to Diocese of Rethymnon, and in autumn 1838, after annexing the neighboring Diocese of Avlopotamos, to Diocese of Rethymnon and Avlopotamos. In 1932 the Diocese of Lampi was annexed to the Diocese of Rethymnon and Avlopotamos, its name being changed to Diocese of Rethymnon, but on October 24, 1935 the Diocese of Lampi was re-established, and the name of the Diocese of Rethymnon reverted to its pre-1932 form.

The Diocese of Rethymnon and Avlopotamos was promoted to a Metropolitanate on September 25, 1962. It is bordered by the Sea of Crete on the north, the area of the Archdiocese of Kriti on the east, the Metropolitanate of Gortyni and the Metropolitanate of Lampi on the south, and the Metropolitanate of Kydonia on the west.

Hierarchs of Rethymnon and Avlopotamos since 1800
(Bishops of Rethymnon before 1838, Metropolitans after 25 Sep 1962)

11. Gerasimus II	Γεράσιμος Β΄		1796 – 1822++	d. 1821
Perdikaris/Kontogiannakis, executed by the Ottomans				
12. Johnnicius	Ιωαννίκιος		1827 – 21 Aug 1838	d≥1840
Lazaridis/Lazaropoulos (to m.Ioannina)				
13. Callinicus	Καλλίνικος		autumn 1838 – 2 Aug 1868+	1804-1868
Nikoletakis (ex b.Avlopotamos)				
14. Hilarion	Ιλαρίων		10 May 1869 – Jan 1881	1808-1884
Katsoulis (ex b.Ierositia) resigned, Mar 1884+				
15. Dionysius	Διονύσιος	(1st time)	8 Mar 1881 – 20 Dec 1882	1856-1910
Kastrinogiannakis (to b.Cherronisos)				
16. Hierotheus	Ιερόθεος		20 Dec 1882 – 1896+	1836-1896
Praoudakis/Bragoudakis (ex b.Kydonia)				
---. Dionysius	Διονύσιος	(2nd time)	11 Mar 1896 – 12 Jun 1910+	1856-1910
Kastrinogiannakis (ex b.Cherronisos)				
17. Chrysanthus	Χρύσανθος		*28 Oct* 1910 – 14 Oct 1915+	1863-1915
Tsepetakis				
18. Timothy	Τιμόθεος		28 Mar 1916 – 22 Jul 1933	1876-1941
Venieris (to m.Kriti)				
19. Athanasius II	Αθανάσιος Β΄		16 Feb 1936 – 1 Apr 1968	1892-1981
Apostolakis, resigned, 15 Mar 1981+				
20. Titus	Τίτος		17 May 1970 – 11 Sep 1987+	1929-1987
Silligardakis				
21. Theodore	Θεόδωρος		6 Oct 1987 – 27 Feb 1996+	1933-1996
Tzedakis (ex m.Lampi)				
22. Anthimus II	Άνθιμος Β΄		2 Nov 1996 –	b. 1953
Syrianos				

A NOTE ON THE FORMER DIOCESE OF AVLOPOTAMOS

The Diocese of Eleftherna (Grk Ελεύθερνα, located 23 km southeast of Rethymnon) was established under the jurisdiction of the Metropolitanate of Gortyna before 451 AD, and was abolished after the Arab occupation of 826. After Crete's Roman reconquest of 961, the Diocese of Avlopotamos (Grk Αυλοπόταμος) or Mylopotamos (Grk Μυλοπόταμος), today the village of Episkopi Mylopotamou (Grk Επισκοπή

Μυλοποτάμου, located 27 km east of Rethymnon), was established in place of the former Diocese of Eleftherna.

Abolished in 1211 by the Venetians, the Diocese of Avlopotamos was re-established after the Ottoman Turks occupied the area in November 1646. During the eighteenth century the Diocese's See moved 7 km north to the village of Melidonion (Grk Μελιδόνιον). On October 6, 1779 the area of Sfakia (then under the direct jurisdiction of the Metropolitanate of Kriti, today part of the Metropolitanate of Lampi) was granted for life to the Bishop of Avlopotamos, Parthenius (died 1820), who was named "Bishop of Avlopotamos and Exarch of Sfakia."

In autumn 1838 (probably September), the Diocese of Avlopotamos was annexed to the Diocese of Rethymnon, hence renamed the Diocese of Rethymnon and Avlopotamos.

Bishops of Avlopotamos since 1800

5. Parthenius also Exarch of Sfakia after 6 Oct 1779	Παρθένιος	before 1777 – 1820+	d. 1820
6. Callinicus Nikoletakis (to b.Rethymnon)	Καλλίνικος	2 Feb 1832 – autumn 1838	1804-1868

SECTION I:
METROPOLITANATES IN WESTERN EUROPE

ARCHDIOCESE OF THYATIRA AND GREAT BRITAIN
ΑΡΧΙΕΠΙΣΚΟΠΗ ΘΥΑΤΕΙΡΩΝ ΚΑΙ ΜΕΓΑΛΗΣ ΒΡΕΤΑΝΙΑΣ

Archbishop of Thyatira and Great Britain,
most honorable and Exarch of Western Europe and Ireland

The city of Thyatira (Grk Θυάτειρα, Trk Akhisar, located 85 km northeast of Smyrni) was called Pelopia (Grk Πελόπια) until 290 BC, when the Macedonian-Greek King of Syria Seleucus I renamed it. It came under Roman control in 133 BC, and became a Diocese under the Metropolitanate of Sardis in 325 AD. The city fell to the Ottoman Turks in 1307, and its Diocese was abolished soon thereafter.

The Metropolitanate of Thyatira was re-established in March 24, 1922 with its See in London, having jurisdiction in all Western and Central Europe. It was renamed the Metropolitanate of Thyatira and Great Britain on April 15, 1924, during a short-lived attempt to create a Metropolitanate of Hungary for Central Europe, and was promoted to an Archdiocese in 1954. It reverted to a Metropolitanate on February 5, 1963, a few days before the establishment of the three new Metropolitanates of Austria, Germany, and France (February 17, 1963), with Great Britain, Ireland, Malta, Norway, Sweden, and Iceland remaining under its jurisdiction.

On February 24, 1968 the Metropolitanate was again promoted to an Archdiocese, while on August 12, 1969 the jurisdiction over Sweden, Norway, and Iceland was transferred to the new Metropolitanate of Sweden; on April 4, 2005 the jurisdiction over Malta was transferred to the Metropolitanate of Italia. Over the course of the Archdiocese's history many assistant Bishops were consecrated in order to accommodate the vast area under its jurisdiction (especially before 1963), and were stationed in various European countries. Today the Archdiocese of Thyatira and Great Britain has jurisdiction in Great Britain and Ireland.

Hierarchs of Thyatira and Great Britain
(Metropolitans 1922-1954 and 1963-1968, Archbishops 1954-1963 and after 24 Feb 1968)

1. Germanus	Γερμανός	24 Mar 1922 – 23 Jan 1951+	1872-1951
Strinopoulos (ex t.m.Selefkia *28 Jun* 1912)			
2. Athenagoras I	Αθηναγόρας Α'	12 Apr 1951 – 15 Oct 1962+	1885-1962
Kavadas (ex m.Philadelphia)			
3. Athenagoras II	Αθηναγόρας Β'	10 Dec 1963 – 9 Sep 1979+	1912-1979
Kokkinakis (ex t.b.Elaia 14 Sep 1950, t.m.Elaia 6 Sep 1960)			
4. Methodius	Μεθόδιος	9 Oct 1979 – 16 Apr 1988	1925-2006
Fougias (ex m.Axomi/Axum, Patriarchate of Alexandria) suspended (to former, to m.Pisidia)			
5. Gregory	Γρηγόριος	16 Apr 1988 –	b. 1928
Theocharous/Chatzifotis (ex t.b.Tropaion 12 Dec 1970)			

METROPOLITANATE OF AUSTRIA
ΜΗΤΡΟΠΟΛΙΣ ΑΥΣΤΡΙΑΣ

Metropolitan of Austria, most honorable and Exarch of Hungary and Middle Europe

On April 15, 1924 a new Metropolitanate of Hungary was established, encompassing all Central Europe, but on August 12, 1924 it was abolished and reunited with the Metropolitanate of Thyatira, although the former Metropolitan of Hungary remained in Vienna as Exarch of Central Europe until 1935. The Metropolitanate of Austria, with its See in Vienna, was established on February 17, 1963 in areas previously under the jurisdiction of the Archdiocese of Thyatira. It had jurisdiction in Austria, Hungary, Switzerland, Italy, and Liechtenstein. On October 10, 1982 its jurisdiction over Switzerland and Liechtenstein was transferred to the new Metropolitanate of Helvetia, while on November 5, 1991 the new Metropolitanate of Italia was established. Today the Metropolitanate of Austria has jurisdiction in Austria and Hungary.

Metropolitans of Austria
(Metropolitan of Hungary in 1924)

1. Germanus	Γερμανός	15 Apr 1924 – 12 Aug 1924	1866-1935
Karavangelis (ex m.Ioannina) (to m.Amasia and Exarch of Central Europe) 10 Feb 1935+			
2. Chrysostom	Χρυσόστομος	22 Oct 1963 – 5 Nov 1991	1903-1995
Tsiter (ex t.b.Thermes 6 Nov 1955) resigned, 1 Apr 1995+			
3. Michael	Μιχαήλ	5 Nov 1991 –	b. 1946
Staïkos (ex t.b.Christoupolis 12 Jan 1986)			

METROPOLITANATE OF BELGIUM
ΜΗΤΡΟΠΟΛΙΣ ΒΕΛΓΙΟΥ

Metropolitan of Belgium, most honorable and Exarch of Netherlands and Luxemburg

The Metropolitanate of Belgium, with its See in Brussels, was established on August 12, 1969 in areas previously under the jurisdictions of the Metropolitanate of Germany (Netherlands) and the Metropolitanate of France (Belgium and Luxemburg). It has jurisdiction in Belgium, the Netherlands, and Luxemburg.

Metropolitans of Belgium

1. Aemilian	Αιμιλιανός	12 Aug 1969 – 14 Dec 1982	b. 1915
Zacharopoulos (ex t.m.Selefkia 14 Jun 1959, expelled from Turkey on 21 Apr 1964) (to m.Kos)			
2. Panteleimon	Παντελεήμων	23 Dec 1982 –	b. 1935
Kontogiannis (ex t.b.Apollonias 19 Aug 1974)			

METROPOLITANATE OF FRANCE
ΜΗΤΡΟΠΟΛΙΣ ΓΑΛΛΙΑΣ

Metropolitan of France, most honorable and Exarch of Europe

The Metropolitanate of France, with its See in Paris, was established on February 5, 1963 in areas previously under the jurisdiction of the Archdiocese of Thyatira. It had jurisdiction in France, Spain, Portugal, Belgium, and Luxemburg. On August 12, 1969 its jurisdiction over Belgium and Luxemburg was transferred to the new Metropolitanate of Belgium, while on January 20, 2003 the new Metropolitanate of Spain and Portugal was established. Today the Metropolitanate of France has jurisdiction in France and Monaco.

Metropolitans of France

1. Meletius   Μελέτιος   22 Oct 1963 – 9 Jun 1988   1914-1993
   Karabinis (ex t.b.Rigion 27 Jun 1953) resigned, 19 Apr 1993+
2. Jeremias   Ιερεμίας   9 Jun 1988 – 20 Jan 2003   b. 1935
   Kalligiorgis (ex t.b.Sasima 31 Jan 1971) (to m.Helvetia)
3. Emmanuel   Εμμανουήλ   20 Jan 2003 –   b. 1958
   Adamakis (ex t.b.Rigion 11 Nov 1996)

METROPOLITANATE OF GERMANY
ΜΗΤΡΟΠΟΛΙΣ ΓΕΡΜΑΝΙΑΣ

Metropolitan of Germany, most honorable and Exarch of Central Europe

The Metropolitanate of Germany, with its See in Bonn, was established on February 5, 1963 in areas previously under the jurisdiction of the Archdiocese of Thyatira. It had jurisdiction in West Germany, East Germany, the Netherlands, and Denmark. On August 12, 1969 its jurisdiction over the Netherlands was transferred to the new Metropolitanate of Belgium, and its jurisdiction over Denmark to the new Metropolitanate of Sweden. Today the Metropolitanate of Germany has jurisdiction in the united Germany; the See remains in Bonn.

Metropolitans of Germany

1. Polyeuctus   Πολύευκτος   22 Oct 1963 – 26 Jun 1968   1912-1988
   Finfinis (ex t.b.Tropaion 3 Nov 1955, t.m.Tropaion 6 Sep 1960) (to m.Ilioupolis)
2. Jacob   Ιάκωβος   12 Aug 1969 – 3 Dec 1971+   1920-1971
   Tzanavaris/Papaïoannou (ex m.Philadelphia)
3. Irenaeus   Ειρηναίος   16 Dec 1971 – 1980   b. 1911
   Galanakis (ex m.Kissamos) suspended (to former, to m.Kissamos)
4. Augustine   Αυγουστίνος   29 Sep 1980 –   b. 1938
   Labardakis (ex t.b.Elaia 26 Mar 1972)

METROPOLITANATE OF HELVETIA (SWITZERLAND)
ΜΗΤΡΟΠΟΛΙΣ ΕΛΒΕΤΙΑΣ

Metropolitan of Helvetia, most honorable and Exarch of Europe

The Metropolitanate of Helvetia, with its See in Chambésy (located on the west shore of Lake Geneva, 3 km north of Geneva), was established on October 10, 1982, in area previously under the jurisdiction of the Metropolitanate of Austria. It has jurisdiction in Switzerland and Liechtenstein.

Metropolitans of Helvetia

1. Damascenus Papandreou (ex t.m.Tranoupolis) (to m.Adrianoupolis)	Δαμασκηνός	2 Oct 1982 – 20 Jan 2003	b. 1936
2. Jeremias Kalligiorgis (ex m.France)	Ιερεμίας	20 Jan 2003 –	b. 1935

METROPOLITANATE OF ITALIA AND MELITE
ΜΗΤΡΟΠΟΛΙΣ ΙΤΑΛΙΑΣ ΚΑΙ ΜΕΛΙΤΗΣ

Metropolitan of Italia and Melite, most honorable and Exarch of all Thrace

The Metropolitanate of Italia, with its See in Venice, was established on November 5, 1991 in areas previously under the jurisdiction of the Metropolitanate of Austria. On April 20, 2005 jurisdiction over Malta was transferred from the Archdiocese of Thyatira to the Metropolitanate of Italia, now renamed Metropolitanate of Italia and Melite. It has jurisdiction in Italy, Malta, and San Marino.

Metropolitans of Italia and Melite

1. Spyridon Papageorgiou (ex t.b.Apamia 24 Nov 1985) (to a.America)	Σπυρίδων	5 Nov 1991 – 30 Jul 1996	b. 1940
2. Gennadius Zervos (ex t.b.Kratia 17 Jan 1971)	Γεννάδιος	26 Aug 1996 –	b. 1937

METROPOLITANATE OF SPAIN AND PORTUGAL
ΜΗΤΡΟΠΟΛΙΣ ΙΣΠΑΝΙΑΣ ΚΑΙ ΠΟΡΤΟΓΑΛΙΑΣ

Metropolitan of Hispania and Portugal,
most honorable and Exarch of Mediterranean Sea

The Metropolitanate of Spain and Portugal, with its See in Madrid, was established on January 10, 2003, in areas previously under the jurisdiction of the Metropolitanate of France. It has jurisdiction in Spain (incuding the Canary Islands) and Portugal.

Metropolitans of Spain and Portugal

1. Epiphanius Perialas (to m.Vryoula)	Επιφάνιος	4 May 2003 – 30 Apr 2007	b. 1935

2. Polycarp   Πολύκαρπος   6 May 2007 –   b. 1963
   Stavropoulos

METROPOLITANATE OF SWEDEN AND ALL SCANDINAVIA
ΜΗΤΡΟΠΟΛΙΣ ΣΟΥΗΔΙΑΣ ΚΑΙ ΠΑΣΗΣ ΣΚΑΝΔΙΝΑΥΪΑΣ

Metropolitan of Sweden and all Scandinavia
most honorable and Exarch of Northern Lands

The Metropolitanate of Sweden, with its See in Stockholm, was established on August 12, 1969 in areas previously under the jurisdictions of the Archdiocese of Thyatira (Sweden, Norway, Iceland) and the Metropolitanate of Germany (Denmark). It has jurisdiction in Sweden, Norway, Denmark, and Iceland.

Metropolitans of Sweden

1. Polyeuctus   Πολύευκτος   12 Aug 1969 – 30 Apr 1974   1912-1988
   Finfinis (ex m.Ilioupolis) (to m.Anea)
2. Paul   Παύλος   12 May 1974 –   b. 1935
   Menevisoglou

SECTION J:
METROPOLITANATES IN AMERICA

ARCHDIOCESE OF AMERICA
ΑΡΧΙΕΠΙΣΚΟΠΗ ΑΜΕΡΙΚΗΣ

Archbishop of America, most honorable and Exarch of Oceans Atlantic and Pacific

The Autonomous Archdiocese of North and South America, with its See in New York, was established on April 26, 1922, having jurisdiction over the whole American continent. Its three initial Dioceses (Boston, Chicago, and San Francisco) were abolished on January 10, 1931, when the Autonomous status of the Archdiocese was revoked due to serious internal disputes.

In order to accommodate the vast area under the Archdiocese's jurisdiction, many assistant Bishops were consecrated, being stationed in various States of the United States of America and other Central and South American countries. However, on March 15, 1979 the three abolished Dioceses were re-established, along with seven new (Buenos Aires, Charlotte, Denver, Detroit, New Jersey, Pittsburg, and Toronto).

On July 30, 1996, the Dioceses of Buenos Aires and Toronto were promoted to Metropolitanates, and a new Metropolitanate of Panamá was established, with the Archdiocese, now renamed Archdiocese of America, retaining jurisdiction only inside the United States of America. On December 20, 2002, all eight Dioceses remaining under the jurisdiction of the Archdiocese of America were promoted to Metropolitanates; thus, today the Holy Synod of the Archdiocese of America is comprised of eight Metropolitans, and is headed by the Archbishop.

The Archdiocese has direct jurisdiction over the southern part of the State of New York, the western part of the State of Connecticut, and the District of Columbia, where the capital of the United States of America, Washington, DC, is situated.

Archbishops of America
(Archbishops of North and South America before 30 Jul 1996)

1. Alexander   Αλέξανδρος   26 Apr 1922 – 19 Jun 1930   1876-1942
   Dimoglou (ex t.b.Rhodostolon 21 Oct 1907) suspended (to former, to m.Kerkyra, Church of Greece)
2. Athenagoras   Αθηναγόρας   12 Aug 1930 – 1 Nov 1948   1886-1972
   Spyrou (ex m.Kerkyra, Church of Greece) (to p.Constantinople)
3. Timothy   Τιμόθεος   7 Jun 1949 – 20 Sep 1949   1880-1949
   Evangelinidis (ex m.Rhodes) (to m.Rhodes)
4. Michael   Μιχαήλ   11 Oct 1949 – 13 Jul 1958+   1892-1958
   Konstantinidis (ex m.Korinthos, Church of Greece)
5. Jacob   Ιάκωβος   14 Feb 1959 – 30 Jul 1996   1911-2005
   Koukouzis (ex t.b.Meliti 6 Feb 1955, t.m.Meliti 4 Apr 1956) resigned, 10 Apr 2005+

6. Spyridon   Σπυρίδων   30 Jul 1996 – 19 Aug 1999   b. 1940
  Papageorgiou (ex m.Italia) (to m.Chaldia)

7. Demetrius   Δημήτριος   19 Aug 1999 –   b. 1928
  Trakatellis (ex t.b.Vrestheni 17 Sep 1967, t.m.Vrestheni 20 Aug 1991, Church of Greece)

METROPOLITANATE OF ATLANTA
ΜΗΤΡΟΠΟΛΙΣ ΑΤΛΑΝΤΑΣ

The Diocese of Charlotte was established on March 15, 1979, and renamed the Diocese of Atlanta in 1981. It has jurisdiction in the States of Georgia, North Carolina, South Carolina, Alabama, Mississippi, Florida, and parts of the States of Louisiana and Tennessee. On December 20, 2002 it was promoted to a Metropolitanate. The See is in Atlanta, Georgia.

Hierarchs of Atlanta
(Bishop of Charlotte before 1981, Bishops of Atlanta 1981-2002, Metropolitan after 20 Dec 2002)

1. John   Ιωάννης   15 Mar 1979 – 15 Mar 1988   b. 1928
  Kalogerakis (ex t.b.Thermes 17 Jan 1971) resigned (to former, to t.b.Amorion on 15 Oct 1992)

2. Philip   Φίλιππος   2 Apr 1992 – 29 Dec 1995+   1929-1995
  Koutoufas (ex t.b.Daphnousia 1 Aug 1982)

3. Alexius   Αλέξιος   13 Mar 1999 –   b. 1943
  Panagiotopoulos (ex t.b.Troas 17 May 1987)

METROPOLITANATE OF BOSTON
ΜΗΤΡΟΠΟΛΙΣ ΒΟΣΤΩΝΗΣ

The Diocese of Boston was established on May 17, 1922, but was abolished on January 10, 1931, before being re-established on March 15, 1979. It has jurisdiction in the States of Massachusetts, Maine, New Hampshire, Vermont, Rhode Island, and the eastern part of Connecticut. On December 20, 2002 it was promoted to a Metropolitanate. The See is in Boston, Massachusetts.

Hierarchs of Boston
(Bishops until 20 Dec 2002, Metropolitan afterwards)

1. Joachim   Ιωακείμ   28 Jun 1923 – Aug 1930   1873-1959
  Alexopoulos, resigned (to former, to m.Phokis, Church of Greece)

2. Athenagoras   Αθηναγόρας   5 Jun 1938 – 7 Jun 1949   1885-1962
  Kavvadas, Titular Bishop (to m.Thyatira and Great Britain)

3. Anthimus   Άνθιμος   15 Mar 1979 – 15 Nov 1983   b. 1934
  Drakonakis (ex t.b.Christoupolis 17 Apr 1977) (to b.Denver)

4. Methodius   Μεθόδιος   13 Mar 1984 –   b. 1946
  Tournas (ex t.b.Skopelos 18 Jul 1982) see note 1

1. On 24 Nov 1997 Bishop Methodius was elected Metropolitan of Anea, continuing to head the Diocese of Boston as president. On 20 Dec 2002 he was elected Metropolitan of Boston.

METROPOLITANATE OF CHICAGO
ΜΗΤΡΟΠΟΛΙΣ ΣΙΚΑΓΟΥ

The Diocese of Chicago was established on May 17, 1922, but was abolished on January 10, 1931, before being re-established on March 15, 1979. It has jurisdiction in the States of Illinois, Wisconsin, Minnesota, Iowa, and parts of Missouri and Indiana. On December 20, 2002 it was promoted to a Metropolitanate. The See is in Chicago, Illinois.

Hierarchs of Chicago
(Bishops until 20 Dec 2002, Metropolitan afterwards)

1. Philaretus	Φιλάρετος	21 Jun 1923 – Jul 1930	1886-1961
Ioannidis, resigned (to former, to m.Syros, Church of Greece)			
2. Gerasimus	Γεράσιμος	*26 Jan* 1943 – 28 Feb 1954+	1874-1954
Ilias, Titular Bishop			
3. Jacob	Ιάκωβος	15 Mar 1979 –	b. 1928
Gkarmatis (ex t.b.Apamia 25 Dec 1969) see note 1			

1. On 24 Nov 1997 Bishop Jacob was elected Metropolitan of Krini, continuing to head the Diocese of Chicago as president. On 20 Dec 2002 he was elected Metropolitan of Chicago.

METROPOLITANATE OF DENVER
ΜΗΤΡΟΠΟΛΙΣ ΝΤΕΝΒΕΡ

The Diocese of Denver was established on March 15, 1979. It has jurisdiction in the States of Colorado, Idaho, Kansas, Montana, Nebraska, New México, Oklahoma, North Dakota, South Dakota, Texas, Utah, Wyoming, and in parts of Missouri and Louisiana. On December 20, 2002 it was promoted to a Metropolitanate. The See is in Denver, Colorado.

Hierarchs of Denver
(Bishops until 20 Dec 2002, Metropolitan afterwards)

1. Anthimus	Άνθιμος	15 Nov 1983 – 1988	b. 1934
Drakonakis (ex b.Boston) resigned (to former, to t.b.Olympos 15 Oct 1992)			
2. Isaiah	Ησαΐας	23 Jun 1992 –	b. 1931
Chronopoulos (ex t.b.Aspendos 25 May 1986) see note 1			

1. On 24 Nov 1997 Bishop Isaiah was elected Metropolitan of Prikonnisos, continuing to head the Diocese of Denver as president. On 20 Dec 2002 he was elected Metropolitan of Denver.

METROPOLITANATE OF DETROIT
ΜΗΤΡΟΠΟΛΙΣ ΝΤΗΤΡΟΪΤ

The Diocese of Detroit was established on March 15, 1979. It has jurisdiction in the States of Michigan, Arkansas, Kentucky, and parts of New York, Indiana, Tennessee, and Ohio. On December 20, 2002 it was promoted to a Metropolitanate. The See is in Detroit, Michigan.

Hierarchs of Detroit
(Bishops until 20 Dec 2002, Metropolitan afterwards)

1. Timothy   Τιμόθεος   15 Mar 1979 – 1 Aug 1995   1924-1998
   Negrepontis (ex t.b.Pamphilos 20 Jan 1974) resigned, 11 Dec 1998+
2. Nicholas   Νικόλαος   3 Apr 1999 –   b. 1953
   Pissaris

METROPOLITANATE OF NEW JERSEY
ΜΗΤΡΟΠΟΛΙΣ ΝΕΑΣ ΥΕΡΣΕΗΣ

The Diocese of New Jersey was established on March 15, 1979. It has jurisdiction in the States of New Jersey, Delaware, Maryland, Virginia, and part of Pennsylvania. On December 20, 2002 it was promoted to a Metropolitanate. The See is in Kenilworth, New Jersey.

Hierarchs of New Jersey
(Bishops until 20 Dec 2002, Metropolitan afterwards)

1. Silas   Σίλας   15 Mar 1979 – 15 Oct 1996   1919-2000
   Koskinas (ex t.b.Amphipolis 9 Oct 1960) promoted to Metropolitan 24 Jan 1980 (to m.Saranta Ekklisies)
2. George   Γεώργιος   13 Mar 1999 – 22 Nov 1999+   1933-1999
   Papaïoannou (ex t.b.Komana 31 May 1998)
3. Evangelus   Ευάγγελος   10 May 2003 –   b. 1961
   Kourounis

METROPOLITANATE OF PITTSBURGH
ΜΗΤΡΟΠΟΛΙΣ ΠΙΤΣΒΟΥΡΓΟΥ

The Diocese of Pittsburgh was established on March 15, 1979. It has jurisdiction in the State of Western Virginia and in parts of Pennsylvania and Ohio. On December 20, 2002 it was promoted to a Metropolitanate. The See is in Pittsburgh, Pennsylvania.

Hierarchs of Pittsburgh
(Bishop until 20 Dec 2002, Metropolitan afterwards)

1. Maximus   Μάξιμος   15 Mar 1979 –   b. 1935
   Agiorgousis (ex t.b.Dioklia 18 Jun 1978) see note 1

1. On 24 Nov 1997 Bishop Maximus was elected Metropolitan of Ainos, continuing to head the Diocese of Pittsburgh as president. On 20 Dec 2002 he was elected Metropolitan of Pittsburgh.

METROPOLITANATE OF SAN FRANCISCO
ΜΗΤΡΟΠΟΛΙΣ ΑΓΙΟΥ ΦΡΑΓΚΙΣΚΟΥ

The Diocese of San Francisco was established on May 17, 1922, but was abolished on January 10, 1931, before being re-established on March 15, 1979. It has jurisdiction in the States of California, Oregon, Washington, Nevada, Arizona, Alaska, and Hawaii. On

December 20, 2002 it was promoted to a Metropolitanate. The See is in San Francisco, California.

Hierarchs of San Francisco
(Bishops until 20 Dec 2002, Metropolitans afterwards)

1. Callistus	Κάλλιστος	7 Aug 1927 – Nov 1940+	1878-1940
Papageorgopoulos, Titular Bishop of San Francisco after 10 Jan 1931			
2. Irenaeus	Ειρηναίος	*18 Nov* 1941 – 2 Jun 1944+	d. 1944
Tsourounakis, Titular Bishop			
3. Anthony	Αντώνιος	15 Mar 1979 – 25 Dec 2004+	1935-2004
Gergiannakis (ex t.b.Amisos 21 May 1978) see note 1			
4. Gerasimus	Γεράσιμος	22 Feb 2005 –	b. 1945
Michaleas (ex t.b.Kratia 9 Feb 2002)			

1. On 24 Nov 1997 Bishop Anthony was elected Metropolitan of Dardanellia, continuing to head the Diocese of San Francisco as president. On 20 Dec 2002 he was elected Metropolitan of San Francisco.

METROPOLITANATE OF BUENOS AIRES
ΜΗΤΡΟΠΟΛΙΣ ΜΠΟΥΕΝΟΣ ΑΫΡΕΣ

Metropolitan of Buenos Aires, most honorable and Exarch of South America

The Diocese of Buenos Aires was established on March 15, 1979, under the jurisdiction of the Archdiocese of North and South America. On July 30, 1996 the Diocese was promoted to a Metropolitanate, while on the same date the jurisdiction of the Archdiocese was confined within the borders of the United States of America. The Metropolitanate of Buenos Aires has jurisdiction in Argentina, Brazil, Uruguay, Chile, Paraguay, Peru, Bolivia, Ecuador, Suriname, Guyana, and French Guiana. The See is in Buenos Aires, Argentina.

Hierarchs of Buenos Aires
(Bishops until 30 Jul 1996, Metropolitan afterwards)

1. Gennadius	Γεννάδιος	8 Apr 1979 – 30 Apr 2001	b. 1924
Chrysoulakis, resigned			
2. Tarasius	Ταράσιος	3 Jun 2001 –	b. 1956
Antonopoulos			

METROPOLITANATE OF MÉXICO
ΜΗΤΡΟΠΟΛΙΣ ΜΕΞΙΚΟΥ

Metropolitan of México, most honorable and Exarch of Central America and Caribbean Islands

The Metropolitanate of Panamá was established on July 30, 1996, with its See located temporarily in México City, México. It was later decided that the See should remain in México City, and on October 13, 2005 the name of the Metropolitanate was changed to Metropolitanate of México. The Metropolitanate of México has jurisdiction in Panamá, Costa Rica, Nicaragua, Honduras, El Salvador, Guatemala, Belize, México, Colombia, Venezuela, Bahamas, Bermuda, Turks and Caicos Islands, Cuba, Haiti, Dominican Republic, Puerto Rico, Cayman Islands, Jamaica, US Virgin Islands, British Virgin Islands, Anguilla, Antigua and Barbuda, Montserrat, Saint Kitts and Nevis, Guadeloupe, Dominica, Martinique, Santa Lucia, Saint Vincent and the Grenadines, Grenada, Barbados, Trinidad and Tobago, Netherlands Antilles, and Aruba.

Metropolitans of México
(Metropolitan of Panamá until 13 Oct 2005)

1. Athenagoras	Αθηναγόρας	2 Dec 1996 –	b. 1941
Anastasiadis (ex t.b.Dorylaion 22 Aug 1982)			

METROPOLITANATE OF TORONTO
ΜΗΤΡΟΠΟΛΙΣ ΤΟΡΟΝΤΟ

Metropolitan of Toronto, most honorable and Exarch of all Canada

The Diocese of Toronto was established on March 15, 1979, under the jurisdiction of the Archdiocese of North and South America. On July 30, 1996 the Diocese was promoted to a Metropolitanate, while on the same date the jurisdiction of the Archdiocese was confined within the borders of the United States of America. The Metropolitanate of Toronto has jurisdiction in all Canada. The See is in Toronto, Ontario.

Hierarchs of Toronto
(Bishop until 30 Jul 1996, Metropolitan afterwards)

1. Soterius	Σωτήριος	15 Mar 1979 –	b. 1936
Athanasoulas (ex t.b.Konstantia 27 Jan 1974)			

SECTION K:
METROPOLITANATES IN OCEANIA
AND THE FAR EAST

ARCHDIOCESE OF AUSTRALIA
ΑΡΧΙΕΠΙΣΚΟΠΗ ΑΥΣΤΡΑΛΙΑΣ

Archbishop of Australia, most honorable and Exarch of all Oceania

The Metropolitanate of Australia, with its See in Sydney, New South Wales, was established on February 9, 1924, having jurisdiction in Australia and all the islands of Oceania. On November 3, 1947 the name of the Metropolitanate changed to the Metropolitanate of Australia and New Zealand, and it was promoted to an Archdiocese on September 10, 1959. In order to accommodate the vast area under the Archdiocese's jurisdiction, many assistant Bishops were consecrated, being stationed in various States of Australia and in New Zealand. On January 10, 1970, a Metropolitanate of New Zealand was established, while the Archdiocese, renamed Archdiocese of Australia, retained jurisdiction in Australia and Papua-New Guinea only.

Hierarchs of Australia
(Australia and New Zealand during 1947-1970. Metropolitans until 10 Sep 1959, Archbishops afterwards)

1. Christopher	Χριστόφορος	(1st time)	9 Feb 1924 – 17 Apr 1926	1872-1958
Knitis (ex m.Serres) suspended (to former, to m.Australia)				
2. Joachim	Ιωακείμ		17 Apr 1926 – 24 Jun 1926	1883-1962
Apostolidis (ex m.Servia) suspended (to former, to m.Servia)				
–. Christopher	Χριστόφορος	(2nd time)	24 Jun 1926 – 4 Feb 1928	1872-1958
Knitis (ex former m.Australia) (to m.Vizyi)				
3. Timothy	Τιμόθεος		30 Nov 1931 – 16 Jan 1947	1880-1949
Evangelinidis (to m.Rhodes)				
4. Theophylactus	Θεοφύλακτος		24 Aug 1947 – 2 Aug 1958+	1891-1958
Papathanasopoulos				
5. Ezekiel	Ιεζεκιήλ	(1st time)	24 Feb 1959 – 27 Feb 1968	1913-1987
Tsoukalas (ex t.b.Nazianzos 17 Sep 1950) resigned (to former, to a.Australia)				
–. Ezekiel	Ιεζεκιήλ	(2nd time)	12 Aug 1969 – 5 Aug 1974	1913-1987
Tsoukalas (ex former a.Australia) (to m.Pisidia)				
6. Stylianus	Στυλιανός		13 Feb 1975 –	b. 1935
Charkianakis (ex t.m.Militoupolis 6 Dec 1970)				

METROPOLITANATE OF HONG KONG
ΜΗΤΡΟΠΟΛΙΣ ΧΟΓΚ ΚΟΓΚ

Metropolitan of Hong Kong, most honorable and Exarch of Far East

The Metropolitanate of Hong Kong, with its See in Hong Kong, China, was established on August 12, 1969 in areas previously under the jurisdiction of the Metropolitanate of New Zealand. It has jurisdiction in China, Taiwan, Mongolia, Vietnam, Laos, Cambodia, Thailand, Philippines, and Myanmar (Burma). On January 9, 2008, the new Metropolitanate of Singapore was established, taking under its jurisdiction the southeastern areas of the Metropolitanate of Hong Kong.

Metropolitans of Hong Kong

1. Nicetas Loulias (to m.Dardanellia)	Νικήτας	14 Dec 1996 – 29 Aug 2007	b. 1955
2. Nectarius Tsilis	Νεκτάριος	20 Jan 2008 –	b. 1969

METROPOLITANATE OF KOREA
ΜΗΤΡΟΠΟΛΙΣ ΚΟΡΕΑΣ

Metropolitan of Korea, most honorable and Exarch of Japan

The Metropolitanate of Korea, with its See in Seoul, South Korea, was established on April 20, 2004 in areas previously under the jurisdiction of the Metropolitanate of New Zealand. It has jurisdiction in South Korea, North Korea, and Japan.

Metropolitans of Korea

1. Soterius Trabas (ex t.b.Zila 21 Mar 1993)(to m.Pisidia)	Σωτήριος	20 Apr 2004 – 27 May 2008	b. 1929
2. Ambrose Zografos (ex t.b.Zila 5 Feb 2006)	Αμβρόσιος	27 May 2008 –	b. 1960

METROPOLITANATE OF NEW ZEALAND
ΜΗΤΡΟΠΟΛΙΣ ΝΕΑΣ ΖΗΛΑΝΔΙΑΣ

Metropolitan of New Zealand, most honorable and Exarch of Oceania

The Metropolitanate of New Zealand, with its See in Wellington, was established on January 8, 1970 in areas previously under the jurisdiction of the Archdiocese of Australia. On July 30, 1996 its jurisdiction in Asia (except Korea and Japan) was transferred to the new Metropolitanate of Hong Kong, while on April 20, 2004 its jurisdiction in Korea and Japan was transferred to the new Metropolitanate of Korea.

Today the Metropolitanate of New Zealand has jurisdiction in New Zealand, New Caledonia, Vanuatu, Solomon Islands, Tuvalu, Wallis and Futuna, Fiji, Tokelau, Samoa, American Samoa, Tonga, Niue, Cook Islands, French Polynesia, Pitcairn, Kiribati, Nauru, Marshall Islands, Micronesia, Palau, Guam, and the Northern Mariana Islands.

Metropolitans of New Zealand

1. Dionysius   Διονύσιος   8 Jan 1970 – 21 Jul 2003   1916-2008
   Psiachas (ex t.b.Nazianzos 6 Dec 1959) (to m.Prousa)
2. Joseph   Ιωσήφ   21 Jul 2003 – 13 Oct 2005   b. 1955
   Charkiolakis (ex t.b.Arianzos 3 Dec 1989) resigned (to former, to m.Prikonnisos)
3. Amphilochius   Αμφιλόχιος   13 Oct 2005 –   b. 1938
   Tsoukos (ex t.b.Erythres 9 Jul 2005)

METROPOLITANATE OF SINGAPORE
ΜΗΤΡΟΠΟΛΙΣ ΣΙΓΚΑΠΟΥΡΗΣ

Metropolitan of Singapore, most honorable and Exarch of Far East

The Metropolitanate of Singapore, with its See in Singapore, was established on January 9, 2008 in areas previously under the jurisdiction of the Metropolitanate of Hong Kong. It has jurisdiction in Singapore, Malaysia, Brunei, Indonesia, India, Bangladesh, Nepal, Bhutan, Pakistan, Afghanistan, Sri Lanka, and the Maldives. No Metropolitan had been appointed as of the beginning of 2009.

SECTION L:
AUTONOMOUS CHURCH OF FINLAND

ARCHDIOCESE OF KARELIA AND ALL FINLAND
ΑΡΧΙΕΠΙΣΚΟΠΗ ΚΑΡΕΛΙΑΣ ΚΑΙ ΠΑΣΗΣ ΦΙΝΛΑΝΔΙΑΣ

The area of Finland was initially under the jurisdiction of the Diocese of Novgorod (Church of Russia). Following the annexation of Finland by the Russian Empire (March 17, 1809), it was transferred to the jurisdiction of the Metropolitanate of Saint Petersburg, from which it was separated on October 24, 1892, when the Diocese of Vyborg and Finland was created (the city of Vyborg is located on the northeast shore of the Gulf of Finland, 130 km northwest of Saint Petersburg).

On December 6, 1917 Finland declared its independence from Russia, while the Diocese of Vyborg and All Finland was declared Autonomous under the Russian Church on November 26, 1918. The Russian Church, being in a dire situation at the time, officially gave Autonomy to the Church of Finland in February 1921. Due to the political situation, contact with the Russian Orthodox Church became exceedingly difficult, and the Orthodox Church of Finland turned to the Ecumenical Patriarchate, asking to come under its jurisdiction. This request was granted on July 7, 1923, and in 1925 the title of the Archdiocese changed to "Karelia and All Finland," with its See moving 170 km northeast of Viipuri (Vyborg) to the city of Sortavala, situated on the northern shore of Lake Ladoga.

During the Second World War, the Soviet Union annexed the southeastern areas of Finland, including Vyborg and Sortavala, causing a major relocation of Finnish Orthodox, who resettled in various areas of western Finland. The See was likewise moved westwards, today being located in the city of Kuopio, situated in central Finland, 300 km northwest of Sortavala and 400 km northeast of Helsinki. The Russian Church re-established relations with the Finnish Orthodox Church on May 7, 1957.

The area under the direct jurisdiction of the Archdiocese is bordered by the Metropolitanate of Oulu on the north, the Metropolitanate of Petrozavodsk (Russian Church) on the east, the Metropolitanate of Helsinki on the south, and the Metropolitanate of Helsinki and the Metropolitanate of Oulu on the west.

Archbishops of Karelia and All Finland
(Assistant Bishop of Karelia until 1925)

1. Germanus	Γερμανός	8 Jul 1923 – 1 Jul 1960	1878-1961
Aav, resigned, 15 Jan 1961+			
2. Paul	Παύλος	29 Aug 1960 – 16 Sep 1987	1914-1989
Olmari (ex t.b.Laponia 17 Nov 1958) resigned, 2 Dec 1989+			
3. John	Ιωάννης	15 Oct 1987 – 30 Sep 2001	b. 1923
Rinne (ex m.Helsinki) (to former, to m.Nikaia)			
4. Leo	Λέων	27 Oct 2001 –	b. 1948
Makkonen (ex m.Helsinki)			

METROPOLITANATE OF HELSINKI
ΜΗΤΡΟΠΟΛΙΣ ΕΛΣΙΝΚΙΟΥ

The Diocese of Vyborg and Finland was established by the Russian Church on October 24, 1892, becoming the Autonomous Archdiocese of Vyborg and All Finland in February 1921. In 1925 it became the Diocese of Vyborg under the jurisdiction of the Autonomous Archdiocese of Karelia and All Finland. After the area of Vyborg was annexed by the Soviet Union in 1940, the See of the Diocese was moved 230 km west to the city of Helsinki. On February 1, 1972 the Diocese of Helsinki was promoted to a Metropolitanate. The Metropolitanate of Helsinki is bordered by the Metropolitanate of Oulu and the area under the Archdiocese of Karelia on the north, the Metropolitanate of Saint Petersburg (Russian Church) and the Metropolitanate of Petrozavodsk (Russian Church) on the east, the Gulf of Finland on the south, and the Gulf of Bothnia on the west.

Metropolitans of Helsinki
(Archbishop of Vyborg and All Finland until 1925, Bishops of Vyborg afterwards, Bishops of Helsinki 1940-1972)

1. Seraphim   Σεραφείμ   Feb 1921 – 1927   1879-1959
Lukyanov, (ex t.b.Serdobol 7 Sep 1914, b.Vyborg 17 Jan 1918, a.Vyborg 1920) (to ROCOR) 18 Feb 1959+ see note 1

2. Alexander   Αλέξανδρος   *18 Jun* 1935 – 13 Oct 1969+   1883-1969
Karpin, moved to Helsinki in 1940

3. John   Ιωάννης   1970 – 15 Oct 1987   b. 1923
Rinne (ex t.b.Laponia 26 May 1969) promoted to Metropolitan 1 Feb 1972 (to a.Karelia)

4. Tychon   Τύχων   17 Mar 1988 – 14 May 1996   1928-2000
Tajakka (ex b.Joensuu) resigned, 12 Aug 2000+

5. Leo   Λέων   14 May 1996 – 27 Oct 2001   b. 1948
Makkonen (ex m.Oulu) (to a.Karelia)

6. Ambrose   Αμβρόσιος   1 Feb 2002 –   b. 1945
Jaaskelainen (ex m.Oulu)

1. Archbishop Seraphim headed the Finnish Orthodox Church until 1924, when he was forcibly retired by the Finnish government. In 1927 he joined the Synod in exile of the Russian Orthodox Church Outside of Russia (ROCOR), returning to the Russian Orthodox Church on August 31, 1945. On August 9, 1946 he was promoted to Metropolitan and appointed Russian Exarch of Western Europe, a position he held until his retirement of November 15, 1949.

METROPOLITANATE OF OULU
ΜΗΤΡΟΠΟΛΙΣ ΟΟΥΛΟΥ

The city of Oulu is located on the shore of the Bothnian Gulf, 290 km northwest of Kuopio and 580 km north of Helsinki. The Metropolitanate of Oulu was established on January 1, 1980. It is bordered by the Metropolitanate of Sweden on the north, the Metropolitanate of Murmansk (Russian Church) and the Metropolitanate of Petrozavodsk (Russian Church) on the east, the area of the Archdiocese of Karelia and the Metropolitanate Helsinki on the south, and the Gulf of Bothnia and the Metropolitanate of Sweden on the west.

Metropolitans of Oulu

1. Leo Makkonen (ex b. Joensuu) (to m.Helsinki)	Λέων	1 Jan 1980 – 14 May 1996	b. 1948
2. Ambrose Jaaskelainen (ex b. Joensuu) (to m.Helsinki)	Αμβρόσιος	May 1996 – 1 Feb 2002	b. 1945
3. Panteleimon Sarho (ex b. Joensuu)	Παντελεήμων	1 Apr 2002 –	b. 1949

DIOCESE OF JOENSUU
ΕΠΙΣΚΟΠΗ ΓΙΟΕΝΣΟΥ

The Diocese of Joensuu, a city located 140 km southeast of Kuopio, was created in February 1979 as an assistant Bishop's See inside the area of the Archdiocese of Karelia.

Bishops of Joensuu

1. Leo Makkonen (to m.Oulu)	Λέων	25 Feb 1979 – 1 Jan 1980	b. 1948
2. Alexius Rantala	Αλέξιος	2 Mar 1980 – 22 Jan 1984+	1941-1984
3. Tychon Tajakka (to m.Helsinki)	Τύχων	26 May 1984 – 17 Mar 1988	1928-2000
4. Ambrose Jaaskelainen (to m.Oulu)	Αμβρόσιος	20 Nov 1988 – May 1996	b. 1945
5. Panteleimon Sarho (to m.Oulu)	Παντελεήμων	16 Mar 1997 – 1 Apr 2002	b. 1949
6. Arsenius Heikkinen	Αρσένιος	23 Jan 2005 –	b. 1957

SECTION M:
AUTONOMOUS CHURCH OF ESTONIA

METROPOLITANATE OF TALLINN AND ALL ESTONIA
ΜΗΤΡΟΠΟΛΙΣ ΤΑΛΛΙΝΗΣ ΚΑΙ ΠΑΣΗΣ ΕΣΘΟΝΙΑΣ

The area of Estonia was initially under the jurisdiction of the Metropolitanate of Saint Petersburg (Church of Russia), and after May 1865 under the jurisdiction of the Diocese of Riga. On February 12, 1918 Estonia declared its independence from Russia, and on March 21, 1919 the General Assembly of the Estonian Orthodox decided to establish the Diocese of Tallinn (the capital city of Estonia) and to request Autonomy for the Estonian Orthodox Church. The Russian Church, being in a dire situation at the time, accepted their request on April 17, 1920, and officially gave Autonomy to the Church of Estonia on June 15, 1920, creating the Archdiocese of Tallinn and All Estonia. Due to the political situation, contact with the Russian Orthodox Church became exceedingly difficult, and the Orthodox Church of Estonia turned to the Ecumenical Patriarchate, asking to come under its jurisdiction. This request was granted on July 7, 1923 by the Ecumenical Patriarchate, who simultaneously elevated the Archdiocese of Tallin to a Metropolitanate.

In June 1940 the forces of the Soviet Union occupied Estonia, and on February 24, 1941 the Russian Church created the Baltic Exarchate, incorporating the former Dioceses of Estonia and Latvia. It was decided that the existing Hierarchs of the former Autonomous Churches of Estonia and Latvia would become assistant Bishops to the new Russian Exarch, whose See was set in Riga, Latvia. Metropolitan Alexander of Tallinn and All Estonia was summoned in Moscow, where on March 30, 1941 he was forced to sign a degree recognizing the new situation. The Russian Church officially abolished the Autonomy of the Orthodox Estonian Church on the next day, March 31.

Soon afterwards Germany invaded the Soviet Union, the German army occupying Petseri on July 8, 1941 and Tallinn on August 28, 1941. On September 3, 1941 Metropolitan Alexander declared the re-establishment of the Autonomous Estonian Church under the Ecumenical Patriarchate. In September 1944 the Russian Army entered Estonia, and Metropolitan Alexander along with many members of the Estonian Orthodox Church were forced to exile in Germany and soon afterwards in Sweden, where a Synod in exile was created. On March 6, 1945 the Autonomy of the Estonian Church was officially abolished, and the Tallinn Diocese of the Russian Church was established.

The Ecumenical Patriarchate continued to recognize the Autonomy of the Estonian Orthodox Church, appointing Archbishop Athenagoras of Thyatira and Great Britain *Locum Tenens* of the Estonian Church after the death of Metropolitan Alexander. However, under pressure by the Russian Church the Autonomy of the Estonian Church was deemed inactive in April 1978.

On August 20, 1991 the new Republic of Estonia declared its independence, and after requests from the Estonian Orthodox, on February 20, 1996 the Ecumenical Patriarchate reactivated the Autonomous status of the Estonian Orthodox Church, appointing

Archbishop John of Karelia and All Finland as *Locum Tenens* until the election of a new Metropolitan became possible. The Russian Church objected to these moves and although negotiations ensued, leading to agreement on some matters, today there are two parallel jurisdictions in Estonia, one under the Ecumenical Patriarchate and one under the Russian Church.

Metropolitans of Tallinn and All Estonia
(Archbishop until 7 Jul 1923)

1. Alexander Paulus, in exile after Sep 1944	Αλέξανδρος	5 Dec 1920 – 18 Oct 1953+	1872-1953
2. Stephen Charalampidis (ex t.b.Nazianzos 25 Jul 1987)	Στέφανος	13 Mar 1999 –	b. 1940

DIOCESE OF PÄRNU AND SAAREMAA
ΕΠΙΣΚΟΠΗ ΠΙΑΡΝΟΥ ΚΑΙ ΣΑΑΡΕΜΑ

On July 7, 1923, the Ecumenical Patriarchate created two Dioceses inside the Estonian Church: Petseri and Saaremaa. Due to local reasons, however, on September 24, 1923 the Diocese of Narva and Izborsk (Irboska) was established instead of the Diocese of Saaremaa. The city of Narva is situated in the northeastern border with Russia, 210 km east of Tallinn. The city of Irboska (today Izborsk, inside the Russian Federation), located 296 km southeast of Tallinn, was situated near the southeastern border.

On October 21, 2008 the See was reactivated as the Diocese of Pärnu and Saaremaa. Pärnu is a port on the Gulf of Riga, 125 km south of Tallinn. Saaremaa is the largest island of Estonia, having an area of 2,673 km².

Bishops of Pärnu and Saaremaa
(Bishops of Narva and Irboska 1925-42)

1. Eusebius Grozdov (ex t.b. Uglichsk 28.5.1906, t.b. Rybinsk 27.2.09, b.Tobolsk 18.3.10, b.Pskov 17.4.12, a.Pskov 12.4.18)	Ευσέβιος	1 Dec 1925 – 12 Aug 1929+	1866-1929
2. Paul Dmitrovski, suspended (to a.Narva/Russian Church 21 Dec 1942, to a.Tallin 9 Mar 1945) 1 Feb 1946+	Παύλος	3 Oct 1937 – Aug 1942	1872-1946
3. Alexander Hopjorski	Αλέξανδρος	12 Jan 2009 –	b. 1964

DIOCESE OF TARTU
ΕΠΙΣΚΟΠΗ ΤΑΡΤΟΥ

The Diocese of Petseri was established on July 7, 1923 by the Ecumenical Patriarchate; however, it functioned as an assistant bishop's See inside the area of the Metropolitanate of Estonia, until in July 1943 the Diocese of Tartu and Petseri was created, encompassing southeastern Estonia. The city of Tartu is situated 180 km southeast of Tallinn, while the city of Petseri (today Pechory inside the Russian Federation) is located 95 km southeast of Tartu and 20 km northwest of Irboska. On October 21, 2008 the Diocese of Tartu was reactivated.

Bishops of Tartu
(Bishops of Petseri 1926-40, Bishop of Tartu and Petseri 1943-48)

1. John   Ιωάννης   25 Apr 1926 – 30 Dec 1932   1893-1941
   Bulin, Titular Bishop, suspended, 30 Jul 1941+
2. Nicholas   Νικόλαος   2 Apr 1933 – Jul 1940   d. 1947
   Leysman, Titular Archbishop, resigned
3. Peter   Πέτρος   25 Jul 1943 – 20 Aug 1948++   1875-1948
   Pahkel, imprisoned 26 Jun 1945-20 Aug 1948
4. Elias   Ηλίας   10 Jan 2009 –   b. 1977
   Ojaperv

SECTION N:
FORMER AUTONOMOUS CHURCH OF LATVIA

METROPOLITANATE OF RIGA AND ALL LATVIA
ΜΗΤΡΟΠΟΛΙΣ ΡΙΓΑΣ ΚΑΙ ΠΑΣΗΣ ΛΑΤΒΙΑΣ

The area of Latvia was under the jurisdiction of the Diocese of Pskov (Church of Russia) until the establishment of the Diocese of Riga and Mitau on March 11, 1850. On November 15, 1918 Latvia declared its independence from Russia, and on February 27, 1920 the General Assembly of the Latvian Orthodox Church requested the appointment of Archbishop John Pommer (of Latvian descent) to the Diocese of Riga. The Russian Church, at the request of Archbishop John, officially granted Autonomy to the Church of Estonia on July 6, 1921, creating the Archdiocese of Riga and All Latvia. After the brutal murder of Archbishop John (October 12, 1934) and due to the political situation of the time, the Orthodox Church of Latvia turned to the Ecumenical Patriarchate, asking to come under its jurisdiction. This request was granted in February 1936 by the Ecumenical Patriarchate, which simultaneously elevated the Archdiocese of Riga to a Metropolitanate.

In June 1940 the forces of the Soviet Union occupied Latvia, and on February 24, 1941 the Russian Church created the Baltic Exarchate, incorporating the former Dioceses of Estonia and Latvia. It was decided that the existing Hierarchs of the former Autonomous Churches of Estonia and Latvia would become assistant Bishops to the new Russian Exarch, whose See was set in Riga. Metropolitan Augustine of Riga and All Estonia was summoned in Moscow, where on March 28, 1941 he was forced to sign a degree recognizing the new situation. The Russian Church officially abolished the Autonomy of the Orthodox Latvian Church three days later, March 31.

Soon afterwards Germany invaded the Soviet Union, the German army completely occupying Latvia by July 10, 1941. On July 20, 1941 Metropolitan Augustine declared the re-establishment of the Autonomous Latvian Church under the Ecumenical Patriarchate. However, the German forces supported the Exarch of the Russian Church, and Metropolitan Augustine was not able to re-establish his authority in many parishes.

In September 1944 the Russian Army entered Latvia, and Metropolitan Augustine, along with many members of the Estonian Orthodox Church, were forced into exile in West Germany, where a Synod in exile was created. The Ecumenical Patriarchate continued to recognize the Autonomy of the Latvian Orthodox Church even after the death of Metropolitan Augustine. However, under pressure by the Russian Church, the Autonomy of the Latvian Church was deemed inactive in April 1978.

Metropolitans of Riga and All Latvia
(Archbishop before Mar 1936)

1. John   Ἰωάννης   6 Jul 1921 – 14 Oct 1934++   1876-1934
   Pommer (ex t.b.Slutsk 11 Feb 1912, t.b.Taganrog 4 Apr 1913, t.b.Starita 7 Sep 1917, a.Penza 9 Apr 1918)
2. Augustine   Αὐγουστίνος   29 Mar 1936 – 5 Oct 1955+   1873-1955
   Peterson, in exile after Sep 1944

DIOCESE OF JELGAVA
ΕΠΙΣΚΟΠΗ ΕΛΓΑΒΑΣ

The Diocese of Jelgava, a city located 46 km southwest of Riga, was created on September 3, 1936 as an assistant Bishop's See inside the Metropolitanate of Latvia.

1. Jacob   Ἰάκωβος   27 Sep 1936 – 13 Oct 1943+   d. 1943
   Carp, promoted to Archbishop in 1942 by the Russian Exarch

DIOCESE OF JERSIKA
ΕΠΙΣΚΟΠΗ ΖΕΡΖΙΚΑΣ

The Diocese of Jersika with its See in Daugavpils, a city located 220 km southeast of Riga, was created on May 31, 1938 as an assistant Bishop's See inside the Metropolitanate of Latvia. In 1939 the See of Diocese was moved 140 km north to the city of Madona, located 140 km east of Riga. Jersika, located 170 km southeast of Riga and 50 km northwest of Daugavpils, was an important city and a Principality in the middle ages.

1. Alexander   Ἀλέξανδρος   17 Jul 1938 – 30 Jul 1942+   1876-1942
   Adam Vitold

SECTION O:
EXTRA-TERRITORIAL JURISDICTION

ALBANIAN ORTHODOX DIOCESE IN THE USA

At the request of Archbishop Michael of North and South America, a Bishop of Albanian descent was elected on August 31, 1950 by the Ecumenical Patriarchate to represent the Albanian Orthodox in the United States of America.

Bishops of the Albanian Orthodox Diocese

1. Mark	Μάρκος	10 Sep 1950 – 11 Mar 1982+	1919-1982
Lippa, t.b.Lefki			
2. Elias	Ηλίας	10 May 2002 –	b. 1937
Katre, t.b.Philomilion			

CARPATHORUSSIAN ORTHODOX DIOCESE IN THE USA

The Carpathorussian immigrants in the United States of America, although being Uniate, decided in their General Assembly of November 23, 1937 to return to Orthodoxy, and petitioned the Ecumenical Patriarchate to receive them under its jurisdiction. Their request was granted on September 14, 1938, with the whole community, then numbering 75,000 people, returning to the jurisdiction of the Ecumenical Patriarchate.

Hierarchs of the Carpathorussian Orthodox Diocese

1. Orestes	Ορέστης	18 Sep 1938 – 17 Feb 1977+	1883-1977
Chornock, t.b.Agathonikia until 1 Jan 1966, t.m.Agathonikia afterwards			
2. Peter	Πέτρος	22 Oct 1963 – 17 May 1964+	d. 1964
Shymansky, t.b. Syrakousai			
3. John	Ιωάννης	6 Oct 1966 – 30 Sep 1984+	1931-1984
Martin, t.b. Nyssa, heading the Diocese since 1977			
4. Nicholas	Νικόλαος	13 Mar 1983 –	b. 1936
Smisko, t.b. Amisos until 24 Nov 1997, t.m.Amisos afterwards, heading the Diocese since 20 Mar 1985			

EXARCHATE OF RUSSIAN ORTHODOX
PARISHES IN WESTERN EUROPE

The Provisional Administration of Russian Parishes in Western Europe was established by Patriarch Tikhon of Russia on April 8, 1921, who appointed Metropolitan Eulogius of Volynsk as its head. In 1930, after Metropolitan Eulogius openly criticized an outburst of persecution against the Church that was happening in Russia, he was suspended by the Russian Church (June 10, 1930). Metropolitan Eulogius refused to recognize this action, and requested permission to enter the jurisdiction of the Ecumenical Patriarchate, which accepted this request and on February 13, 1931 established the Provisional Exarchate of Russian Parishes in Western Europe.

During 1945 Metropolitan Eulogius entered into negotiations with the Russian Church to return to Russian jurisdiction, but his successor discontinued them. The Ecumenical Patriarchate, under pressure by the Russian Church, abolished the Exarchate on November 22, 1965; however, the Hierarchs refused to return to the jurisdiction of the Russian Church, and so the Ecumenical Patriarchate on January 22, 1971 established in its place the Archdiocese of Russian Parishes in Western Europe. On June 19, 1999 the Ecumenical Patriarchate re-established the Exarchate under the title Exarchate of Parishes of Russian Tradition in Western Europe.

Hierarchs heading the Parishes of Russian Tradition in Western Europe

1. Eulogius   Εὐλόγιος   17 Feb 1931 – 12 Aug 1946+   1868-1946
   Georgievsky (ex t.b.Lublin 12 Jan 1903, b.Kholm 18 Jul 1905, a.Kholm 20 May 1912, a.Volynsky 14 May 1917, a.Russian Exarch Western Europe 8 Apr 1921, promoted to Metropolitan Jan 1922) Metropolitan Exarch
2. Vladimir   Βλαδίμηρος   6 Mar 1947 – 18 Dec 1959+   1873-1959
   Tikhonitsky (ex t.b.Bialystok 3 Jun 1907, t.a.Bialystok 30 Nov 1923, deported from Poland in 1924, assistant in France Feb 1925) Archbishop Exarch until 8 Jul 1947, Metropolitan Exarch afterwards
3. George I   Γεώργιος Α´   10 Oct 1960 – 22 Mar 1981+   1893-1981
   Tarasov (ex t.b.Syrakousai 4 Oct 1953) Archbishop Exarch until 22 Nov 1965, t.a.Syrakousai afterwards
4. George II   Γεώργιος Β´   1 May 1981 – 6 Apr 1993+   1930-1993
   Wagner (ex t.b.Evdokias 3 Oct 1971) t.a.Evdokias
5. Sergius   Σέργιος   27 Jun 1993 – 22 Jan 2003+   1941-2003
   Konovalov, t.a.Efkarpia until 19 Jun 1999, afterwards t.a.Efkarpia and Exarch
6. Gabriel   Γαβριήλ   3 May 2003 –   b. 1946
   De Vylder (ex t.b.Komana 24 Jun 2001) t.a.Komana and Exarch

UKRAINIAN ORTHODOX CHURCH OF AMERICA AND THE DIASPORA

A community of nineteen Uniate Ukrainian parishes in the United States of America decided in their General Assembly of April 9, 1929 to return to Orthodoxy, and petitioned the Ecumenical Patriarchate to receive them under its jurisdiction. Their request was granted on December 14, 1930, with the whole community returning to the jurisdiction of the Ecumenical Patriarchate.

At the request of Archbishop Athenagoras of North and South America, a Bishop of Ukrainian descent was elected on January 28, 1937 by the Ecumenical Patriarchate for the Ukrainian Orthodox in the United States of America, heading about fifty additional parishes that had requested to come under the Ecumenical Patriarchate's jurisdiction.

A larger body of Ukrainian Orthodox, numbering some 180 parishes, had organized themselves as the Ukrainian Orthodox Church of America and the Diaspora (Western Europe and Australia). They too requested to enter the jurisdiction of the Ecumenical Patriarchate, and their request was granted on March 11, 1995. The existing Ukrainian Diocese under the jurisdiction of the Ecumenical Patriarchate (headed by Bishop Vsevolod) was integrated in this larger ecclesiastic entity.

Metropolitans of the Ukrainian Orthodox Church of America

1. Constantine   Κωνσταντίνος   11 Mar 1995 –   b. 1936
   Buggan, t.m.Irinoupolis (ex bishop 7 May 1972, archbishop 1976, metropolitan 15 Oct 1993)

Hierarchs of the former Ukrainian Diocese in the USA

1. Theodore   Θεόδωρος (aka Bogdan)   28 Feb 1937 – 1 Nov 1965+   1892-1965
   Spylka, t.b.Efkarpia
2. Andrew   Ανδρέας   28 Jan 1967 – 18 Nov 1986+   1901-1986
   Kushchak, t.b.Efkarpia until 1983, t.m.Efkarpia afterwards
3. Pangratius   Παγκράτιος (Vsevolod)   27 Sep 1987 – 11 Mar 1995   1927-2007
   Majdanski, t.b.Skopelos (part of UOC of America after 11 Mar 1995, t.a.Skopelos from 11 Apr 2000)

UKRAINIAN ORTHODOX CHURCH OF CANADA

Since 1937 the Ukrainian Orthodox Diocese of America, headed by Bishop Bogdan, included parishes in Canada. However, the main body of Ukrainian Orthodox in Canada had organized themselves as the Ukrainian Orthodox Church of Canada. On September 23, 1987 they officially requested to enter the jurisdiction of the Ecumenical Patriarchate, and after the initial positive reply of January 21, 1989, their request was granted on April 1, 1990.

Metropolitans of Canada

1. Basil   Βασίλειος   1 Apr 1990 – 10 Jan 2005+   1909-2005
   Fedak (ex t.b.Saskatoon 16 Jul 1978, a.Toronto Nov 1983, a.Winnipeg and m.Canada 15 Jul 1985)
2. John   Ιωάννης   20 Nov 2005 –   b. 1935
   Stinka (ex t.b.Saskatoon 27 Nov 1983, b.Edmonton 15 Jul 1985, a.Edmonton 8 Jul 1990)

SECTION P:
METROPOLITANATES IN THE NEW LANDS OF GREECE

On September 4, 1928, the management of all the Ecumenical Patriarchate's Metropolitanates located inside the New Lands annexed by Greece in 1912 was entrusted to the Church of Greece. Since that date their Metropolitans have been elected by the Synod of the Greek Church; therefore, these Metropolitanates will be examined in detail in a future work regarding the Greek Church. A brief list follows here for reference.

I. METROPOLITANATES IN THE NORTHERN AEGEAN ISLANDS

METROPOLITANATE OF CHIOS, PSARA, AND INOUSSES
ΜΗΤΡΟΠΟΛΙΣ ΧΙΟΥ, ΨΑΡΩΝ ΚΑΙ ΟΙΝΟΥΣΣΩΝ

Metropolitan Dionysius of Chios, Psara, and Inousses, most honorable and Exarch of all Ionia

METROPOLITANATE OF LIMNOS
ΜΗΤΡΟΠΟΛΙΣ ΛΗΜΝΟΥ

Metropolitan Hierotheus of Lemnos, most honorable and Exarch of all Aegean Sea

METROPOLITANATE OF MITHYMNA
ΜΗΤΡΟΠΟΛΙΣ ΜΗΘΥΜΝΗΣ

Metropolitan Chrysostom of Methymna, most honorable and Exarch of Lesvos

METROPOLITANATE OF MYTILINI, ERESOS, AND PLOMARION
ΜΗΤΡΟΠΟΛΙΣ ΜΥΤΙΛΗΝΗΣ, ΕΡΕΣΟΥ ΚΑΙ ΠΛΩΜΑΡΙΟΥ

Metropolitan Jacob of Mytilene, Eresus, and Plomarion, most honorable and Exarch of all Lesvos

METROPOLITANATE OF SAMOS AND IKARIA
ΜΗΤΡΟΠΟΛΙΣ ΣΑΜΟΥ ΚΑΙ ΙΚΑΡΙΑΣ

Metropolitan Eusebius of Samos and Icaria, most honorable and Exarch of Cyclades Islands

II. METROPOLITANATES IN WESTERN THRACE

METROPOLITANATE OF ALEXANDROUPOLIS
ΜΗΤΡΟΠΟΛΙΣ ΑΛΕΞΑΝΔΡΟΥΠΟΛΕΩΣ

Metropolitan Anthimus of Alexandrople, most honorable and Exarch of Rhodope

METROPOLITANATE OF DIDYMOTICHON AND ORESTIAS
ΜΗΤΡΟΠΟΛΙΣ ΔΙΔΥΜΟΤΕΙΧΟΥ ΚΑΙ ΟΡΕΣΤΙΑΔΟΣ

Metropolitan Nicephorus of Didymotichon and Orestias,
most honorable and Exarch of all Rhodope

METROPOLITANATE OF MARONIA AND KOMOTINI
ΜΗΤΡΟΠΟΛΙΣ ΜΑΡΩΝΕΙΑΣ ΚΑΙ ΚΟΜΟΤΗΝΗΣ

Metropolitan Damascene of Maronia and Comotene, most honorable and Exarch of Rhodope

METROPOLITANATE OF XANTHI AND PERITHEORION
ΜΗΤΡΟΠΟΛΙΣ ΞΑΝΘΗΣ ΚΑΙ ΠΕΡΙΘΕΩΡΙΟΥ

Metropolitan Panteleimon of Xanthe and Peritheorion, most honorable and Exarch of Western Thrace

III. METROPOLITANATES IN MACEDONIA

METROPOLITANATE OF DRAMA
ΜΗΤΡΟΠΟΛΙΣ ΔΡΑΜΑΣ

Metropolitan Paul of Drama, most honorable and Exarch of Macedonia

METROPOLITANATE OF EDESSA, PELLA, AND ALMOPIA
ΜΗΤΡΟΠΟΛΙΣ ΕΔΕΣΣΗΣ, ΠΕΛΛΗΣ ΚΑΙ ΑΛΜΩΠΙΑΣ

Metropolitan Ioel of Edessa, Pella, and Almopia, most honorable and Exarch of Central Macedonia

METROPOLITANATE OF ELASSON
ΜΗΤΡΟΠΟΛΙΣ ΕΛΑΣΣΩΝΟΣ

Metropolitan Basil of Elasson, most honorable and Exarch of Olympus

METROPOLITANATE OF ELEFTHEROUPOLIS
ΜΗΤΡΟΠΟΛΙΣ ΕΛΕΥΘΕΡΟΥΠΟΛΕΩΣ

Metropolitan Chrysostom of Eleutheropolis, most honorable and Exarch of Pangaion

METROPOLITANATE OF FLORINA, PRESPES, AND EORDAIA
ΜΗΤΡΟΠΟΛΙΣ ΦΛΩΡΙΝΗΣ, ΠΡΕΣΠΩΝ ΚΑΙ ΕΟΡΔΑΙΑΣ

Metropolitan Theocletus of Florina, Prespes, and Eordaia,
most honorable and Exarch of Upper Macedonia

METROPOLITANATE OF GOUMENISSA, AXIOUPOLIS, AND POLYKASTRON
ΜΗΤΡΟΠΟΛΙΣ ΓΟΥΜΕΝΙΣΣΗΣ, ΑΞΙΟΥΠΟΛΕΩΣ ΚΑΙ ΠΟΛΥΚΑΣΤΡΟΥ

Metropolitan Demetrius of Goumenissa, Axiopolis, and Polycastron,
most honorable and Exarch of Western Macedonia

METROPOLITANATE OF GREVENA
ΜΗΤΡΟΠΟΛΙΣ ΓΡΕΒΕΝΩΝ

Metropolitan Sergius of Grevena, most honorable and Exarch of Southern Macedonia

METROPOLITANATE OF IERISSOS, AGION OROS, AND ARDAMERION
ΜΗΤΡΟΠΟΛΙΣ ΙΕΡΙΣΣΟΥ, ΑΓΙΟΥ ΟΡΟΥΣ ΚΑΙ ΑΡΔΑΜΕΡΙΟΥ

Metropolitan Nicodemus of Hierissus, Hagion Oros, and Ardamerion,
most honorable and Exarch of all Chalcidice

METROPOLITANATE OF KASSANDRIA
ΜΗΤΡΟΠΟΛΙΣ ΚΑΣΣΑΝΔΡΕΙΑΣ

Metropolitan Nicodemus of Cassandria, most honorable and Exarch of Thermaicus Gulf

METROPOLITANATE OF KASTORIA
ΜΗΤΡΟΠΟΛΙΣ ΚΑΣΤΟΡΙΑΣ

Metropolitan Seraphim of Castoria, most honorable and Exarch of Upper Macedonia

METROPOLITANATE OF KITROS AND KATERINI
ΜΗΤΡΟΠΟΛΙΣ ΚΙΤΡΟΥΣ ΚΑΙ ΚΑΤΕΡΙΝΗΣ

Metropolitan Agathonicus of Citrus and Caterine, most honorable and Exarch of Pieria

METROPOLITANATE OF LANGADA
ΜΗΤΡΟΠΟΛΙΣ ΛΑΓΚΑΔΑ

Metropolitan Spyridon of Langada, most honorable and Exarch of Central Macedonia

METROPOLITANATE OF NEAPOLIS AND STAVROUPOLIS
ΜΗΤΡΟΠΟΛΙΣ ΝΕΑΠΟΛΕΩΣ ΚΑΙ ΣΤΑΥΡΟΥΠΟΛΕΩΣ

Metropolitan Barnavas of Neapolis and Stauropolis,
most honorable and Exarch of Central Macedonia

METROPOLITANATE OF NEW KRINI AND KALAMARIA
ΜΗΤΡΟΠΟΛΙΣ ΝΕΑΣ ΚΡΗΝΗΣ ΚΑΙ ΚΑΛΑΜΑΡΙΑΣ

Metropolitan Procopius of New Crene and Calamaria, most honorable and Exarch of Chalcidice

METROPOLITANATE OF PHILIPPI, NEAPOLIS, AND THASOS
ΜΗΤΡΟΠΟΛΙΣ ΦΙΛΙΠΠΩΝ, ΝΕΑΠΟΛΕΩΣ ΚΑΙ ΘΑΣΟΥ

Metropolitan Procopius of Philippi, Neapolis, and Thasos,
most honorable and Exarch of Eastern Macedonia

METROPOLITANATE OF POLYANI AND KILKISION
ΜΗΤΡΟΠΟΛΙΣ ΠΟΛΥΑΝΗΣ ΚΑΙ ΚΙΛΚΙΣΙΟΥ

Metropolitan Apostolus of Polyane and Cilcision, most honorable and Exarch of Macedonia

METROPOLITANATE OF SERRES AND NIGRITA
ΜΗΤΡΟΠΟΛΙΣ ΣΕΡΡΩΝ ΚΑΙ ΝΙΓΡΙΤΗΣ

Metropolitan Theologus of Serres and Nigrita, most honorable and Exarch of all Macedonia

METROPOLITANATE OF SERVIA AND KOZANI
ΜΗΤΡΟΠΟΛΙΣ ΣΕΡΒΙΩΝ ΚΑΙ ΚΟΖΑΝΗΣ

Metropolitan Paul of Serbia and Cozane, most honorable and Exarch of Western Macedonia

METROPOLITANATE OF SIDIROKASTRON
ΜΗΤΡΟΠΟΛΙΣ ΣΙΔΗΡΟΚΑΣΤΡΟΥ

Metropolitan Macarius of Siderocastron, most honorable and Exarch of Macedonia

METROPOLITANATE OF SISANION AND SIATISTA
ΜΗΤΡΟΠΟΛΙΣ ΣΙΣΑΝΙΟΥ ΚΑΙ ΣΙΑΤΙΣΤΗΣ

Metropolitan Paul of Sisanion and Siatista, most honorable and Exarch of Macedonia

METROPOLITANATE OF THESSALONIKI
ΜΗΤΡΟΠΟΛΙΣ ΘΕΣΣΑΛΟΝΙΚΗΣ

Metropolitan Anthimus of Thessalonica, most honorable and Exarch of all Thessaly

METROPOLITANATE OF VERIA AND NAOUSA
ΜΗΤΡΟΠΟΛΙΣ ΒΕΡΟΙΑΣ ΚΑΙ ΝΑΟΥΣΗΣ

Metropolitan Panteleimon of Beroea and Naousa, most honorable and Exarch of Thessaly

METROPOLITANATE OF ZICHNA AND NEVROKOPION
ΜΗΤΡΟΠΟΛΙΣ ΖΙΧΝΩΝ ΚΑΙ ΝΕΥΡΟΚΟΠΙΟΥ

Metropolitan Hierotheus of Zichna and Neurocopion, most honorable and Exarch of Pangaion

IV. METROPOLITANATES IN EPIRUS

METROPOLITANATE OF DRYINOUPOLIS, POGONIANI, AND KONITSA
ΜΗΤΡΟΠΟΛΙΣ ΔΡΥΪΝΟΥΠΟΛΕΩΣ, ΠΩΓΩΝΙΑΝΗΣ ΚΑΙ ΚΟΝΙΤΣΗΣ

Metropolitan Andrew of Dryinopolis, Pogoniane, and Konitsa,
most honorable and Exarch of Northern Eperus

METROPOLITANATE OF IOANNINA
ΜΗΤΡΟΠΟΛΙΣ ΙΩΑΝΝΙΝΩΝ

Metropolitan Theocletus of Joannina, most honorable and Exarch of all Eperus and Corfu

METROPOLITANATE OF NIKOPOLIS AND PREVEZA
ΜΗΤΡΟΠΟΛΙΣ ΝΙΚΟΠΟΛΕΩΣ ΚΑΙ ΠΡΕΒΕΖΗΣ

Metropolitan Meletius of Nicopolis and Preveza, most honorable and Exarch of Old Eperus

METROPOLITANATE OF PARAMYTHIA, PHILIATAI, AND GIROMERION
ΜΗΤΡΟΠΟΛΙΣ ΠΑΡΑΜΥΘΙΑΣ, ΦΙΛΙΑΤΩΝ ΚΑΙ ΓΗΡΟΜΕΡΙΟΥ

Metropolitan Titus of Paramythia, Philiatai, and Geromerion, most honorable and Exarch of Thesprotia

SECTION Q:
TITULAR HIERARCHS

The practice of electing Hierarchs with titles of long-dissolved eparchies of the Ecumenical Patriarchate started some years before the fall of Constantinople, "for the names of the old Metropolitanates not to be forgotten." Titular Metropolitans stayed mostly in Constantinople, while titular Bishops usually served as assistants to Hierarchs of the existing Metropolitanates. During the last two centuries the number of titular Hierarch elections increased significantly, as their presence has become essential in the Ecumenical Patriarchate's organization. This section lists all titular Metropolitans and titular Archbishops elected by the Ecumenical Patriarchate. In addition, some 500 titular Bishops have been elected to this day.

TITULAR METROPOLITANS

1. Jacob of Myra/ Μυρέων	. . . – 18 Jan 1600+	d. 1600
2. Matthew of Myra/ Μυρέων	Dec 1606 – 1624+	1550-1624
3. Seraphim of Sevastia/Σεβαστείας	Jul 1617 – . . .	d. ?
4. Longinus of Synnada/Συννάδων	May 1618 – 1628+	d. 1628
5. Nicephorus of Laodikia/Λαοδικείας	before 1620 – 4 Oct 1628+	d. 1628
6. Meletius of Synnada/Συννάδων	Oct 1628 – 1637+	d. 1637
7. Joseph of Sevastia/Σεβαστείας	May 1629 – . . .	d. ?
8. (unknown) of Laodikia/Λαοδικείας	Aug 1630 – 1643?	d. 1643?
9. Meletius of Efchaita/Ευχαΐτων	Aug 1632 – . . .	d. ?
10. Jeremy of Myra/ Μυρέων (to former, m.Drystra)	Aug 1633 – before Oct 1637	d≥1638
11. Meletius of Neapolis/Νεαπόλεως	26 Jan 1636 – . . .	d. ?
12. Jacobus of Sidi/Σίδης (to m.Ganos)	. . . – 7 Aug 1637	d≥1639
13. Callinicus of Sidi/Σίδης	7 Aug 1637 – . . .	d. ?
14. Matthew of Synnada/Συννάδων (ex t.b.Chimarra)	11 Sep 1637 – 1640 +	d. 1640
15. Callistus of Synnada/Συννάδων	5 Aug 1640 – . . .	d. ?
16. Zacharias of Myra/ Μυρέων (to m.Kaisaria)	. . . – Nov 1642	d≥1649
17. Sophronius of Laodikia/Λαοδικείας	4 Sep 1643 – . . .	d. ?
18. Benedict of Selefkia/Σελευκείας	8 Jan 1653 – 1663+	d. 1663
19. Jacob of Efchaita/Ευχαΐτων	Dec 1656 – . . .	d. ?
20. Matthew of Selefkia/Σελευκείας	Oct 1663 – . . .	d. ?
21. Pangratius of Myra/ Μυρέων	1666	d. ?
22. Parthenius of Efchaita/Ευχαΐτων (to m.Old Patra)	. . . – Apr 1674	d≥1677
23. Joasaph of Efchaita/Ευχαΐτων	24 Jul 1674 – . . .	d. ?
24. Ephrem of Sardis/Σάρδεων	1677	d. ?
25. Anthimus of Sevastia/Σεβαστείας	1693	d. ?
26. Macarius of Klavdioupolis/Κλαυδιουπόλεως	. . . – Aug 1695	d≥1703

(to m.Paronaxia)

27. Neophytus of Sevastia/Σεβαστείας	*Jun* 1696 – . . .	d. ?
28. Macarius of Klavdioupolis/Κλαυδιουπόλεως	. . . – 17 Feb 1699	d≥1713
Dapontes (to a.Andros)		
29. Cosmas of Klavdioupolis/Κλαυδιουπόλεως	2 Feb 1706 – Jan 1712	d. 1736
(ex a.Sina) (to p.Alexandria)		
30. Anthimus of Stavroupolis/Σταυρουπόλεως	*Jul* 1743 – . . .	d. ?
31. Nicodemus of Sardis/Σάρδεων	*Dec* 1749 – 1764?	d. 1764?
32. Philaretus of Myra/Μυρέων (to p.d.Rimnikon)	. . . – Mar 1780	d. 1792
33. Athanasius of Stavroupolis/Σταυρουπόλεως	*Jan* 1790 – . . .	d. ?
34. Gregory of Laodikia/Λαοδικείας	*Feb* 1792 – 11 Mar 1812+	d. 1812
Xenos		
35. Dorotheus of Stavroupolis/Σταυρουπόλεως	*Jun* 1800 – . . .	d. ?
36. Macarius of Avydos/Αβύδου	*Nov* 1800 – . . .	d. ?
37. Dionusius of Edessa/Εδέσσης	*Nov* 1801 – Jan 1834	d. 1838
Delazaris (to m.Zakynthos)		
38. Gregory of Irinoupolis/Ειρηνουπόλεως	11 Jan 1802 – 1 Jan 1846+	1761-1846
Pataras/Kouimntzoglou (signing as Metropolitan of "Irinoupolis and Vatopedion")		
39. Hierotheus of Avgoustoupolis/Αυγουστουπόλεως	*Dec* 1802 – after 1812	d≥1812
40. Nectarius of Sardis/Σάρδεων	1792 – 12 Jun 1831+	d. 1831
Thomaïdis		
41. Neophytus of Stavroupolis/Σταυρουπόλεως	*Jun* 1805 – . . .	d. ?
42. Joseph of Melitini/Μελιτηνής	*Aug* 1806 – Jul 1814	c.1750-1820
Lefakis (to m.Mesimvria)		
43. Neophytus of Efkarpia/Ευκαρπίας	*Jan* 1813 – . . .	d. ?
44. Benjamin of Myron/ Μύρων	*Mar* 1817 – . . .	d. ?
45. Joachim of Keltzini/Κελτζηνής	*Aug* 1817 – . . .	d. ?
46. Theodosius of Zichnai/Ζιχνών (to m.Angyra)	*Mar* 1821 – Oct 1827	d. 1834
47. Meletius of Stavroupolis/Σταυρουπόλεως	*Dec* 1826 – . . .	d. ?
48. Meletius of Sardis/Σάρδεων	1836, 1840	d. ?
49. Constantine of Stavroupolis/Σταυρουπόλεως	*Aug* 1848 – 21 Nov 1868+	1795-1868
Typaldos		
50. Acacius of Ierapolis/Ιεραπόλεως	*27 Sep* 1856 – . . .	d. ?
51. Άνθιμος of Selefkia/Σελευκείας	*20 Apr* 1866 – 1868+	c.1800-1868
Mazarakis		
52. Apostolus of Stavroupolis/Σταυρουπόλεως	6 *Jul* 1901 – 29 Jun 1906	1850-1917
Christodoulou (to m.Veria)		
53. Michael of Sardis/Σάρδεων	15 Jul 1901 – 23 Feb 1918+	1848-1918
Kleovoulos		
54. Germanus of Selefkia/Σελευκείας	*28 Jun* 1912 – 24 Mar 1922	1872-1951
Strinopoulos (to m.Thyatira/Great Britain)		
55. Basil of Selefkia/Σελευκείας	*26 Jan* 1926 – 27 Jan 1928	1884-1969
Papadopoulos (to m.Giannitsa)		
56. Joachim of Stavroupolis/Σταυρουπόλεως	24 Jun 1926 – 12 Dec 1931	1892-1950
Pelekanos (to m.Derki)		
57. Leontius of Theodoroupolis/Θεοδωρουπόλεως	17 Dec 1927 – 8 Feb 1964+	1872-1964
Liverios (ex t.b.Theodoroupolis 6 Nov 1906)		
58. Constantine of Irinoupolis/Ειρηνουπόλεως	17 Dec 1927 – 5 May 1961+	1892-1961
Alatopoulos (ex t.b.Irinoupolis 30 Jan 1925)		

59. Meletius of Christoupolis/Χριστουπόλεως Loukakis (ex t.b.Christoupolis 13 Apr 1926)	17 Dec 1927 – 21 Jul 1946+	1862-1946
60. Polycarp of Myron/ Μύρων Dimitriadis (to m.Prousa)	25 Dec 1927 – 28 Jan 1936	1892-1953
61. Dorotheus of Laodikia/Λαοδικείας Georgiadis (to m.Pringiponnisa)	1 Jan 1928 – 12 Mar 1946	1891-1974
62. Maximus of Laodikia/Λαοδικείας Georgiadis	17 Oct 1946 – 10 Dec 1979+	1908-1979
63. Jacobus of Meliti/Μελίτης Koukouzis (ex t.b.Meliti 6 Feb 1955) (to a.America)	4 Apr 1956 – 14 Feb 1959	1911-2005
64. Aemilian of Selefkia/Σελευκείας Zacharopoulos (to m.Belgium)	14 Jun 1959 – 12 Aug 1969	b. 1915
65. Athenagoras of Elaia/Ελαίας Kokkinakis (ex t.b.Elaia 14 Sep 1950) (to m.Thyatira/Great Britain)	6 Sep 1960 – 10 Dec 1963	1912-1979
66. Polyeuctus of Tropaion/Τροπαίου Finfinis (ex t.b.Tropaion 3 Nov 1955) (to m.Germany)	6 Sep 1960 – 22 Oct 1963	1912-1988
67. Maximus of Stavroupolis/Σταυρουπόλεως Repanellis	26 Feb 1961 – 4 Jan 1991+	1919-1991
68. Chrysostomus of Myron/ Μύρων Konstantinidis (to m.Ephesos)	5 Mar 1961 – 10 Dec 1991	1921-2006
69. Germanus of Ierapolis/Ιεραπόλεως Polyzoïdis (ex t.b.Nyssa 30 Sep 1941)	17 Apr 1962 – 13 Jul 1993+	1897-1993
70. Jacobus of Christoupolis/Χριστουπόλεως Virvos (ex t.b.Apamia 13 May 1956)	10 Dec 1963 – 17 Dec 1976+	1901-1976
71. Nathanael of Militoupolis/Μιλητουπόλεως Dikaios (ex t.b.Militoupolis 7 May 1956) (to m.Kos)	1963 – 23 May 1967	1919-1979
72. Symeon of Irinoupolis/Ειρηνουπόλεως Amaryllios (to m.Pringiponnisa)	26 Apr 1964 – 9 Jun 1987	1916-2003
73. Aemilian of Militos/Μιλήτου Tsakopoulos (ex t.b.Militos 28 Jun 1959)	1964 – 24 Jul 1985+	1915-1985
74. Aemilian of Kalavria/Καλαβρίας Timiadis (ex t.b.Meloi 25 Sep 1960) (to m.Silyvria)	30 Mar 1965 – 15 Nov 1977	1916-2008
75. Orestes of Agathonikia/Αγαθονικείας Chornock, (ex t.b.Agathonikia 18 Sep 1938)	1 Jan 1966 – 17 Feb 1977+	1883-1977
76. Emmanuel of Mesimvria/Μεσημβρίας Karpathios (ex m.Kos)	23 May 1967 – 5 Aug 1972+	1887-1972
77. Agapius of Sozopolis/Σωζοπόλεως Ioannidis (to m.Pringiponnisa)	29 Nov 1970 – 22 Mar 1977	1923-1979
78. Evangelus of Pergi/Πέργης Galanis	30 Nov 1970 –	b. 1928
79. Callinicus of Lystra/Λύστρων (1st time) Alexandridis (to m.Pringiponnisa)	6 Dec 1970 – 18 Sep 1979	b. 1926
80. Stylianus of Militoupolis/Μιλητουπόλεως Charkianakis (to a.Australia)	6 Dec 1970 – 13 Feb 1975	b. 1935
81. Damascene of Tranoupolis/Τρανουπόλεως Papandreou (to m.Helvetia)	6 Dec 1970 – 2 Oct 1982	b. 1936
82. Panteleimon of Tyana/Τυάνων Rodopoulos (to m.Tyroloi)	9 Jun 1974 – 15 Nov 1977	b. 1929
83. Cosmas of Kampania/Καμπανίας Papadopoulos (ex t.b.Dervi 18 Jul 1965)	13 Aug 1976 – 15 Nov 1992+	1923-1992
84. Athanasius of Elenoupolis/ Ελενουπόλεως	8 Nov 1976 – 2 Oct 1990	b. 1936

Papas (ex t.b.Elenoupolis 24 Sep 1972) (to m.Ilioupolis)

85. Joachim of Melitini/Μελιτηνής   27 Jun 1977 – 10 Dec 1991   b. 1942
Nerantzoulis (ex t.b.Melitini 23 Sep 1973) (to m.Chalkidon)

86. Andrew of Efkarpia/Ευκαρπίας   1983 – 18 Nov 1986+   1901-1986
Kuschak (ex t.b.Efkarpia 28 Jan 1967)

87. Philip of Tyana/Τυάνων   11 Mar 1984 – 18 Oct 1997+   1941-1997
Kapetanidis

88. Cyril of Selefkia/Σελευκείας   27 Oct 1985 – 5 Sep 2002   b. 1942
Dragounis (to m.Imvros)

---. Callinicus of Lystra/Λύστρων   (2nd time)   5 Nov 1985 –   b. 1926
Alexandridis (ex m.Pringiponnisa)

89. Timothy of Efchaita/Ευχαΐτων   5 Feb 1987 – 8 Jan 1993+   1910-1993
Pazaridis (ex t.b.Trachia 2 Aug 1964)

90. Germanus of Tranoupolis/Τρανουπόλεως   5 Feb 1987 –   b. 1931
Chaviaropoulos (ex t.b.Trallis 14 Jan 1973)

91. Germanus of Theodoroupolis/Θεοδωρουπόλεως   5 Feb 1987 –   b. 1930
Athanasiadis (ex t.b.Arianzos 6 Feb 1972)

92. Theocletus of Amphipolis/Αμφιπόλεως   5 Feb 1987 – 8 Jun 1993   1939-2004
Rokas (ex t.b.Sevastia 22 May 1977) (to m.Metres)

93. Ιάκωβος of Laodikia/Λαοδικείας   25 Dec 1987 – 9 Jul 2002   b. 1947
Sofroniadis (to m.Pringiponnisa)

94. Apostolus of Militos/Μιλήτου   15 Jan 1990 –   b. 1948
Voulgaris (ex t.b.Militos 3 Nov 1985)

95. Demetrius of Sevastia/Σεβαστείας   4 Nov 1990 –   b. 1952
Kommatas

96. Constantine of Irinoupolis/Ειρηνουπόλεως   11 Mar 1995 –   b. 1936
Buggan (ex bishop 7 May 1972, archbishop 1976, metropolitan 15 Oct 1993)

97. Anatolius of Sozopolis/Σωζοπόλεως   11 Mar 1995 – 28 Oct 1997+   1912-1997
Dublansky (ex bishop 31 May 1981, Metropolitan 1994)

98. Irenaeus of Evdokias/Ευδοκιάδος   21 Nov 1995 – 4 Sep 2000   b. 1951
Ioannidis (to m.Myriophyton)

99. Chrysostomus of Myron/ Μύρων   25 Nov 1995 –   b. 1946
Kalaïtzis

100. Apostolus of Agathonikia/Αγαθονικείας   26 Nov 1995 – 4 Sep 2000   b. 1952
Daniilidis (to m.Moschonesia)

101. Gennadius of Sasima/Σασίμων   1 Jun 1997 –   b. 1951
Lymouris

102. Nicholas of Amisos/Αμισού   24 Nov 1997 –   b. 1936
Smisko (ex t.b. Amisos 13 Mar 1983)

103. Païsius of Tyana/Τυάνων   11 Apr 1998 –   b. 1945
Loulourgas

104. Callistus of Dioklia/Διοκλείας   30 Mar 2007 –   b. 1934
Ware (ex t.b.Dioklia 6 Jun 1982)

TITULAR ARCHBISHOPS

1. George of Syrakousai/ Συρακουσών   10 Oct 1960 – 22 Mar 1981+   1893-1981
Tarasov(ex t.b.Syrakousai 4 Oct 1953)

2. George of Evdokias/Ευδοκιάδος   1 May 1981 – 6 Apr 1993+   1930-1993
Wagner (ex t.b.Evdokias 3 Oct 1971)

3. Sergius of Efkarpia/Ευκαρπίας   27 Jun 1993 – 22 Jan 2003+   1941-2003
    Konovalov

4. Anthony of Ierapolis/Ιεραπόλεως   11 Mar 1995 –   b. 1947
    Scharba (ex bishop 6 Oct 1985)

5. Pangratius (Vsevolod) of Skopelos/ Σκοπέλου   11 Apr 2000 – 16 Dec 2007+   1927-2007
    Majdanski (ex t.b.Skopelos 27 Sep 1987)

6. Gabriel of Komana/Κομάνων   3 May 2003 –   b. 1946
    De Vylder (ex t.b.Komana 24 Jun 2001)

SECTION R:
THE APPENDICES

APPENDIX A

LISTS OF HIERARCHS BEFORE 1800 AD

The lists of hierarchs prior to 1800 are often incomplete, due to records of the Byzantine and early Ottoman periods having been lost. Largely reconstructed by directly or indirectly consulting sources of the era, they present catalogs of known hierarchs rather than catalogs of all past hierarchs of each Eparchy. Some of the listed dates reflect just the year or years that a certain hierarch is mentioned in the sources, being a middle point of his tenure as Metropolitan rather than a beginning or end. With further research in the Byzantine and early Ottoman periods pending (the pre-Ottoman parts of the listings presented here being preliminary), these catalogs will be updated in a future edition of this work, which will also expand the detailed listings (presently stopping in the year 1800) as far back as 1600.

SECTION A: METROPOLITANATES IN EASTERN THRACE

Known Hierarchs of Adrianople

1. Eutropius	Ευτρόπιος	. . . – 336
2. Lucius	Λούκιος	before 341 – 348
3. Philip I	Φίλιππος Α΄	. . . – 362
4. Ammonius	Αμμώνιος	394, 399
5. Gregory I	Γρηγόριος Α΄	451, 459
6. John	Ιωάννης	553
7. Sabbas	Σάββας	
8. Constantine	Κωνσταντίνος	
9. Daniel	Δανιήλ	
10. Sergius	Σέργιος	
11. Pantherius	Πανθήριος	
12. Eustace I	Ευστάθιος Α΄	
13. Myron	Μύρων	
14. Joseph I	Ιωσήφ Α΄	. . . – 787
15. Manuel	Μανουήλ	787 – 813
16. Theophylactus	Θεοφύλακτος	
17. Philip II	Φίλιππος Β΄	879
18. Stephen	Στέφανος	914 – 924
19. Athanasius I	Αθανάσιος Α΄	942

20. Nicholas I	Νικόλαος Α'	975
21. Michael	Μιχαήλ	succeeded Nicholas I
22. Agapetus	Αγαπητός	1025 – 1043
23. Eusebius	Ευσέβιος	1053
24. Nicholas II	Νικόλαος Β'	1082
25. Leo	Λέων	1157 – 1170
26. George	Γεώργιος	1173
27. Christodoulus	Χριστόδουλος	
28. Eustace II	Ευστάθιος Β'	
29. Theodosius	Θεοδόσιος	
30. Theodore	Θεόδωρος	
31. Gerasimus I	Γεράσιμος Α'	
32. Germanus	Γερμανός	1260 – 25 May 1265 (to p.Const)
33. Basil or Barlaam	Βασίλειος ή Βαρλάαμ	1265 – . . .
34. Theoctistus	Θεόκτιστος	after 1278 – 1283
35. Arsenius I	Αρσένιος Α'	1299
36. Ignatius	Ιγνάτιος	1324 – . . .
37. Joseph II	Ιωσήφ Β'	1334, 1347
38. Gerasimus II	Γεράσιμος Β'	
39. Polycarp I	Πολύκαρπος Α'	. . . – 1361
. . . vacant		1361 – 1380
40. Matthew I	Ματθαίος Α'	Jun 1380 – after 1389
41. Melanion	Μελανίων	May 1401 – . . .
42. Nicephorus I	Νικηφόρος Α'	1410?- 1420
43. Gerasimus III	Γεράσιμος Γ'	1433 – 1457?
44. Mark	Μάρκος	1465 – . . .
45. Macarius	Μακάριος	1467
46. Theophanes	Θεοφάνης	1474
47. Matthew II	Ματθαίος Β'	1499
48. Sophronius	Σωφρόνιος	after 1500
49. Joasaph	Ιωάσαφ	1535 – Aug 1556 (to p.Const)
50. Arsenius II	Αρσένιος Β'	1561, 1567
51. Jeremias	Ιερεμίας	1572, 1580
52. Callistus	Κάλλιστος	before 1590 – 26 Apr 1594
53. Anthimus	Άνθιμος	9 Jun 1600 – 18 Jun 1623 (to p.Const)
54. Parthenius I	Παρθένιος Α'	19 Jun 1623 – 1 Jul 1639 (to p.Const)
55. Parthenius II	Παρθένιος Β'	7 Jul 1639 – 8 Sep 1644 (to p.Const)
56. Neophytus I	Νεόφυτός Α'	Sep 1644 – 1688 (later to p.Const)
57. Clement	Κλήμης	1688 – 1692
58. Athanasius II	Αθανάσιος Β'	Oct 1692 – May 1709 (to p.Const)
59. Athanasius III	Αθανάσιος Γ'	1709 – 1739
60. Dionysius I	Διονύσιος Α'	Sep 1739 – 1 Feb 1774
61. Nicephorus II	Νικηφόρος Β'	21 Feb 1774 – 26 Sep 1780
62. Callinicus I	Καλλίνικος Α'	8 Oct 1780 – Sep 1792
63. Gabriel	Γαβριήλ	Sep 1792 – 1810

Known Hierarchs of Ainos

1. George	Γεώργιος	691
2. John I	Ἰωάννης Α'	879
3. John II	Ἰωάννης Β'	1025 – 1043
4. Michael	Μιχαήλ	1084
5. John III	Ἰωάννης Γ'	1166
6. Basil	Βασίλειος	1259, 1260
7. Sabbas	Σάββας	1310
8. Arsenius	Ἀρσένιος	1315 (m. of Pergamos, president)
9. Theodosius	Θεοδόσιος	1329 (m. of Melitini, president)
10. Daniel I	Δανιήλ Α'	1351, 1355
11. Dionysius	Διονύσιος	May 1369 – after 1371
12. Mark	Μάρκος	1381
13. Athanasius	Ἀθανάσιος	before 1393 – 1395
. . . vacant		1395 – 1467?
14. Dorotheus	Δωρόθεος Α'	1467
15. Nephon	Νήφων	1484
16. Isidore	Ἰσίδωρος	1567
17. Matthew I	Ματθαίος Α'	1575, 1578, 1583
18. Pachomius	Παχώμιος	1590
19. Parthenius I	Παρθένιος Α'	28 Feb 1601 – 1602
20. Meletius I	Μελέτιος Α'	28 Mar 1602 – 1612
21. Daniel II	Δανιήλ Β'	1612 – 1621
22. Parthenius II	Παρθένιος Β'	Jan 1622 – 1 Mar 1652
23. Nicephorus	Νικηφόρος	Mar 1652 – Nov 1654
24. Macarius	Μακάριος	2 Nov 1654 – after 1658
25. Gideon	Γεδεών	1672, 1676, 1704
26. Jeremias I	Ἰερεμίας	1706
27. Joachim I	Ἰωακείμ Α'	1708
28. Neophytus	Νεόφυτος	1713
29. Daniel III	Δανιήλ Γ'	1716
30. Jeremias II	Ἰερεμίας Β'	1721 (could be 2nd time of Jeremias I)
31. Methodius	Μεθόδιος	1738 – 1760
32. Timothy	Τιμόθεος	Jan 1760 – 1772
33. Dionysius	Διονύσιος	Jul 1772 – 1807

Known Hierarchs of Derki

1. Gregory I	Γρηγόριος Α'	783, 786, 787
2. Macarius I	Μακάριος Α'	. . . – 879
3. Neophytus I	Νεόφυτος Α'	879 – . . .
4. John I	Ἰωάννης Α'	997
5. John II	Ἰωάννης Β'	1166
6. Michael	Μιχαήλ	1171
7. George	Γεώργιος	1192

8. Gregory II	Γρηγόριος Β΄	1197
9. Constantine I	Κωνσταντίνος Α΄	1276
10. Constantius	Κωνστάντιος	1278
11. Theodulus	Θεόδουλος	1316 (a.Nymphaion, as president)
12. Luke	Λουκάς	1324, 1329
13. Neophytus II	Νεόφυτος Β΄	1354, 1355 (m.Vizyi, as president)
14. Methodius	Μεθόδιος	1365 (m.Iraklia, as president)
15. Paul	Παύλος	1379, 1381
16. Joseph	Ιωσήφ	1389
17. Acacius	Ακάκιος	1443
Eparchy abolished		1453 – Jun 1655
18. Daniel	Δανιήλ (titular)	1634
19. Athanasius	Αθανάσιος	Jun 1655 – Dec 1660
20. Chrysanthus	Χρύσανθος	Dec 1660 – Sep 1673
21. Macarius II	Μακάριος Β΄	11 Sep 1673 – Sep 1688
22. Nicodemus	Νικόδημος	Sep 1688 – Dec 1731
23. Samouel	Σαμουήλ	27 Dec 1731 – 24 May 1763 (to p.Const)
24. Dionysius	Διονύσιος	Aug 1763 – Oct 1772
25. Ananias	Ανανίας	Feb 1773 – Mar 1791
26. Gerasimus I	Γεράσιμος Α΄	26 Mar 1791 – 3 Mar 1794 (to p.Const)
27. Macarius III	Μακάριος Γ΄	4 Mar 1794 – Jun 1801

Known Hierarchs of Ganos and Chora

1. Constantine I	Κωνσταντίνος Α΄	1324, 1325 (m.Pigai, as president)
2. Menas I	Μηνάς Α΄	1329, 1330
3. Joseph	Ιωσήφ	. . . – Sep 1347
4. Athanasius	Αθανάσιος	Sep 1347 – . . . (m.Kyzikos, as pres.)
5. Menas II	Μηνάς Β΄	. . . – after May 1387
6. Nicandrus	Νίκανδρος	before Nov 1387 – after 1389
7. Gennadius	Γεννάδιος	1437, 1439
8. Gregory I	Γρηγόριος Α΄	1450
9. Matthew I	Ματθαίος Α΄	1467
10. Nicephorus	Νικηφόρος	1499
11. Theophanes	Θεοφάνης	1561
12. Pachomius	Παχώμιος	1572, 1576, 1578
13. Dionysius I	Διονύσιος Α΄	1585, 1593, 1596, 1597
14. Macarius I	Μακάριος Α΄ (1st time)	Dec 1601 – Sep 1609
15. Neophytus I	Νεόφυτος Α΄	1609 – 1613
---. Macarius I	Μακάριος Α΄ (2nd time)	Jan 1613 – 1616
16. Ignatius	Ιγνάτιος	1616 – 1 Apr 1624
17. Johnnicius	Ιωαννίκιος	29 Apr 1624 – summer 1636
18. Jacob	Ιάκωβος	7 Aug 1637 – 21 Aug 1639
19. Païsius I	Παΐσιος Α΄	18 Sep 1639 – 18 Mar 1648
20. Gabriel	Γαβριήλ (1st time)	23 Mar 1648 – 26 Nov 1651
21. Cosmas	Κοσμάς (1st time)	2 Mar 1652 – 1654

---. Gabriel	Γαβριήλ	(2nd time)	1654 – 23 Apr 1657 (to p.Const)
22. Jeremias	Ιερεμίας		1663
---. Cosmas	Κοσμάς	(2nd time)	1664, 1668, 1669
23. Christopher	Χριστόφορος		1669/70 – Jan 1672
24. Leontius I	Λεόντιος Α΄		Oct 1672 – after 1674
25. Matthew II	Ματθαίος Β΄		1682
26. Germanus	Γερμανός		1684, 1688, 1690
27. Constantius I	Κωνστάντιος Α΄		1692, 1699, 1705, 1707
28. Anthimus	Άνθιμος		1708?- 3 Sep 1716
29. Gregory II	Γρηγόριος Β΄		1716 – 1728
30. Bartholomew	Βαρθολομαίος	(1st time)	Oct 1728 – 1733?
31. Hierotheus	Ιερόθεος		1733
---. Bartholomew	Βαρθολομαίος	(2nd time)	. . . – 5 Mar 1744
32. Neophytus II	Νεόφυτος Β΄		Mar 1744 – 13 Sep 1759
33. Procopius	Προκόπιος		3 Oct 1759 – Jan 1770
34. Païsius II	Παΐσιος Β΄		Jan 1770 – Mar 1780
35. Cyril I	Κύριλλος Α΄		Mar 1780 – 31 Aug 1798
36. Gerasimus	Γεράσιμος		Sep 1798 – 28 May 1821

Known Hierarchs of Iraklia

1. Apelles	Απελλής	c. 100
2. Domitius	Δομίτιος	138 – 161
3. Philip	Φίλιππος	264 – 305
4. Paiderus	Παιδέρως	325 – 343
5. Theodore	Θεόδωρος	343 – 358?
6. Hypatianus	Υπατιανός	358
7. Dorotheus	Δωρόθεος	369
8. Paul	Παύλος	382 – 402
9. Serapion	Σεραπίων	402
10. Eugene	Ευγένιος	
11. Fritilas	Φριτίλας	431
12. Sabbinus	Σαββίνος	449
13. Cyriacus	Κυριακός	451
14. John I	Ιωάννης Α΄	459
15. Theophilus I	Θεόφιλος Α΄	518
16. John II	Ιωάννης Β΄	520
17. Constantine	Κωνσταντίνος	536 – 552
18. Megethius	Μεγέθιος	553
19. Theophilus II	Θεόφιλος Β΄	680
20. Leo I	Λέων Α΄	783 – 806
21. John III	Ιωάννης Γ΄	879 – 889
22. Demetrius	Δημήτριος	905
23. Anastasius	Αναστάσιος	933
24. Nicephorus	Νικηφόρος	959
25. John IV	Ιωάννης Δ΄	997

26. Nicetas I	Νικήτας Α΄		1066 – 1090	
27. Peter	Πέτρος		1147	
28. Michael	Μιχαήλ		1156	
29. Manuel	Μανουήλ		1169 – 1177	
30. Thomas	Θωμάς		1190	
31. Gerasimus I	Γεράσιμος Α΄		12th/13th century	
32. Nicetas II	Νικήτας Β΄		1260	
33. Philotheus I	Φιλόθεος Α΄		1261 – 1263	
34. Leo II	Λέων Β΄		1263 – 1281	
35. Germanus I	Γερμανός Α΄		1281	
36. John V	Ιωάννης Ε΄		1316	
37. Barlaam	Βαρλαάμ		1340	
38. Philotheus II	Φιλόθεος Β΄	(1st time)	1347 – Nov 1353 (to p.Const)	
39. Metrophanes	Μητροφάνης		1355	
---. Philotheus II	Φιλόθεος Β΄	(2nd time)	1360 – 1362 (later to p.Const)	
41. Joseph I	Ιωσήφ Α΄		1380 – 1389	
42. Gennadius I	Γεννάδιος Α΄		1392	
43. Theophanes	Θεοφάνης		1400	
44. Anthony	Αντώνιος		1434 – 1450	
45. Galaction	Γαλακτίων		1474	
46. Callistus	Κάλλιστος		1484	
47. Joseph II	Ιωσήφ Β΄		1499	
48. Cyril	Κύριλλος		1546, 1561, 1565, 1567	
49. Gerasimus II	Γεράσιμος Β΄		1575	
50. Dionysius I	Διονύσιος Α΄	(1st time)	1580 – 1591?	
51. Gregory I	Γρηγόριος Α΄		1591	
---. Dionysius I	Διονύσιος Α΄	(2nd time)	1593, 1600, 1606	
52. Neophytus I	Νεόφυτος Α΄		1610	
53. Germanus II	Γερμανός Β΄		1613	
54. Gabriel	Γαβριήλ		1615	
55. Timothy	Τιμόθεος	(1st time)	1616 – 1617	
56. Bartholomew I	Βαρθολομαίος Α΄		1617 – 1618	
---. Timothy	Τιμόθεος	(2nd time)	1618 – 1622	
57. Neophytus II	Νεόφυτος Β΄	(1st time)	2 Feb 1622 – after May 1635	
58. Jeremias	Ιερεμίας		before Mar 1636 – Jun 1636	
---. Neophytus II	Νεόφυτος Β΄	(2nd time)	Jun 1636	(to p.Const)
59. Johnnicius I	Ιωαννίκιος Α΄		summer 1636 – 16 Nov 1646 (to p.Const)	
60. Methodius I	Μεθόδιος Α΄		17 Dec 1646 – 5 Jan 1668 (to p.Const)	
61. Bartholomew II	Βαρθολομαίος Β΄		Jan/Feb 1668 – 1688	
62. Sophronius	Σωφρόνιος		1688	
63. Macarius	Μακάριος		Sep 1688 – 1689	
64. Neophytus III	Νεόφυτος Γ΄		15 May 1689 – 1711	
65. Athanasius	Αθανάσιος		18 Oct 1711 – Jan 1714	
65. Gennadius II	Γεννάδιος Β΄		25 Feb 1714 – 18 Oct 1716	
66. Callinicus	Καλλίνικος		Oct 1716 – 19 Nov 1726 (to p.Const)	
67. Gerasimus III	Γεράσιμος Γ΄		22 Nov 1726 – 6 Nov 1760	

68. Methodius II	Μεθόδιος Β᾽	6 Nov 1760 – Nov 1794
69. Meletius	Μελέτιος	Nov 1794 – 19 Sep 1821

Known Hierarchs of Kallipolis

1. Cyril	Κύριλλος	431
2. Harmonius	Αρμόνιος	536
3. Melchisedek	Μελχισεδέκ	787
4. Joseph	Ιωσήφ	1351, 1354
5. Meletius	Μελέτιος	. . . – Dec 1651
6. Macarius	Μακάριος	. . . – 1668
7. Philotheus	Φιλόθεος	1668 – 20 Nov 1676
8. Athanasius	Αθανάσιος	20 Nov 1676 – 1680
9. Jeremias	Ιερεμίας	1680 – 1728
10. Gregory I	Γρηγόριος Α᾽	1776
11. Joachim	Ιωακείμ	1795 – Dec 1834

Known Hierarchs of Metres and Athyra
(the first four listed were Bishops of Athyra only)

1. Porphyras	Πορφύρας	
2. Orestes	Ορέστης	1st/2nd century
3. Dionysius I	Διονύσιος Α᾽	. . . – 1369
4. Theophanes	Θεοφάνης	after 1399
5. Procopius	Προκόπιος	1564, 1565
6. Dionysius II	Διονύσιος Β᾽	1577, 1581
7. Germanus	Γερμανός	1582, 1587
8. Theonas	Θεωνάς	1590
9. Methuselah	Μαθουσάλας	1593
10. Manasses	Μανασσής	1598
11. Joasaph	Ιωάσαφ	1600, 1612
12. Neophytus I	Νεόφυτος Α᾽	1616, 1620, 1621
13. Hierotheus	Ιερόθεος	1633, 1637, 1639
14. Neophytus II	Νεόφυτος Β᾽	1648
15. Pangratius	Παγκράτιος	1653
16. Timothy	Τιμόθεος	before 1673 – Aug 1675
17. Raphael	Ραφαήλ	12 Aug 1675 – . . .
18. Anthimus I	Άνθιμος Α᾽	1683
19. Dionysius III	Διονύσιος Γ᾽	. . . – 1685
20. Gideon	Γεδεών	. . . – 1695
21. Macarius	Μακάριος	26 May 1695 – 19 Feb 1697
22. Nilus	Νείλος	19 Feb 1697 – 1711
23. Metrophanes	Μητροφάνης	20 May 1711 – May 1723
24. Sylvester	Σίλβεστρος	May 1723 – May 1744
25. Dorotheus	Δωρόθεος	1744 – 17 Nov 1745
26. Methodius	Μεθόδιος	16 Jan 1746 – 6 Nov 1760

27. Gerasimus	Γεράσιμος	1 Feb 1761 – 20 Jun 1783 (to p.Alex)
28. Sophronius	Σωφρόνιος	21 Sep 1783 – 1816

Known Hierarchs of Myriophyton and Peristasis

1. Sergius	Σέργιος	1580
2. Euthymius	Ευθύμιος	1590
3. Gabriel	Γαβριήλ	. . . – Sep 1622
4. Laurentius	Λαυρέντιος	Dec 1622, 1628, 1629, 1630, 1636, 1637
5. Symeon	Συμεών	1646, 1658
6. Neophytus	Νεόφυτος Α'	before 1661 – Apr 1675
7. Theodosius	Θεοδόσιος	29 Apr 1675 – . . .
8. Joasaph	Ιωάσαφ	1708, 1714
9. Jacob	Ιάκωβος	1728
10. Nicodemus I	Νικόδημος Α'	1743, 1751, 1752, 1754
11. Callinicus I	Καλλίνικος Α'	1767, 1784
12. Meletius	Μελέτιος	1788 – Nov 1794
13. Neophytus II	Νεόφυτος Β'	1795 – May 1821

Known Hierarchs of Silyvria

1. Sergius I	Σέργιος Α'	325
2. Theosebius	Θεοσέβιος	after 325
3. Philip	Φίλιππος	
4. Romanus	Ρωμανός	448 – 451
5. Auxentius	Αυξέντιος	536 – 553
6. Sergius II	Σέργιος Β'	680
7. George	Γεώργιος	692
8. Epiphanius	Επιφάνιος	
9. Symeon	Συμεών	879
10. Antipater	Αντίπατρος	1030 – 1038
11. Jacob I	Ιάκωβος Α'	
12. Artemius	Αρτέμιος	1090
13. John	Ιωάννης	1156
14. Theodulus	Θεόδουλος	1166 – 1171
15. Nicephorus	Νικηφόρος	1260
16. Thomas	Θωμάς	1262
17. Hilarion	Ιλαρίων	1283
18. Gregory I	Γρηγόριος Α'	1327
19. Ignatius I	Ιγνάτιος Α'	1330
20. Methodius	Μεθόδιος	1347
21. Isaiah	Ησαΐας	1347 – 1355
22. Philotheus	Φιλόθεος	1355 – 1375
23. Theophilus	Θεόφιλος	1389
24. Ignatius II	Ιγνάτιος Β'	1431
25. Jacob II	Ιάκωβος Β'	c. 1450

26. Joseph	Ἰωσήφ	1474, 1484
27. Athanasius I	Ἀθανάσιος Α´	1514 – 1541
28. Anthimus	Ἄνθιμος	1564
29. Athanasius II	Ἀθανάσιος Β´	1578 – after 1600
30. Theophanes	Θεοφάνης	before 1608 – 1618
31. Jeremias	Ἰερεμίας	10 Nov 1618 – 1623
32. Macarius I	Μακάριος Α´	Aug 1623 – Apr 1624
33. Laurentius I	Λαυρέντιος Α´	29 Apr 1624 – Feb 1638
34. Sophronius I	Σωφρόνιος Α´	Feb 1638 – 8 Oct 1645
35. Macarius II	Μακάριος Β´	20 Dec 1645 – 1646
36. Meletius I	Μελέτιος Α´	14 Mar 1646 – 1654
37. Metrophanes	Μητροφάνης	1655
38. Laurentius II	Λαυρέντιος Β´	1675
39. Nectarius	Νεκτάριος	1681
40. Gregory II	Γρηγόριος Β´	before 1684
41. Arsenius	Ἀρσένιος	1688, 1689
42. Macarius III	Μακάριος Γ´	. . . – 10 May 1701
43. Leontius	Λεόντιος	May 1701 – 1726
44. Macarius IV	Μακάριος Δ´	1726 – 1744
45. Theocletus	Θεόκλητος	2 May 1744 – 1764
46. Parthenius	Παρθένιος	Jul 1764 – May 1777
47. Chrysanthus	Χρύσανθος	May 1777 – 1790
48. Callinicus	Καλλίνικος	Dec 1790 – Aug 1816

Known Hierarchs of Tyroloi and Serention

1. Theonas	Θεωνάς	1565, 1579, 1580
2. Anthimus	Ἄνθιμος	. . . – 1 Jun 1616
3. Chariton	Χαρίτων	1630
4. Nectarius	Νεκτάριος	1708 – 1714
5. Neophytus I	Νεόφυτος Α´	1714 – 1716
6. Porphyrius	Πορφύριος	1751 – 1781
7. Neophytus II	Νεόφυτος Β´	1781 – 1808

Known Hierarchs of Vizyi and Midia
(Hierarchs of Vizyi before 1682, Vizyi and Midia afterwards)

1. George I	Γεώργιος Α´	325
2. Euprepius	Εὐπρέπιος	431
3. Lucian	Λουκιανός	451
4. John I	Ἰωάννης Α´	533
5. Theodore I	Θεόδωρος Α´	553
6. Theodosius	Θεοδόσιος	650/656
7. George II	Γεώργιος Β´	680
8. Theodore II	Θεόδωρος Β´	783
9. Michael	Μιχαήλ	869

10. Peter	Πέτρος	879
11. Euthymius	Εὔθυμος	902
12. Nicetas I	Νικήτας Α´	1028
13. Leo	Λέων	1082
14. Theodore III	Θεόδωρος Γ´	1156 – 1166
15. John II	Ἰωάννης Β´	1170
16. Nicholas I	Νικόλαος Α´	1191 – 1192
17. Nicetas II	Νικήτας Β´	1192
18. Demetrius	Δημήτριος	c. 1200 – 1250
19. John III	Ἰωάννης Γ´	1260 – 1278
20. Nicholas II	Νικόλαος Β´	1283 – 1329 (m.Prousa, president)
21. Neophytus I	Νεόφυτος Α´	1356 – 1368
22. Joachim I	Ἰωακείμ Α´	1565
23. Dionysius	Διονύσιος	1567
24. Daniel	Δανιήλ	1572
25. Cyril	Κύριλλος	1575
26. Jeremias I	Ἰερεμίας Α´	1578
27. Laurentius	Λαυρέντιος	before 1614 – 1616
28. Anthimus I	Ἄνθιμος Α´	1 Jun 1616 – 1631
29. Damascene	Δαμασκηνός	8 Mar 1631 – 1/22 Jul 1641
30. Gabriel	Γαβριήλ	1641 – Mar 1648
31. Gregory I	Γρηγόριος Α´	Mar 1648 – Jan 1671
32. Cosmas I	Κοσμάς Α´	Jan 1671 – 1674
33. Gerasimus I	Γεράσιμος Α´	14 Mar 1674 – 1682
34. Zacharias	Ζαχαρίας	1682 – after 1691
35. Joachim II	Ἰωακείμ Β´	1708 – after 1719
36. Parthenius I	Παρθένιος Α´	. . . – Dec 1727
37. Dorotheus I	Δωρόθεος Α´	Dec 1727 – . . .
38. Gennadius	Γεννάδιος	. . . – Nov 1751
39. Gerasimus II	Γεράσιμος Β´ (1st time)	17 Nov 1751 – Jul 1752
40. Agapius	Ἀγάπιος	Jul 1752 – Feb 1762
---. Gerasimus II	Γεράσιμος Β´ (2nd time)	28 Feb 1762 – Feb 1783
41. Parthenius II	Παρθένιος Β´	14 Feb 1783 – 1792
42. Daniel II	Δανιήλ Β´	Jun 1792 – Aug 1813

SECTION B: METROPOLITANATES IN THE ISLANDS

Known Hierarchs of Imvros

1. Jacob I	Ἰάκωβος Α´	1321 – 1324
2. Joseph I	Ἰωσήφ Α´	1324 – 1329
3. Chariton	Χαρίτων	1346
4. George	Γεώργιος	1397 – 1415
5. Dorotheus	Δωρόθεος	1455 – 1464
6. Leontius	Λεόντιος	1541 – 1567
7. Joachim I	Ἰωακείμ Α´	1567 – 1584

8. Arsenius	Ἀρσένιος		1584?- 1596
9. Parthenius I	Παρθένιος Α΄		1596 – after 1610
10. Macarius	Μακάριος		before 1616 – 1619
11. Athanasius I	Ἀθανάσιος Α΄		1619 – 1621
12. Joachim II	Ἰωακείμ Β΄		before Jul 1624 – . . .
13. Christopher	Χριστόφορος		Aug 1626 – 1627
14. Sophronius	Σωφρόνιος	(1ˢᵗ time)	10 Apr 1627 – 27 Jul 1635
15. Abramius	Ἀβράμιος		1636 – 1638
16. Parthenius II	Παρθένιος Β΄		1639 – 1640
---. Sophronius	Σωφρόνιος	(2ⁿᵈ time)	1640 – 1652
17. Nicodemus	Νικόδημος		24 Mar 1652 – 1660
18. Theodosius	Θεοδόσιος		1660 – 1672
19. Païsius I	Παΐσιος Α΄		1672 – 1700
20. Germanus	Γερμανός		1700 – 1708
21. Gregory I	Γρηγόριος Α΄		1708 – 1710
22. Daniel	Δανιήλ		1711 – 1721
23. Gregory II	Γρηγόριος Β΄		1721 – 1727
24. Dionysius	Διονύσιος		1728 – 1733
25. Meletius I	Μελέτιος Α΄		Apr 1733 – 14 May 1743
26. Joachim III	Ἰωακείμ Γ΄		14 May 1743 – Feb/Mar 1745
27. Meletius II	Μελέτιος Β΄		2 Mar 1745 – Aug 1745
28. Athanasius II	Ἀθανάσιος Β΄		17 Aug 1745 – Nov 1759
29. Nicephorus I	Νικηφόρος Α΄		Nov 1759 – 14 Feb 1762
30. Neophytus I	Νεόφυτος Α΄		15 Feb 1762 – Mar 1785
31. Ignatius	Ἰγνάτιος		Mar 1785 – Jan 1793
32. Nicephorus II	Νικηφόρος Β΄		Jan 1793 – Feb 1825

Known Hierarchs of Prikonnisos

1. John	Ἰωάννης	431
2. Acacius	Ἀκάκιος	451
3. Stratocles	Στρατοκλῆς	459
4. Nicetas	Νικήτας	787
5. Ignatius	Ἰγνάτιος	879
6. Leo	Λέων	10ᵗʰ/11ᵗʰ century
7. Dionysius I	Διονύσιος Α΄	1027, 1028
8. Cosmas	Κοσμᾶς	1078
9. Isaacius	Ἰσαάκιος	1166
10. Basil	Βασίλειος	before 1250
11. Nicholas	Νικόλαος	1280
12. Nephon	Νήφων	1311 (m.Kyzikos, president)
---. administered by Ecumenical Patriarch John XIII		1315 – 1319/20
13. Manuel	Μανουήλ	1329, 1330
14. Macarius	Μακάριος	1548, 1552
15. Anthimus	Ἄνθιμος	1580
16. Clement I	Κλήμης Α΄	1585

17. Dionysius II	Διονύσιος Β'	c. 1600
18. Clement II	Κλήμης Β'	before Aug 1605 – after Jul 1626
19. Daniel I	Δανιήλ Α'	before 1629 – Jun 1638
20. Gregory	Γρηγόριος	Jun 1638 – Jul 1639
21. Jeremias	Ιερεμίας	Jul 1639 – Jul 1660
22. Gerasimus	Γεράσιμος	Jul 1660 – 1665?
23. Daniel II	Δανιήλ Β'	3 Nov 1665 – 1668?
24. Constantius	Κωνστάντιος	1668 – 1677?
25. Metrophanes	Μητροφάνης	1677 – Mar 1702
26. Theocletus	Θεόκλητος	15 Mar 1702 – c. 1731
27. Gabriel	Γαβριήλ	before 1739 – Jan 1745
28. Nicephorus I	Νικηφόρος Α'	23 Jan 1745 – 25 Mar 1759
29. Ananias	Ανανίας	27 Mar 1759 – Aug 1791
30. Arsenius	Αρσένιος	17 Aug 1791 – Aug 1795
31. Nicephorus II	Νικηφόρος Β'	Aug 1795 – Jun 1821

SECTION C: METROPOLITANATES IN NORTHWEST ASIA MINOR

Known Hierarchs of Chalkidon

1. Theocritus	Θεόκριτος	2nd century?
2. Adrian	Αδριανός	2nd century?
3. Maris	Μάρις	325 – 362
4. Theodulus I	Θεόδουλος Α'	381
5. Cyrinus	Κυρίνος	c. 400 – 405
6. Philotheus	Φιλόθεος	Jun 405 – ...
7. Eulalius	Ευλάλιος	426?- 450
8. Eleutherius	Ελευθέριος	451 – 475?
9. Heraclian	Ηρακλειανός	509 – 518
10. Martian	Μαρτιανός	518, 520
11. Photinus	Φωτεινός	530, 536
12. Constantine I	Κωνσταντίνος Α'	553
13. Peter	Πέτρος	c. 600
14. Probus	Πρόβος	7th century
15. John I	Ιωάννης Α'	681, 692
16. Nicetas I	Νικήτας Α'	8th century
17. Andrew	Ανδρέας	780 – 787
18. Stauracius	Σταυράκιος	787 – ...
19. Cosmas	Κοσμάς	c. 813 – 820
20. John II	Ιωάννης Β'	8th or 9th century
21. Damian	Δαμιανός	8th or 9th century
22. Basil	Βασίλειος (1st time)	... – 858
23. Zacharias I	Ζαχαρίας Α' (1st time)	858 – 870
---. Basil	Βασίλειος (2nd time)	870 – 877
---. Zacharias I	Ζαχαρίας Α' (2nd time)	877 – ...

24. Nicon	Νίκων		before 899
25. Stephen	Στέφανος		. . . – 903
26. Michael I	Μιχαήλ Α'		10th century
27. John III	Ιωάννης Γ'		10th century
28. Daniel	Δανιήλ		997
29. Theodore	Θεόδωρος		1027
30. Nicetas II	Νικήτας Β'		1058
31. Leo	Λέων	(1st time)	1080 – 1086
32. Michael II	Μιχαήλ Β'		1086 – 1090
---. Leo	Λέων	(2nd time)	1090 – . . .
33. John IV	Ιωάννης Δ'		1147
34. Constantius I	Κωνστάντιος Α'		1156
35. Constantine II	Κωνσταντίνος Β'		1171
36. John V	Ιωάννης Ε'		1191/2
37. Nicholas I	Νικόλαος Α'		1275, 1278
38. Theognostus	Θεόγνωστος		1294
39. Symeon	Συμεών		1303
40. Theodulus II	Θεόδουλος Β'		1315 – 1337 (m.Maronia, presid.)
41. Jacob	Ιάκωβος		1351 – 1379
42. Matthew	Ματθαίος		1387 – 1389? (m.Kyzikos, presid.)
43. Gabriel I	Γαβριήλ Α'		1389 – 1397
44. Joseph I	Ιωσήφ Α'		1477, 1484
45. Gabriel II	Γαβριήλ Β'		1499
46. Euthymius I	Ευθύμιος Α'		1546, 1565
47. Dorotheus	Δωρόθεος	(1st time)	1570, 1572
48. Sisinnius	Σισίννιος		1580
---. Dorotheus	Δωρόθεος	(2nd time)	1583, 1584, 1593
49. Timotheus	Τιμόθεος	(1st time)	1593 – 1617
50. Jeremias I	Ιερεμίας Α'		1617
---. Timotheus	Τιμόθεος	(2nd time)	1617 – Jun 1620
51. Joseph II	Ιωσήφ Β'		Jun 1620 – 1622
---. Timotheus	Τιμόθεος	(3rd time)	1622 – 18 May 1623
52. Joasaph	Ιωάσαφ		29 May 1623 – Mar 1626
53. Gregory I	Γρηγόριος Α'		24 Mar 1626 – before April 1628
54. Isaacius	Ισαάκιος		after April 1628 – May 1630
55. Nectarius	Νεκτάριος		10 Jun 1630 – 1637
56. Pachomius	Παχώμιος	(1st time)	1 Feb 1637 – 20 Jun 1638
57. Dionysius I	Διονύσιος Α'		20 Jun 1638 – before 1 Jul 1639
---. Pachomius	Παχώμιος	(2nd time) bef.1 Jul 1639 – 1647	
58. Gabriel III	Γαβριήλ Γ'		1647 – after 1662
59. Euthymius II	Ευθύμιος Β'		. . . – 7 Apr 1671
60. Jeremias II	Ιερεμίας Β'		7 Apr 1671 – 1685?
61. Dionysius II	Διονύσιος Β'	(president)	Mar 1685 – Mar 1686 (ex/to p.Const)
62. Clement	Κλήμης		1686 – 1688
63. Gabriel IV	Γαβριήλ Δ'		1688 – Aug 1702 (to p.Const)

64. Constantius II	Κωνστάντιος Β'	Oct 1702 – 1719/20
65. Parthenius I	Παρθένιος Α'	1719/20 – 1726
66. Nicodemus	Νικοδημος	Dec 1726 – 1731
67. Callinicus I	Καλλίνικος Α'	1731 – Apr 1746
68. Gabriel V	Γαβριήλ Ε'	Apr 1746 – Sep 1747
69. Johnnicius I	Ιωαννίκιος Α'	Sep 1747 – 26 Mar 1761 (to p.Const)
70. Johnnicius II	Ιωαννίκιος Β'	27 Mar 1761 – Jan 1770
71. Parthenius II	Παρθένιος Β'	Jan 1770 – May 1777
72. Parthenius III	Παρθένιος Γ'	May 1777 – Nov 1790
73. Jeremias III	Ιερεμίας Γ'	Nov 1790 – Nov 1810

Known Hierarchs of Kyzikos

1. Aphrodisius	Αφροδίσιος		3rd century
2. Theodosius I	Θεοδόσιος Α'		
3. Theonas	Θεωνάς		325
4. Ascholius	Ασχόλιος		c. 330
5. Germinius	Γερμίνιος		
6. Eleusius	Ελεύσιος	(1st time)	. . . – 359
7. Eunomius	Ευνόμιος		360
–. Eleusius	Ελεύσιος	(2nd time)	
8. Proclus	Πρόκλος		428?
9. Dalmatius	Δαλμάτιος		431
10. Diogenes	Διογένης		449
11. Evethius	Ευήθιος		458
12. Basiliscus	Βασιλίσκος		494, 518
13. Eusebius	Ευσέβιος		536
14. Euprepius	Ευπρέπιος		553
15. Stephen	Στέφανος		610
16. John I	Ιωάννης Α'		7th century
17. Germanus	Γερμανός		705/6 – 11 Aug 715 (to p.Const)
18. Emilian	Αιμιλιανός		c. 730
19. Nicholas	Νικόλαος		787
20. John II	Ιωάννης Β'		825
21. Anthony	Αντώνιος		869
22. Amphilochius	Αμφιλόχιος		
23. Barnabas	Βαρνάβας		869
24. Gregory I	Γρηγόριος Α'		879
25. Theodore I	Θεόδωρος Α'		959
26. Demetrius	Δημήτριος		1028
27. Romanus	Ρωμανός		c. 1050
28. Euthymius	Ευθύμιος		1082
29. Symeon	Συμεών		1107
30. Theophilus	Θεόφιλος		1147
31. John III	Ιωάννης Γ'		1156
32. Basil	Βασίλειος		1166

33. John IV	Ιωάννης Δ'		1170
34. George I	Γεώργιος Α'		1191
35. George II	Γεώργιος Β'		1254
36. Theodore II	Θεόδωρος Β'		1270, 1283
37. Daniel	Δανιήλ		1285, 1288
38. Nicon	Νίκων		
39. Nicetas	Νικήτας		c. 1300
40. Nephon	Νήφων		1303 – 9 May 1310 (to p.Const)
---. administered by Ecumenical Patr. Nephon I			9 May 1310 – 11 Apr 1314
41. Athanasius I	Αθανάσιος Α'		1324, 1347
42. Arsenius	Αρσένιος		1350, 1368
43. Theodoretus	Θεοδώρητος		1370
44. Sebastian	Σεβαστιανός		1381 – after 1384
45. Matthew I	Ματθαίος Α'		Nov 1387 – Nov 1397 (to p.Const)
46. Theognostus	Θεόγνωστος		Dec 1399 – . . .
47. Metrophanes I	Μητροφάνης Α'		before 1437 – 4/5 May 1440 (to p.Const)
48. Theodosius II	Θεοδόσιος Β'		1528
49. Joasaph	Ιωάσαφ		1560, 1565, 1576
50. Achillius	Αχίλλειος		1580, 1586
51. Damascene	Δαμασκηνός		1593
52. Gabriel	Γαβριήλ		1606
53. Parthenius	Παρθένιος		before 1618 – Nov 1633
54. Anthimus I	Άνθιμος Α'		14 Nov 1633 – Aug 1655
55. Païsius	Παΐσιος		Aug 1655 – 1656 (ex former p.Const)
56. Metrophanes II	Μητροφάνης Β'		Sep 1656 – after 1673
57. Cyril	Κύριλλος		before 1685 – Dec 1711 (to p.Const)
58. Auxentius	Αυξέντιος		1712 – after 1727
59. Ananias	Ανανίας		before 1734 – after 1754
60. Gerasimus I	Γεράσιμος Α '		before 1763 – 6 Nov 1768
61. Anthimus II	Άνθιμος Β'		12 Nov 1768 – Jul 1769
62. Gerasimus II	Γεράσιμος Β '		Jul 1769 – Feb 1778
63. Agapius	Αγάπιος		Feb 1778 – Sep 1794
64. Joachim I	Ιωακείμ Α'		Sep 1794 – 14 Mar 1806

Known Hierarchs of Nikaia

1. Theognius	Θεόγνιος	(1st time)	. . . – 325
2. Chrestus	Χρήστος		325 – 328
–. Theognius	Θεόγνιος	(2nd time)	328 – 344
3. Eugene	Ευγένιος		355 – 370
4. Hypatius I	Υπάτιος Α'		. . . – 379
5. Dorotheus	Δωρόθεος		381
6. Anastasius I	Αναστάσιος Α'		431 – 451
7. Peter I	Πέτρος Α'		459 – 490
8. Appion	Αππίων		c. 490
9. Anastasius II	Αναστάσιος Β'		518 – 553

10. Stephen	Στέφανος	553
11. Theophanes I	Θεοφάνης Α΄	590
12. Theophilus	Θεόφιλος	602
13. Anastasius III	Αναστάσιος Γ΄	640 – 680
14. Photius	Φώτιος	680
15. Theognis	Θέογνις	680?
16. George I	Γεώργιος Α΄	692
17. Anastasius IV	Αναστάσιος Δ΄	c. 700
18. John I	Ιωάννης Α΄	715
19. Hypatius II	Υπάτιος Β΄	783 – 787?
20. Peter II	Πέτρος Β΄	c. 816
21. Theophanes II	Θεοφάνης Β΄	842 – 845
22. Ignatius	Ιγνάτιος	845 – . . .
23. John II	Ιωάννης Β΄	864
24. Nicephorus	Νικηφόρος	869 – 879?
25. Amphilochius	Αμφιλόχιος	880
26. Gregory I	Γρηγόριος Α΄	880 – 886
27. John III	Ιωάννης Γ΄	c. 900
28. Alexander	Αλέξανδρος	before 925 – 944/5
29. Constantine	Κωνσταντίνος	997 – 1028
30. John IV	Ιωάννης Δ΄	1050
31. Theodore	Θεόδωρος	11th century
32. Eustratius	Ευστράτιος	before 1110 – after 1117
33. Nicetas	Νικήτας	12th century
34. Leo	Λέων	1147, 1151
35. George II	Γεώργιος Β΄	1166
36. Gerasimus I	Γεράσιμος Α΄	after 1166
37. Nicholas	Νικόλαος	1183, 1185
38. Theophanes III	Θεοφάνης Γ΄	before 1272 – 1283
39. Peter III	Πέτρος Γ΄	1283 – 1320
40. Callistratus	Καλλίστρατος	1327
41. Manasses	Μανασσής	1355, 1360
42. Theophanes IV	Θεοφάνης Δ΄	before 1370 – 1381
43. Alexius	Αλέξιος	1381 – after 1393
44. Bessarion	Βησσαρίων	1436 – 1440 (latin p.Const 1463-72)
45. Neophytus	Νεόφυτος	1440 – after 1451
46. Stauracius	Σταυράκιος	1452 – . . .
47. Macarius I	Μακάριος Α΄	1474
48. Joseph I	Ιωσήφ Α΄	1497
49. Cyril	Κύριλλος	1564, 1565, 1572, 1590
50. Parthenius	Παρθένιος	1606
51. Macarius II	Μακάριος Β΄	1610 – Jan 1612
52. Porphyrius I	Πορφύριος Α΄	Jan 1612 – Jun 1640
53. Porphyrius II	Πορφύριος Β΄ (1st time)	Jun 1640 – Aug 1645
---. Porphyrius II	Πορφύριος Β΄ (2nd time)	1647 – Apr 1653
54. Gregory II	Γρηγόριος Β΄	22 Apr 1653 – Apr 1657

55. Nathaniel	Ναθαναήλ	Apr 1657 – Sep 1657
56. Philotheus	Φιλόθεος	Sep 1657 – Jul 1662
57. Damascene	Δαμασκηνός	12 Jul 1662 – 1 Feb 1676
58. Sophronius I	Σωφρόνιος Α΄	1 Feb 1676 – 1688
59. Johnnicius I	Ιωαννίκιος Α΄	before 1692 – Mar 1696
60. Gennadius	Γεννάδιος	Mar 1696 – after 1712
61. Gerasimus II	Γεράσιμος Β΄	before 1718 – 22 Nov 1726
62. Callinicus I	Καλλίνικος Α΄	Nov/Dec 1726 – 7 May 1752
63. Jeremias	Ιερεμίας	31 May 1752 – May 1764
64. Anthimus	Άνθιμος	May 1764 – 14 Feb 1783
65. Gabriel	Γαβριήλ	14 Feb 1783 – Sep 1792
66. Callinicus II	Καλλίνικος Β΄	Sep 1792 – 17 Jun 1801 (to p.Const)

Known Hierarchs of Nikomidia

1. Prochorus	Πρόχορος		1st century
2. Evander	Εύανδρος		2nd century
3. Cyril I	Κύριλλος Α΄		c. 290
4. Anthimus I	Άνθιμος Α΄		. . . – 303/4+
5. Eustolius	Ευστόλιος		c. 314 – 318
6. Eusebius	Ευσέβιος	(1st time)	318 – 325
7. Amphion	Αμφίων		325 – 329
–. Eusebius	Ευσέβιος	(2nd time)	328 – 339 (to a.Const)
8. Marathonius	Μαραθώνιος		342 – . . .
–. Amphion	Αμφίων	(2nd time)	347
9. Cecropius	Κεκρόπιος		351 – 358
10. Onesimus	Ονήσιμος		after 369
11. Euphrasius	Ευφράσιος		381
12. Patricius	Πατρίκιος		381
13. Gerontius	Γερόντιος		390 – 400?
14. Pamphilius	Παμφίλιος		401?
15. Pansophius	Πανσόφιος		c. 405
16. Diodorus	Διόδωρος		(succesor of Pansophius)
17. Hemerius	Ημέριος		431?
18. Eusemius	Ευσήμιος		after 431
19. Polychronius	Πολυχρόνιος		451
20. Stephen I	Στέφανος Α΄		518, 520
21. Thalassius	Θαλάσσιος		536 – 553?
22. John I	Ιωάννης Α΄		553
23. Joseph	Ιώσηπος		553 – 560?
24. George I	Γεώργιος Α΄		606 – 630
25. Peter I	Πέτρος Α΄		680, 692
26. John II	Ιωάννης Β΄		754 – 764?
27. Constantine I	Κωνσταντίνος Α΄		764?
28. Peter II	Πέτρος Β΄		783, 787
29. Theophylactus I	Θεοφύλακτος Α΄		800 – 845

30. John III	Ἰωάννης Γ´	867
31. George II	Γεώργιος Β´	860 – 879?
32. Stephen II	Στέφανος Β´	997 – 1009?
33. Anthony	Ἀντώνιος	1028 – 1043?
34. Constantine II	Κωνσταντίνος Β´	1084
35. Basil	Βασίλειος	1085 – 1118
36. Nicetas	Νικήτας	1135
37. John IV	Ἰωάννης Δ´	1145 – 1151
38. Theophylactus II	Θεοφύλακτος Β´	1156
39. Michael	Μιχαήλ	1166
40. John V	Ἰωάννης Ε´	1283 – 1295
41. Caracallus	Καράκαλλος	c. 1300
42. Cyril II	Κύριλλος Β´	1315
43. Maximus I	Μάξιμος Α´	1324, 1327
44. Macarius I	Μακάριος Α´	1387, 1389, 1393
45. Macarius II	Μακάριος Β´	before 1437 – after 1451
46. Dorotheus	Δωρόθεος	1474
47. Maximus II	Μάξιμος Β´	1497, 1498
48. Dionysius I	Διονύσιος Α´	1516 – 17 Apr 1546 (to p.Const)
49. Timothy I	Τιμόθεος Α´	between 1546/1572
50. Sisinnius	Σισίννιος	4 May 1572 – after 1593
51. Metrophanes	Μητροφάνης	1596
52. Gabriel I	Γαβριήλ Α´	before 1610 – Jun 1617
53. Neophytus I	Νεόφυτος Α´	7 Jun 1617 – 4 May 1639
54. Cyril III	Κύριλλος Γ´	6 May 1639 – 26 Mar 1659
55. Timothy II	Τιμόθεος Β´	26 Mar 1659 – . . .
56. Neophytus II	Νεόφυτος Β´	before 1667 – 17 Jul 1680
57. Meletius I	Μελέτιος Α´	1 Sep 1680 – after Jan 1691
58. Parthenius	Παρθένιος	9 Mar 1692 – 27 Oct 1714
59. Païsius	Παΐσιος	before 1716 – 20 Nov 1726 (to p.Const)
60. Seraphim	Σεραφείμ	Nov/Dec 1726 – Mar 1733 (to p.Const)
61. Theocletus	Θεόκλητος	1733 – Dec 1744
62. Gabriel II	Γαβριήλ Β´ (1st time)	1/16 Jan 1745 – 6/21 Jan 1745 (6 days)
63. Cyril IV	Κύριλλος Δ´	22 Jan 1745 – 28 Sep 1748 (to p.Const)
---. Gabriel II	Γαβριήλ Β´ (2nd time)	23 Oct 1748 – 25 Mar 1759
64. Nicephorus	Νικηφόρος	31 Mar 1759 – 1776
65. Meletius II	Μελέτιος Β´ (1st time)	Jul 1776 – 5 Jan 1783
66. Gerasimus	Γεράσιμος	14 Feb 1783 – 26 Mar 1791
67. Meletius II	Μελέτιος Β´ (2nd time)	26 Mar 1791 – Nov 1791
68. Athanasius	Ἀθανάσιος	Nov 1791 – 10 Apr 1821

Known Hierarchs of Pergamos

1. Gaius	Γάιος	1st century
2. Antipas	Ἀντίπας	1st century
3. Theodotus	Θεόδοτος	2nd century

4. Carpus	Κάρπος	249 – 252
5. Eusebius	Ευσέβιος	340 – 347
6. Dracontius	Δρακόντιος	359 – 361
7. Barlaamius	Βαρλαάμιος	363, 364
8. Philip	Φίλιππος	431
9. Eutropius	Ευτρόπιος	449
10. John I	Ιωάννης Α΄	6th century
11. Theodore	Θεόδωρος	680/1
12. Basil	Βασίλειος	787
13. Methodius	Μεθόδιος	879
14. George	Γεώργιος	1256 – 1303
15. Arsenius	Αρσένιος	1303 – 1315

Known Hierarchs of Prousa

1. Alexander	Αλέξανδρος	
2. Patricius	Πατρίκιος	200
3. George	Γεώργιος	. . . – 325
4. Timothy	Τιμόθεος	325 – 363
5. Eustace	Ευστάθιος	381
6. Peter	Πέτρος	431
7. Stephen	Στέφανος	459
8. Theoctistus	Θεόκτιστος	553
9. Cosmas I	Κοσμάς Α΄	610 – 642
10. Polychronius	Πολυχρόνιος	680, 681
11. Theodore	Θεόδωρος	787
12. Nicetas	Νικήτας	879
13. Cosmas II	Κοσμάς Β΄	before 1000
14. Maximus	Μάξιμος	
15. Leo	Λέων	1232
16. Nicholas I	Νικόλαος Α΄	1256
17. Neophytus I	Νεόφυτος Α΄	1283
18. Nicholas II	Νικόλαος Β΄	1315, 1329, 1331
19. Alexius	Αλέξιος	1381 (m.Nikaia, presid.)
20. Theodoretus	Θεοδώρητος	1416
21. Metrophanes	Μητροφάνης	1467
22. Neophytus II	Νεόφυτος Β΄	1477
23. Theodulus	Θεόδουλος	. . . – 1484
24. Macarius	Μακάριος	1484 – . . .
25. Païsius	Παΐσιος	1497
26. Gregory I	Γρηγόριος Α΄	before 1559 – 1580
27. Neophytus III	Νεόφυτος Γ΄	1580 – after 1593
28. Joasaph	Ιωάσαφ (1st time)	May 1605 – Aug 1634
29. Chrysanthus I	Χρύσανθος Α΄	Aug 1634 – 1643
30. Clement	Κλήμης	Jun 1643 – Jan 1655
31. Parthenius	Παρθένιος (1st time)	21 Jan 1655 – 1 May 1657 (to p.Const)

32. Meletius I	Μελέτιος Α΄	3 May 1657 – 1658
33. Gabriel	Γαβριήλ	1658 – 3 Dec 1659++ (ex p.Const)
34. Dionysius I	Διονύσιος Α΄ (m.Larissa, pr.)	Dec 1659 – 29 Jun 1662 (to p.Const)
---. Parthenius	Parthenius (2nd time)	Jun 1662 – 21 Oct 1665 (ex/to p.Const)
35. Anthimus I	Άνθιμος Α΄	before 1668 – after Jan 1672
36. Callinicus	Καλλίνικος	before Jun 1672 – 3 Mar 1688 (to p.Const)
37. Cyril	Κύριλλος	Oct 1689 – after Jun 1724
38. Gregory II	Γρηγόριος Β΄	before 1731 – Apr 1749
39. Meletius II	Μελέτιος Β΄	30 Apr 1749 – Jul 1776
40. Anthimus II	Άνθιμος Β΄	Jul 1776 – 1807

SECTION D: METROPOLITANATES
IN SOUTHWEST ASIA MINOR

Known Hierarchs of Anea

1. Olivian	Ολιβιανός	c. 300 – 312
2. Paul	Παύλος	325
3. Modestus	Μόδεστος	431
4. Zoticus	Ζωτικός	451
5. Marcellus	Μάρκελλος	536
6. John	Ιωάννης	
7. Sabbas	Σάββας	787
8. Joseph	Ιωσήφ	869
9. Athanasius I	Αθανάσιος Α΄	879
10. George	Γεώργιος	1167
11. Athanasius II	Αθανάσιος Β΄	1230

Known Hierarchs of Ephesos

1. Timothy	Τιμόθεος	c. 50
2. John I	Ιωάννης Α΄	60 – 103
3. Onesimus	Ονήσιμος	104 – 110
4. Demas	Δήμας	116?
5. Polycrates	Πολυκράτης	190/193 – 202
6. Apollonius	Απολλώνιος	. . . – 203
7. Isaac I	Ισαάκ Α΄	
8. Theodotus	Θεόδοτος	250
9. Ananias	Ανανίας	3rd century
10. Solomon	Σολομών	3rd century
11. Menophantus	Μηνόφαντος	325/340
12. Metrophanes	Μητροφάνης	
13. Agapius	Αγάπιος	340 – 350
14. Abramius I	Αβράμιος Α΄	360 – 380
15. Evethius	Ευήθιος	380 – 381
16. Myrtinus	Μυρτίνος	

17. Agapetus	Αγαπητός		
18. Macarius I	Μακάριος Α΄		391
19. Antoninus	Αντωνίνος		391 – 400
20. Heraclides	Ηρακλείδης		401 – 403
21. Catinus	Κατίνος		403?
22. Marinus	Μαρίνος		408
23. Memnon	Μέμνων		431
24. Basil I	Βασίλειος Α΄		431 – 435
25. Bassian	Βασσιανός		435 – 439
26. Stephen I	Στέφανος Α΄		439 – 451
27. John II	Ιωάννης Β΄		451 – 459
28. Paul	Παύλος	(1st time)	459
29. John	Ιωάννης		
---. Paul	Παύλος	(2nd time)	475 – 477
30. Theosebius I	Θεοσέβιος Α΄		518
31. Aetherius	Αιθέριος		531
32. Hypatius I	Υπάτιος Α΄		532, 536, 552?
33. Procopius	Προκόπιος		6th century
34. Andrew	Ανδρέας		553
35. Theosebius II	Θεοσέβιος Β΄		553 – 558?
36. John III	Ιωάννης Γ΄		559 – 565?
37. Abramius II	Αβράμιος Β΄		566 – 597?
38. Rufinus	Ρουφίνος		597
39. Theodore I	Θεόδωρος Α΄		680/1
40. Stephen II	Στέφανος Β΄		691/2
41. Hypatius II	Υπάτιος Β΄		. . . – 730+
42. Theodosius	Θεοδόσιος		754
43. John IV	Ιωάννης Δ΄		787
44. Theophilus	Θεόφιλος		816
45. Mark I	Μάρκος Α΄		833
46. Theodore II	Θεόδωρος Β΄		8th/9th century
47. Basil II	Βασίλειος Β΄		869
48. Gregory I	Γρηγόριος Α΄		879
49. Stephen III	Στέφανος Γ΄		. . . – 945
50. Theodore III	Θεόδωρος Γ΄		1019
51. Cyriacus	Κυριακός		1028 – . . .
52. Theodore IV	Θεόδωρος Δ΄		c. 1050, 1066
53. Nicephorus I	Νικηφόρος Α΄		1071
54. Theodore V	Θεόδωρος Ε΄		1073
55. Euthymius	Ευθύμιος		
56. Michael	Μιχαήλ		1078 – . . .
57. Nicephorus II	Νικηφόρος Β΄		
58. John V	Ιωάννης Ε΄		1081 – 1108
59. Neophytus I	Νεόφυτος Α΄		1113 – 1125
60. Leontius	Λεόντιος		1143

61. John VI	Ἰωάννης ΣΤ'		1144/7
62. Constantine I	Κωνσταντίνος Α'		c. 1160
63. Nicholas I	Νικόλαος Α'		1167, 1169, 1177
64. George	Γεώργιος		1191, 1192
65. John VII	Ἰωάννης Ζ'		1195
66. Nicholas II	Νικόλαος Β'		1213/6
67. Jasites	Ἰασίτης		1217, 1224
68. John VII	Ἰωάννης Η'		1227/9
69. Nicephorus III	Νικηφόρος Γ'		1230
70. Constantine II	Κωνσταντίνος Β'		1237/8, 1239
71. Nicephorus IV	Νικηφόρος Δ'		1240 – 1260 (to p.Const)
72. Isaac II	Ἰσαάκ Β'		1260 – 1279
73. John IX	Ἰωάννης Θ'		1283 – 1289
74. John X	Ἰωάννης Ι'		1300
75. Matthew I	Ματθαῖος Α'		before 1329 – Jun 1351
76. Neophytus II	Νεόφυτος Β'		1368
77. Theodoretus	Θεοδώρητος		1368, 1388
78. Maximus I	Μάξιμος Α'		1390 – 1393
79. Myron	Μύρων		1393
80. Joseph	Ἰωσήφ		1393 – 21 May 1416 (to p.Const)
81. Matthew II	Ματθαῖος Β'		1426, 1427
82. Manuel	Μανουήλ		1431 – 1437
83. Joasaph I	Ἰωάσαφ Α'		1437
84. Mark II	Μάρκος Β'		1437 – 23 Jun 1444/5
85. Neophytus III	Νεόφυτος Γ'		before 1467 – after 1477
86. Daniel I	Δανιήλ Α'		before 1484 – after 1488
87. Joasaph II	Ἰωάσαφ Β'		1522, 1523
88. Luke	Λουκᾶς		1561
89. Gregory II	Γρηγόριος Β'		1564
90. Athanasius I	Ἀθανάσιος Α'		before 1568 – 1577
91. Sophronius	Σωφρόνιος		1577 – after 1606
92. Gabriel I	Γαβριήλ Α'	(1st time)	before 1613 – 1625
93. Ignatius I	Ἰγνάτιος Α'		1625 – Dec 1626
---. Gabriel I	Γαβριήλ Α'	(2nd time)	Dec 1626 – 1627
94. Sylvester	Σίλβεστρος		1 Oct 1627 – Apr 1631
95. Meletius I	Μελέτιος Α'	(1st time)	28 Apr 1631 – May 1639
96. Anthimus I	Ἄνθιμος Α'		May 1639 – after July 1639
---. Meletius I	Μελέτιος Α'	(2nd time)	1639 – Feb 1642
97. Païsius I	Παΐσιος Α'	(1st time)	16 Feb 1642 – 10 Sep 1645
98. Ignatius II	Ἰγνάτιος Β'		10 Sep 1645 – after 1655
---. Païsius I	Παΐσιος Α'	(2nd time)	1656 – after 1672?
(ex p.Const and president m.Kyzikos, as president)			
99. Athanasius II	Ἀθανάσιος Β'		1683
100. Theophanes	Θεοφάνης		before 1688 – 1704
101. Parthenius	Παρθένιος		1704 – . . .
102. Cyprian	Κυπριανός		1710 (ex/to p.Const, president.)

103. Cyril	Κύριλλος	1712, 1725
104. Gabriel II	Γαβριήλ Β΄	1745 – Apr 1746
105. Joachim I	Ιωακείμ Α΄	Apr 1746 – 1747
106. Dionysius I	Διονύσιος Α΄	19 Aug 1747 – 1753
107. Nathaniel	Ναθαναήλ	23 Nov 1753 – Feb 1762
108. Dionysius II	Διονύσιος Β΄	27 Feb 1762 – 24 May 1763
109. Meletius II	Μελέτιος Β΄	31 May 1763 – Feb 1780
110. Samuel	Σαμουήλ	Feb 1780 – Jun 1801

Known Hierarchs of Philadelphia

1. Lucius	Λούκιος	1st century
2. Demetrius	Δημήτριος	1st century
3. Zacharias	Ζαχαρίας	109
4. Theodosius I	Θεοδόσιος Α΄	302
5. Crinon	Κρίνων	320
6. Etimasius	Ετοιμάσιος	325
7. Cyriacus	Κυριακός	344
8. Theodosius II	Θεοδόσιος Β΄	359
9. Theophanes I	Θεοφάνης Α΄	431
10. Metellus	Μέτελλος	451
11. Asianus	Ασιανός	458
12. Eustace	Ευστάθιος	518
13. John I	Ιωάννης Α΄	680
14. Leontius I	Λεόντιος Α΄	705
15. Lycastus	Λύκαστος	783
16. Stephen I	Στέφανος Α΄	787
17. Michael	Μιχαήλ	879
18. Agapetus	Αγαπητός	10th century
19. Manuel	Μανουήλ	1193, 1197
20. Nicholas	Νικόλαος	1213, 1216
21. Phocas	Φωκάς	1228, 1246
22. Johnnicius I	Ιωαννίκιος Α΄	1256, 1260
23. Theoleptus	Θεόληπτος	1292, 1321
24. Macarius I	Μακάριος Α΄	1345, 1348, 1351, 1354, 1355
25. Aaron	Ααρών	1369
26. Paul	Παύλος	1393
27. Macarius II	Μακάριος Β΄	1454, 1456
28. Joachim	Ιωακείμ	1497
29. Neophytus	Νεόφυτος	1546
30. Gabriel I	Γαβριήλ Α΄	1560, 1561
31. Sophronius I	Σωφρόνιος Α΄	1572, 1575, 1577
32. Gabriel II	Γαβριήλ Β΄	18 Jul 1577 – 21 Oct 1616 (in Venice)
33. Theophanes II	Θεοφάνης Β΄	14 Mar 1617 – 29 Feb 1632 (in Venice)
34. Nicodemus	Νικόδημος	12 Apr 1632 – 28 Apr 1635 (in Venice)
35. Athanasius	Αθανάσιος	6 May 1635 – 10 Apr 1656 (in Venice)

36. Meletius I	Μελέτιος Α'	25 Mar 1657 – 25 Jul 1677	(in Venice)
37. Methodius	Μεθόδιος (ex f.p.Const)	19 Dec 1677 – 29 Aug 1679	(in Venice)
38. Gerasimus	Γεράσιμος	3 Sep 1679 – 24 Mar 1685	(in Venice)
39. Meletius II	Μελέτιος Β'	28 Mar 1685 – Jun 1712	(in Venice)
40. Macarius III	Μακάριος Γ'	1721?	
41. Joannicius II	Ιωαννίκιος Β'	1725	
42. Joseph	Ιωσήφ	. . . – 1733	
43. Dionysius I	Διονύσιος Α'	. . . – Jul 1759	
44. Anatole	Ανατόλιος	Jul 1759 – 8 Jul 1765	
45. Jacob I	Ιάκωβος Α'	9 Jul 1765 – 1805	
46. Sophronius II	Σωφρόνιος Β'	3 Sep 1780 – 30 Nov 1790	(in Venice)

Known Hierarchs of Pisidia

1. Eudoxus	Εύδοξος	c. 290
2. Optatus	Οπτάτος	
3. Anthimus	Άνθιμος	
4. Cyprian	Κυπριανός	
5. Sergian	Σεργιανός	314
6. Optimus	Όπτιμος	373, 381
7. Tranquillinus	Τρανκυλλίνος	431
8. Erechthius	Ερέχθιος	c. 440
9. Candidian	Κανδιδιανός	448, 449
10. Pergamius	Περγάμιος	451, 458
11. John	Ιωάννης	518
12. Polydeuces	Πολυδεύκης	520
13. Bacchus	Βάκχος	536
14. Theodore	Θεόδωρος	553
15. Stephen	Στέφανος	681, 692
16. George	Γεώργιος	787
17. Gregory I	Γρηγόριος Α'	847
18. Zacharias	Ζαχαρίας	847
19. Theophylactus	Θεοφύλακτος	997
20. Michael I	Μιχαήλ Α'	1143, 1147
21. Michael II	Μιχαήλ Β'	1256
22. Macarius I	Μακάριος Α'	1264
23. Gregory II	Γρηγόριος Β'	1315, 1331
24. Athanasius	Αθανάσιος	Aug 1369 – . . .
25. Metrophanes	Μητροφάνης	1484
26. Macarius II	Μακάριος Β'	before 1527
27. Daniel or Gabriel	Δανιήλ or Γαβριήλ	1575, 1583, 1590
28. Païsius I	Παΐσιος Α'	1617
29. Euthymius	Ευθύμιος	. . . – 1649
30. Sylvester	Σίλβεστρος	Sep 1649 – 1661
31. Joachim	Ιωακείμ	Sep 1661 – . . .
32. Methodius I	Μεθόδιος Α'	before Jul 1671 – c. Jun 1673

33. Païsius II	Παΐσιος Β΄	c. Jun 1673 – 21 Dec 1673
34. Cyril I	Κύριλλος Α΄	21 Dec 1673 – Jan 1676
35. Leontius	Λεόντιος	28 Jan 1676 – Mar 1719
36. Cosmas I	Κοσμάς Α΄	28 Mar 1719 – 1734 (later p.Alexandria)
37. Cosmas II	Κοσμάς Β΄	before 1746 – 14 Mar 1747
38. Païsius III	Παΐσιος Γ΄	16 Mar 1747 – Jul 1757
39. Ignatius	Ιγνάτιος	Jul 1757 – 22 Jul 1757
40. Dorotheus	Δωρόθεος	23 Jul 1757 – Nov 1768
41. Benedict I	Βενέδικτος Α΄	12 Nov 1768 – Aug 1780
42. Cyril II	Κύριλλος Β΄	Aug 1780 – Jan 1814

Known Hierarchs of Sardis

1. Meliton	Μελίτων	c. 150
2. Artemidorus	Αρτεμίδωρος	325
3. Leontius	Λεόντιος	359
4. Eortasius	Εορτάσιος	. . . – 360
5. Meonius	Μεώνιος	431
6. Florentius	Φλωρέντιος	449, 451
7. Aetherius	Αιθέριος	c. 465
8. Julian	Ιουλιανός	553
9. Marinus	Μαρίνος	680, 681
10. Euthymius	Ευθύμιος	787 – Dec 824
11. John I	Ιωάννης Α΄	824
12. Peter I	Πέτρος Α΄	858 – Feb 869
13. Theophylactus	Θεοφύλακτος	879
14. Peter II	Πέτρος Β΄	c. 880
15. John II	Ιωάννης Β΄	c. 900
16. Peter III	Πέτρος Γ΄	. . . – 912?
17. Anthony	Αντώνιος	912?- . . .
18. Leo	Λέων	996?
19. John III	Ιωάννης Γ΄	1114
20. Nicetas	Νικήτας	1116
21. Nicephorus I	Νικηφόρος Α΄	c. 1210
22. Alexius	Αλέξιος	1216
23. Andronicus	Ανδρόνικος	1261
24. Jacob	Ιάκωβος	1274
25. Gerasimus	Γεράσιμος	1284, 1285 (m.Kerkyra, as pres.)
26. Clement	Κλήμης	13th century
27. Theodore	Θεόδωρος	14th century
28. Nicephorus II	Νικηφόρος Β΄	14th century
29. Gregory	Γρηγόριος	1315, 1341
30. Dionysius	Διονύσιος	(titular bishop) 1437 – 13 Apr 1438
31. Nicholas	Νικόλαος	(titular bishop) c. 1450
32. Ephraim	Εφραίμ	(titular metr.) 1677
33. Nicodemus	Νικόδημος	(titular metr.) Dec 1749 – 1764?

34. Timothy	Τιμόθεος	(titular bishop)	1780
35. Nectarius	Νεκτάριος	(titular metr.)	1792 – 12 Jun 1831

Known Hierarchs of Smyrni

1. Aristion I	Ἀριστίων Α΄	1st century
2. Strataius	Στραταίος	
3. Aristion II	Ἀριστίων Β΄	
4. Bucolus	Βουκόλος	
5. Polycarp	Πολύκαρπος	. . . – 155/6
6. Papyrius	Παπύριος	
7. Camerius	Καμέριος	
8. Thraseas	Θρασέας	
9. Eudaimon	Εὐδαίμων	
10. Eutychius	Εὐτύχιος	325
11. Idduas	Ἰδδούας	431
12. Aetherichus	Αἰθέριχος	451
13. Cyrus	Κύρος	455/460
14. Kalloas	Καλλόας	536
15. Photius	Φώτιος	546
16. Stephen	Στέφανος	692
17. Metrophanes	Μητροφάνης	c. 850
18. Nicetas I	Νικήτας Α΄	879
19. Nicetas II	Νικήτας Β΄	10th century
20. John I	Ἰωάννης Α΄	1043
21. Anthony I	Ἀντώνιος Α΄	12th century
22. Constantine	Κωνσταντίνος	1207, 1208, 1225
23. George I	Γεώργιος Α΄	c. 1225 – 1240?
24. George II	Γεώργιος Β΄	1250
25. Theodore	Θεόδωρος	1256
26. Calophorus	Καλοφόρος	1261
27. Isaac	Ἰσαάκ	1261?
28. John II	Ἰωάννης Β΄	1274 – 1283
29. Thomas	Θωμάς	1283
30. Xenophon I	Ξενοφῶν Α΄	1324, 1326
31. Gregory I	Γρηγόριος Α΄	
32. Macarius I	Μακάριος Α΄	1347 (m.Philadelphia, pres.)
33. Dionysius	Διονύσιος	1389
34. Anthony II	Ἀντώνιος Β΄	1393
35. Daniel	Δανιήλ	1476
36. Neophytus I	Νεόφυτος Α΄	1484
37. Gabriel I	Γαβριήλ Α΄	1572
38. Macarius II	Μακάριος Β΄	1585
39. Methodius	Μεθόδιος	1592
40. Gabriel II	Γαβριήλ Β΄	6 Nov 1605 – . . .
41. Xenophon II	Ξενοφῶν Β΄	1618, 1619

42. Jacob	Ἰάκωβος	(1st time)	1620?- Feb 1638
43. Jeremias	Ἰερεμίας		Feb 1638 – 1639/40
---. Jacob	Ἰάκωβος	(2nd time)	1639/40 – Nov 1652
44. Nathaniel	Ναθαναήλ		Nov 1652?- May 1653?
45. Macary III	Μακάριος Γ'		May 1653 – after 1676
46. Ignatius	Ἰγνάτιος		. . . – 30 Jun 1688
47. Athanasius I	Ἀθανάσιος Α'		1688 – 1689/90
48. Gregory II	Γρηγόριος Β'		1689/90 – May 1698
49. Cyprian	Κυπριανός		15 Jun 1698 – 14 Oct 1707
50. Parthenius	Παρθένιος		15 Oct 1707 – after Oct 1717
51. Ananias	Ἀνανίας		1720, 1721
52. Neophytus II	Νεόφυτος Β'		24 Jan 1731 – Sep 1765
53. Callinicus	Καλλίνικος		1 Oct 1765 – Jan 1770
54. Procopius	Προκόπιος		Jan 1770 – 29 Jun/1 Jul 1785 (p.Const)
55. Gregory III	Γρηγόριος Γ'		19 Aug 1785 – 19 Apr 1797 (to p.Const)
56. Anthimus I	Ἄνθιμος Α'		11 May 1797 – 20 Oct 1821

SECTION E: METROPOLITANATES IN CENTRAL ASIA MINOR

Known Hierarchs of Amasia

1. Nicetius	Νικήτιος	1st century
2. Phaidimus	Φαίδιμος	235, 238, 240
3. Athenodorus	Ἀθηνόδωρος	270
4. Meletius I	Μελέτιος Α'	297
5. Basileus	Βασιλεύς	314 – 322
6. Eutychianus	Εὐτυχιανός	325
7. Eulalius	Εὐλάλιος	343
8. Basil	Βασίλειος	347 – 354
9. Eulabius	Εὐλάβιος	360
10. Eusebius	Εὐσέβιος	
11. Marcellus	Μάρκελλος	378
12. Asterius I	Ἀστέριος Α'	380 – 410
13. Palladius	Παλλάδιος	431
14. Seleucus I	Σέλευκος Α'	448, 449, 451, 456
15. Mammas	Μάμας	491 – 518
16. Meletius II	Μελέτιος Β'	515 – . . .
17. Seleucus II	Σέλευκος Β'	. . . – 553
18. Stephen I	Στέφανος Α'	553 – . . .
19. John	Ἰωάννης	680 – 692
20. Theodore	Θεόδωρος	692
21. Asterius II	Ἀστέριος Β'	. . . – 783
22. Daniel I	Δανιήλ Α'	783 – 787
23. Theophylactus	Θεοφύλακτος	792
24. Nicephorus	Νικηφόρος	868
25. Michael I	Μιχαήλ Α'	900

26. Stephen II	Στέφανος Β´		. . . – 29 Jun 925 (to p.Const)
27. Michael II	Μιχαήλ Β´		1167
28. Nicetas	Νικήτας		1168
29. Leo	Λέων		1168, 1177
30. Michael III	Μιχαήλ Γ´		c. 1190
31. Stephen III	Στέφανος Γ´		1193, 1197
32. Callistus	Κάλλιστος		1316, 1317
33. Michael IV	Μιχαήλ Δ´		1370, 1371, 1379, 1381, 1387
34. Joseph	Ιωσήφ		1384
35. Joasaph I	Ιωάσαφ Α´		1434, 1439
36. Daniel II	Δανιήλ Β´		1450 – . . .
37. Theophilus	Θεόφιλος		1488
38. Sabbatius	Σαββάτιος		1546, 1547
39. Gennadius	Γεννάδιος		1561, 1563
40. Joasaph II	Ιωάσαφ Β´		1572, 1575, 1578
41. Anthimus I	Άνθιμος Α´		1590
42. Gerasimus I	Γεράσιμος Α´		. . . – Jun 1617
43. Gregory	Γρηγόριος		Jun 1617 – 12 Apr 1623 (to p.Const)
44. Meletius III	Μελέτιος Γ´	(1st time)	15 Jun 1623 – Jul 1626
45. Zacharias	Ζαχαρίας		Jul 1626 – Oct 1633
---. Meletius III	Μελέτιος Γ´	(2nd time)	1633 – Mar 1635
46. Ezekiel	Ιεζεκιήλ		13 Mar 1635 – Jan 1641
47. Metrophanes	Μητροφάνης		Jan 1641 – 1644
48. Arsenius	Αρσένιος		Feb 1644 – 24 Mar 1652
49. Cosmas	Κοσμάς	(1st time)	31 Mar 1652 – Nov 1656
50. Gerasimus II	Γεράσιμος Β´	(1st time)	Nov 1656 – after 1665
---. Cosmas	Κοσμάς	(2nd time)	1666, 1667
---. Gerasimus II	Γεράσιμος Β´	(2nd time)	1668?- after 1672
51. Joasaph III	Ιωάσαφ Γ´		before 1688 – 2 Jun 1696
52. Johnnicius	Ιωαννίκιος		Jun 1696 – 7 Aug 1702
53. Dionysius I	Διονύσιος Α´		7 Aug 1702 – after 1719
54. Agapetus	Αγαπητός		1721, 1725
55. Callinicus I	Καλλίνικος Α´		before 1740 – May 1746
56. Benjamin	Βενιαμίν	(1st time)	May 1746 – before 1751
57. Gabriel	Γαβριήλ		1751, 1756
---. Benjamin	Βενιαμίν	(2nd time)	after 1756 – 30 Jul 1764
58. Dionysius II	Διονύσιος Β´		10 Aug 1764 – Sep 1780
59. Païsius	Παΐσιος		Sep 1780 – 1809

Known Hierarchs of Ankyra

1. Theodore (?)	Θεόδωρος		3rd century
2. Clement I	Κλήμης Α´		285 – 304
3. Marcellus	Μάρκελλος	(1st time)	314 – 335
4. Basil I	Βασίλειος Α´	(1st time)	335 – 348
–. Marcellus	Μάρκελλος	(2nd time)	348 – 350

–. Basil I	Βασίλειος Α΄	(2nd time)	351 – 360
5. Athanasius I	Αθανάσιος Α΄		360 – 370
6. Arabian	Αραβιανός		394 – 400
7. Clement II	Κλήμης Β΄		400 – 401
8. Leo	Λέων		401 – 430
9. Theodotus	Θεόδοτος		c. 430 – before 446
10. Eusebius	Ευσέβιος		before 446 – 451
11. Anastasius	Αναστάσιος		458, 459
12. Theodosius I	Θεοδόσιος Α΄		490
13. Dorotheus	Δωρόθεος		513
14. Elpidius	Ελπίδιος		536
15. Dometian	Δομετιανός		539
16. Frontinus	Φροντίνος		562
17. Paul	Παύλος	(1st time)	578 – 582
---. Paul	Παύλος	(2nd time)	595 – 606
18. Plato	Πλάτων		680
19. Stephen I	Στέφανος Α΄		692
20. Basil II	Βασίλειος Β΄		787
21. Theodulus	Θεόδουλος		869, 870
22. Daniel	Δανιήλ		879 – 891
23. Theophylactus	Θεοφύλακτος		892
24. Gabriel	Γαβριήλ		907 – 912
25. John	Ιωάννης		997
26. Michael I	Μιχαήλ Α΄		1032
27. Nicholas I	Νικόλαος Α΄		1043
28. Michael II	Μιχαήλ Β΄		1050
29. Nicetas	Νικήτας		1099 ,1101
30. Stephen II	Στέφανος Β΄		1156, 1157
31. Michael III	Μιχαήλ Γ΄		between 1168/1177
32. Christopher	Χριστόφορος		after 1232
33. Gregory I	Γρηγόριος Α΄		1260
34. Babylas	Βαβύλας		1320
35. Macarius I	Μακάριος Α΄		1391, 1404
36. Constantine I	Κωνσταντίνος Α΄		1450
37. Macarius II	Μακάριος Β΄		1460
38. Gerasimus I	Γεράσιμος Α΄		1561
39. Matthew I	Ματθαίος Α΄		1590
40. Sabbatius	Σαββάτιος		before 1596 – 1602
41. Parthenius	Παρθένιος	(1st time)	24 Sep 1602 – before 1617
42. Gregory II	Γρηγόριος Β΄		1617
43. Parthenius	Παρθένιος	(2nd time)	after 1617 – Aug 1631
44. Laurentius	Λαυρέντιος		11 Aug 1631 – Jul 1655
45. Germanus	Γερμανός		1655, 1665
46. Gerasimus II	Γεράσιος Β΄		1668, before 1674

47. Seraphim I	Σεραφείμ Α'	1670
48. Athanasius II	Αθανάσιος Β'	1674, 1679
49. Joachim	Ιωακείμ	1698, 1699
50. Macarius III	Μακάριος Γ'	1711
51. Meletius I	Μελέτιος Α'	1713
52. Neophytus	Νεόφυτος	1721
53. Johnnicius I	Ιωαννίκιος Α'	before 1741 – 22 Jan 1745
54. Jeremias	Ιερεμίας	23 Jan 1745 – 12 Apr 1754
55. Anthimus	Άνθιμος	12 Apr 1754 – after 1766
56. Seraphim II	Σεραφείμ Β'	16 Dec 1773 – 15 Jun 1779
57. Johnnicius II	Ιωαννίκιος Β'	Jul 1799 – Mar 1811

Known Hierarchs of Ikonion

1. Sosipater	Σωσίπατρος	1st century
2. Terentius	Τερέντιος	1st century
3. Caruatus	Καρουάτος	
4. Celsus	Κέλσος	
5. Nicomas	Νικωμάς	268
6. Peter	Πέτρος	314
7. Eulielius	Ευλιέλιος	325
8. Faustinus	Φαυστίνος	. . . – c.370
9. John I	Ιωάννης Α'	c. 370 – c. 372
10. Amphilochius	Αμφιλόχιος	c. 372 – after 394
11. Valerian	Βαλεριανός	431
12. Onesiphorus	Ονησιφόρος	451
13. Palladius	Παλλάδιος	c. 465
14. Theodulus	Θεόδουλος	535
15. Pastor	Πάστωρ	after 536
16. Theodore I	Θεόδωρος Α'	c. 550
17. Paul	Παύλος	680, 681
18. Elias	Ηλίας	692
19. Leo	Λέων	787
20. Theophylactus	Θεοφύλακτος	c. 870
21. Theophilus	Θεόφιλος	c. 880
22. Phocas	Φωκάς	c. 960
23. Basil	Βασίλειος	997
24. John II	Ιωάννης Β'	1027
25. Eustace	Ευστάθιος	1082
26. Nicetas	Νικήτας	
27. John III	Ιωάννης Γ'	1166, 1170
28. Nicholas	Νικόλαος	1191
29. Marcellus	Μάρκελλος	before 1370 – Jun 1380
30. Theodosius	Θεοδόσιος	1392, 1393
31. Matthew	Ματθαίος	1439
32. Theodore II	Θεόδωρος Β'	1450

33. Amphilochius	Ἀμφιλόχιος	1484, 1488
34. Joasaph	Ἰωάσαφ	between 1572/1594
35. Anthimus I	Ἄνθιμος Α'	1611
36. Leontius	Λεόντιος	. . . – 1 Oct 1625
37. Athanasius I	Ἀθανάσιος Α'	1 Oct 1625 – Oct 1630
38. Abercius	Ἀβέρκιος	9 Oct 1630 – . . .
39. Parthenius I	Παρθένιος Α'	. . . – 30 Aug 1638
40. Laurentius	Λαυρέντιος	30 Aug 1638 – . . .
41. Clement	Κλήμης	(1ˢᵗ time) . . . – Sep 1655
---. union with M. Pisidia		15 Sep 1655 – possibly Sep 1661
42. Athanasius II	Ἀθανάσιος Β'	1666, 1667
---. Clement	Κλήμης	(2ⁿᵈ time) 1667 – 9 Sep 1667 (to p.Const)
43. Meletius I	Μελέτιος Α'	. . . – 1691/3
44. Pachomius	Παχώμιος	1691/3 – after Feb 1699
45. Anthimus II	Ἄνθιμος Β'	before May 1699 – after 1712
46. Parthenius II	Παρθένιος Β'	1715
47. Sylvester	Σίλβεστρος	1721, 1728
48. Joachim I	Ἰωακείμ Α'	before 1734 – Jul 1749
49. Dionysius	Διονύσιος	8 Jul 1749 – Jul 1780
50. Raphael	Ραφαήλ	Jul 1780 – Sep 1803

Known Hierarchs of Kaisaria

1. Primian (?)	Πριμιανός	1ˢᵗ century
2. Apollos (?)	Ἀπολλώς	1ˢᵗ century
3. Theocritus I	Θεόκριτος Α'	c. 160
4. Alexander	Ἀλέξανδρος	170 – 211
5. Firmilian I	Φιρμιλιανός Α'	236 – 268/9
6. Theoctistus	Θεόκτιστος	258
7. Firmilian II	Φιρμιλιανός Β'	269
8. Leontius I	Λεόντιος Α'	285
9. Agricolaus	Ἀγρικόλαος	314
10. Eusebius I	Εὐσέβιος Α'	315 – 320
11. Leontius II	Λεόντιος Β'	325
12. Eusebius II	Εὐσέβιος Β'	335
13. Dianius I	Διάνιος Α'	336
14. Eusebius III	Εὐσέβιος Γ'	340
15. Eulabius	Εὐλάβιος	341
16. Hermogenes	Ἑρμογένης	341
17. Dianius II	Διάνιος Β'	341 – 362
18. Eusebius IV	Εὐσέβιος Δ'	362 – 370
19. Basil I	Βασίλειος Α'	370 – 378/9
20. Heracleides	Ἡρακλείδης	379 – 380
21. Helladius	Ἑλλάδιος	380 – 396
22. Pharetrius	Φαρέτριος	396 – 404
23. Archelaus	Ἀρχέλαος	404 – 431

24. Firmus	Φίρμος	431 – 438
25. Thalassius I	Θαλάσσιος Α΄	438 – 451
26. Alypius I	Αλύπιος Α΄	458
27. Thalassius II	Θαλάσσιος Β΄	469
28. Andrew	Ανδρέας	485
29. Alypius II	Αλύπιος Β΄	513
30. Arethas I	Αρέθας Α΄	518
31. Elias	Ηλίας	c. 530
32. Soterius	Σωτήριος	535, 537
33. Theodore I	Θεόδωρος Α΄	538 – 550
34. Arethas II	Αρέθας Β΄	550
35. Soterichus	Σωτήριχος	553
36. Theocritus II	Θεόκριτος Β΄	c. 560
37. Philalethes	Φιλαλήθης	680, 681
38. Cyriacus	Κυριακός	691
39. Agapius I	Αγάπιος Α΄	783, 787
40. Nicholas I	Νικόλαος Α΄	806
41. Thomas	Θωμάς	812
42. Euschemon I	Ευσχήμων Α΄	857, 859
43. Euthemius I	Ευθύμιος Α΄	c. 865
44. Paul	Παύλος	867
45. Procopius	Προκόπιος	879, 880
46. Theophanes I	Θεοφάνης Α΄	886
47. Euschemon II	Ευσχήμων Β΄	889
48. Arethas III	Αρέθας Γ΄	910
49. Basil II	Βασίλειος Β΄	912 – 918
50. Theophanes II	Θεοφάνης Β΄	918 – 933
51. Basil III	Βασίλειος Γ΄	933 – . . .
52. Arethas IV	Αρέθας Δ΄	945
53. Eusebius V	Ευσέβιος Ε΄	950
54. Basil IV	Βασίλειος Δ΄	950 – 980
55. Cosmas	Κοσμάς	. . . – 1084
56. Stephen I	Στέφανος Α΄	1084 – . . .
57. Abraham	Αβραάμ	11th/12th century
58. Constantine	Κωνσταντίνος	1143 – 1147
59. Stephen II	Στέφανος Β΄	1156, 1166, 1171, 1177
60. Demetrius	Δημήτριος	1190, 1192
61. Metrophanes I	Μητροφάνης Α΄	1242?- 1260?
62. Basil V	Βασίλειος Ε΄	Oct 1352 – 1363
63. Methodius I	Μεθόδιος Α΄	1365, 1368
64. Athanasius	Αθανάσιος	c. 1370
65. Euthymius II	Ευθύμιος Β΄	1378
66. Arsenius	Αρσένιος	1438, 1439, 1440, 1443
67. Agapius II	Αγάπιος Β΄	1450
68. Macarius I	Μακάριος Α΄	1468
69. Metrophanes II	Μητροφάνης Β΄ (1st time) 7 Nov 1546 – 1549	

70. Pachomius I	Παχώμιος Α'		1549 – after 1554
---. Metrophanes II	Μητροφάνης Β'	(2nd time)	before 1558 – Jan/Feb 1565 (to p.Const)
71. Joasaph	Ιωάσαφ		1574, 1575
72. Pachomius II	Παχώμιος Β'		1583?- 22 Feb 1584 (to p.Const)
73. Euthymius III	Ευθύμιος Γ'		Feb 1584 – . . .
74. Gregory I	Γρηγόριος Α'	(1st time)	before 1602 – Sep 1623
75. Meletius I	Μελέτιος Α'		Sep 1623 – 1624
---. Gregory I	Γρηγόριος Α'	(2nd time)	1624 – Jun 1627
76. Epiphanius	Επιφάνιος	(1st time)	Jun 1627 – Jun 1630
77. Isaac	Ισαάκ		8 Jun 1630 – 1631
---. Epiphanius	Επιφάνιος	(2nd time)	1631 – 1642
78. Macarius II	Μακάριος Β'		1642?- Nov 1643?
79. Zacharias	Ζαχαρίας		Nov 1643?- Dec 1649
80. Anthimus	Άνθιμος		Dec 1649 – 1663
81. Neophytus I	Νεόφυτος Α'		1671
82. Gregory II	Γρηγόριος Β'	(1st time)	1672 – 5 Oct 1674
83. Germanus	Γερμανός		5 Oct 1674 – May 1676
---. Gregory II	Γρηγόριος Β'	(2nd time)	May 1676 – 1687
84. Cyprian	Κυπριανός		1687 – 25 Oct 1707 (to p.Const)
85. Jeremias	Ιερεμίας		Nov 1707 – 23/25 Mar 1716 (to p. Const)
86. Neophytus II	Νεόφυτος Β'		1716 – 27 Sep 1734 (to p.Const)
87. Parthenius	Παρθένιος		1734 – Jul 1757
88. Païsius I	Παΐσιος Α'		Jul 1757 – Sep 1766
89. Macarius III	Μακάριος Γ'		2 Sep 1766 – 2 Mar 1773
90. Gregory III	Γρηγόριος Γ'		27 Mar 1773 – Jul 1796
91. Leontius III	Λεόντιος Γ'		Jul 1796 – 1 Oct 1801

Known Hierarchs of Neokaisaria

1. Gregory I	Γρηγόριος Α'	c. 240 – c. 270
2. Longinus	Λογγίνος	314, 325
3. Theodulus	Θεόδουλος	343
4. Mousonius	Μουσώνιος	371
5. Atarbius	Ατάρβιος	381
6. Eleusius	Ελεύσιος	431
7. Dorotheus	Δωρόθεος	449, 451
8. Evippus	Εύιππος	458
9. Bosporius	Βοσπόριος	536, 553
10. Gregory II	Γρηγόριος Β'	754
11. Thomas	Θωμάς	812
12. Stylian	Στυλιανός	880, 886
13. Nicephorus I	Νικηφόρος Α'	931/47
14. Theophylactus	Θεοφύλακτος	1028
15. Gregory III	Γρηγόριος Γ'	1082
16. Abraham	Αβραάμ	
17. Nicephorus II	Νικηφόρος Β'	1143

18. Constantine	Κωνσταντίνος		1153, 1156
19. Basil	Βασίλειος		1166, 1171
20. Monoconstantine	Μονοκωνστάντινος		1264
21. Gregory IV	Γρηγόριος Δ'		1450
---. unknown			. . . – May 1607
22. Metrophanes I	Μητροφάνης Α'		28 May 1607 – before 1610
23. Benjamin	Βενιαμίν		Oct 1610 – . . .
24. Benedict	Βενέδικτος		before May 1616 – 20 Jan 1623
25. Metrophanes II	Μητροφάνης Β'		18 May 1623 – . . .
26. Parthenius	Παρθένιος		. . . – 19 Jan 1630
27. Macarius	Μακάριος		19 Jan 1630 – Sep 1643
28. Christopher	Χριστόφορος		25 Sep 1643 – May 1645
29. Samouel	Σαμουήλ		18 May 1645 – 1 Nov 1655
30. Cyril I	Κύριλλος Α'		26 Nov 1655 – Oct 1677
31. Arsenius	Αρσένιος		13 Oct 1677 – . . .
32. Cyprian	Κυπριανός		. . . – 1687
33. Ignatius I	Ιγνάτιος Α'		1687 – Sep 1695
34. Jacob	Ιάκωβος	(1st time)	Sep 1695 – 19 Dec 1696
35. Gregory V	Γρηγόριος Ε'		17 Jan 1697 – . . .
---. Jacob	Ιάκωβος	(2nd time)	. . . – c. 1710
---. unknown			. . . – 1721
36. Methodius	Μεθόδιος		1721 – after 1728
37. Dionysius	Διονύσιος		before 1742 – 19 Aug 1747
38. Cosmas	Κοσμάς		21 Aug 1747 – . . .
39. Gerasimus	Γεράσιμος		before 1756 – 31 May 1758
40. Cyril II	Κύριλλος Β'		31 May 1758 – Mar 1767
41. Daniel	Δανιήλ		5 Mar 1767 – 1 Nov 1773
42. Ignatius II	Ιγνάτιος Β'		17 Nov 1773 – 29 Apr 1793
43. Isaiah	Ησαΐας		May 1793 – 1801

SECTION F: METROPOLITANATES IN NORTHEAST ASIA MINOR

Known Hierarchs of Chaldia

1. Macarius	Μακάριος	1520
2. Daniel	Δανιήλ	1560
3. Theoleptus	Θεόληπτος	1610?- 1624?
4. Sylvester I	Σίλβεστρος Α'	1624?- 1653
5. Euthymius	Ευθύμιος	Dec 1653 – after 1660
6. Germanus	Γερμανός	1667
7. Gregory I	Γρηγόριος Α'	before 1680 – 1683
8. Gregory II	Γρηγόριος Β'	25 Dec 1684 – Jul 1694
9. Philotheus	Φιλόθεος	13 Jul 1694 – 27 Jul 1717
10. Ignatius I	Ιγνάτιος Α'	12 Sep 1717 – 17 Apr 1734
11. Ignatius II	Ιγνάτιος Β'	1734 – 26 Oct 1749
12. Païsius	Παΐσιος	1749 – after 1755

13. Dionysius	Διονύσιος	before 1767 – 1783
14. Theophanes	Θεοφάνης	Nov 1783 – 1790
15. Sophronius	Σωφρόνιος	Nov 1790 – 13 Nov 1818

Known Hierarchs of Nikopolis

1. Theodotus	Θεόδοτος	372 – 375
2. Fronton	Φρόντων	375
3. Euphronius	Ευφρόνιος	375 – . . .
4. Panestius	Πανέστιος	
5. John	Ιωάννης	449, 451, 458
6. Photius	Φώτιος	692
7. Tarasius	Ταράσιος	869, 870
8. Nicholas I	Νικόλαος Α´	879, 880
9. Gregory	Γρηγόριος	c. 1000
10. Nicholas II	Νικόλαος Β´	1147

Known Hierarchs of Kolonia

1. Euphonius	Ευφώνιος	375, 376
2. Eustace	Ευστάθιος	458
3. John I	Ιωάννης Α´	481
4. Proclus	Πρόκλος	518
5. John II (?)	Ιωάννης Β´	553
6. Callinicus	Καλλίνικος	680, 692
7. Nicetas	Νικήτας	787
8. Constantine	Κωνσταντίνος	879, 880
9. Thomas	Θωμάς	c. 1000
10. Theophilus	Θεόφιλος	1071
11. John III	Ιωάννης Γ´	1082
12. Theodore	Θεόδωρος	1177

Known Hierarchs of Trapezous

1. Domnus	Δόμνος	325
2. Atarbius	Ατάρβιος	451
3. Antipater	Αντίπατρος	518
4. Anthimus I	Ἄνθιμος Α´	532, 535, 536
5. Uranius	Ουράνιος	542
6. Theodore	Θεόδωρος	680
7. Christopher	Χριστόφορος	787
8. Nicephorus	Νικηφόρος	c. 825
9. Athanasius	Αθανάσιος	867 – 886
10. Basil	Βασίλειος	913, 914
11. Constantine I	Κωνσταντίνος Α´	1027, 1028
12. Leo	Λέων	1054

13. Stephen	Στέφανος	1126 – 1140
14. Michael	Μιχαήλ	1166
15. David	Δαυΐδ	after 1238 – before 1263
16. Barnabas	Βαρνάβας	1311 – 1333
17. Gregory I	Γρηγόριος Α΄	1333 – 1339
18. Acacius	Ακάκιος	1339 – 1351
19. Nephon	Νήφων	1351 – 1364
20. Joseph	Ιωσήφ	1364 – 1368
21. Theodosius	Θεοδόσιος	1370 – 1391
22. Hilarion	Ιλαρίων	1394
23. Anthony	Αντώνιος	1395 – 1400
24. Symeon	Συμεών	1401 – 1402
25. Theodulus	Θεόδουλος	1403 – 1408
26. Dositheus	Δοσίθεος	1408 – 1422
27. Dorotheus I	Δωρόθεος Α΄	1422 – after 1439
28. Pangratius	Παγκράτιος	1471, 1472
29. Dorotheus II	Δωρόθεος Β΄	1472
30. Gennadius I (?)	Γεννάδιος Α΄	1500, 1501
31. Gerasimus I	Γεράσιμος Α΄	1506
32. Gennadius II	Γεννάδιος Β΄	1564
33. Maximus	Μάξιμος	1570
34. Anthimus II	Άνθιμος Β΄	1583
35. Theophanes	Θεοφάνης	1591, 1593
36. Gerasimus II	Γεράσιμος Β΄	1596 – 1610
37. Ignatius I	Ιγνάτιος Α΄	1610 – 1620
38. Xenophon	Ξενοφών	1620 – Aug 1628
39. Cyril	Κύριλλος	5 Aug 1628 – 1638
40. Anthimus III	Άνθιμος Γ΄	1638/9 – 1640
41. Laurentius	Λαυρέντιος	1640/1 – Dec 1659
42. Philotheus	Φιλόθεος	24 Dec 1659 – 1665
43. Johnnicius	Ιωαννίκιος	3 Nov 1665 – 10 Mar 1689
44. Nectarius	Νεκτάριος	Apr 1689 – 1705/6
45. Païsius	Παΐσιος	before Mar 1706 – after Jun 1717
46. Ignatius II	Ιγνάτιος Β΄	1721
47. Ananias I	Ανανίας Α΄	Sep 1722 – 1736
48. Ananias II	Ανανίας Β΄	Mar 1736 – 1764
49. Dorotheus III	Δωρόθεος Γ΄	17 Aug 1764 – 1798
50. Parthenius	Παρθένιος	Mar 1798 – 1830

SECTION G: METROPOLITANATES IN THE DODECANESE

Known Hierarchs of Karpathos

1. Philon	Φίλων	383 – 400
2. Zoticus	Ζωτικός	520
3. Menas	Μηνάς	553

4. John	Ἰωάννης	680
5. Leo	Λέων	783 – 787
6. Philip	Φίλιππος	879
7. Johnnicius	Ἰωαννίκιος	1562 – 25 Jul 1576
8. Macarius I	Μακάριος Α΄	1576 – 1583
9. Joasaph	Ἰωάσαφ	1583 – 1590
10. Theodulus	Θεόδουλος	1590 – 1601
11. Hierotheus	Ἱερόθεος	1601 – 1622
---. vacant		1622 – 1636
12. Damascenus	Δαμασκηνός	1636 – 1643
13. Athanasius	Ἀθανάσιος	1643 – 1665
14. Leontius	Λεόντιος	1665 – 1674
15. Macarius II	Μακάριος Β΄	1674 – 1680
16. Neophytus I	Νεόφυτος Α΄	1680 – 1723
17. Nicephorus I (?)	Νικηφόρος Α΄	1723 – 1730
18. Nicephorus II	Νικηφόρος Β΄	1736 – 1744
19. Parthenius I	Παρθένιος Α΄	1744 – 1755
20. Macarius III	Μακάριος Γ΄	1755 – 1760
21. Païsius	Παΐσιος	1760 – 1764
22. Daniel	Δανιήλ	1764 – 1780
23. Parthenius II	Παρθένιος Β΄	1780 – 1793
24. Neophytus II	Νεόφυτος Β΄	Jun 1793 – 1832

Known Hierarchs of Kos

1. Meliphron	Μελίφρων	325
2. Hedesotus	Ἐδέσοτος	343, 344
3. Julian	Ἰουλιανός	448, 451
4. Dorotheus	Δωρόθεος	518
5. George	Γεώργιος	680, 681
6. Constantine	Κωνσταντίνος	879
7. Athanasius I	Ἀθανάσιος Α΄	11th century
8. Gerasimus I	Γεράσιμος Α΄	1330
9. Nicandrus	Νίκανδρος	. . . – 1584
10. Dionysius	Διονύσιος	1590
11. Jacob	Ἰάκωβος	. . . – 1595
12. Gabriel	Γαβριήλ	1596 – 1616
13. Christopher	Χριστόφορος	1 Jan 1616 – 1625
14. Anthony	Ἀντώνιος	Nov 1625 – 1626
15. Seraphim	Σεραφείμ	1626 – 1638
16. Joachim I	Ἰωακείμ Α΄	Jan 1638 – . . .
17. Cosmas	Κοσμάς	1648 – . . .
18. Zacharias	Ζαχαρίας Α΄	1660 – . . .
19. Macarius	Μακάριος	1670 – . . .
20. Cyril I	Κύριλλος Α΄	1701 – 1720
21. Neophytus	Νεόφυτος	1720 – 1748

22. Meletius I	Μελέτιος Α΄	22 Aug 1748 – 27 Mar 1761
23. Theocletus	Θεόκλητος	27 Mar 1761 – 1763
24. Meletius II	Μελέτιος Β΄	1763 – 1765
25. Joseph	Ιωσήφ	1766 – 1768
26. Callinicus I	Καλλίνικος Α΄	1768 – 1774
27. Parthenius	Παρθένιος	1774 – 1790
28. Zacharias II	Ζαχαρίας Β΄	1790 – 1801

Known Hierarchs of Leros

1. John I	Ιωάννης Α΄	553
2. Sergius	Σέργιος	787
3. Joseph	Ιωσήφ	869
4. Constantine	Κωνσταντίνος	1158
5. Constantius	Κωνστάντιος	1187
6. Nilus	Νείλος	c. 1255
7. Callistus	Κάλλιστος	1577 – 1584
8. Symeon I	Συμεών Α΄	. . . – 1603
9. Philotheus	Φιλόθεος	. . . – 1635
10. Pachomius	Παχώμιος	1637 – 1643
11. Symeon II	Συμεών Β΄	1717 – 1730
12. Ignatius I	Ιγνάτιος Α΄	May 1756 – 1800

Known Hierarchs of Rhodes

1. Prochorus	Πρόχορος		1st century
2. Euphranor (?)	Ευφράνωρ		2nd century
3. Photinus	Φωτεινός		296
4. Euphrosinus	Ευφρόσυνος		325
5. Hellanodicus	Ελλανόδικος		431
6. John I	Ιωάννης Α΄		449, 451
7. Agapetus	Αγαπητός		459
8. Isaiah	Ησαΐας		. . . – 528
9. Theodosius I	Θεοδόσιος Α΄		553 – . . .
10. Isidore	Ισίδωρος		680, 681
11. Leo I	Λέων Α΄		783, 787
12. Theophanes	Θεοφάνης		814, 832
13. Nilus I	Νείλος Α΄		833 – . . .
14. Michael	Μιχαήλ	(1st time)	. . . – 858
15. Leontius	Λεόντιος	(1st time)	858 – 868
---. Michael	Μιχαήλ	(2nd time)	868 – 879
---. Leontius	Λεόντιος	(2nd time)	879 – . . .
16. Theodore	Θεόδωρος		997 – . . .
17. John II	Ιωάννης Β΄		between 1070/1100
18. Nicephorus	Νικηφόρος		1147
20. Leo II	Λέων Β΄		1166

21. George	Γεώργιος	12th/13th century
22. Theodulus	Θεόδουλος	1256
19. John III	Ιωάννης Γ'	before 1350 – Apr 1357
24. Nilus II	Νείλος Β'	1357 – 1376
26. Nathaniel I	Ναθαναήλ Α'	1437 – 1439
27. Macarius	Μακάριος	1450 – 1455
28. Nilus III	Νείλος Γ'	1455 – 1470
29. Metrophanes I	Μητροφάνης Α'	1471 – 1498
30. Metrophanes II	Μητροφάνης Β'	1498 – 1511
31. Jeremias I	Ιερεμίας Α'	1511 – 1522
32. Clement	Κλήμης	1522 – 1523
33. Euthemius	Ευθύμιος	1523 – 1525?
34. Theodosius II	Θεοδόσιος Β'	1541 – 1548?
35. Callistus	Κάλλιστος	1572 – 1594
36. Païsius I	Παΐσιος Α'	1595 – Dec 1603
37. Jeremias II	Ιερεμίας Β'	1603 – Mar 1604
38. Philotheus	Φιλόθεος	1604 – 1610
39. Ignatius II	Ιγνάτιος Β'	1610 – 1612
40. Pachomius	Παχώμιος	1612 – 1637
41. Meletius I	Μελέτιος Α'	14 Aug 1637 – 1639
42. Païsius II	Παΐσιος Β'	1639 – 1643
43. Meletius II	Μελέτιος Β'	1643 – 1651
44. Gregory I	Γρηγόριος Α'	1651 – 1652
45. Nathaniel II	Ναθαναήλ Β'	1652 – 1665
46. Joachim I	Ιωακείμ Α'	1666 – 1676
47. Parthenius	Παρθένιος	1676 – 1691
48. Constantius	Κωνστάντιος	1692 – Oct 1702
49. Ignatius III	Ιγνάτιος Γ'	1702 – 1722
50. Neophytus	Νεόφυτος	1722 – 1733
51. Jeremias III	Ιερεμίας Γ'	1733 – 1758
52. Callinicus I	Καλλίνικος Α'	1758 – 1792
53. Agapius	Αγάπιος	1792 – 1827

Special Section: Patriarchal Exarchs of Patmos (incl. surnames)

1. Methodius	Μεθόδιος	(Kalogeras)	1715 – 1718	(1st time)	1748+
2. Callinicus	Καλλίνικος	(Papageorgas)	1718 – 1721+		1721+
3. Athanasius I	Αθανάσιος Α'	(Kotis)	1722 – 1724	(1st time)	1740+
4. Ignatius	Ιγνάτιος	(Simos)	1725 – 1727	(1st time)	1734+
–. Athanasius I	Αθανάσιος Α'	(Kotis)	1728 – 1729	(2nd time)	1740+
–. Ignatius	Ιγνάτιος	(Simos)	1729 – 1731	(2nd time)	1734+
–. Methodius	Μεθόδιος	(Kalogeras)	1731	(2nd time)	1748+
–. Ignatius	Ιγνάτιος	(Simos)	1732 – 1734+	(3rd time)	1734+
5. Theophylactus	Θεοφύλακτος	(Grimanis)	1734 – 1737		1742+
6. Neophytus	Νεόφυτος	(Fasolas)	1738 – 1740+		1740+
7. Nectarius I	Νεκτάριος Α'	(Thomaos)	1741 – 1742		1751+

8. Joachim	Ιωακείμ	(Simon)	1743 – 1748		1763+
9. Parthenius I	Παρθένιος Α'	(Sigalas)	1748 – 1750		1752+
10. Christopher	Χριστόφορος	(Saliermos)	1752 – 1757	(1st time)	1788+
11. Germanus	Γερμανός	(Pangalos)	1757	(1st time)	1778+
---. Christopher	Χριστόφορος	(Saliermos)	1758 – 1762	(2nd time)	1788+
12. Joasaph I	Ιωάσαφ Α'	(Kalogeras)	1762 – 1763	(1st time)	1801+
---. Christopher	Χριστόφορος	(Saliermos)	1763 – 1765	(3rd time)	1788+
13. Parthenius II	Παρθένιος Β'	(Germanos)	1765 – 1766	(1st time)	1790+
14. Jacob I	Ιάκωβος Α'	(Grimanis)	1767		1771+
---. Parthenius II	Παρθένιος Β'	(Germanos)	1768 – 1770	(2nd time)	1790+
---. Germanus	Γερμανός	(Pangalos)	1770 – 1774	(2nd time)	1778+
---. Joasaph I	Ιωάσαφ Α'	(Kalogeras)	1774 – 1790	(2nd time)	1801+
15. Gabriel	Γαβριήλ	(Pankostas)	1790 – 1791		1792+
16. Symeon I	Συμεών Α'	(Mandis)	1791 – 1793		1812+
17. Parthenius III	Παρθένιος Γ'	(Chazakos)	1793 – 1794	(1st time)	1797+
18. Athanasius II	Αθανάσιος Β'	(Metalas)	1794 – 1796		1799+
---. Parthenius III	Παρθένιος Γ'	(Chazakos)	1796 – 1797+	(2nd time)	1797+
19. Macarius I	Μακάριος Α'	(Loungas)	1797	(1st time)	1828+
---. Joasaph I	Ιωάσαφ Α'	(Kalogeras)	1797 – 1799	(3rd time)	1801+
20. Macarius II	Μακάριος Β'	(Palaiologos)	1800 – 1801		1804+
21. Parthenius IV	Παρθένιος Δ'	(Amprouzis)	1801 – 1804		1812+
---. Macarius I	Μακάριος Α'	(Loungas)	1804	(2nd time)	1828+
22. Gerasimus	Γεράσιμος	(Mavrodis)	1804 – 1806		1820+
23. Gregory I	Γρηγόριος Α'	(Adeletis)	1806 – 1808		1832+
24. Jacob II	Ιάκωβος Β'	(Kefalianos)	1808 – 1813		1814+
25. Jacob III	Ιάκωβος Γ'	(Meligiannis)	1813 – 1818	(1st time)	1831+
26. Benjamin I	Βενιαμίν Α'	(Grimanis)	1818 – 1820	(1st time)	1856+
27. Daniel I	Δανιήλ Α'	(Palaiologos)	1820	(1st time)	1824+
---. Jacob III	Ιάκωβος Γ'	(Meligiannis)	1820 – 1823	(2nd time)	1831+
---. Daniel I	Δανιήλ Α'	(Palaiologos)	1823 – 1824+	(2nd time)	1824+
28. Gregory II	Γρηγόριος Β'	(Pitilos)	1824 – 1825	(1st time)	1834+
---. Jacob III	Ιάκωβος Γ'	(Meligiannis)	1825 – 1827	(3rd time)	1831+
---. Benjamin I	Βενιαμίν Α'	(Grimanis)	1827 – 1831	(2nd time)	1856+
---. Gregory II	Γρηγόριος Β'	(Pitilos)	1831 – 1834	(2nd time)	1834+
---. Benjamin I	Βενιαμίν Α'	(Grimanis)	1834 – 1849	(3rd time)	1856+
29. Daniel II	Δανιήλ Β'	(Sychnis)	1849 – 1863	(1st time)	1870+
30. Parthenius V	Παρθένιος Ε'	(Kalligas)	1863 – 1865	(1st time)	1874+
---. Daniel II	Δανιήλ Β'	(Sychnis)	1865 – 1867	(2nd time)	1870+
---. Parthenius V	Παρθένιος Ε'	(Kalligas)	1867 – 1870	(2nd time)	1874+
31. Gregory III	Γρηγόριος Γ'	(Papadopoulos)	1870 – 1874	(1st time)	1878+
32. Hilarion	Ιλαρίων	(Γαλάνης)	1874 – 1876		1877+
---. Gregory III	Γρηγόριος Γ'	(Papadopoulos)	1876 – 1878+	(2nd time)	1878+
33. Jacob IV	Ιάκωβος Δ'	(Pantelakis)	1878 – 1880	(1st time)	1899+
34. Joasaph II	Ιωάσαφ Β'	(Xenos)	1880 – 1882		1888+
35. Constantius	Κωνστάντιος	(Glavaridis)	1882 – 1884	(1st time)	1891+
---. Jacob IV	Ιάκωβος Δ'	(Pantelakis)	1884 – 1886	(2nd time)	1899+

36. Benjamin II	Βενιαμίν Β'	(Meligiannis)	1886 – 1888	(1st time)	1896+
---. Constantius	Κωνστάντιος	(Glavaridis)	1888 – 1890	(2nd time)	1891+
---. Benjamin II	Βενιαμίν Β'	(Meligiannis)	1890 – 1892	(2nd time)	1896+
---. Jacob IV	Ιάκωβος Δ'	(Pantelakis)	1892 – 1894	(3rd time)	1899+
37. Nectarius II	Νεκτάριος Β'	(Ioannidis)	1894 – 1896	(1st time)	1912+
---. Jacob IV	Ιάκωβος Δ'	(Pantelakis)	1896 – 1898	(4th time)	1899+
38. Meletius I	Μελέτιος Α'	(Kotzanis)	1898 – 1899+		1899+
39. Theophanes I	Θεοφάνης Α'	(Skopelitis)	1899 – 1901		1905+
40. Païsius	Παΐσιος	(Ferentinos)	1901 – 1903	(1st time)	1926+
41. Agathangelus	Αγαθάγγελος	(Vatikas)	1903 – 1907	(1st time)	1934+
---. Nectarius II	Νεκτάριος Β'	(Ioannidis)	1907 – 1909	(2nd time)	1912+
42. Gregory IV	Γρηγόριος Δ'	(Pteris)	1909 – 1911	(1st time)	1926+
---. Agathangelus	Αγαθάγγελος	(Vatikas)	1911 – 1915	(2nd time)	1934+
---. Gregory IV	Γρηγόριος Δ'	(Pteris)	1915 – 1917	(2nd time)	1926+
---. Païsius	Παΐσιος	(Ferentinos)	1917 – 1918	(2nd time)	1926+
---. Agathangelus	Αγαθάγγελος	(Vatikas)	1918 – 1922	(3rd time)	1934+
43. Gregory V	Γρηγόριος Ε'	(Genis)	1922 – 1930		1960+
44. Jeremias I	Ιερεμίας Α'	(Vallas)	1930 – 1932		1934+
45. Theophanes II	Θεοφάνης Β'	(Krikris)	1933		1966+
46. Amphilochius I	Αμφιλόχιος Α'	(Makris)	1935 – 1937		1970+
47. Epiphanius	Επιφάνιος	(Kalogiannis)	1937 – 1943		1966+
48. Nicodemus	Νικόδημος	(Kanakis)	1943 – 1945		1946+
49. Symeon II	Συμεών Β'	(Revithis)	1946 – 1951		1959+
50. Meletius II	Μελέτιος Β'	(Margiolos)	1951 – 1957		1975+
51. Jeremias II	Ιερεμίας Β'	(Vastas)	1957 – 1961		1991+
52. Paul	Παύλος	(Nikitaras)	1961 – 1963		1999+
53. Theodoretus	Θεοδώρητος	(Bournis)	1963 – 1975	(1st time)	1986+
54. Isidore	Ισίδωρος	(Krikris)	1975 – 1981	(1st time)	2007+
---. Theodoretus	Θεοδώρητος	(Bournis)	1981 – 1986+	(2nd time)	1986+
---. Isidore	Ισίδωρος	(Krikris)	1986 – 1997	(2nd time)	2007+
55. Amphilochius II	Αμφιλόχιος Β'	(Kamitsis)	1997 – 2000	b. 1953	
56. Antipas	Αντίπας	(Nikitaras)	2000 –	b. 1962	

SECTION H: SEMI-AUTONOMOUS CHURCH OF CRETE

Known Hierarchs of Crete (Gortyna before c.1000 AD)

1. Titus I	Τίτος Α'	1st century
2. Artemas	Αρτεμάς	
3. Philip	Φίλιππος	c. 160/170
4. Dioscorus	Διόσκορος	
5. Cresces	Κρήσκης	256
6. Cyril	Κύριλλος	303
7. Peter	Πέτρος	
8. Iconius	Εικόνιος	431
9. Martyrius	Μαρτύριος	451

10. Theodore	Θεόδωρος	553	
11. John I	Ιωάννης Α΄	597	
12. Paul	Παύλος	667	
13. Eumenius I	Ευμένιος Α΄	668	
14. Basil I	Βασίλειος Α΄	680, 692	
15. Andrew	Ανδρέας	711 – 726?	
16. Elias I	Ηλίας Α΄	787	
17. John II	Ιωάννης Β΄		
18. Stephen I	Στέφανος Α΄		
19. Nicetas I	Νικήτας Α΄		
20. Nicetas II	Νικήτας Β΄		
21. Basil II	Βασίλειος Β	823, 828 (in exile)	
22. Basil III	Βασίλειος Γ΄	879 (in exile)	
23. Elias II	Ηλίας Β΄	before 961 (in exile)	
24. Andrew II	Ανδρέας Β΄	c. 1000	
25. Nicetas III	Νικήτας Γ΄		
26. Stephen II	Στέφανος Β΄	1028	
27. John III	Ιωάννης Γ΄	1166 – 1172?	
28. Leo	Λέων		
29. Michael	Μιχαήλ		
30. Constantine I	Κωνσταντίνος Α΄		
31. Elias III	Ηλίας Γ΄		
32. Basil IV	Βασίλειος Δ΄		
33. Constantine II	Κωνσταντίνος Β΄		
34. Nicholas I	Νικόλαος Α΄		
35. John IV	Ιωάννης Δ΄		
36. Manuel I	Μανουήλ Α΄		
37. Manuel II	Μανουήλ Β΄		
38. Nicholas II	Νικόλαος Β΄	c. 1200 – after 1224 (exiled aft.1211)	
39. Nicephorus I	Νικηφόρος Α΄	after 1285, 1303/4, 1316, 1322 (in exile)	
40. Macarius	Μακάριος	1357 (in exile)	
41. Anthimus	Άνθιμος	. . . – 1366 (m.Athina, president)	
42. Ignatius	Ιγνάτιος	1381 (m.Old Patra, president)	
43. Prochorus	Πρόχορος	1410 (m.Stavroupolis, president)	
44. Belisarius	Βελισάριος	1499 (b.Koroni, president)	
45. Neophytus	Νεόφυτος	1646 – 1679	
46. Nicephorus II	Νικηφόρος Β΄	1679 – 1683	
47. Callinicus I	Καλλίνικος Α΄	1683 – 1684?	
48. Arsenius I	Αρσένιος Α΄	1684?- 1685	
49. Athanasius	Αθανάσιος	1687;- 3 Feb 1697	
50. Callinicus II	Καλλίνικος Β΄	1697 – 1699?	
51. Arsenius II	Αρσένιος Β΄	1699 – 1701?	
52. Joasaph	Ιωάσαφ	1704 – 1710?	
53. Constantius	Κωνστάντιος (1st time)	1711?- 1716	
54. Gerasimus I	Γεράσιμος Α΄	1716 – 1718	
---. Constantius	Κωνστάντιος (2nd time)	7 Dec 1718 – 1722	

55. Daniel	Δανιήλ	1723 – 1725
56. Gerasimus II	Γεράσιμος Β'	1725 – 2 Jan 1756
57. Gerasimus III	Γεράσιμος Γ'	6 Feb 1756 – Jul 1769
58. Zacharias	Ζαχαρίας	Jul 1769 – May 1786
59. Maximus	Μάξιμος	19 May 1786 – 4 May 1800

Known Hierarchs of Knossos

1. Pinytus	Πινυτός	170
2. Myron	Μύρων	249
3. Zenobius	Ζηνόβιος	431
4. Gennadius	Γεννάδιος	451, 457
5. Anastasius	Ἀναστάσιος	787
6. Paul	Παῦλος	1204
7. Constantine	Κωνσταντίνος	10th/12th century
8. Parthenius	Παρθένιος	. . . – 2 Nov 1716+
9. Methodius	Μεθόδιος	1717 – . . .
10. Gerasimus I	Γεράσιμος Α'	1743 – 10 Jan 1781+
11. Philotheus	Φιλόθεος	5 Mar 1781 – 1782+ (ex b. Iera)
12. Gerasimus II	Γεράσιμος Β'	Dec 1782 – 5 Apr 1819+

Known Hierarchs of Arkadia (now Gortyna and Arkadia)

1. John I	Ἰωάννης Α'		787
2. John II	Ἰωάννης Β'		1205, 1216 (in exile after 1211)
3. Theophanes	Θεοφάνης		. . . – 30 Mar 1659 (to m.Chios)
4. Parthenius	Παρθένιος		1681
5. Athanasius	Ἀθανάσιος	(1st time)	1706 – 1734
–. Athanasius	Ἀθανάσιος	(2nd time)	1735 – . . .
6. Cyril I	Κύριλλος Α'		before 1754 – 31 May 1758 (to m.Neokaisaria)
7. Gabriel	Γαβριήλ		1758 – 1763+
8. Methodius	Μεθόδιος		1763 – . . .+
9. Cyril II	Κύριλλος Β'		. . . – . . .+
10. Gerasimus	Γεράσιμος		before 1793 – 20 Jun 1803

Known Hierarchs of Iera (now Ierapytna and Sitia)

1. Symphorus	Σύμφορος	343
2. Euphronius	Εὐφρόνιος	457
3. Athanasius I	Ἀθανάσιος Α'	1671
4. Raphael	Ραφαήλ	. . . – 1689
5. Athanasius II	Ἀθανάσιος Β'	1689 – . . .
6. Meletius	Μελέτιος	before 1696 – 5 Apr 1713+
7. Athanasius III	Ἀθανάσιος Γ'	1731?- . . .+ (see note 1)
8. Jeremias	Ἰερεμίας	Aug 1763 – 1773
9. Philotheus I	Φιλόθεος Α'	30 Dec 1773 – 5 Mar 1781 (to b.Knossos)

10. Auxentius	Αυξέντιος	1781 – after 1790+
11. Gideon	Γεδεών	before 1793 – 8 Oct 1810+

1. Athanasius III officiated during the consecration of the Metropolitan of Derki, Samuel, later Ecumenical Patriarch, which occurred on December 27, 1731 (Μανουήλ Γεδεών, *Πατριαρχικοί Πίνακες*, 1st reprint by Σύλογος προς Διάδοσιν Ωφέλιμων Βιβλίων, Athens 1996, p.552).

Known Hierarchs of Sitia

1. Meletius	Μελέτιος	
2. Parthenius	Παρθένιος	
3. Gregory	Γρηγόριος	
4. Athanasius	Αθανάσιος	
5. Dionysius	Διονύσιος	
6. Joseph	Ιωσήφ	
7. Gerasimus	Γεράσιμος	before 1777 (to b.Cherronisos)
8. Constantius	Κωνστάντιος	before 1777 – 1785+
9. Theophylactus	Θεοφύλακτος	before 1793 – 20 Jun 1803 (to b.Arkadia)

Known Hierarchs of Kissamos

1. Eucissus	Εύκισσος	343
2. Theopemptus	Θεόπεμπτος	691, 692
3. Leo	Λέων	787
4. Gerasimus I	Γεράσιμος Α'	c. 1470 (permitted to reside on the island)
5. Philotheus	Φιλόθεος	before 1684
6. Gerasimus II	Γεράσιμος Β'	before 1711
7. Gerasimus III	Γεράσιμος Γ'	. . . – 1716 (to m.Kriti)
8. Parthenius I	Παρθένιος Α'	. . . – 5 Jul 1731+
9. Anthimus I	Άνθιμος Α'	1731 – 1750
10. Parthenius II	Παρθένιος Β'	1750/1 – 1770/1+
11. Païsius	Παΐσιος	1771 – 1777
12. Sophronius	Σωφρόνιος	1777 – 1790/2+
13. Joasaph	Ιωάσαφ	1790/2 – 1808

Known Hierarchs of Kydonia

1. Cydonius	Κυδώνιος	343
2. Sivon	Σίβων	458
3. Nicetas	Νικήτας	692
4. Meliton	Μελίτων	787
5. Porphyrius I	Πορφύριος Α'	1061
6. Dionysius	Διονύσιος	before 1679
7. Callinicus I	Καλλίνικος Α'	1684
8. Gennadius	Γεννάδιος	1685
9. Arsenius	Αρσένιος (1st time)	
10. Porphyrius II	Πορφύριος Β'	. . . – Aug 1699

---. Arsenius	Ἀρσένιος	(2nd time)	Aug 1699 – 1705
11. Ephraim	Ἐφραίμ		1705/6 – . . .
12. Daniel	Δανιήλ		. . . – 1 Jul 1714 (to m.Chios)
13. Macarius	Μακάριος		
14. Joasaph	Ἰωάσαφ		before 1777 – . . .+
15. Martinianus	Μαρτινιανός		. . . – Mar 1780 (deposed, d≥1783)
16. Gerasimus	Γεράσιμος		Mar 1780 – 30 Jan 1815

Known Hierarchs of Lampi

1. Paul	Παύλος	431
2. Demetrius	Δημήτριος	451
3. Prosdocius	Προσδόκιος	457
4. John	Ἰωάννης	667, 681
5. Epiphanius	Ἐπιφάνιος	787
6. Nectarius	Νεκτάριος	before 1723 – 1729+
7. Manasses	Μανασσής	between 1768/1777 – 1779+
8. Matthew	Ματθαίος	1779/80 – . . . (resigned or deposed)
9. Pamphilus	Πάμφιλος	. . . – 1788+
10. Methodius	Μεθόδιος	1788?- 9 Jul 1793++ (murdered)
11. Hierotheus	Ἱερόθεος	1793/5 – 24 Jun 1821++

Known Hierarchs of Petra

1. George	Γεώργιος	1205, 1216 (in exile after 1211)
2. Raphael	Ραφαήλ	. . . – 1688
3. Athanasius	Ἀθανάσιος	1688 – . . .
4. Gerasimus I	Γεράσιμος Α´	1703
5. Meletius I	Μελέτιος Α´	before 1734 – . . . +
6. Gerasimus II	Γεράσιμος Β´	before 1777 – . . . +

Known Hierarchs of Cherronisos

1. Anderius	Ἀνδήριος	431
2. Euphratas	Εὐφράτας	457
3. Sisinnius I	Σισίννιος Α´	691, 692
4. Sisinnius II	Σισίννιος Β´	787
5. Raphael	Ραφαήλ	before 1699
6. Anthimus	Ἄνθιμος	1696
7. Nicephorus	Νικηφόρος	1701
8. Theodosius	Θεοδόσιος	1705
9. Nectarius	Νεκτάριος	before 1742 – after 1752+
10. Macarius	Μακάριος	after 1752 – . . . +
11. Gerasimus I	Γεράσιμος Α´	before 1777 – 29 Apr 1806+

Known Hierarchs of Rethymnon

1. Cyril	Κύριλλος	(of Syvritos)	451
2. Theodore	Θεόδωρος	(of Syvritos)	787
3. Basil	Βασίλειος	(of Agrion)	1260 (permitted to reside on the island)
4. Alexander	Ἀλέξανδρος	(of Kalliergipolis)	1322 – 1324 (p. to reside on the island)
5. Macarius	Μακάριος		1671 – 1680
6. Philotheus	Φιλόθεος		before 1683
7. Athanasius I	Ἀθανάσιος Α΄		1688 – before 1708 (1708+)
8. Daniel	Δανιήλ		before 1719 – 1723 (to m.Kriti)
9. Anthimus I	Ἄνθιμος Α΄		1731
10. Gerasimus I	Γεράσιμος Α΄		before 1777 – after 1789+
11. Gerasimus II	Γεράσιμος Β΄		1796 – 1822++

Known Hierarchs of Avlopotamos

1. Euphratas	Ευφράτας	(of Eleftherna)	451
2. Epiphanius	Επιφάνιος	(of Eleftherna)	787
3. Gideon	Γεδεών		2 Sep 1713 – 1753 (resigned, 22/9/1754+)
4. Neophytus	Νεόφυτος		20 Nov 1755 – before 1777 (resigned)
5. Parthenius	Παρθένιος		before 1777 – 1820+

SECTION I: METROPOLITANATES IN WESTERN EUROPE

Known Hierarchs of Thyatira (in Asia Minor)

1. Carpus	Κάρπος	250++
2. Sozon	Σώζων	325
3. Phoscus	Φώσκος	431
4. Diamonius	Διαμόνιος	458
5. Basil	Βασίλειος	879

APPENDIX B
EPARCHIES OF THE ECUMENICAL PATRIARCHATE

Listed here are all the Eparchies of the Ecumenical Patriarchate that exist or existed after 1800. Where the Eparchy is not a Metropolitanate, it is specifically so noted (for example, "Vella, Diocese Ioannina" means that the Eparchy of Vella was a Diocese under the Metropolitanate of Ioannina). Any change in the status of the Eparchies after 1800 is also noted. The geographical location of each Eparchy is given, along with the year it passed into the jurisdiction of another church, if that is the case (*e.g.*, Serbia 1879). Abbreviations used: est. (established), abol. (abolished), M. (Metropolitanate), A. (Archdiocese), canon. (canonically).

If the name of the city after which the Eparchy is named has since been changed, the current name of the city is included inside parentheses. If the Eparchy is in Western Europe, America, the Far East, or Oceania, it is listed under its international name.

Changes in the Metropolitanates of the New Lands are stated even after the transfer of their management to the Church of Greece in 1928, since, although the Church of Greece elects the Hierarchs of these Metropolitanates, they remain Metropolitanates of the Ecumenical Patriarchate.

Names of Eparchies abolished before 1800 (not listed here), are still used for the Titular Metropolitans and Titular Bishops of the Ecumenical Throne.

Adrianoupolis (Edirne), (Adrianople), East Thrace
Agathoupolis (Akhtopol), Archdiocese, abol.1808, re-est.1813, abol.1831, East Thrace
Ainos (Enez), East Thrace
Aigina, Archdiocese, M.1813, South Aegean Sea, Greece 1833 de facto, 1850 canon
Akova, Archdiocese, abol.1819, Peloponnese, Greece
Alexandroupolis, West Thrace, est.1924, Greece 1928 (New Lands)
Almyros, Diocese Larissa, est.1833, abol.1844, Thessaly, Greece
Amasia (Amasya), Central Asia Minor
America, Archdiocese, est.1922, North America
Amykles, Diocese Lakedaimonia, abol.1804, Peloponnese, Greece
Anchialos (Pomorie), Bulgaria 1908 de facto, 1945 canon
Andros, Archdiocese, M.1810, South Aegean Sea, Greece 1833 de facto, 1850 canon
Androussa, Diocese Monemvasia, Peloponnese, Greece 1833 de facto, 1850 canon
Androuvista, Diocese Monemvasia, Peloponnese, Greece 1833 de facto, 1850 canon
Anea (Soke), Diocese Ephesos, est.1883, M.1917, Southwest Asia Minor
Ankyra (Ankara), Central Asia Minor
Ardamerion, Diocese Thessalonica, abol.1923, re-est+M.1924, Macedonia, Greece 1928 (New
    Lands), abol.1934
Argyrokastron (Gjirokastra), est.1937, North Epirus, Albania 1937
Arkadia (named Gortyna and Arkadia 1961), Diocese Kriti, M.1962, Crete
Arkalochorion Kastellion and Viannos, est.2001, Crete
Arta, South Epirus, est.1826, Greece 1882
Artzi (Arges), Diocese Oungrovlachia, Romania 1864 de facto, 1885 canon
Athina (Athens) and Livadia, Central Hellas, Greece 1833 de facto, 1850 canon
Atlanta (Charlotte until 1981), Diocese America, est.1979, M.2002, North America
Australia, Archdiocese, est.M.1924, A.1959, Oceania
Austria, est.1963, West Europe

Avlopotamos, Diocese Kriti, abol.1838, Crete
Belgium, est.1969, West Europe
Boston, Diocese America, est.1922, abol.1931, re-est.1979, M.2002, North America
Bozeon (Buzau), Diocese Oungrovlachia, Romania 1864 de facto, 1885 canon
Buenos Aires, Diocese America, est.1979, M.1996, South America
Chaldia (Gumushane), Northeast Asia Minor
Chalkidon (Kadikoy), Northwest Asia Minor
Charlotte, see Atlanta
Cherronisos, Diocese Kriti, abol.1831, re-est.1843, abol.1900, Crete
Chicago, Diocese America, est.1922, abol.1931, re-est.1979, M.2002, North America
Chimarra and Delvinon, Diocese Ioannina, abol.1832, North Epirus, Albania
Chios, North Aegean Sea, Greece 1928 (New Lands)
Chousion (Husi), Diocese Moldavia, Romania 1864 de facto, 1885 canon
Christianoupolis, Peloponnese, Greece 1833 de facto, 1850 canon
Damala and Polyfengon, Diocese Korinthos, Peloponnese, Greece 1833 de facto, 1850 canon
Dardanellia (Canakkale) and Lampsakos (Lapseki), est.1913, Northwest Asia Minor
Denver, Diocese America, est.1979, M.2002, North America
Derki (Durusu), East Thrace
Detroit, Diocese America, est.1979, M.2002, North America
Devres (Debar), North Macedonia, Serbia 1920
Didymotichon, West Thrace, Greece 1928 (New Lands)
Dimitrias and Zagora, Thessaly, Greece 1882
Dimitsana, Archdiocese, Peloponnese, Greece 1833 de facto, 1850 canon
Diskati, Archdiocese, est.1882, M.1887, abol.1896, Macedonia, Greece
Drama, see Philippi and Drama
Dryinoupolis, Diocese Ioannina, M.1835, South Epirus, Greece 1928 (New Lands)
Drystra (Silistra), Bulgaria 1872 de facto, 1945 canon
Dyrachion (Durres), North Epirus, Albania 1922 de facto, 1937 canon
Edessa (Vodena until 1922), Macedonia, Greece 1928 (New Lands)
Elasson, Archdiocese, M.1814, Macedonia, Greece 1928 (New Lands)
Eleftheroupolis, Diocese Filippi, M.1889, Macedonia, Greece 1928 (New Lands)
Elos, Diocese Monemvasia, Peloponnese, Greece 1833 de facto, 1850 canon
Ephesos (Kusadasi), West Asia Minor
Ersekion (Herzegovina), Bosnia-Herzegovina, Serbia 1920
Evripos (Euboea), Central Hellas, Greece 1833 de facto, 1850 canon
Fersala, Archdiocese, abol.1820, Thessaly, Greece, see Phanariofersala
Florina (Moglena to 1925), Macedonia, Greece 1928 (New Lands)
France, est.1963, West Europe
Ganos (Guzelkoy) and Chora (Hoskoy), East Thrace
Gardikion, Diocese Larissa, Thessaly, Greece 1882
Giannitsa and Goumenissa, est.1924, Macedonia, Greece 1928 (New Lands), named Pella 1930, abol.1932
Giromerion, Diocese Ioannina, est.1800, abol.1803, South Epirus, Greece
Gortyna and Arkadia (Arkadia until 1961), Diocese Kriti, M.1962, Crete
Goumenissa Axioupolis and Polykastron, est.1991, Macedonia, Greece (New Lands)
Grevena, Macedonia, Greece 1928 (New Lands)
Germany, est.1963, West Europe
Halepion (Haleb), Syria, Antioch 1888
Helsinki (Vyborg until 1940), (Diocese Karelia, est.1925, M.1972, Finland
Helvetia (Switzerland), est.1982, West Europe
Hong Kong, est.1996, East Asia
Hungary, est.1924, abol.1924, East Europe
Iera, Diocese Kriti, abol.1831, see Iera and Sitia
Iera and Sitia (alternatively called Ierositia until 1900, named Ierapytna and Sitia 1961),
    Diocese Kriti, est.1831, abol.1932, re-est.1935, M.1962, Crete, see Neapolis, see Iera, see Sitia
Ierapytna and Sitia (Iera and Sitia until 1961), Diocese Kriti, est.1831, abol.1932, re-est.1935,
    M.1962, Crete, see Neapolis, see Iera, see Sitia
Ierissos and Agion Oros, Diocese Thessalonica, M.1924, Macedonia, Greece 1928 (New Lands)
Ierositia (see Iera and Sitia)
Ikaria, est.1924, South Aegean Sea, Greece 1928 (New Lands), abol.1931
Ikonion (Konya), Central Asia Minor
Ilioupolis (Aydin) and Thira (Tire), Diocese Ephesos, M.1901, Southwest Asia Minor
Imvros (Gokceada) and Tenedos (Bosca Ada), North Aegean Sea

Ioannina, South Epirus, Greece 1928 (New Lands)
Iraklia (Marmaraereglisi), (Heraclia), East Thrace
Italia and Melite (Italy and Malta), est.1991, West Europe
Ithaki (Ithaca), Diocese Kefallinia, est.1817, Ionian Sea, Greece 1865
Kaisaria (Kayseri), (Caesaria), Central Asia Minor
Kallipolis (Gelibolu) and Madytos (Eceabat), Diocese Iraklia, M.1901, East Thrace
Kampania, Diocese Thessalonica, abol.1879, re-est.1882, M.1924, Greece 1928 (New Lands),
    abol.1930
Kardamyla, est.1924, North Aegean Sea, Greece 1928 (New Lands), abol.1933
Karelia, Archdiocese, est.1925, Finland
Karpathos and Kasos, Archdiocese, M.1865, South Aegean Sea, Dodecanese
Karyoupolis, Diocese Lakedaimonia, Peloponnese, Greece 1833 de facto, 1850 canon
Karystos, Diocese Athina, Central Hellas, Greece 1833 de facto, 1850 canon
Kassandria, Macedonia, Greece 1928 (New Lands)
Kastoria, Macedonia, Greece 1928 (New Lands)
Kavala and Nestos, est.1924, Macedonia, Greece 1928 (New Lands), named Philippi and Neapolis 1930
Kefallinia (Cephallenia), Archdiocese, M.1799, Ionian Sea, Greece 1865
Kerkyra (Corfu), re-est.1799, Ionian Sea, Greece 1865
Kernitzi and Kalavryta, Diocese Old Patra, Peloponnese, Greece 1833 de facto, 1850 canon
Kestentilion (Kyustendil), Bulgaria 1872 de facto, 1945 canon
Kissamos and Selinon, Diocese Kriti, abol.1831, re-est.1860, M.1962, Crete
Kitros and Katerini, Diocese Thessalonica, M.1924, Macedonia, Greece 1928 (New Lands)
Knossos, Diocese Kriti, abol.1831, Crete
Kolonia (Koyulhisar), est.1889, Northeast Asia Minor, see Nikopolis
Korea, est.2004, East Asia
Korinthos (Corinth), Peloponnese, Greece 1833 de facto, 1850 canon
Koritsa (Korce), Albania 1922 de facto, 1937 canon
Koroni, Diocese Old Patra, Peloponnese, Greece 1833 de facto, 1850 canon
Kos and Nisyros (Kos until 2004), Archdiocese, M.1838, South Aegean Sea, Dodecanese
Krini (Cesme), Diocese Ephesos, est.1806, M.1903, West Asia Minor
Kriti (Crete), A.1967, South Aegean Sea
Kydonia (named Kydonia and Kissamos 1831, named Kydonia and Apokoronon 1900),
    Diocese Kriti, M.1962, Crete
Kydonies (Ayvalik), est.1908, Northwest Asia Minor
Kyklades, est.1924, abol.1924, South Aegean Sea, Dodecanese (see Symi)
Kythira (Cythera), Diocese Philadelphia, A.1817, South Aegean Sea, Greece 1865
Kyzikos (Balkiz), Northwest Asia Minor
Lagia, Diocese Monemvasia, est.1810, Peloponnese, Greece 1833 de facto, 1850 canon
Lampi Syvritos and Sphakia (Lampi and Sphakia until 2000), Diocese Kriti, abol.1845,
    re-est.1863, M.1962, Crete
Langada, est.1924, Macedonia, Greece 1928 (New Lands), abol.1932, re-est.1966
Lakedaimonia (Lacedaemonia), Peloponnese, Greece 1833 de facto, 1850 canon
Larissa, Thessaly, Greece 1882
Lefkas and Agia Mavra, Archdiocese, M.1799, Ionian Sea, Greece 1865
Lerna (named Leros and Kalymnos 1888), Diocese Rhodes, M.1888, South Aegean Sea,
    Dodecanese
Leros and Kalymnos (Lerna to 1888), Diocese Rhodes, M.1888, South Aegean Sea, Dodecanese
Lidorikion, Diocese Larissa, Central Hellas, Greece 1833 de facto, 1850 canon
Limnos, North Aegean Sea, Greece 1928 (New Lands)
Lititza (Ivaylovgrad), Archdiocese, M.1855, West Thrace, Bulgaria 1913 de facto, 1945 canon
Litza and Agrapha, Diocese Larissa, Central Hellas, Greece 1833 de facto, 1850 canon
Loftsa (Lovetch), Diocese Tornovo, Bulgaria 1872 de facto, 1945 canon
Maltzini, Diocese Lakedaimonia, Peloponnese, Greece 1833 de facto, 1850 canon
Mani, Diocese Monemvasia, Peloponnese, Greece 1833 de facto, 1850 canon
Maronia and Komotini, West Thrace, Greece 1928 (New Lands)
Melenikon (named Sidirokastron 1922), Macedonia, Greece 1928 (New Lands)
Mendenitsa, Diocese Athina, Central Hellas, Greece 1833 de facto, 1850 canon
Mesimvria (Nesebur), abol.1830, re-est.1835, Bulgaria 1908 de facto, 1945 canon
Methoni, Diocese Old Patra, Peloponnese, Greece 1833 de facto, 1850 canon
Metres (Catalca) and Athyra (Buyukcekmece), Diocese Iraklia, M.1909, East Thrace
Metsovon, est.1924, South Epirus, Greece 1928 (New Lands), abol.1931
Mexiko (Panamá until 2005), est.1996, Central America

Milea, Diocese Monemvasia, Peloponnese, Greece 1833 de facto, 1850 canon
Mithymna, North Aegean Sea, Greece 1928 (New Lands)
Moglena (named Florina 1925), Macedonia, Greece 1928 (New Lands)
Moldavia, Romania 1864 de facto, 1885 canon
Monemvasia, Peloponnese, Greece 1833 de facto, 1850 canon
Moschonisia (Alibey Adalar), Diocese Smyrni, M.1922, North Aegean Sea
Myriophyton (Murefte) and Peristasis (Sarkoy), Diocese Iraklia, M.1909, East Thrace
Mytilini, North Aegean Sea, Greece 1928 (New Lands)
Nafpaktos, abol.1808, re-est.1813, Central Hellas, Greece 1833 de facto, 1850 canon
Nafplion and Argos, Peloponnese, Greece 1833 de facto, 1850 canon
Narva and Irboska, see Pärnu and Saaremaa
Neapolis, Diocese Kriti, est.1932, abol.1935, see Iera and Sitia
Neapolis and Stavroupolis, est.1974, Macedonia, Greece (New Lands)
Neokaisaria (Niksar), Central Asia Minor
Nevrokopion, Archdiocese, est.1882, M.1887, Macedonia, Greece 1928 (New Lands), named Zichna and Nevrokopion 1965
New Jersey, Diocese America, est.1979, M.2002, North America
New Krini and Kalamaria, est.1974, Macedonia, Greece (New Lands)
New Orestias, est.1924, West Thrace, Greece 1928 (New Lands), abol.1931
New Patra (Ypati), Central Hellas, Greece 1833 de facto, 1850 canon
New Pelagonia, est.1924, Macedonia, Greece 1928 (New Lands), named Ptolemaïs and
    Eordaia 1930, abol.1935
New Zealand, est.1970, Oceania
Nigrita, est.1924, Macedonia, Greece 1928 (New Lands), abol.1935
Nikaia (Iznik), (Nicaea), Northwest Asia Minor
Niklon, Diocese Monemvasia, abol.1800, Peloponnese, Greece
Nikomidia (Izmit), Northwest Asia Minor
Nikopolis (Sebinkarahisar), Diocese Neokaisaria, abol.1889, Northeast Asia Minor, see
    Kolonia
Nikopolis and Preveza, South Epirus, est.1881, Greece 1928 (New Lands)
Nyssa (Nis) (called Nyssonysava 1820-23), Bulgaria 1872 de facto, Serbia 1879
Nyssava (Pirot), Archdiocese, abol.1820, re-est.M.1823, Bulgaria 1872 de facto, Serbia 1879
Nyssonysava (Nis and Pirot), est.1820, abol.1823, see Nyssa, see Nyssava
Old Patra, Peloponnese, Greece 1833 de facto, 1850 canon
Oleni, Peloponnese, Greece 1833 de facto, 1850 canon
Oulu, est.1980, Finland
Oungrovlachia (Hungaro-Walachia), Romania 1864 de facto, 1885 canon
Ouzitsa (Uzice) and Voliovo (Valjevo), Serbia 1831
Paramythia, Diocese Ioannina, M.1895, South Epirus, Greece 1928 (New Lands)
Pärnu and Saaremaa (Narva and Irboska until 2008), Diocese Tallinn, est. 1923, Estonia
Paronaxia (Paros and Naxos), South Aegean Sea, Greece 1833 de facto, 1850 canon
Patmos (Exarchate), South Aegean Sea, Dodecanese
Paxi, Diocese Kerkyra, est.1817, Ionian Sea, Greece 1865
Petseri, see Tartu
Pelagonia (Bitola), North Macedonia, Serbia 1920
Pella, see Giannitsa and Goumenissa
Pergamos (Bergama) and Adramytion (Edremit), est.1922, Northwest Asia Minor
Petra, Diocese Thessalonica, abol.1896, Macedonia, Greece
Petra and Cherronisos (Petra until 2000), Diocese Kriti, abol.1932, re-est.1935, M.1962, Crete,
    see Neapolis
Panamá (named Mexiko 2005), est.1996, Central America
Phanariofersala, est.1820, Thessaly, Greece 1882
Phanarion, Archdiocese, abol.1820, Thessaly, Greece, see Phanariofersala
Philadelphia (Alasehir), West Asia Minor
Philiatai and Giromerion, est.1925, South Epirus, Greece 1928 (New Lands), abol.1928
Philippi and Drama, Macedonia, Greece 1928 (New Lands), named Drama 1930
Philippi and Neapolis, see Kavala and Nestos
Philippoupolis (Plovdiv), Bulgaria 1908 de facto, 1945 canon
Pisidia (Isparta), Southwest Asia Minor
Pittsburgh, Diocese America, est.1979, M.2002, North America
Platamon, Diocese Thessalonica, Thessaly, Greece 1882
Platza, Diocese Monemvasia, Peloponnese, Greece 1833 de facto, 1850 canon

Plomarion, est.1924, North Aegean Sea, Greece 1928 (New Lands), abol.1934
Pogoniani, Archdiocese, abol.1828, re-est.M.1842, abol.1863, South Epirus, Greece
Polyani and Kilkision, Diocese Thessalonica, M.1924, Macedonia, Greece 1928 (New Lands)
Preslava (Preslav), Diocese Tornovo, M.1831, Bulgaria 1872 de facto, 1945 canon
Prespes and Ochrida, North Macedonia, Serbia 1920
Prikonnisos (Marmara Adasi), Archdiocese, M.1823, Sea of Marmara
Pringiponnisa (Kuzil Adalar), (Princes' Islands), est.1924, Sea of Marmara
Proilavos (Braila), abol.1813, Romania
Prousa (Bursa), Northwest Asia Minor
Ptolemaïs and Eordaia, see New Pelagonia
Radaouzion (Radauti), Diocese Moldavia, Romania 1864 de facto, 1885 canon
Radovisdion, Diocese Larissa, abol.1830, South Epirus, Greece
Raskoprezreni (Raska and Prizren), Kosovo, Serbia 1920
Reontas and Prastos, Archdiocese, M.1812, Peloponnese, Greece 1833 de facto, 1850 canon
Rethymnon and Avlopotamos, Diocese Kriti, M.1962, Crete
Riga, est.1936, abol.1978, Latvia
Rimnikon (Ramnic), Diocese Oungrovlachia, Romania 1864 de facto, 1885 canon
Rhodopolis (Macka), Archdiocese, est.1863, abol.1867, re-est.M.1902, Northeast Asia Minor
Rhodes, South Aegean Sea, Dodecanese
Romanon (Roman), Diocese Moldavia, Romania 1864 de facto, 1885 canon
Salona (Amfissa), Diocese Athina, Central Hellas, Greece 1833 de facto, 1850 canon
Samakovion (Samokov), Bulgaria 1872 de facto, 1945 canon
Samos, Archdiocese, M.1841, South Aegean Sea, Greece 1928 (New Lands)
San Francisco, Diocese America, est.1922, abol.1931, re-est.1979, M.2002, North America
Santorini (Thira), Archdiocese, M.1814, South Aegean Sea, Greece 1833 de facto, 1850 canon
Sapaski (Sabac), Diocese Ouzitsa, Serbia 1831
Saranta Ekklisies (Kirklareli), est.1906, East Thrace
Sardis (Sartmahmut), est.1924, Southwest Asia Minor
Serres, Macedonia, Greece 1928 (New Lands)
Servia and Kozani, Diocese Thessalonica, M.1882, Macedonia, Greece 1928 (New Lands)
Sidirokastron (Melenikon until 1922), Macedonia, Greece 1928 (New Lands)
Sifnos and Milos, South Aegean Sea, Greece 1833 de facto, 1850 canon
Sitia, Diocese Kriti, abol.1831, Crete, see Iera and Sitia
Siyvria (Silivri), East Thrace
Sisanion and Siatista, Macedonia, Greece 1928 (New Lands)
Skiathos and Skopelos, Diocese Larissa, North Aegean Sea, Greece 1833 de facto, 1850 canon
Skopia (Skopje), North Macedonia, Serbia 1920
Skyros, Diocese Athina, North Aegean Sea, Greece 1833 de facto, 1850 canon
Smyrna (Izmir), West Asia Minor
Sophia (Sofia), Bulgaria 1872 de facto, 1945 canon
Souflion, est.1924, West Thrace, Greece 1928 (New Lands), abol.1934
Sozoagathoupolis (Sozopol and Akhtopol), est.1808, abol.1813, re-est. 1831, East Thrace,
    Bulgaria 1913 de facto, 1945 canon, see Sozopolis, see Agathoupolis
Switzerland (Helvetia), est.1982, West Europe
Sozopolis (Sozopol), abol. 1808, re-est. 1813', abol. 1831, see Sozoagathoupolis
Spain and Portugal, est.2003, West Europe
Stagi, Diocese Larissa, Thessaly, Greece 1882
Stromnitsa (Strumica), North Macedonia, Serbia 1920
Svornikion (Zvornik), Bosnia-Herzegovina, Serbia 1920
Sweden, est.1969, West Europe
Symi, est.2004, South Aegean Sea, Dodecanese
Talantion and Diavlia, Diocese Athina, Central Hellas, Greece 1833 de facto, 1850 canon
Tallinn, est.1923, abol.1978, re-est.1996, Estonia
Tartu (Petseri until 1943, Tartu and Petseri until 2008), Diocese Tallinn, est.1923, Estonia
Thasos, est.1924, North Aegean Sea, Greece 1928 (New Lands), abol.1932
Thavmakos, Diocese Larissa, Thessaly, Greece 1882
Thessaloniki, Macedonia, Greece 1928 (New Lands)
Thiva (Thebes), Central Hellas, Greece 1833 de facto, 1850 canon
Thyatira and Great Britain (Thyatira and Megali Vretania), est.1922, A.1954, M.1963, A.1968,
    West Europe
Tinos, Archdiocese, M.1810, South Aegean Sea, Greece 1833 de facto, 1850 canon
Tornovo (Veliko Tarnovo), Bulgaria 1872 de facto, 1945 canon

Toronto, Diocese America, est.1979, M.1996, North America

Trapezous (Trabzon), Northeast Asia Minor

Trikki (Trikala), Diocese Larissa, Thessaly, Greece 1882

Tripolis and Amykles, est.1804, Peloponnese, Greece 1833 de facto, 1850 canon

Tyroloï (Corlu) and Serention (Binkilic), Diocese Iraklia, M.1840, abol.1848, re-est.1907, East Thrace

Tzervenos (Cherven), Diocese Tornovo, M.1865, Bulgaria 1872 de facto, 1945 canon

Tzia (Kea) and Thermia (Kythnos), Archdiocese, M.1819, South Aegean Sea, Greece 1833 de facto, 1850 canon

Vanialouka (Banja Luka) and Vichatsi (Bihac), est.1900, Bosnia-Herzegovina, Serbia 1920

Varna, Bulgaria 1908 de facto, 1945 canon

Velegrades (Berat), Albania 1922 de facto, 1937 canon

Veligradion (Belgrade), Serbia 1831

Velissos (Veles), Archdiocese, M.1842, abol.1880, North Macedonia

Vella, Diocese Ioannina, M.1834, abol.1842, Diocese Ioannina 1863, M.1895, South Epirus, Greece 1928 (New Lands), abol.1936

Veria (Beroea), Macedonia, Greece 1928 (New Lands)

Vidyni (Vidin), Bulgaria 1872 de facto, 1945 canon

Vizyi (Vize) and Midia (Kiyikoy), East Thrace

Vodena (named Edessa 1922), Macedonia, Greece 1928 (New Lands)

Vosna (Bosnia), Bosnia-Herzegovina, Serbia 1920

Vratza, Diocese Tornovo, Bulgaria 1872 de facto, 1945 canon

Vrestheni, Diocese Lakedaimonia, Peloponnese, Greece 1833 de facto, 1850 canon

Vryoula (Urla), est.1922, West Asia Minor

Xanthi and Peritheorion, West Thrace, Greece 1928 (New Lands)

Zakynthos (Zante), re-est.1817, Ionian Sea, Greece 1865

Zarnata, Archdiocese, est.1811, M.1819, Peloponnese, Greece 1833 de facto, 1850 canon

Zichna, est.1924, Macedonia, Greece 1928 (New Lands), abol.1951 (see Nevrokopion)

Zitounion (Lamia) and Almyros, Diocese Larissa, Central Hellas, Greece 1833 de facto, 1850 canon, see Almyros

APPENDIX C
PRONUNCIATION GUIDE TO GREEK NAMES

The Greek alphabet has been transliterated to Latin in various ways in the past, most of them failing to make the pronunciation of the transliterated text sound like the way a Greek would pronounce it during the last 1,500 years.

This work uses the common western form for transcribing Hierarch names, and a method close to the standard transliteration method as used in Greek passports for transcribing Eparchy names and Hierarch surnames.

Here follows a guide of Greek letter pronunciation and their Latin transliteration:

Greek written letters as:	pronounced as:	
A, α	A, a	pronounced 'a' as in 'cat'
B, β	V, v	pronounced 'v' as in 'vat'
Γ, γ	G, g	pronounced 'y' as in 'yet'
Δ, δ	D, d	pronounced 'th' as in 'this'
E, ε	E, e	pronounced 'e' as in 'pet'
Z, ζ	Z, z	pronounced 'z' as in 'zebra'
H, η	I, i	pronounced 'i' as in 'pit'
Θ, θ	TH, th	pronounced 'th' as in 'think'
I, ι	I, i	pronounced 'i' as in 'pit'
K, κ	K, k	pronounced 'k' as in 'kit'
Λ, λ	L, l	pronounced 'l' as in 'lit'
M, μ	M, m	pronounced 'm' as in 'mat'
N, ν	N, n	pronounced 'n' as in 'next'
Ξ, ξ	X, x	pronounced 'x' as in 'box', even at the beginning of a word, *i.e.*, Xerxes=Kserkses
O, o	O, o	pronounced 'o' as in 'pot'
Π, π	P, p	pronounced 'p' as in 'pot'
P, ϱ	R, r	pronounced 'r' as in 'red'
Σ, σ, ς	S, s	pronounced 's' as in 'sit', ς used instead of σ at the end of words.
T, τ	T, t	pronounced 't' as in 'top'
Υ, υ	Y, y	pronounced 'i' as in 'pit'
Φ, φ	F, f	pronounced 'f' as in 'fit'
X, χ	CH, ch	pronounced like 'ch' in the Scottish word 'Loch'
Ψ, ψ	PS, ps	pronounced 'ps' as in 'psi'
Ω, ω	O, o	pronounced 'o' as in 'pot'

Diphthongs:

EI, ει   I, i   pronounced 'i' as in 'pit'
OI, οι   I, i   pronounced 'i' as in 'pit'
ΥI, υι   I, i   pronounced 'i' as in 'pit'
AI, αι   AI, ai   pronounced 'e' as in 'pet'
OΥ, ου OU, ou   pronounced 'u' as in 'put'
AΥ, αυ AF, af   pronounced 'af' as in 'affair' if next letter is Θ, Κ, Ξ, Π, Σ, Τ, Φ, Χ,
                       or Ψ
AΥ, αυ AV, av   pronounced 'av' as in 'avenger' in all other cases
EΥ, ευ EF, ef   pronounced 'ef' as in 'effective' if next letter is Θ, Κ, Ξ, Π, Σ, Τ, Φ,
                       Χ, or Ψ
EΥ, ευ EV, ev   pronounced 'ev' as in 'evade' in all other cases

Letter combinations:

ΓΚ, γκ NG, ng pronounced 'g' as in 'golf'
ΓΓ, γγ NG, ng pronounced 'g' as in 'golf'
ΜΠ, μπ B, b   pronounced 'b' as in 'bat'
ΝΤ, ντ NT, nt   pronounced 'd' as in 'den'

Any other same-consonant combination (νν, μμ, ρρ, σσ, etc) is pronounced in the same way that a single consonant is pronounced.

Accented vowels: Ά, ά, Έ, έ, Ή, ή, Ί, ί, Ό, ό, Ύ, ύ, Ώ, ώ

In polysyllabic words, an accent mark on a vowel informs which syllable of the word must be stressed, *i.e.,* Βασίλειος, Βασιλέας, Βασιλικός, Άνθιμος, Νίκαια, Νικομήδεια. No accent mark is put on words written with capital letters.

Accented diphthongs: Εί, εί, Οί, οί, Υί, υί, Αί, αί, Ού, ού, Αύ, αύ, Εύ, εύ

In diphthongs the accent mark is always noted over the second vowel. An accent mark on the first vowel breaks the diphthong, for example Cairo is written Κάιρο in order to be pronounced correctly (Καίρο would have been pronounced Kero).

Dieresis: Ϊ, ϊ, Ϋ, ϋ

Used to break non-accented diphthongs. The dieresis in Παπαϊωάννου means that the surname is pronounced Papa-i-oannou and not Papeoannou. The dieresis in the 'ai' diphthong had been retained in the Latin transliteration of such words, hence the above surname is written Papaïoannou in the lists.

Toned dieresis: ΐ, ΰ

In order to break a diphthong that has an accent mark on its second vowel, the accented dieresis is used. Two common examples are Παΐσιος (pronounced Pa-i-sios instead of Pesios) and Ησαΐας (pronounced Isa-i-as instead of Iseas).

Orthography

The orthography of words has been carried out from Ancient Greek, where each different 'i' and 'o' was pronounced differently. However, starting as early as the fifth century BC, some diphthongs and letters began to lose their different pronunciation, a process more or less completed by 300 AD. By the fifth century AD Greek letters were pronounced as per the above 'modern Greek' guide, applicable to words as spoken in Greece today. Thus, today there are six 'i' forms (η, ι, υ, ει, οι, υι) in the Greek language, all pronounced identically, two 'e' forms (ε, αι) and two 'o' forms (ο, ω). The letters remained in use not for phonetic reasons, but to respect the language's tradition.

Polytonic Greek

There were many ways to pronounce each vowel in ancient Greek, hence one of three accent marks could be noted over a vowel: Oksia (´), Varia (`) and Perispomeni (˜). If the vowel was the first letter of a word, one of two breathing marks, Psili (᾿) and Dasia (῾), was also noted over it. Many accent-breathing mark combinations were possible, including the additional placement of dieresis dots where required.

The accent and breathing marks remained in use, although phonetically useless, after the fifth century AD, until their abolishment on January 12, 1982 by the Greek government. Only a single accent mark was retained (´), to denote the stressed syllable in polysyllabic words. Nevertheless, the polytonic system remains in use in official ecclesiastic documents.

Vowels in the polytonic system can be accented as follows:

Accents:			Breathings:		Accent-Breathing	Accent-Dieresis
Acute	Grave	Circumflex	Smooth	Rough	Combinations:	Combinations:
ά	ὰ	ᾶ	Ἀ, ἀ	Ἁ, ἁ	Ἄἄ Ἂἂ Ἆἆ Ἄἄ Ἂἂ Ἆἆ	
έ	ὲ		Ἐ, ἐ	Ἑ, ἑ	Ἔ ἔ, Ἒ ἒ, Ἔ ἔ, Ἒ ἒ	
ή	ὴ	ῆ	Ἠ, ἠ	Ἡ, ἡ	Ἤἤ Ἢἢ Ἦἦ Ἤἤ Ἢἢ Ἦἦ	
ί	ὶ	ῖ	Ἰ, ἰ	Ἱ, ἱ	Ἴἴ Ἲἲ Ἶἶ Ἴἴ Ἲἲ Ἶἶ	ΐ, ῒ, ῗ
ό	ὸ		Ὀ, ὀ	Ὁ, ὁ	Ὄ ὄ, Ὂ ὂ, Ὄ ὄ, Ὂ ὂ	
ύ	ὺ	ῦ	ὐ	Ὑ, ὑ	ὔ, ὒ, ὖ, Ὕ ὕ, Ὓ ὓ, Ὗ ὗ	ΰ, ῢ, ῧ
ώ	ὼ	ῶ	Ὠ, ὠ	Ὡ, ὡ	Ὤὤ Ὢὢ Ὦὦ Ὤὤ Ὢὢ Ὦὦ	

The consonant 'r' is a unique exception, bearing a rough breathing mark when placed at the beginning of a word (Ῥ, ῥ) or both smooth and rough breathing marks in succession when double 'r' are used inside a word written in lower-case letters (ῤῥ).

The Greek question mark is (;) and the Greek semicolon is an elevated dot (·).

The following table lists most of the Hierarch names in three forms:

Western Form	Polytonic Greek	Transliterated
1. Abbacum	Ἀββακοὺμ	Avvakoum
2. Abercius	Ἀβέρκιος	Averkios
3. Abilius	Ἀβίλιος	Avilios
4. Abraham	Ἀβραὰμ	Avraam

5. Abramius	Ἀβράμιος	Avramios
6. Acacius	Ἀκάκιος	Akakios
7. Achillius	Ἀχίλλειος	Achillios
8. Acylas	Ἀκύλας	Akylas
9. Adrian	Ἀδριανὸς	Adrianos
10. Aemilian/Emilian	Αἰμιλιανὸς	Aimilianos
11. Aetherichus	Αἰθέριχος	Aitherichos
12. Aetherius	Αἰθέριος	Aitherios
13. Aetius	Ἀέτιος	Aetios
14. Agapetus	Ἀγαπητὸς	Agapitos
15. Agapius	Ἀγάπιος	Agapios
16. Agathangelus	Ἀγαθάγγελος	Agathangelos
17. Agathocles	Ἀγαθοκλῆς	Agathoklis
18. Agathodorus	Ἀγαθόδωρος	Agathodoros
19. Agathon	Ἀγάθων	Agathon
20. Agathonicus	Ἀγαθόνικος	Agathonikos
21. Agrippinus	Ἀγριππίνος	Agrippinos
22. Alexander	Ἀλέξανδρος	Alexandros
23. Alexius	Ἀλέξιος	Alexios
24. Alypius	Ἀλύπιος	Alypios
25. Ambrose	Ἀμβρόσιος	Amvrosios
26. Ammon	Ἄμμων	Ammon
27. Ammonius	Ἀμμώνιος	Ammonios
28. Amos	Ἀμῶς	Amos
29. Amphilochius	Ἀμφιλόχιος	Amfilochios
30. Amphion	Ἀμφίων	Amfion
31. Anacletus	Ἀνάκλητος	Anaklitos
32. Ananias	Ἀνανίας	Ananias
33. Anastasius	Ἀναστάσιος	Anastasios
34. Anatole	Ἀνατόλιος	Anatolios
35. Andrew	Ἀνδρέας	Andreas
36. Andromachus	Ἀνδρόμαχος	Andromachos
37. Andronicus	Ἀνδρόνικος	Andronikos
38. Anterus	Ἀντέρως	Anteros
39. Anthemius	Ἀνθέμιος	Anthemios
40. Anthimus	Ἄνθιμος	Anthimos
41. Anthony	Ἀντώνιος	Antonios
42. Antigonus	Ἀντίγονος	Antigonos
43. Antipas	Ἀντίπας	Antipas
44. Antipater	Ἀντίπατρος	Antipatros
45. Antoninus	Ἀντωνίνος	Antoninos
46. Aphrodisius	Ἀφροδίσιος	Afrodisios
47. Apollonius	Ἀπολλώνιος	Apollonios
48. Apostolus	Ἀπόστολος	Apostolos
49. Appion	Ἀππίων	Appion
50. Arethas	Ἀρέθας	Arethas

51. Aristarchus	Ἀρίσταρχος	Aristarchos
52. Archelaus	Ἀρχέλαος	Archelaos
53. Aristion	Ἀριστίων	Aristion
54. Aristobulus	Ἀριστόβουλος	Aristovoulos
55. Aristophorus	Ἀριστοφόρος	Aristoforos
56. Arcadius	Ἀρκάδιος	Arkadios
57. Arsacius	Ἀρσάκιος	Arsakios
58. Arsenius	Ἀρσένιος	Arsenios
59. Artemidorus	Ἀρτεμίδωρος	Artemidoros
60. Artemius	Ἀρτέμιος	Artemios
61. Ascholius	Ἀσχόλιος	Ascholios
62. Asianus	Ἀσιανὸς	Asianos
63. Asterius	Ἀστέριος	Asterios
64. Athanasius	Ἀθανάσιος	Athanasios
65. Athenagoras	Ἀθηναγόρας	Athinagoras
66. Athenodorus	Ἀθηνόδωρος	Athinodoros
67. Atticus	Ἀττικὸς	Attikos
68. Augustine	Αὐγουστίνος	Avgoustinos
69. Auxentius	Αὐξέντιος	Afxentios
70. Barlaam	Βαρλάαμ	Varlaam
71. Barlaamius	Βαρλαάμιος	Varlaamios
72. Barnavas	Βαρνάβας	Varnavas
73. Bartholomew	Βαρθολομαῖος	Vartholomaios
74. Basil	Βασίλειος	Vasilios
75. Basiliscus	Βασιλίσκος	Vasiliskos
76. Bassianus	Βασσιανὸς	Vassianos
77. Belisarius	Βελισάριος	Velisarios
78. Benedict	Βενέδικτος	Venediktos
79. Benjamin	Βενιαμὶν	Veniamin
80. Bessarion	Βησσαρίων	Vissarion
81. Blassius	Βλάσσιος	Vlassios
82. Boniface	Βονιφάτιος	Vonifatios
83. Bosporius	Βοσπόριος	Vosporios
84. Caesarius	Καισάριος	Kaisarios
85. Calandion	Καλανδίων	Kalandion
86. Callinicus	Καλλίνικος	Kallinikos
87. Callistratus	Καλλίστρατος	Kallistratos
88. Callistus	Κάλλιστος	Kallistos
89. Calophorus	Καλοφόρος	Kaloforos
90. Candidianus	Κανδιδιανὸς	Kandidianos
91. Caracallus	Καράκαλλος	Karakallos
92. Carpus	Κάρπος	Karpos
93. Castinus	Καστίνος	Kastinos
94. Cecropius	Κεκρόπιος	Kekropios
95. Cedron	Κέδρων	Kedron

96. Celadion	Κελαδίων	Keladion
97. Celestine	Κελεστίνος	Kelestinos
98. Charalambes	Χαραλάμπης	Charalampis
99. Chariton	Χαρίτων	Chariton
100. Cherubim	Χερουβεὶμ	Cherouvim
101. Christodulus	Χριστόδουλος	Christodoulos
102. Christopher	Χριστόφορος	Christoforos
103. Chrestus	Χρῆστος	Christos
104. Chrysanthus	Χρύσανθος	Chrysanthos
105. Chrysogonus	Χρυσόγονος	Chrysogonos
106. Chrysostom	Χρυσόστομος	Chrysostomos
107. Claudius	Κλαύδιος	Klavdios
108. Clement	Κλήμης	Klimis
109. Cleonicus	Κλεόνικος	Kleonikos
110. Cleopas	Κλέοπας	Kleopas
111. Conon	Κόνων	Konon
112. Constantine	Κωνσταντῖνος	Konstantinos
113. Constantius	Κωνστάντιος	Konstantios
114. Cornelius	Κορνήλιος	Kornilios
115. Cosmas	Κοσμᾶς	Kosmas
116. Crinon	Κρίνων	Krinon
117. Cydonius	Κυδώνιος	Kydonios
118. Cyriacus	Κυριακὸς	Kyriakos
119. Cyprian	Κυπριανὸς	Kyprianos
120. Cyril I	Κύριλλος	Kyrillos
121. Cyrus	Κύρος	Kyros
122. Dalmatius	Δαλμάτιος	Dalmatios
123. Damascene	Δαμασκηνὸς	Damaskinos
124. Damian	Δαμιανὸς	Damianos
125. Daniel	Δανιὴλ	Daniil
126. David	Δαυΐδ	David
127. Demetrius	Δημήτριος	Dimitrios
128. Demophilus	Δημόφιλος	Dimofilos
129. Diamonius	Διαμόνιος	Diamonios
130. Diodorus	Διόδωρος	Diodoros
131. Diogenes	Διογένης	Diogenis
132. Dionysius	Διονύσιος	Dionysios
133. Dioscurus	Διόσκουρος	Dioskouros
134. Dolichian	Δολιχιανὸς	Dolichianos
135. Dometius	Δομέτιος	Dometios
136. Domitius	Δομίτιος	Domitios
137. Domnus	Δόμνος	Domnos
138. Dorotheus	Δωρόθεος	Dorotheos
139. Dositheus	Δοσίθεος	Dositheos
140. Dracontius	Δρακόντιος	Drakontios
141. Eleazar	Ἐλεάζαρ	Eleazar

142. Eleusius	Ἐλεύσιος	Elefsios
143. Eleutherius	Ἐλευθέριος	Eleftherios
144. Elias	Ἠλίας	Ilias
145. Elpidius	Ἐλπίδιος	Elpidios
146. Elpidophorus	Ἐλπιδοφόρος	Elpidoforos
147. Emmanuel	Ἐμμανουὴλ	Emmanouil
148. Eortasius	Ἑορτάσιος	Eortasios
149. Ephrem	Ἐφραὶμ	Efraim
150. Epictetus	Ἐπίκτητος	Epiktitos
151. Epimachus	Ἐπίμαχος	Epimachos
152. Epiphanius	Ἐπιφάνιος	Epifanios
153. Erechthius	Ἐρέχθιος	Erechthios
154. Etimasius	Ἐτοιμάσιος	Etimasios
155. Eubulus	Εὔβουλος	Evvoulos
156. Eucissus	Εὔκισσος	Efkissos
157. Eudaimon	Εὐδαίμων	Evdaimon
158. Eudocimus	Εὐδόκιμος	Evdokimos
159. Eudocius	Εὐδόκιος	Evdokios
160. Eudorus	Εὔδωρος	Evdoros
161. Eudoxius	Εὐδόξιος	Evdoxios
162. Eudoxus	Εὔδοξος	Evdoxos
163. Euethius	Εὐήθιος	Evithios
164. Eugene	Εὐγένιος	Evgenios
165. Eugraphus	Εὔγραφος	Evgrafos
166. Eulabius	Εὐλάβιος	Evlavios
167. Eulalius	Εὐλάλιος	Evlalios
168. Eulogius	Εὐλόγιος	Evlogios
169. Eumenius	Εὐμένιος	Evmenios
170. Eunomius	Εὐνόμιος	Evnomios
171. Euphemius	Εὐφήμιος	Efphimios
172. Euphradius	Εὐφράδιος	Effradios
173. Euphranor	Εὐφράνωρ	Effranor
174. Euphrasius	Εὐφράσιος	Effrasios
175. Euphratas	Εὐφράτας	Effratas
176. Euphronius	Εὐφρόνιος	Effronios
177. Euphrosinus	Εὐφρόσυνος	Effrosynos
178. Euprepius	Εὐπρέπιος	Efprepios
179. Euschemon	Εὐσχήμων	Efschimon
180. Eusebius	Εὐσέβιος	Efsevios
181. Eusemius	Εὐσήμιος	Efsimios
182. Eustace	Εὐστάθιος	Efstathios
183. Eustochius	Εὐστόχιος	Efstochios
184. Eustolius	Εὐστόλιος	Efstolios
185. Eustratius	Εὐστράτιος	Efstratios
186. Euthymius	Εὐθύμιος	Efthymios

187. Eutropius	Εὐτρόπιος	Eftropios
188. Eutychianus	Εὐτυχιανὸς	Eftychianos
189. Eutychius	Εὐτύχιος	Eftychios
190. Euzoius	Εὐζώιος	Evzoios
191. Evagrius	Εὐάγριος	Evagrios
192. Evandrus	Εὔανδρος	Evandros
193. Evangelus	Εὐάγγελος	Evangelos
194. Evarestus	Εὐάρεστος	Evarestos
195. Evelpistius	Εὐέλπιστος	Evelpistos
196. Evethius	Εὐήθιος	Evithios
197. Evilasius	Εὐϊλάσιος	Evilasios
198. Evippus	Εὔιππος	Evippos
199. Ezekiel	Ἰεζεκιὴλ	Iezekiil
200. Felix	Φήλιξ	Filix
201. Firmilianus	Φιρμιλιανὸς	Firmilianos
202. Flacillus	Φλάκιλλος	Flakillos
203. Flavian	Φλαβιανὸς	Flavianos
204. Florentius	Φλωρέντιος	Florentios
205. Fravitas	Φράβιτας	Fravitas
206. Frumentius	Φρουμέντιος	Froumentios
207. Gabriel	Γαβριὴλ	Gavriil
208. Gaius	Γάιος	Gaios
209. Galaction	Γαλακτίων	Galaktion
200. Gideon	Γεδεῶν	Gedeon
211. Gelasius	Γελάσιος	Gelasios
212. Gennadius	Γεννάδιος	Gennadios
213. George	Γεώργιος	Georgios
214. Gerasimus	Γεράσιμος	Gerasimos
215. Germanus	Γερμανὸς	Germanos
216. Germinius	Γερμίνιος	Germinios
217. Gerontius	Γερόντιος	Gerontios
218. Gervase	Γερβάσιος	Gervasios
219. Glycerius	Γλυκέριος	Glykerios
220. Gordius	Γόρδιος	Gordios
221. Gregory	Γρηγόριος	Grigorios
222. Harmonius	Ἁρμόνιος	Armonios
223. Hedesotus	Ἑδέσοτος	Edesotos
224. Helladius	Ἑλλάδιος	Elladios
225. Hellanodicus	Ἑλλανόδικος	Ellanodikos
226. Hemerius	Ἡμέριος	Imerios
227. Heraclianus	Ἡρακλειανὸς	Iraklianos
228. Heraclius	Ἡράκλειος	Iraklios
229. Hermogenes	Ἑρμογένης	Ermogenis
230. Hermon	Ἕρμων	Ermon
231. Hesychius	Ἡσύχιος	Isychios
232. Hieronymus/Jerome	Ἱερώνυμος	Ieronymos

233. Hierotheus	Ἱερόθεος	Ierotheos
234. Hilarion	Ἱλαρίων	Ilarion
235. Hilarus	Ἱλάριος	Ilarios
236. Hippolytus	Ἱππόλυτος	Ippolytos
237. Honorius	Ὀνώριος	Onorios
238. Hosea	Ὡσηὲ	Osie
239. Hyacinth	Ὑάκινθος	Yakinthos
240. Hyginus	Ὑγίνος	Yginos
241. Hymeneus	Ὑμέναιος	Ymenaios
242. Hypatianus	Ὑπατιανὸς	Ypatianos
243. Hypatius	Ὑπάτιος	Ypatios
244. Iconius	Εἰκόνιος	Ikonios
245. Ignatius	Ἰγνάτιος	Ignatios
246. Innocent	Ἰννοκέντιος	Innokentios
247. Irenaeus	Εἰρηναῖος	Irinaios
248. Irenarchus	Εἰρήναρχος	Irinarchos
249. Isaac	Ἰσαὰκ	Isaak
250. Isaacius	Ἰσαάκιος	Isaakios
251. Isaiah	Ἡσαΐας	Isaïas
252. Isidore	Ἰσίδωρος	Isidoros
253. Jacob	Ἰακὼβ	Iakov
254. Jacob/James	Ἰάκωβος	Iakovos
255. Jeremias	Ἱερεμίας	Ieremias
256. Joachim	Ἰωακεὶμ	Ioakim
257. Joasaph	Ἰωάσαφ	Ioasaf
258. Job	Ἰὼβ	Iov
259. Joel	Ἰωὴλ	Ioil
260. John	Ἰωάννης	Ioannis
261. Johnnicius	Ἰωαννίκιος	Ioannikios
262. Jonas	Ἰωνὰς	Ionas
263. Joseph	Ἰωσὴφ	Iosif
264. Josepus	Ἰώσηπος	Iosipos
265. Julian	Ἰουλιανὸς	Ioulianos
266. Julius	Ἰούλιος	Ioulios
267. Justus	Ἰοῦστος	Ioustos
268. Juvenal	Ἰουβενάλιος	Iouvenalios
269. Lamprus	Λάμπρος	Lampros
270. Laurentius/Lawrence	Λαυρέντιος	Lavrentios
271. Leo	Λέων	Leon
272. Leontius	Λεόντιος	Leontios
273. Levis	Λευὴς	Levis
274. Longinus	Λογγίνος	Longinos
275. Lucian	Λουκιανὸς	Loukianos
276. Lucius	Λούκιος	Loukios
277. Luke/Lucas	Λουκᾶς	Loukas

278. Lycastus	Λύκαστος	Lykastos
279. Macarius	Μακάριος	Makarios
280. Macedonius	Μακεδόνιος	Makedonios
281. Manasses	Μανασσὴς	Manassis
282. Manuel	Μανουὴλ	Manouil
283. Marathonius	Μαραθώνιος	Marathonios
284. Marcus/Mark	Μάρκος	Markos
285. Marcellinus	Μαρκελλίνος	Markellinos
286. Marcellus	Μάρκελλος	Markellos
287. Marinus	Μαρίνος	Marinos
288. Martian	Μαρτιανὸς	Martianos
289. Martinian	Μαρτινιανὸς	Martinianos
290. Martinus	Μαρτίνος	Martinos
291. Martyrius	Μαρτύριος	Martyrios
292. Matthew	Ματθαῖος	Matthaios
293. Matthias	Ματθίας	Matthias
294. Maximian	Μαξιμιανὸς	Maximianos
295. Maximus	Μάξιμος	Maximos
296. Mazabanes	Μαζαβάνης	Mazavanis
297. Megethius	Μεγέθιος	Megethios
298. Melanion	Μελανίων	Melanion
299. Melchisedek	Μελχισεδὲκ	Melchisedek
300. Meletius	Μελέτιος	Meletios
301. Meliphron	Μελίφρων	Meliphron
302. Melissenus	Μελισσηνὸς	Melissinos
303. Meliton	Μελίτων	Meliton
304. Memnon	Μέμνων	Memnon
305. Menas	Μηνὰς	Minas
306. Mercurius	Μερκούριος	Merkourios
307. Methodius	Μεθόδιος	Methodios
308. Methuselah	Μαθουσάλας	Mathousalas
309. Metrophanes	Μητροφάνης	Mitrofanis
310. Menophantus	Μηνόφαντος	Minofantos
311. Michael	Μιχαὴλ	Michaïl
312. Miltiades	Μιλτιάδης	Miltiadis
313. Misael	Μισαὴλ	Misaïl
314. Modestus	Μόδεστος	Modestos
315. Moses	Μωυσῆς	Moysis
316. Myron	Μύρων	Myron
317. Myrtinus	Μυρτίνος	Myrtinos
318. Narcissus	Νάρκισσος	Narkissos
319. Nathaniel	Ναθαναὴλ	Nathanaïl
320. Nearchus	Νέαρχος	Nearchos
321. Nectarius	Νεκτάριος	Nektarios
322. Neophytus	Νεόφυτος	Neofytos
323. Nestorius	Νεστόριος	Nestrorios

324. Nestor	Νέστωρ	Nestor
325. Nicandrus	Νίκανδρος	Nikandros
326. Nicephorus	Νικηφόρος	Nikiforos
327. Nicetas	Νικήτας	Nikitas
328. Nicholas	Νικόλαος	Nikolaos
329. Nicodemus	Νικόδημος	Nikodimos
330. Nicon	Νίκων	Nikon
331. Nilus	Νεῖλος	Nilos
332. Niphon	Νήφων	Nifon
333. Oceanus	Ὠκεανός	Okeanos
334. Olivianus	Ὀλιβιανός	Olivianos
335. Olympianus	Ὀλυμπιανός	Olympianos
336. Olympius	Ὀλύμπιος	Olympios
337. Onesimus	Ὀνήσιμος	Onisimos
338. Onuphrius	Ὀνούφριος	Onoufrios
339. Orestes	Ὀρέστης	Orestis
340. Orion	Ὠρίων	Orion
341. Pachomius	Παχώμιος	Pachomios
342. Païsius	Παΐσιος	Païsios
343. Palladius	Παλλάδιος	Palladios
344. Pamphilius	Παμφίλιος	Pamfilios
345. Panaretus	Πανάρετος	Panaretos
346. Pangratius	Παγκράτιος	Pangratios
347. Pansophius	Πανσόφιος	Pansofios
348. Panteleimon	Παντελεήμων	Panteleimon
349. Pantherius	Πανθήριος	Panthirios
350. Paphnutius	Παφνούτιος	Pafnoutios
351. Papyrius	Παπύριος	Papyrios
352. Parthenius	Παρθένιος	Parthenios
353. Paschalius	Πασχάλιος	Paschalios
354. Patricius	Πατρίκιος	Patrikios
355. Paul	Παῦλος	Pavlos
356. Paulinus	Παυλίνος	Pavlinos
357. Pelagius	Πελάγιος	Pelagios
358. Pergamius	Περγάμιος	Pergamios
359. Pertinax	Περτίναξ	Pertinax
360. Peter	Πέτρος	Petros
361. Pharetrius	Φαρέτριος	Faretrios
362. Philadelphus	Φιλάδελφος	Filadelfos
363. Philalethes	Φιλαλήθης	Filalithis
364. Philaretus	Φιλάρετος	Filaretos
365. Philemon	Φιλήμων	Filimon
366. Philip	Φίλιππος	Filippos
367. Philogonius	Φιλογόνιος	Filogonios
368. Philotheus	Φιλόθεος	Filotheos

369. Philumenus	Φιλούμενος	Filoumenos
370. Phocas	Φωκᾶς	Fokas
371. Phoscus	Φῶσκος	Foskos
372. Photinus	Φωτεινὸς	Fotinos
373. Photius	Φώτιος	Fotios
374. Pistus	Πιστὸς	Pistos
375. Plato	Πλάτων	Platon
376. Plutarch	Πλούταρχος	Ploutarchos
377. Politian	Πολιτιανὸς	Politianos
378. Polycarp	Πολύκαρπος	Polykarpos
379. Polychronius	Πολυχρόνιος	Polychronios
380. Polycrates	Πολυκράτης	Polykratis
381. Polydeuces	Πολυδεύκης	Polydefkis
382. Polyeuctus	Πολύευκτος	Polyefktos
383. Pontianus	Ποντιανὸς	Pontianos
384. Porphyrius	Πορφύριος	Porfyrios
385. Praylius	Πραΰλιος	Praylios
386. Primus	Πρίμος	Primos
387. Probus	Πρόβος	Provos
388. Prochorus	Πρόχορος	Prochoros
389. Proclus	Πρόκλος	Proklos
390. Procopius	Προκόπιος	Prokopios
391. Prosdocius	Προσδόκιος	Prosdokios
392. Proterius	Προτέριος	Proterios
393. Psoes	Ψόης	Psois
394. Pyrrhus	Πύρρος	Pyrros
395. Raphael	Ῥαφαὴλ	Rafaïl
396. Rufinus	Ῥουφίνος	Roufinos
397. Romanus	Ῥωμανὸς	Romanos
398. Sabbas	Σάββας	Savvas
399. Sabbatius	Σαββάτιος	Savvatios
400. Sabbinus	Σαββίνος	Savvinos
401. Sallustius	Σαλλούστιος	Salloustios
402. Samuel	Σαμουὴλ	Samouil
403. Sebastian	Σεβαστιανὸς	Sevastianos
404. Sedecion	Σεδεκίων	Sedekion
405. Seleucus	Σέλευκος	Selefkos
406. Senecas	Σένεκας	Senekas
407. Sennuphius	Σεννούφιος	Sennoufios
408. Seraphim	Σεραφεὶμ	Serafim
409. Serapion	Σεραπίων	Serapion
410. Sergius	Σέργιος	Sergios
411. Silas	Σίλας	Silas
412. Simon	Σίμων	Simon
413. Sisinnius	Σισίννιος	Sisinnios
414. Sixtus	Σίξτος	Sixtos

415. Smaragdus	Σμάραγδος	Smaragdos
416. Solomon	Σολομῶν	Solomon
417. Sophronius	Σωφρόνιος	Sofronios
418. Sosipater	Σωσίπατρος	Sosipatros
419. Soterichus	Σωτήριχος	Sotirichos
420. Soterius	Σωτήριος	Sotirios
421. Sozon	Σώζων	Sozon
422. Spyridon	Σπυρίδων	Spyridon
423. Stachys	Στάχυς	Stachys
424. Stauracius	Σταυράκιος	Stavrakios
425. Stephen/Steven	Στέφανος	Stefanos
426. Stratocles	Στρατοκλῆς	Stratoklis
427. Stylianus	Στυλιανὸς	Stylianos
428. Symeon	Συμεὼν	Symeon
429. Symmachus	Σύμμαχος	Symmachos
430. Symphorus	Σύμφορος	Symforos
431. Synetus	Συνετὸς	Synetos
432. Tarasius	Ταράσιος	Tarasios
433. Telesphorus	Τελεσφόρος	Telesforos
434. Thaddeus	Θαδδαῖος	Thaddaios
435. Thalassius	Θαλάσσιος	Thalassios
436. Themistocles	Θεμιστοκλῆς	Themistoklis
437. Theocharistus	Θεοχάριστος	Theocharistos
438. Theocletus	Θεόκλητος	Theoklitos
439. Theocritus	Θεόκριτος	Theokritos
440. Theoctistus	Θεόκτιστος	Theoktistos
441. Theodore	Θεόδωρος	Theodoros
442. Theodoretus	Θεοδώρητος	Theodoritos
443. Theodosius	Θεοδόσιος	Theodosios
444. Theodotus	Θεόδοτος	Theodoros
445. Theodulus	Θεόδουλος	Theodoulos
446. Theognius	Θεόγνιος	Theognios
447. Theognostus	Θεόγνωστος	Theognostos
448. Theoleptus	Θεόληπτος	Theoliptos
449. Theonas	Θεωνᾶς	Theonas
450. Theopemptus	Θεόπεμπτος	Theopemptos
451. Theophanes	Θεοφάνης	Theofanis
452. Theophylactus	Θεοφύλακτος	Theofylaktos
453. Theosebius	Θεοσέβιος	Theosevios
454. Thomas	Θωμὰς	Thomas
455. Thraseas	Θρασέας	Thraseas
456. Timothy	Τιμόθεος	Timotheos
457. Titus	Τίτος	Titos
458. Tobias	Τωβίας	Tovias
459. Tranquillinus	Τρανκυλλίνος	Trankyllinos

460. Triantaphyllus	Τριαντάφυλλος	Triantafyllos
461. Tryphon	Τρύφων	Tryfon
462. Tychon	Τύχων	Tychon
463. Uranius	Οὐράνιος	Ouranios
464. Urban	Οὐρβανὸς	Ourvanos
465. Valerian	Βαλεριανὸς	Valerianos
466. Victor	Βίκτωρ	Viktor
467. Vigilius	Βιγίλιος	Vigilios
468. Vitalian	Βιταλιανὸς	Vitalianos
469. Vitalius	Βιτάλιος	Vitalios
470. Xenophon	Ξενοφῶν	Xenofon
471. Zacharias	Ζαχαρίας	Zacharias
472. Zaccheus	Ζακχαῖος	Zakcheos
473. Zambdas	Ζάμβδας	Zamvdas
474. Zenobius	Ζηνόβιος	Zinovios
475. Zeno	Ζήνων	Zinon
476. Zephyrinus	Ζεφυρίνος	Zefyrinos
477. Zoilus	Ζωίλος	Zoilos
478. Zosimas	Ζωσιμᾶς	Zosimas
479. Zosimus	Ζώσιμος	Zosimos
480. Zoticus	Ζωτικὸς	Zotikos

APPENDIX D
EMPERORS OF THE ROMANS

A. THE ROMAN EMPERORS

1. Augustus   Αύγουστος   16 Jan 27 BC – 19 Aug 14+   63BC-14
Gaius Julius Caesar Octavianus

2. Tiberius I   Τιβέριος Α΄   19 Aug 14 – 16 Mar 37+   42BC-37
Tiberius Claudius Nero Caesar

3. Gaius   Γάιος   16 Mar 37 – 24 Jan 41++   12-41
Gaius Julius Caesar Germanicus, unofficially nicknamed "Caligula"

4. Claudius I   Κλαύδιος Α΄   25 Jan 41 – 13 Oct 54++   10BC-54
Tiberius Claudius Drusus Germanicus

5. Nero   Νέρων   13 Oct 54 – 9 Jun 68++   37-68
Nero Claudius Caesar Drusus Germanicus

6. Galba   Γάλβας   8 Jun 68 – 15 Jan 69++   3BC-69
Servius Sulpicius Galba

7. Otho   Όθων   15 Jan 69 – 16 Apr 69++   32-69
Marcus Salvius Otho

8. Vitellius   Βιτέλλιος   3 Jan 69 – 20 Dec 69++   15-69
Aulus Vitellius, in opposition to 16 Apr 69

9. Vespasian   Βεσπασιανός   1 Jul 69 – 23 Jun 79+   9-79
Titus Flavius Vespasianus, in opposition to 20 Dec 69

10. Titus   Τίτος   23 Jun 79 – 13 Sep 81+   39-81
Titus Flavius Vespasianus

11. Domitian   Δομιτιανός   13 Sep 81 – 18 Sep 96++   51-96
Titus Flavius Domitianus

12. Nerva   Νέρβας   18 Sep 96 – 27 Jan 98+   30-98
Marcus Cocceius Nerva

13. Trajan   Τραϊανός   Oct 97 – 8 Aug 117+   53-117
Marcus Ulpius Nerva Traianus, co-emperor to 27 Jan 98

14. Hadrian   Αδριανός   11 Aug 117 – 10 Jul 138+   76-138
Publius Aelius Hadrianus

15. Antoninus Pius   Αντωνίνος Πίος   10 Jul 138 – 7 Mar 161+   86-161
Titus Aurelius Fulvus Boionius Arrius Hadrianus Antoninus Pius

16. Marcus Aurelius   Μάρκος Αυρήλιος   7 Mar 161 – 17 Mar 180+   121-180
Marcus Aelius Aurelius Verus, co-emperor to Jan/Feb 169

17. Lucius Verus   Λούκιος Βέρος   7 Mar 161 – Jan/Feb 169+   130-169
Lucius Aelius Aurelius Verus Commodus, co-emperor

18. Commodus   Κόμμοδος   177 – 31 Dec 192++   161-192
Lucius Aelius Aurelius Commodus, co-emperor to 17 Mar 180

19. Pertinax   Περτίναξ   1 Jan 193 – 28 Mar 193++   126-193
Publius Helvius Pertinax

20. Didius Julianus (I) Ιουλιανός Α´	29 Mar 193 – 2 Jun 193++	133-193
Marcus Didius Severus Julianus		
21. Septimius Severus Σεπτίμιος Σεβῆρος	9 Apr 193 – 4 Feb 211+	146-211
Lucius Septimius Severus, in opposition to autumn 194 and 195 to 19 Feb 197		
---. Pescennius Niger Πεσκέννιος Νίγηρ	Apr 193 – autumn 194++	135/40-194
Gaius Pescennius Niger Justus, in opposition		
---. Clodius Albinus Κλώδιος Αλβίνος (1st time)	Apr 193 – Jun 193	140/50-197
Decimus Clodius Septimius Albinus, in opposition		
---. Clodius Albinus Κλώδιος Αλβίνος (2nd time)	late 195 – 19 Feb 197++	140/50-197
Decimus Clodius Septimius Albinus, in opposition		
22. Antoninus Αντωνίνος	28 Jan 198 – 8 Apr 217++	188-217
Marcus Aurelius Antoninus, unofficially nicknamed "Caracalla", co-emperor to 1 Feb 212		
23. Geta Γέτας	autumn 209 – 1 Feb 212++	189-212
Lucius Publius Septimius Geta, co-emperor		
24. Macrinus Μακρινός	11 Apr 217 – Jun 218++	c. 164-218
Marcus Opellius Severus Macrinus		
---. Diadumenian Διαδουμενιανός	May 218 – Jun 218++	c. 209-218
Marcus Opellius Diadumenianus Antoninus, co-emperor with his father		
25. Elagabalus Ηλιογάβαλος	8 Jun 218 – 6 Mar 222++	204-222
Marcus Aurelius Antoninus Elagabalus, in opposition during Jun 218		
26. Severus Alexander Σεβῆρος Αλέξανδρος	6 Mar 222 – Mar 235++	208-235
Marcus Aurelius Severus Alexander		
27. Maximinus I Μαξιμίνος Α´	Mar 235 – 24 Jun 238++	c. 173-238
Gaius Julius Verus Maximinus, in opposition during Mar 235		
28. Gordian I Γορδιανός Α´	22 Mar 238 – 12 Apr 238++	c. 157-238
Marcus Antonius Gordianus, in opposition to Maximianus, co-emperor with Gordian II		
29. Gordian II Γορδιανός Β´	22 Mar 238 – 12 Apr 238++	c. 192-238
Marcus Antonius Gordianus, in opposition to Maximianus, co-emperor with Gordian I		
30. Balbinus Βαλβίνος	22 Apr 238 – 29 Jul 238++	c. 180-238
Decimus Caelius Calvinus Balbinus, in opposition to Maximianus to 24 Jun 238, co-emperor with Pupienus		
31. Pupienus Παπιένος	22 Apr 238 – 29 Jul 238++	c. 180-238
Clodius Pupienus Maximus, in opposition to Maximianus to 24 Jun 238, co-emperor with Balbinus		
32. Gordian III Γορδιανός Γ´	29 Jul 238 – 25 Feb 244++	c. 225-244
Marcus Antonius Gordianus		
33. Philip I Φίλιππος	25 Feb 244 – Sep 249++	c. 200-249
Marcus Julius Philippus		
---. Philip II Φίλιππος (Β´)	c. May 247 – Sep 249++	c. 237-249
Marcus Julius Severus Philippus, co-emperor with his father		
34. Trajan Decius Τραϊανός Δέκιος	Sep 249 – 1 Jul 251++	c. 201-251
Gaius Messius Quintus Traianus Decius		
---. Herennius Etruscus Ερέννιος Ετρούσκος	May 251 – Jun 251++	c. 235-251
Quintus Herennius Etruscus Messius Decius, co-emperor with his father Decius		
35. Trebonian Gallus Τρεβονιανός	2 Jul 251 – Jul 253++	c. 210-253
Gaius Vibius Trebonianus Gallus		
---. Hostilian Οστιλιανός	Aug 251 – Nov 251+	c. 238-251
Gaius Valens Hostilianus Messius Quintus, co-emperor (son of Decius)		
---. Volusian Βολουσιανός	Nov 251 – Jul 253++	d. 253
Gaius Valens Hostilianus Messius Quintus, co-emperor with his father Trebonian		
36. Aemilian Αιμιλιανός	c. May 253 – Aug 253++	207/14-253
Marcus Aemilius Aemilianus, in opposition to Jul 253		
37. Valerian Βαλεριανός	c. Jul 253 – Jun 260	c. 193-262?

Publius Licinius Valerianus, captured by the Persians, died in captivity c. 262++

38. Gallienus	Γαλλιηνός	c. Sep 253 – Mar 268++	c. 218-268
Publius Licinius Egnatius Gallienus, co-emperor to Jun 260			
39. Claudius II	Κλαύδιος Β΄	Mar 268 – Jan 270+	213/4-270
Marcus Aurelius Claudius			
40. Quintillus	Κουϊντίλλος	Jan 270 – c. May 270++	aft.214-270
Marcus Aurelius Claudius Quintillus			
41. Aurelian	Αυρηλιανός	c. May 270 – c. Oct 275++	214/5-275
Lucius Domitius Aurelianus, in opposition circa May 270			
42. Tacitus	Τάκιτος	c. Nov 275 – c. Apr 276++	c. 200-275
Marcus Claudius Tacitus			
43. Florian	Φλοριανός	c. Apr 276 – c. Jul 276++	aft. 200-276
Marcus Annius Florianus			
44. Probus	Πρόβος	c. May 276 – c. Sep 282++	232-282
Marcus Aurelius Probus, in opposition to circa Jul 276			
45. Carus	Κάρος	c. Sep 282 – c. Aug 283+	c. 230-283
Marcus Aurelius Carus			
46. Carinus	Καρίνος	c. Aug 283 – c. Jul 285++	c. 249-285
Marcus Aurelius Carinus, co-emperor in the west until c. Nov 284			
47. Numerian	Νουμεριανός	c. Aug 283 – c. Nov 284++	c. 254-284
Marcus Aurelius Numerianus, co-emperor in the east			
48. Diocletian	Διοκλητιανός	20 Nov 284 – 1 May 305	c. 245-311
Gaius Aurelius Valerius Diocletianus, co-emperor in the east after 1 Apr 286, abdicated, 3 Dec 311+			
49. Maximian	Μαξιμιανός (1st time)	1 Apr 286 – 1 May 305	c. 250-310
Marcus Aurelius Valerius Maximianus, co-emperor in the west, abdicated			
50. Constantius I	Κωνστάντιος Α΄	1 May 305 – 25 Jul 306+	c. 250-306
Gaius Flavius Valerius Constantius, co-emperor in the west			
51. Galerius	Γαλέριος	1 May 305 – 5 May 311+	c. 255-311
Gaius Galerius Valerius Maximianus, co-emperor in the east			
52. Valerius Severus	Βαλέριος Σεβήρος	Aug 306 – Mar/Apr 307	d. 307
Flavius Valerius Severus, co-emperor in the west, deposed and imprisoned, 16 Sep 307++			
53. Maxentius	Μαξέντιος	28 Oct 306 – 28 Oct 312++	c. 282-312
Marcus Aurelius Valerius Maxentius, in opposition to Severus to Mar/Apr 307, co-emperor in the west			
---. Maximian	Μαξιμιανός (2nd time)	Nov 306 – Nov 308	c. 250-310
Marcus Aurelius Valerius Maximianus, co-emperor in the west, abdicated, Jul 310++			
54. Constantine I	Κωνσταντίνος Α΄	c. Apr 307 – 22 May 337+	c. 273-337
Flavius Valerius Constantinus, co-emperor in the west until 19 Dec 324			
the government continued to be carried out in the name of the (dead) Emperor Constantine until 9 Sep 337			
55. Licinius	Λικίνιος	11 Nov 308 – 18 Sep 324	c. 263-325
Gaius Valerius Licinianus Licinius, co-emperor in the east, abdicated, early 325++			
56. Maximinus II	Μαξιμίνος Β΄	1 May 310 – Jul 313+	270-313
Gaius Galerius Valerius Maximinus Daia, co-emperor in the east			
57. Constantine II	Κωνσταντίνος Β΄	9 Sep 337 – Mar/Apr 340++	316-340
Flavius Claudius Constantinus, co-emperor in the west			
58. Constantius II	Κωνστάντιος Β΄	9 Sep 337 – 3 Nov 361+	317-361
Flavius Julius Constantius, co-emperor in the east until Jan 350			
59. Constans I	Κώνστας Α΄	9 Sep 337 – Jan 350++	c. 321-350
Flavius Julius Constans, co-emperor in the west			
---. Magnentius	Μαγνέντιος	18 Jan 350 – 11 Aug 353++	c. 300-353
Flavius Magnus Magnentius, usurper in the west			
60. Julian II	Ιουλιανός Β΄	Feb 360 – 26 Jun 363++	332-363

Flavius Claudius Julianus, in opposition to 3 Nov 361

61. Jovian	Ιοβιανός	27 Jun 363 – 16 Feb 364++	331-364

Flavius Jovianus

62. Valentinian I	Βαλεντινιανός A'	26 Feb 364 – 17 Nov 375+	321-375

Flavius Valentinianus, co-emperor in the west after 28 Mar 364

63. Valens	Βάλης	28 Mar 364 – 9 Aug 378++	328-378

Flavius Valens, co-emperor in the east

64. Gratian	Γρατιανός	24 Aug 367 – 25 Aug 383++	359-383

Flavius Gratianus, co-emperor in the west

65. Valentinian II	Βαλεντινιανός B'	22 Nov 375 – 15 May 392++	371-392

Flavius Valentinianus, co-emperor in the west

66. Theodosius I	Θεοδόσιος A'	19 Jan 379 – 17 Jan 395+	c. 346-395

Flavius Theodosius, co-emperor in the east until 15 May 392

---. Magnus Maximus	Μάγνος Μάξιμος	Jul 383 – 28 Jul 388++	d. 388

Magnus Clemens Maximus, usurper in the west

---. Eugene	Ευγένιος	22 Aug 392 – 6 Sep 394++	d. 394

usurper in the west

67. Arcadius	Αρκάδιος	19 Jan 383 – 1 May 408+	377-408

Flavius Arcadius, in the east, co-emperor until 17 Jan 395

68. Honorius	Ονώριος	10 Jan 393 – 25 Aug 423+	384-423

Flavius Honorius, in the west, co-emperor until 17 Jan 395

69. Theodosius II	Θεοδόσιος B'	10 Jan 402 – 28 Jul 450+	401-450

Flavius Theodosius, in the east, co-emperor until 1 May 408

70. Constantius III	Κωνστάντιος Γ'	8 Feb 421 – 2 Sep 421+	d. 421

Flavius Constantius, co-emperor in the west

---. Johannes	Ιωάννης	25 Aug 423 – c. Mar 425++	d. 425

usurper in the west

71. Valentinian III	Βαλεντινιανός Γ'	23 Oct 425 – 16 Mar 455++	419-455

Placidius Valentinianus, in the west

72. Marcianus	Μαρκιανός	25 Aug 450 – 26 Jan 457+	392-457

Flavius Valerius Marcianus, in the east

---. Petronius Maximus	Πετρόνιος Μάξιμος	17 Mar 455 – 31 May 455++	c. 397-455

Flavius Anicius Petronius Maximus, usurper in the west

---. Avitus	Άβιτος	10 Jul 455 – 17 Oct 456	c. 395-457

Marcus Maecilius Flavius Eparchius Avitus, usurper in the west, deposed, 457+

73. Leo I	Λέων A'	7 Feb 457 – 3 Feb 474+	c. 411-474

Flavius Valerius Leo, in the east

74. Majorian	Μαϊοριανός	1 Apr 457 – 2 Aug 461	c. 405-461

Julius Valerius Maiorianus, in the west, deposed, 7 Aug 461++

---. Libius Severus	Λίβιος Σεβήρος	19 Nov 461 – 15 Aug 465+	d. 465

usurper in the west

75. Anthemius	Ανθέμιος	12 Apr 467 – 11 Jul 472++	d. 472

Procopius Anthemius, in the west

---. Olybrius	Ολύβριος	Apr 472 – 23 Oct 472+	d. 472

Anicius Olybrius, usurper in the west

---. Glycerius	Γλυκέριος	5 Mar 473 – 24 Jun 474	d≥480

Flavius Glycerius, usurper in the west, deposed

76. Leo II	Λέων B'	18 Nov 473 – 17 Nov 474+	c. 467-474

Flavius Leo (?), in the east, co-emperor

77. Zeno	Ζήνων	9 Feb 474 – 9 Apr 491+	c. 427-491

formerly Tarasicodissa, in the east, co-emperor to 17 Nov 474

78. Julius Nepos   Ἰούλιος Νέπος   24 Jun 474 – 9 May 480++   d. 480
Flavius Julius Nepos, in the west, forced out of Italy on 28 Aug 475, continued to rule in Dalmatia

---. Basiliscus   Βασιλίσκος   9 Jan 475 – Aug 476   d. 477
usurper in the east, deposed, 477++

---. Romulus Augustus   Ρωμύλος Αύγουστος   31 Oct 475 – 4 Sep 476   c. 464- ?
nicknamed "Augustulus", usurper in the west, abdicated

79. Anastasius I   Ἀναστάσιος Α'   11 Apr 491 – 9 Jul 518+   c. 430-518
Flavius Anastasius

80. Justin I   Ἰουστίνος Α'   10 Jul 518 – 1 Aug 527+   c. 452-527
Flavius Justinus

81. Justinian I   Ἰουστινιανός Α'   4 Apr 527 – 14 Nov 565+   c. 482-565
Flavius Petrus Sabbatius Justinianus

82. Justin II   Ἰουστίνος Β'   15 Nov 565 – 5 Oct 578+   565-578
Flavius Justinus

83. Tiberius II   Τιβέριος Β'   26 Sep 578 – 14 Aug 582+   c. 540-582
Tiberius Constantinus, co-emperor to 5 Oct 578

84. Maurice   Μαυρίκιος   13 Aug 582 – 27 Nov 602++   c. 539-602
Mauricius Flavius Tiberius, co-emperor to 14 Aug 582

---. Theodosius (III)   Θεοδόσιος (Γ')   26 Mar 590 – c. Dec 602++   d. 602
co-emperor with his father Maurice

85. Phocas   Φωκάς   23 Nov 602 – 5 Oct 610++   c. 547-610
in opposition to 27 Nov 602

86. Heraclius   Ἡράκλειος   5 Oct 610 – 11 Jan 641+   c. 575-641
rebelled against Phocas in summer 608 but crowned after Phocas deposition

87. Constantine III   Κωνσταντίνος Γ'   22 Jan 613 – 20 Apr 641+   612-641
Heraclius Constantinus, co-emperor to 11 Jan 641

88. Heracleonas   Ἡρακλέωνας   4 Jul 638 – Oct 641   626- ?
co-emperor to 20 Apr 641, deposed and exiled to Rhodes

89. Constans II   Κώνστας Β'   Oct 641 – 15 Jul 668++   630-668
Flavius Constantinus, co-emperor to Oct 641

---. Mezezius   Μεζέζιος   Jul 668 – early 869++   d. 869
usurper

90. Constantine IV   Κωνσταντίνος Δ'   13 Apr 654 – 10 Jul 685+   c. 652-685
Flavius Constantinus, co-emperor to 15 Jul 668

---. Heraclius (II)   Ἡράκλειος (Β')   2 Jun 659 – Oct/Nov 681   d. ?
Flavius Heraclius, co-emperor with his father Constans II and brother Constantine IV, deposed

---. Tiberius (III)   Τιβέριος (Γ')   2 Jun 659 – Oct/Nov 681   d. ?
Flavius Tiberius, co-emperor with his father Constans II and brother Constantine IV, deposed

91. Justinian II   Ἰουστινιανός Β' (1st time)   10 Jul 685 – Nov/Dec 695   669-711
Flavius Justinianus, deposed and exiled to Cherson

92. Leontius   Λεόντιος   Nov/Dec 695 – Nov/Dec 698   d. 706
deposed and imprisoned, Feb 706++

93. Tiberius III   Τιβέριος Γ'   Nov/Dec 698 – Aug 705   d. 706
formerly Apsimarus, deposed and imprisoned, Feb 706++

---. Justinian II   Ἰουστινιανός Β' (2nd time)   Aug 705 – 4 Nov 711++   669-711
Flavius Justinianus

---. Tiberius (III)   Τιβέριος (Γ')   Nov/Dec 705 – 4 Nov 711++   705-711
co-emperor with his father Justinian II

94. Philippicus   Φιλιππικός   4 Nov 711 – 3 Jun 713   d. 714
formerly Bardanes, deposed and imprisoned, 20 Jan 714++

95. Anastasius II   Ἀναστάσιος Β´   3 Jun 713 – Nov 715   d. 719
    formerly Artemius, deposed and exiled to Thessalonica, 1 Jun 719++

96. Theodosius III   Θεοδόσιος Γ´   Nov 715 – 25 Mar 717   d. ?
    forced to abdicate, became monk

97. Leo III   Λέων Γ´   25 Mar 717 – 18 Jun 741+   c. 680-741
    the Isaurian

98. Constantine V   Κωνσταντίνος Ε´   25 Mar 720 – 14 Sep 775+   718-775
    Isaurian, nicknamed insultingly Copronymus, co-emperor until 18 Jun 741

---. Artabasdas   Ἀρτάβασδος   Jul 742 – 2 Nov 743   d. ?
    usurper, deposed and imprisoned

---. Nicephorus   Νικηφόρος   Jul 742 – 2 Nov 743   d. ?
    usurper, co-emperor with his father Artabasdus, deposed and imprisoned

99. Leo IV   Λέων Δ´   17 May 750 – 8 Sep 780+   750-780
    Isaurian, nicknamed 'the Khazar', co-emperor to 14 Sep 775

100. Constantine VI   Κωνσταντίνος ΣΤ´   24 Apr 776 – 19 Aug 797   771-804?
    Isaurian, co-emperor with his father to 8 Sep 780, deposed by his mother Irene and exiled, died before 805

101. Irene   Ειρήνη   19 Aug 797 – 31 Oct 802   c. 752-803
    regent for her son 8 Sep 780 to Dec 790 and 792 to 19 Aug 797, deposed and exiled to Lesbos, 9 Aug 803+

102. Nicephorus I   Νικηφόρος Α´   1 Nov 802 – 26 Jul 811++   c. 760-811
    killed in battle against the Bulgarians

103. Stauracius   Σταυράκιος   Dec 803 – 2 Oct 811   d. 812
    co-emperor with his father Nicephorus to 26 Jul 811, abdicated, 12 Jan 812+

104. Michael I   Μιχαήλ Α´   2 Oct 811 – 11 Jul 813   d. 844
    Michael Rhangabe, abdicated and became monk, 11 Jan 844+

----. Theophylactus   Θεοφύλακτος   25 Dec 811 – 11 Jul 813   d. ?
    Theophylactus Rhangabe, co-emperor with his father Michael, abdicated

105. Leo V   Λέων Ε´   11 Jul 813 – 25 Dec 820++   d. 820
    the Armenian

----. Constantine (VII)   Κωνσταντίνος (Ζ´)   25 Dec 813 – 25 Dec 820   d. ?
    former name Symbatius, co-emperor with his father Leo V, deposed and exiled

106. Michael II   Μιχαήλ Β´   25 Dec 820 – 2 Oct 829+   d. 829
    the Amorian

----. Thomas   Θωμάς   Jan 821 – Oct 823++   c. 760-823
    the Slav, usurper

107. Theophilus   Θεόφιλος   12 May 821 – 20 Jan 842+   812/3-842
    Amorian, co-emperor with his father Michael II to 2 Oct 829

----. Constantine (VII)   Κωνσταντίνος (Ζ´)   5 Jun 830 – c. 832+   d. 832?
    Amorian, co-emperor with his father Theophilus

108. Michael III   Μιχαήλ Γ´   1 Sep 840 – 23 Sep 867++   840-867
    Amorian, co-emperor with his father Theophilus to 20 Jan 842

109. Basil I   Βασίλειος Α´   26 May 866 – 28 Aug 886+   c. 835-886
    the Macedonian, co-emperor to 23 Sep 867

----. Constantine (VII)   Κωνσταντίνος (Ζ´)   10 Feb 868 – 3 Sep 877+   c. 859-877
    Macedonian, co-emperor with his father Basil I

110. Leo VI   Λέων ΣΤ´   6 Jan 870 – 11 May 912+   866-912
    Macedonian, byname 'the Wise', co-emperor to 28 Aug 886

111. Alexander   Ἀλέξανδρος   Sep 877 – 6 Jun 913+   871-912
    Macedonian, co-emperor to 11 May 912

112. Constantine VII   Κωνσταντίνος Ζ´   15 May 908 – 9 Nov 959+   905-959
    Macedonian, byname 'Porphyrogenitus', co-emperor to 6 Jun 913 and 17 Dec 920 to 27 Jan 945

113. Romanus I   Ρωμανός Α´   17 Dec 920 – 16 Dec 944   c. 870-948

Lecapenus, co-emperor with his son-in-law Constantine VII, deposed and exiled, 15 Jun 948+

----. Christopher   Χριστόφορος   20 May 921 – Aug 931+   d. 931
     Lecapenus, co-emperor with his father Romanus I

----. Stephen   Στέφανος   25 Dec 924 – 27 Jan 945   d. ?
     Lecapenus, co-emperor with his father Romanus I to 16 Dec 944, deposed and exiled

----. Constantine (VIII)   Κωνσταντίνος (Η')   25 Dec 924 – 27 Jan 945   d. ?
     Lecapenus, co-emperor with his father Romanus I to 16 Dec 944, deposed and exiled

114. Romanus II   Ρωμανός Β'   6 Apr 945 – 15 Mar 963+   938-963
     Macedonian, co-emperor to 9 Nov 959

115. Nicephorus II   Νικηφόρος Β'   16 Aug 963 – 10 Dec 969++   c. 912-969
     Phocas

116. John I   Ιωάννης Α'   11 Dec 969 – 10 Jan 976+   924-976
     Tzimisces

117. Basil II   Βασίλειος Β'   22 Apr 960 – 15 Dec 1025+   958-1025
     Macedonian, byname 'Bulgar-slayer', co-emperor to 15 Mar 963 and 16 Aug 963 to 10 Jan 976

118. Constantine VIII   Κωνσταντίνος Η'   30 Mar 962 – 11 Nov 1028+   960/1-1028
     Macedonian, co-emperor to 15 Mar 963 and 16 Aug 963 to 15 Dec 1025

119. Romanus III   Ρωμανός Γ'   12 Nov 1028 – 11 Apr 1034++   c. 968-1034
     Argyrus

120. Michael IV   Μιχαήλ Δ'   12 Apr 1034 – 10 Dec 1041+   d. 1041
     the Paphlagonian

121. Michael V   Μιχαήλ Ε'   10 Dec 1041 – 21 Apr 1042   d. ?
     byname 'Kalaphates (Caulker)', deposed and exiled

122. Zoë   Ζωή   21 Apr 1042 – 12 Jun 1042   c. 978-1050
     Macedonian, co-empress with her sister Theodora, abdicated

123. Theodora   Θεοδώρα   (1st time)   21 Apr 1042 – 12 Jun 1042   c. 976-1056
     Macedonian, co-empress with her sister Zoe, abdicated

123. Constantine IX   Κωνσταντίνος Θ'   12 Jun 1042 – 11 Jan 1055+   c. 1000-1055
     Monomachus

----. Theodora   Θεοδώρα   (2nd time)   11 Jan 1055 – 21 Aug 1056+   c. 976-1056
     Macedonian

124. Michael VI   Μιχαήλ ΣΤ'   22 Aug 1056 – 31 Aug 1057   d. 1058?
     Bringas, byname 'Stratioticus', deposed, c.1058+

125. Isaac I   Ισαάκιος Α'   1 Sep 1057 – 21/2 Nov 1059   c. 1007-1061
     Comnenus, abdicated

126. Constantine X   Κωνσταντίνος Ι'   23/4 Nov 1059 – 21 May 1067+   c. 1006-1067
     Ducas

----. Constantius (IV)   Κωνστάντιος (Δ')   1060 – 24 Oct 1071   1060- ?
     Ducas, co-emperor with his father Constantine and brother Michael VII, deposed

127. Eudocia   Ευδοκία   (1st time)   21 May 1067 – 31 Dec 1067   c. 1021-1096?
     Ducas, family name Macrembolitissa, co-empress with her sons Michael and Constantius, abdicated

128. Romanus IV   Ρωμανός Δ'   1 Jan 1068 – 19 Aug 1071   d. 1072
     Diogenes, deposed, 4 Aug 1072++

----. Andronicus   Ανδρόνικος   1 Jan 1068 – 24 Oct 1071   c. 1055- ?
     Ducas, co-emperor with stepfather Romanus and brothers Michael VII and Constantius, deposed

----. Eudocia   Ευδοκία   (2nd time)   19 Aug 1071 – 24 Oct 1071   c. 1021-1096?
     Ducas, co-empress with her sons Michael VII/Constantius/Andronicus, deposed

129. Michael VII   Μιχαήλ Ζ'   1060 – 31 Mar 1078   c. 1050-c. 1090
     Ducas, co-emperor to 24 Oct 1071, deposed, consecrated m.Ephesos in 1078 but soon retired

130. Nicephorus III   Νικηφόρος Γ'   10 Oct 1077 – 1 Apr 1081   1001/2-c. 1081
     Botaniates, in opposition to 31 Mar 1078, deposed, probably late 1081+

----. Nicephorus (IV)   Νικηφόρος (Δ')   late 1080 – Apr 1081   d. 1104
Melissenus, in opposition to Nicephorus III, abdicated in favor of Alexius I

131. Alexius I   Αλέξιος Α'   1 Apr 1081 – 15 Aug 1118+   c. 1057-1118
Comnenus, crowned 4 Apr 1081

----. Constantine (XI)   Κωνσταντίνος (ΙΑ')   1081 – c. 1092+   d. c. 1092
Ducas, son of Michael VII, co-emperor

132. John II   Ιωάννης Β'   1092 – 8 Apr 1143+   1087-1143
Comnenus, co-emperor to 15 Aug 1118

133. Manuel I   Μανουήλ Α'   8 Apr 1143 – 24 Sep 1180+   1118-1180
Comnenus

134. Alexius II   Αλέξιος Β'   1171 – Sep 1183++   1169-1183
Comnenus, co-emperor to 24 Sep 1180

135. Andronicus I   Ανδρόνικος Α'   Sep 1183 – 12 Sep 1185++   c. 1118-1185
Comnenus, regent from 16 May 1182

136. Isaac II   Ισαάκιος Β'   (1st time)   12 Sep 1185 – 8 Apr 1195   c. 1156-1204
Angelus, deposed

137. Alexius III   Αλέξιος Γ'   8 Apr 1195 – 17 Jul 1203   c. 1153-1211/2
Angelus, deposed

----. Isaacius II   Ισαάκιος Β'   (2nd time)   18 Jul 1203 – 28 Jan 1204+   c. 1156-1204
Angelus

138. Alexius IV   Αλέξιος Δ'   Aug 1203 – 28 Jan 1204   c. 1182-1204
Angelus, co-emperor with his father Isaacius II (dominant emperor after Nov 1203), deposed, 8 Feb 1204++

139. Alexius V   Αλέξιος Ε'   28 Jan 1204 – 12 Apr 1204   d. 1204
Ducas, nicknamed 'Mourtzouphlos', deposed by the Crusaders, Dec 1204++

140. Theodore I   Θεόδωρος Α'   summer 1205 – Nov 1222+   c. 1174-1222
Lascaris, in Nicaea, crowned 30 Mar/5 Apr 1208

141. John III   Ιωάννης Γ'   Nov 1222 – 3 Nov 1254+   c. 1192-1254
Ducas-Vatatzes, in Nicaea

142. Theodore II   Θεόδωρος Β'   3 Nov 1254 – 16 Aug 1258+   1221-1258
Lascaris, in Nicaea

143. John IV   Ιωάννης Δ'   16 Aug 1258 – 25 Dec 1261   1250-c. 1305
Lascaris, in Nicaea, deposed and imprisoned

144. Michael VIII   Μιχαήλ Η'   1 Dec 1258 – 11 Dec 1282+   1224-1282
Palaiologus, in Nicaea until 15 Aug 1261, co-emperor to 25 Dec 1261

145. Andronicus II   Ανδρόνικος Β'   8 Nov 1272 – 24 May 1328   1259-1332
Palaiologus, co-emperor to 11 Dec 1282, deposed, 13 Feb 1332+

146. Michael IX   Μιχαήλ Θ'   21 May 1295 – 12 Oct 1320+   1277-1320
Palaiologus, co-emperor

147. Andronicus III   Ανδρόνικος Γ'   Jun 1321 – 15 Jun 1341+   1297-1341
Palaiologus, crowned 2 Feb 1325, co-emperor to 24 May 1328

148. John V   Ιωάννης Ε'   (1st time)   15 Jun 1341 – 12 Aug 1376   1332-1391
Palaiologus, deposed and imprisoned

149. John VI   Ιωάννης ΣΤ'   26 Oct 1341 – Dec 1354   c. 1295-1383
Cantacuzenus, in opposition to 8 Feb 1347, co-emperor afterwards, deposed, 15 Jun 1383+

150. Matthew   Ματθαίος   Feb 1354 – 1356   c. 1325-1383
Cantacuzenus, co-emperor, in opposition Dec 1354 to 1356, deposed, 15 Jun 1383+

151. Manuel II   Μανουήλ Β'   (1st time)   25 Sep 1373 – 12 Aug 1376   1350-1425
Palaiologus, co-emperor, deposed and imprisoned

152. Andronicus IV   Ανδρόνικος Δ'   12 Aug 1376 – 1 Jul 1379   1297-1385
Palaiologus, crowned 1 Oct 1376, deposed

----. John V   Ιωάννης Ε'   (2nd time)   1 Jul 1379 – 16 Feb 1391+   1332-1391

Palaiologus
----. Manuel II   Μανουήλ Β΄   (2nd time)   1 Jul 1373 – 21 Jul 1425+   1350-1425
  Palaiologus, co-emperor to 16 Feb 1391, retired
152. John VII   Ἰωάννης Ζ΄   14 Apr 1390 – 17 Sep 1390   c. 1370-1408
  Palaiologus, in opposition, deposed, regent for absent Manuel: Dec 1399 to 13 Sep 1402, 22 Sep 1408+
154. John VIII   Ἰωάννης Η΄   19 Jan 1421 – 31 Oct 1448+   1392-1448
  Palaiologus, co-emperor to 21 Jul 1425
155. Constantine XI Κωνσταντίνος ΙΑ΄   31 Oct 1448 – 29 May 1453++   1405-1453
  Palaiologus, crowned 6 Jan 1449, died fighting the Ottomans on the walls of Constantinople

B. THE OTTOMAN EMPERORS

1. Mehmed II   Μωάμεθ Β΄   29 May 1453 – 3 May 1481+   1432-1481
  had been Sultan of the Ottomans from 3 Feb 1451
2. Bayezid II   Βαγιαζήτ Β΄   3 May 1481 – 25 April 1512   1447/8-1512
  abdicated, 26 May 1512+
3. Selim I   Σελίμ Α΄   25 Apr 1512 – 22 Sep 1520+   1465-1520
4. Suleyman I   Σουλεϊμάν Α΄   22 Sep 1520 – 6 Sep 1566+   1494-1566
5. Selim II   Σελίμ Β΄   6 Sep 1566 – 12 Dec 1574+   1524-1574
6. Murad III   Μουράτ Γ΄   12 Dec 1574 – 15 Jan 1595+   1546-1595
7. Mehmed III   Μωάμεθ Γ΄   15 Jan 1595 – 22 Dec 1603+   1566-1603
8. Ahmed I   Αχμέτ Α΄   22 Dec 1603 – 22 Nov 1617+   1590-1617
9. Mustafa I   Μουσταφά Α΄   (1st time) 22 Nov 1617 – 26 Feb 1618   1592-1639
  deposed and imprisoned
10. Osman II   Οσμάν Β΄   26 Feb 1618 – 20 May 1622++   1604-1622
---. Mustafa I   Μουσταφά Α΄   (2nd time) 20 May 1622 – 10 Sep 1623   1592-1639
  deposed and imprisoned, 20 Jan 1639+
11. Murad IV   Μουράτ Δ΄   10 Sep 1623 – 9 Feb 1640+   1612-1640
12. Ibrahim I   Ιμπραήμ Α΄   9 Feb 1640 – 8 Aug 1648   1615-1648
  deposed, 12 Aug 1648++
13. Mehmed IV   Μωάμεθ Δ΄   8 Aug 1648 – 8 Nov 1687   1642-1693
  deposed and imprisoned, 6 Jan 1693+
14. Suleyman II   Σουλεϊμάν Β΄   8 Nov 1687 – 23 Jun 1691+   1642-1691
15. Ahmed II   Αχμέτ Β΄   23 Jun 1691 – 6 Feb 1695+   1643-1695
16. Mustafa II   Μουσταφά Β΄   6 Feb 1695 – 22 Aug 1703   1664-1703
  deposed, 28 Dec 1703+
17. Ahmed III   Αχμέτ Γ΄   22 Aug 1703 – 1 Oct 1730   1673-1736
  deposed, 1 Jul 1736+
18. Mahmud I   Μαχμούτ Α΄   2 Oct 1730 – 13 Dec 1754+   1696-1754
19. Osman III   Οσμάν Γ΄   14 Dec 1754 – 30 Oct 1757+   1699-1757
20. Mustafa III   Μουσταφά Γ΄   30 Oct 1757 – 21 Jan 1774+   1717-1774
21. Abdulhamid I   Αβδουλχαμίτ Α΄   21 Jan 1774 – 7 Apr 1789+   1725-1789
22. Selim III   Σελίμ Γ΄   7 Apr 1789 – 29 May 1807   1761-1808
  deposed, 29 Jul 1808++
23. Mustafa IV   Μουσταφά Δ΄   29 May 1807 – 28 Jul 1808   1779-1808
  deposed, 15 Nov 1808++
24. Mahmud II   Μαχμούτ Β΄   28 Jul 1808 – 1 Jul 1839+   1785-1839
25. Abdulmecid I   Αβδουλμετζίτ Α΄   1 Jul 1839 – 25 Jun 1861+   1823-1861
26. Abdulaziz   Αβδουλαζίζ   25 Jun 1861 – 30 May 1876   1830-1876

deposed, 4 Jun 1876++

27. Murad V	Μουράτ Ε'	30 May 1876 – 31 Aug 1876	1840-1904

deposed, 29 Aug 1904+

28. Abdulhamid II	Αβδουλχαμίτ Β'	31 Aug 1876 – 27 Apr 1909	1842-1918

deposed, 10 Feb 1918+

29. Mehmed V	Μωάμεθ Ε'	27 Apr 1909 – 3 Jul 1918+	1844-1918
30. Mehmed VI	Μωάμεθ ΣΤ'	3 Jul 1918 – 1 Nov 1922	1861-1926

deposed, left Turkey on 17 Nov 1922, 16 May 1926+

---. Abdulmecid II	Αβδουλμετζίτ Β'	19 Nov 1922 – 3 Mar 1924	1868-1944

Caliph only, deposed and exiled on 4 Mar 1924, 23 Aug 1944+

APPENDIX E
THE PATRIARCHS OF ROME

This listing is written from an Orthodox perspective, noting Rome's unilateral deviations from the common faith which are considered heretical by the Orthodox Church.

A. BISHOPS OF ROME

1. Apostle Peter	Πέτρος ο Απόστολος	c.60 – c.64++	d. 64?
2. Linus	Λίνος	c.65 – c.78+	d. 78?
3. Anacletus I	Ανέγκλητος Α᾽	c.79 – c.91+	d. 91?
4. Clement I	Κλήμης Α᾽	c.91 – c.101+	d. 101?
5. Evaristus	Ευάρεστος	c.101 – c.109+	d. 109?
6. Alexander I	Αλέξανδρος Α᾽	c.109 – c.116+	d. 116?
7. Xystus I	Ξύστος Α᾽	c.116 – c.125+	d. 125?
8. Telesphorus	Τελεσφόρος	c.125 – c.136++	d. 136?
9. Hyginus	Υγίνος	c.138 – c.142+	d. 142?
10. Pius I	Πίος Α᾽	c.142 – c.155+	d. 155?
11. Anicetus	Ανίκητος	c.155 – c.166+	d. 166?
12. Soter	Σωτήρ	c.166 – c.174+	d. 174?
13. Eleutherius	Ελευθέριος	c.174 – c.189+	d. 189?
14. Victor I	Βίκτωρ Α᾽	189 – 198+	d. 198
15. Zephyrinus	Ζεφυρίνος	198/9 – 217+	d. 217
16. Callistus I	Κάλλιστος Α᾽	217 – 14 Oct 222+	d. 222
---. Hippolytus	Ιππόλυτος	217 – c. Sep 235	d. 235
in opposition, imprisoned c. Mar 235 and exiled to Sardinia, resigned, late 235++			
17. Urban I	Ουρβανός Α᾽	c. Oct 222 – 23 May 230+	d. 230
18. Pontian	Ποντιανός	21 Jul 230 – 28 Sep 235	d. 235
imprisoned c. Mar 235 exiled to Sardinia, resigned, Oct 235++			
19. Anterus	Αντέρως	21 Nov 235 – 3 Jan 236+	d. 236
20. Fabian	Φαβιανός	10 Jan 236 – 20 Jan 250++	d. 250
died in prison			
21. Cornelius	Κορνήλιος	Mar 251 – Jun 253++	d. 253
died in prison			
---. Novatian	Νοβατιανός	Mar 251 – Oct 251	d. 258?
in opposition, heresiarch of Novatianism, deposed			
22. Lucius I	Λούκιος Α᾽	25 Jun 253 – 5 Mar 254+	d. 254
23. Stephen I	Στέφανος Α᾽	12 May 254 – 2 Aug 257+	d. 257
24. Xystus II	Ξύστος Β᾽	30 Aug 257 – 6 Aug 258++	d. 258
executed by the Roman authorities			
25. Dionysius	Διονύσιος	22 Jul 260 – 26 Dec 268+	d. 268
26. Felix I	Φήλιξ Α᾽	5 Jan 269 – 30 Dec 274+	d. 274

27. Eutychian	Ευτυχιανός	4 Jan 275 – 7 Dec 283+	d. 283
28. Gaius	Γάιος	17 Dec 283 – 22 Apr 296+	d. 296
29. Marcellinus	Μαρκελλίνος	30 Jun 296 – 25 Oct 304+	d. 304
30. Marcellus I	Μάρκελλος Α΄	Nov/Dec 306 – 16 Jan 308++	d. 308
died in exile			
31. Eusebius	Ευσέβιος	18 Apr 310 – 21 Oct 310++	d. 310
died in exile			
32. Miltiades	Μιλτιάδης	2 Jul 311 – 11 Jan 314+	d. 314
called Melchiades in some records; died in exile			

B. METROPOLITANS OF ROME

33. Sylvester I	Σίλβεστρος Α΄	31 Jan 314 – 31 Dec 335+	d. 335
Metropolitan from summer 325			
34. Marcus	Μάρκος	18 Jan 336 – 7 Oct 336+	d. 336
35. Julius I	Ιούλιος Α΄	6 Feb 337 – 12 Apr 352+	d. 352
36. Liberius	Λιβέριος	17 May 352 – 24 Sep 366+	d. 366
exiled to Beroea (Veria in Greece) c. Nov 355, returned to Rome in 358			
---. Felix II	Φήλιξ Β΄	c. Nov 355 – 22 Nov 365+	d. 365
in opposition, Arian, moved out of Rome in 358			
---. Ursinus	Ουρσίνος	24 Sep 366 – 378	d. 385?
exiled to Gaul mid Oct 366, returned Sep 367, expelled from Rome 12 Jan 368, deposed			

C. PATRIARCHS OF ROME

37. Damasus I	Δάμασος Α΄	1 Oct 366 – 11 Dec 384+	c. 304-384
facing opposition from Ursinus to 378, Patriarch from May 381			
38. Siricius	Σιρίκιος	Dec 384 – 26 Nov 399+	c. 334-399
39. Anastasius I	Αναστάσιος Α΄	27 Nov 399 – 19 Dec 401+	d. 401
40. Innocent I	Ιννοκέντιος Α΄	22 Dec 401 – 12 Mar 417+	d. 417
41. Zosimus	Ζώσιμος	18 Mar 417 – 26 Dec 418+	d. 418
42. Boniface I	Βονιφάτιος Α΄	28 Dec 418 – 4 Sep 422+	d. 422
---. Eulalius	Ευλάλιος	28 Dec 418 – Apr 419	d. 423
deposed and exiled to Campania			
43. Celestine I	Κελεστίνος Α΄	10 Sep 422 – 27 Jul 432+	d. 432
44. Xystus III	Ξύστος Γ΄	31 Jul 432 – 19 Aug 440+	d. 440
45. Leo I	Λέων Α΄	29 Sep 440 – 10 Nov 461+	d. 461
46. Hilarus	Ιλάριος	19 Nov 461 – 29 Feb 468+	d. 468
47. Simplicius	Σιμπλίκιος	3 Mar 468 – 10 Mar 483+	d. 483
48. Felix III	Φήλιξ Γ΄	13 Mar 483 – 1 Mar 492+	d. 492
49. Gelasius I	Γελάσιος Α΄	1 Mar 492 – 21 Nov 496+	d. 496
50. Anastasius II	Αναστάσιος Β΄	24 Nov 496 – 19 Nov 498+	d. 498
51. Symmachus	Σύμμαχος	22 Nov 498 – 19 Jul 514+	d. 514
imprisoned 501-506			
---. Laurentius	Λαυρέντιος (1st time)	22 Nov 498 – c. Dec 498	d. ?
in opposition, resigned			
---. Laurentius	Λαυρέντιος (2nd time)	501 – c. 506	d. ?
in opposition, deposed			

52. Hormisdas	Ορμίσδας	20 Jul 514 – 6 Aug 523+	d. 523
53. Ιωάννης Α΄ died in prison	John I	13 Aug 523 – 18 May 526++	d. 526
54. Felix IV	Φήλιξ Δ΄	12 Jul 526 – 22 Sep 530+	d. 530
---. Dioscorus	Διόσκορος	22 Sep 530 – 14 Oct 530+	d. 530
55. Boniface II in opposition to 14 Oct 530	Βονιφάτιος Β΄	22 Sep 530 – 17 Oct 532+	d. 532
56. John II former name: Mercurius	Ιωάννης Β΄	2 Jan 533 – 8 May 535+	d. 535
57. Agapetus I	Αγαπητός Α΄	13 May 535 – 22 Apr 536+	d. 536
58. Silverius deposed and exiled to Patara in Asia Minor, resigned 11 Nov 537, 2 Dec 537++	Σιλβέριος	1 or 8 Jun 536 – 11 Mar 537	d. 537
59. Vigilius	Βιγίλιος	29 Mar 537 – 7 Jun 555+	d. 555
60. Pelagius I	Πελάγιος Α΄	16 Apr 556 – 4 Mar 561+	d. 561
61. John III former name: Catelinus	Ιωάννης Γ΄	17 Jul 561 – 13 Jul 574+	d. 574
62. Benedict I	Βενέδικτος Α΄	2 Jun 575 – 30 Jul 579+	d. 579
63. Pelagius II election confirmed on 26 Nov 579	Πελάγιος Β΄	Aug 579 – 7 Feb 590+	d. 590
64. Gregory I	Γρηγόριος Α΄	3 Sep 590 – 12 Mar 604+	c. 540-604
65. Sabinian	Σαβινιανός	13 Sep 604 – 22 Feb 606+	d. 606
66. Boniface III	Βονιφάτιος Γ΄	19 Feb 607 – 12 Nov 607+	d. 607
67. Boniface IV	Βονιφάτιος Δ΄	25 Aug 608 – 8 May 615+	d. 615
68. Deusdedit	Θεόδοτος	19 Oct 615 – 8 Nov 618+	d. 618
69. Boniface V	Βονιφάτιος Ε΄	23 Dec 619 – 25 Oct 625+	d. 625
70. Honorius I adopted heresy of monothelitism	Ονώριος Α΄	27 Oct 625 – 12 Oct 638+	d. 638
71. Severinus elected in Oct 638	Σεβερίνος	28 May 640 – 2 Aug 640+	d. 640
72. John IV	Ιωάννης Δ΄	24 Dec 640 – 12 Oct 642+	d. 642
73. Theodore I	Θεόδωρος Α΄	24 Nov 642 – 14 May 649+	d. 649
74. Martin I deposed and imprisoned, exiled to Cherson in Crimea, 16 Sep 655++	Μαρτίνος Α΄	5 Jul 649 – 15 Jun 653	d. 655
75. Eugene I	Ευγένιος Α΄	10 Aug 654 – 2 Jun 657+	d. 657
76. Vitalian	Βιταλιανός	30 Jul 657 – 27 Jan 672+	d. 672
77. Adeodatus	Αδεοδάτος	11 Apr 672 – 17 Jun 676+	d. 676
78. Donus	Δόνος	2 Nov 676 – 11 Apr 678+	d. 678
79. Agatho	Αγάθων	27 Jun 678 – 10 Jan 681+	c. 577-681
80. Leo II	Λέων Β΄	17 Aug 682 – 3 Jul 683+	d. 683
81. Benedict II	Βενέδικτος Β΄	26 Jun 684 – 8 May 685+	d. 685
82. John V	Ιωάννης Ε΄	23 Jul 685 – 2 Aug 686+	d. 686
83. Conon	Κόνων	21 Oct 686 – 21 Sep 687+	d. 687
---. Paschal (I) in opposition, deposed and imprisoned	Πασχάλιος (Α΄)	21 Sep 687 – late Dec 687	d. 692
---. Theodore (II) in opposition, resigned	Θεόδωρος (Β΄)	21 Sep 687 – 15 Dec 687	d. ?
84. Sergius I	Σέργιος Α΄	15 Dec 687 – 8 Sep 701+	d. 701
85. John VI	Ιωάννης ΣΤ΄	30 Oct 701 – 11 Jan 705+	d. 705

86. John VII	Ἰωάννης Ζ'	1 Mar 705 – 18 Oct 707+	d. 707
87. Sisinnius	Σισίννιος	15 Jan 708 – 4 Feb 708+	d. 708
88. Constantine I	Κωνσταντίνος Α'	25 Mar 708 – 9 Apr 715+	d. 715
89. Gregory II	Γρηγόριος Β'	19 May 715 – 11 Feb 731+	669-731
90. Gregory III	Γρηγόριος Γ'	18 Mar 731 – 28 Nov 741+	d. 741
91. Zacharias	Ζαχαρίας	10 Dec 741 – 22 Mar 752+	d. 752
---. Stephen II not consecrated	Στέφανος Β'	22/3 Mar 752 – 25/6 Mar 752+	d. 752
92. Stephen III	Στέφανος Γ'	26 Mar 752 – 26 Apr 757+	d. 757
93. Paul I	Παῦλος Α'	29 May 757 – 28 Jun 767+	d. 767
---. Constantine II deposed and imprisoned	Κωνσταντίνος Β'	5 Jul 767 – late Jul 768	d. ?
---. Philip deposed	Φίλιππος	31 Jul 768 – 1 Aug 768	d. ?
94. Stephen IV	Στέφανος Δ'	7 Aug 768 – 24 Jan 772+	c. 720-772
95. Hadrian I	Ἀδριανός Α'	9 Feb 772 – 25 Dec 795+	d. 795
96. Leo III	Λέων Γ'	27 Dec 795 – 12 Jun 816+	d. 816
97. Stephen V	Στέφανος Ε'	22 Jun 816 – 24 Jan 817+	d. 817
98. Paschal I	Πασχάλιος Α'	25 Jan 817 – 11 Feb 824+	d. 824
99. Eugene II	Εὐγένιος Β'	c. 11 May 824 – c. 27 Aug 827+	d. 827
100. Valentine	Βαλεντίνος	c. 28 Aug 827 – Sep 827+	d. 827
101. Gregory IV	Γρηγόριος Δ'	29 Mar 828 – 25 Jan 844+	d. 844
----. John (VIII) unconsecrated, deposed, and imprisoned	Ἰωάννης (Η')	25 Jan 844 – end Jan 844	d. ?
102. Sergius II	Σέργιος Β'	end Jan 844 – 27 Jan 847+	d. 847
103. Leo IV elected 27 Jan 847	Λέων Δ'	10 Apr 847 – 17 Jul 855+	d. 855
----. Anastasius (III) byname Bibliothecarius, unconsecrated, deposed	Ἀναστάσιος (Γ')	Sep 855 (3 days)	d. 878?
104. Benedict III	Βενέδικτος Γ'	29 Sep 855 – 17 Apr 858+	d. 858
105. Nicholas I	Νικόλαος Α'	24 Apr 858 – 13 Nov 867+	c. 820-867
106. Hadrian II	Ἀδριανός Β'	14 Dec 867 – 14 Dec 872+	792-872
107. John VIII	Ἰωάννης Η'	14 Dec 872 – 16 Dec 882++	d. 882
108. Marinus I	Μαρῖνος Α'	16 Dec 882 – 15 May 884+	d. 884
109. Hadrian III	Ἀδριανός Γ'	17 May 884 – Sep 885+	d. 885
110. Stephen VI	Στέφανος ΣΤ'	Sep 885 – 14 Sep 891+	d. 891
111. Formosus	Φορμόσος	6 Oct 891 – 4 Apr 896+	c. 816-896
112. Boniface VI	Βονιφάτιος ΣΤ'	c. 11 Apr 896 – c. 26 Apr 896+	d. 896
113. Stephen VII murdered in prison	Στέφανος Ζ'	May 896 – Jul/Aug 897++	d. 897
114. Romanus deposed or resigned	Ρωμανός	Aug 897 – Nov 897	d. ?
115. Theodore II died after 20 days	Θεόδωρος Β'	Nov 897 – Dec 897+	d. 897
----. Sergius III deposed	Σέργιος Γ' (1st time)	Dec 897 – Jan 898	d. 911
116. John IX	Ἰωάννης Θ'	Jan 898 – Jan 900+	d. 900
117. Benedict IV	Βενέδικτος Δ'	Feb 900 – Jul 903+	d. 903

118. Leo V	Λέων Ε'		Jul/Aug 903 – Sep 903	d. 904/5
deposed and imprisoned, murdered in prison				
----. Christopher	Χριστόφορος		Sep 903 – Jan 904	d. 904/5
deposed and imprisoned, murdered in prison				
119. Sergius III	Σέργιος Γ'	(2nd time)	29 Jan 904 – 14 Apr 911+	d. 911
120. Anastasius III	Αναστάσιος Γ'		c. Jun 911 – c. Aug 913+	d. 913
121. Lando (Landus)	Λάνδος		c. Aug 913 – c. Mar 914+	d. 914
122. John X	Ιωάννης Ι'		Mar/Apr 914 – May 928	d. 929
deposed and imprisoned, murdered in prison, early 929++				
123. Leo VI	Λέων ΣΤ'		May 928 – Dec 928+	d. 928
124. Stephen VIII	Στέφανος Η'		Dec 928 – Feb 931+	d. 931
125. John XI	Ιωάννης ΙΑ'		Mar 931 – Dec 935/Jan 936+	921-935
126. Leo VII	Λέων Ζ'		3 Jan 936 – 13 Jul 939+	d. 939
127. Stephen IX	Στέφανος Θ'		14 Jul 939 – Oct 942++	d. 942
died in prison				
128. Marinus II	Μαρίνος Β'		30 Oct 942 – May 946+	d. 946
129. Agapetus II	Αγαπητός Β'		10 May 946 – Dec 955+	d. 955
130. John XII	Ιωάννης ΙΒ'	(1st time)	16 Dec 955 – 4 Dec 963	c. 937-964
former name: Octavian, deposed				
131. Leo VIII	Λέων Η'	(1st time)	6 Dec 963 – 26 Feb 964	d. 965
deposed				
----. John XII	Ιωάννης ΙΒ'	(2nd time)	26 Feb 964 – 14 May 964+	c. 937-964
132. Benedict V	Βενέδικτος Ε'		22 May 964 – 23 Jun 964	d. 966
deposed, 4 Jul 966				
----. Leo VIII	Λέων Η'	(2nd time)	23 Jun 964 – 1 Mar 965+	d. 965
133. John XIII	Ιωάννης ΙΓ'		1 Oct 965 – 6 Sep 972+	d. 972
134. Benedict VI	Βενέδικτος ΣΤ'		19 Jan 973 – Jun 974	d. 974
deposed and imprisoned, murdered in prison, Jul 974++				
----. Boniface VII	Βονιφάτιος Ζ'	(1st time)	Jun 974 – Jul 974	d. 985
former name: Franco, deposed				
135. Benedict VII	Βενέδικτος Ζ'		Oct 974 – 10 Jul 983+	d. 983
136. John XIV	Ιωάννης ΙΔ'		Dec 983 – Apr 984	d. 984
Peter Canepanova, deposed and imprisoned, 20 Aug 984++				
----. Boniface VII	Βονιφάτιος Ζ'	(2nd time)	Apr 984 – 20 Jul 985+	d. 985
137. John XV	Ιωάννης ΙΕ'		Aug 985 – Mar 996+	d. 996
138. Gregory V	Γρηγόριος Ε'		3 May 996 – 18 Feb 999+	972-999
former name: Bruno				
----. John XVI	Ιωάννης ΙΣΤ'		Feb 997 – Apr 998	d. 1013?
in opposition, deposed, died in prison				
139. Sylvester II	Σίλβεστρος Β'		2 Apr 999 – 12 May 1003+	c. 945-1003
former name: Gerbert				
140. John XVII	Ιωάννης ΙΖ'		16 May 1003 – 6 Nov 1003+	d. 1003
Sicco				
141. John XVIII	Ιωάννης ΙΗ'		25 Dec 1004 – Jun/Jul 1009+	d. 1009
former name: Fasanius, may have resigned shortly before his death				
142. Sergius IV	Σέργιος Δ'		31 Jul 1009 – 12 May 1012+	d. 1012
Peter Boccapecora, adopted filioque				
----. Gregory (VI)	Γρηγόριος (ΣΤ')		May 1012 – Dec 1012	d. ?
in opposition after 18 May 1012, deposed, filioque?				

143. Benedict VIII	Βενέδικτος Η΄	18 May 1012 – 9 Apr 1024+	c. 980-1024
former name: Theophylactus, filioque			
144. John XIX	Ιωάννης ΙΘ΄	19 Apr 1024 – 20 Oct 1032+	d. 1032
former name: Romanus, filioque			
145. Benedict IX	Βενέδικτος Θ΄ (1st time)	21 Oct 1032 – Sep 1044	d. 1055
former name: Theophylactus, filioque, deposed			
146. Sylvester III	Σίλβεστρος Γ΄	20 Jan 1045 – 10 Mar 1045	d. 1063
former name: John, filioque, deposed			
----. Benedict IX	Βενέδικτος Θ΄ (2nd time)	10 Mar 1045 – 1 May 1045	d. 1055
filioque, resigned			
147. Gregory VI	Γρηγόριος ΣΤ΄	5 May 1045 – 20 Dec 1046	d. 1047
John Gratian, filioque, deposed, late 1047+			
148. Clement II	Κλήμης Β΄	25 Dec 1046 – 9 Oct 1047+	d. 1047
former name: Suidger, filioque			
----. Benedict IX	Βενέδικτος Θ΄ (3rd time)	8 Nov 1047 – 16 Jul 1048	d. 1055
filioque, deposed, Nov/Dec 1055+			
149. Damasus II	Δάμασος Β΄	17 Jul 1048 – 9 Aug 1048+	d. 1048
former name: Poppo, filioque			
150. Leo IX	Λέων Θ΄	12 Feb 1049 – 19 Apr 1054+	1002-1054
former name: Bruno, filioque			
151. Victor II	Βίκτωρ Β΄	13 Apr 1055 – 28 Jul 1057+	c. 1018-1057
former name: Gebhard, filioque			
152. Stephen X	Στέφανος Ι΄	2 Aug 1057 – 29 Mar 1058+	c. 1000-1058
former name: Frederick, filioque			
----. Benedict X	Βενέδικτος Ι΄	5 Apr 1058 – Jan 1059	d. 1080?
former name: John, filioque, deposed			
153. Nicholas II	Νικόλαος Β΄	6 Dec 1058 – 27 Jul 1061+	c. 1010-1061
former name: Gerard, filioque, in opposition to Jan 1059			
154. Alexander II	Αλέξανδρος Β΄	30 Sep 1061 – 21 Apr 1073+	d. 1073
former name: Anselm, filioque			
----. Honorius (II)	Ονώριος (Β΄)	28 Oct 1061 – May 1064	c. 1009-1072
former name: Cadalus, filioque, in opposition, deposed			

D. POPES OF ROME

155. Gregory VII	Γρηγόριος Ζ΄	30 Jun 1073 – 25 May 1085+	c. 1020-1085
former name: Hilderbrand, filioque, decreed universalism ('universal jurisdiction') in Mar 1075			
restricted use of title 'Pope' (formerly all western bishops were addressed with the title 'Pope')			
----. Clement (III)	Κλήμης (Γ΄)	25 Jun 1080 – 8 Sep 1100+	c. 1025-1100
former name: Guibert, filioque-universalism, in opposition			
156. Victor III	Βίκτωρ Γ΄	9 May 1087 – 16 Sep 1087+	c. 1027-1087
former name: Desiderius, born Daufer, filioque-universalism			
157. Urban II	Ουρβανός Β΄	12 Mar 1088 – 29 Jul 1099+	c. 1042-1099
former name: Odo, filioque-universalism			
158. Paschal II	Πασχάλιος Β΄	14 Aug 1099 – 21 Jan 1118+	d. 1118
former name: Ranierus, filioque-universalism			
----. Theodoric	Θεοδώριχος	Sep 1100 – Jan 1101	d. 1102
filioque-universalism, in opposition, deposed and imprisoned			
----. Albert	Αλβέρτος	Jan 1101 (days)	d. ?
filioque-universalism, in opposition, deposed and imprisoned			

----. Sylvester IV   Σίλβεστρος Δ΄   18 Nov 1105 – 11 Apr 1111   d. ?
  former name: Maginulf, filioque-universalism, in opposition, resigned

----. Gregory (VIII)   Γρηγόριος (Η΄)   8 Mar 1118 – Apr 1121   d. 1137
  former name: Mauritius, filioque-universalism, deposed and imprisoned

159. Gelasius II   Γελάσιος Β΄   10 Mar 1118 – 28 Jan 1119+   d. 1119
  former name: John, filioque-universalism, in opposition

160. Callistus II   Κάλλιστος Β΄   2 Feb 1119 – 13 Dec 1124+   1050-1124
  former name: Guy, filioque-universalism, in opposition to Apr 1121

----. Celestine (II)   Κελεστίνος (Β΄)   15 Dec 1124 – 21 Dec 1124   d. ?
  Theobald Buccapeco, filioque-universalism, not consecrated, forced to resign

161. Honorius II   Ονώριος Β΄   15 Dec 1124 – 13 Feb 1130+   d. 1130
  Lambert Scannabecchi, filioque-universalism, in opposition to 21 Dec 1124

----. Anacletus II   Ανέγκλητος Β΄   23 Feb 1130 – 25 Jan 1138+   d. 1138
  Peter Pierleoni, filioque-universalism

162. Innocent II   Ιννοκέντιος Β΄   23 Feb 1130 – 24 Sep 1143+   d. 1143
  Gregory Papareschi, filioque-universalism, in opposition to 25 Jan 1138

----. Victor IV   Βίκτωρ Δ΄   Mar 1138 – 29 May 1138   d. 1140?
  Gregory Conti, filioque-universalism, in opposition, resigned

163. Celestine II   Κελεστίνος Β΄   3 Oct 1143 – 8 Mar 1144+   d. 1144
  former name: Guy, filioque-universalism

164. Lucius II   Λούκιος Β΄   12 Mar 1144 – 15 Feb 1145++   d. 1145
  Gerard Caccianemici, filioque-universalism, killed in battle

165. Eugene III   Ευγένιος Γ΄   18 Feb 1145 – 8 Jul 1153+   d. 1153
  Bernard Paganelli, filioque-universalism

166. Anastasius IV   Αναστάσιος Δ΄   12 Jul 1153 – 3 Dec 1154+   c. 1073-1154
  former name: Conrad, filioque-universalism

167. Hadrian IV   Αδριανός Δ΄   4 Dec 1154 – 1 Sep 1159+   c. 1100-1159
  Nicholas Breakspeare, filioque-universalism

168. Alexander III   Αλέξανδρος Γ΄   20 Sep 1159 – 30 Aug 1181+   c. 1105-1181
  Roland Bandinelli, filioque-universalism

----. Victor V   Βίκτωρ Ε΄   4 Oct 1159 – 20 Apr 1164+   d. 1164
  former name: Octavian, filioque-universalism, in opposition

----. Paschal III   Πασχάλιος Γ΄   22 Apr 1164 – 20 Sep 1168+   d. 1168
  former name: Guy, filioque-universalism, in opposition

----. Callistus (III)   Κάλλιστος (Γ΄)   Sep 1168 – 29 Aug 1178   d≤1184
  former name: John, filioque-universalism, in opposition, resigned

----. Innocent (III)   Ιννοκέντιος (Γ΄)   29 Sep 1179 – Jan 1180   d. ?
  former name: Lando, filioque-universalism, in opposition, deposed and imprisoned

169. Lucius III   Λούκιος Γ΄   1 Sep 1181 – 25 Nov 1185+   c. 1097-1185
  Humbald Allucingoli, filioque-universalism

170. Urban III   Ουρβανός Γ΄   25 Nov 1185 – 20 Oct 1187+   d. 1187
  Humbert Crivelli, filioque-universalism

171. Gregory VIII   Γρηγόριος Η΄   25 Oct 1187 – 17 Dec 1187+   c. 1100-1187
  Albert de Morra, filioque-universalism

172. Clement III   Κλήμης Γ΄   19 Dec 1187 – c.25 Mar 1191+   d. 1191
  Paul Scolari, filioque-universalism

173. Celestine III   Κελεστίνος Γ΄   14 Apr 1191 – 8 Jan 1198+   c. 1106-1198
  Hyacinth Bobone, filioque-universalism

174. Innocent III   Ιννοκέντιος Γ΄   22 Feb 1198 – 16 Jul 1216+   1160/1-1216
  Lothair di Segni, filioque-universalism

175. Honorius III   Ονώριος Γ'   24 Jul 1216 – 18 Mar 1227+   d. 1227
Cencius Savelli, filioque-universalism

176. Gregory IX   Γρηγόριος Θ'   19 Mar 1227 – 22 Aug 1241+   c. 1170-1241
Hugolin di Segni, filioque-universalism

177. Celestine IV   Κελεστίνος Δ'   25 Oct 1241 – 10 Nov 1241+   d. 1241
Geoffrey Castiglioni, filioque-universalism

178. Innocent IV   Ιννοκέντιος Δ'   28 Jun 1243 – 7 Dec 1254+   c. 1200-1254
Sinibald Fieschi, filioque-universalism

179. Alexander IV   Αλέξανδρος Δ'   12 Dec 1254 – 25 May 1261+   1199-1261
Reginald di Segni, filioque-universalism

180. Urban IV   Ουρβανός Δ'   29 Aug 1261 – 2 Oct 1264+   c. 1200-1264
Jacques Pantaléon, filioque-universalism

181. Clement IV   Κλήμης Δ'   5 Feb 1265 – 29 Nov 1268+   d. 1268
Guy Foulques, filioque-universalism

182. Gregory X   Γρηγόριος Ι'   27 Mar 1272 – 10 Jan 1276+   1210-1276
Theobald Visconti, filioque-universalism, dogmatized teaching of purgatory in 1274

183. Innocent V   Ιννοκέντιος Ε'   21 Jan 1276 – 22 Jun 1276+   c. 1224-1276
Peter de Tarentaise, filioque-universalism-purgatory

184. Hadrian V   Αδριανός Ε'   11 Jul 1276 – 18 Aug 1276+   c. 1205-1276
Ottobon Fieschi, filioque-universalism-purgatory, not consecrated

185. John XXI   Ιωάννης Κ'   8 Sep 1276 – 20 May 1277+   c. 1210-1277
Peter Juliao, filioque-universalism-purgatory

186. Nicholas III   Νικόλαος Γ'   26 Dec 1277 – 22 Aug 1280+   c. 1220-1280
John Gaetano, filioque-universalism-purgatory

187. Martin II   Μαρτίνος Β'   23 Mar 1281 – 28 Mar 1285+   c. 1215-1285
Dimon de Brie, filioque-universalism-purgatory

188. Honorius IV   Ονώριος Δ'   20 May 1285 – 3 Apr 1287+   c. 1210-1287
James Savelli, filioque-universalism-purgatory

189. Nicholas IV   Νικόλαος Δ'   22 Feb 1288 – 4 Apr 1292+   1227-1292
Jerome Masci, filioque-universalism-purgatory

190. Celestine V   Κελεστίνος Ε'   29 Aug 1294 – 13 Dec 1294   c. 1210-1296
Peter del Murrone, filioque-universalism-purgatory, resigned, 19 May 1296+

191. Boniface VIII   Βονιφάτιος Η'   23 Jan 1295 – 11 Oct 1303+   c. 1235-1303
Benedict Caetani, filioque-universalism-purgatory

192. Benedict XI   Βενέδικτος ΙΑ'   22 Oct 1303 – 7 Jul 1304+   1240-1304
Nicholas Boccasini, filioque-universalism-purgatory

193. Clement V   Κλήμης Ε'   5 Jun 1305 – 20 Apr 1314+   c. 1264-1314
Bertrand de Got, filioque-universalism-purgatory, moved to Avignon in 1309

194. John XXII   Ιωάννης ΚΑ'   7 Aug 1316 – 4 Dec 1334+   c. 1244-1334
Jack Duese, filioque-universalism-purgatory, in Avignon

----. Nicholas (V)   Νικόλαος (Ε')   22 May 1328 – 25 Aug 1330   d. 1333
Peter Rainalducci, filioque-universalism-purgatory, in opposition, in Rome, resigned, 16 Oct 1333+

195. Benedict XII   Βενέδικτος ΙΒ'   8 Jan 1335 – 25 Apr 1342+   1285-1342
Jack Fournier, filioque-universalism-purgatory, in Avignon

196. Clement VI   Κλήμης ΣΤ'   7 May 1342 – 6 Dec 1352+   c. 1290-1352
Peter Roger, filioque-universalism-purgatory, in Avignon

197. Innocent VI   Ιννοκέντιος ΣΤ'   18 Dec 1352 – 12 Sep 1362+   c. 1282-1362
Stephan Aubert, filioque-universalism-purgatory, in Avignon

198. Urban V   Ουρβανός Ε'   6 Nov 1362 – 19 Dec 1370+   c. 1310-1370
William de Grimoard, filioque-universalism-purgatory,
in Avignon to 30 Apr 1367, in Rome from 16 Oct 1367, returned to Avignon 27 Sep 1370

199. Gregory XI   Γρηγόριος ΙΑ'   4 Jan 1371 – 27 Mar 1378+   c. 1330-1378
   Peter Roger de Beaufort, filioque-universalism-purgatory, moved to Rome 17 Jan 1377

200. Urban VI   Ουρβανός ΣΤ'   8 Apr 1378 – 15 Oct 1389+   c. 1318-1389
   Bartholomew Prignano, filioque-universalism-purgatory

----. Clement (VII)   Κλήμης (Ζ')   20 Sep 1378 – 16 Sep 1394+   1342-1394
   former name: Robert, filioque-universalism-purgatory, in Avignon, in opposition

201. Boniface IX   Βονιφάτιος Θ'   9 Nov 1389 – 1 Oct 1404+   c. 1350-1404
   Peter Tomacelli, filioque-universalism-purgatory

----. Benedict (XIII)   Βενέδικτος (ΙΓ')   11 Oct 1394 – 23 May 1423+   c. 1328-1423
   Peter de Luna, filioque-universalism-purgatory, in Avignon, in opposition

202. Innocent VII   Ιννοκέντιος Ζ'   17 Oct 1404 – 6 Nov 1406+   c. 1336-1406
   Cosma de Migliorati, filioque-universalism-purgatory

203. Gregory XII   Γρηγόριος ΙΒ'   30 Nov 1406 – 4 Jul 1415   c. 1325-1417
   Angelo Corraro, filioque-universalism-purgatory, resigned, 18 Oct 1417+

----. Alexander V   Αλέξανδρος Ε'   26 Jun 1409 – 3 May 1410+   c. 1340-1410
   Peter Philargos, filioque-universalism-purgatory, in opposition

----. John XXIII   Ιωάννης ΚΒ'   25 May 1410 – 29 May 1415   c. 1370-1419
   Balthazar Cossa, filioque-universalism-purgatory, in opposition, deposed, 22 Nov 1419+

204. Martin III   Μαρτίνος Γ'   14 Nov 1417 – 20 Feb 1431+   1368-1431
   Oddo Colonna, filioque-universalism-purgatory

----. Clement (VIII)   Κλήμης (Η')   20 Jun 1423 – 26 Jul 1429   c. 1370-1446
   Gil Sanchez Munoz, filioque-universalism-purgatory, in opposition, resigned, 28 Dec 1446+

----. Benedict (XIV)   Βενέδικτος (ΙΔ')   12 Nov 1425 – c. 1430+   d. 1430?
   Bernard Garnier, filioque-universalism-purgatory, in opposition

205. Eugene IV   Ευγένιος Δ'   11 Mar 1431 – 23 Feb 1447+   c. 1383-1447
   Gabriel Condulmaro, filioque-universalism-purgatory

----. Felix V   Φήλιξ Ε'   24 Jul 1440 – 7 Apr 1449   1383-1451
   former name: Amadeus, filioque-universalism-purgatory, in opposition, resigned, 7 Jan 1451+

206. Nicholas V   Νικόλαος Ε'   6 Mar 1447 – 24 Mar 1455+   1397-1455
   Thomas Parentucelli, filioque-universalism-purgatory

207. Callistus III   Κάλλιστος Γ'   8 Apr 1455 – 6 Aug 1458+   1378-1458
   Alfonsus Borgia, filioque-universalism-purgatory

208. Pius II   Πίος Β'   19 Aug 1458 – 15 Aug 1464+   1405-1464
   Aeneas Silvius Piccolomini, filioque-universalism-purgatory

209. Paul II   Παύλος Β'   30 Aug 1464 – 26 Jul 1471+   1417-1471
   Peter Barbo, filioque-universalism-purgatory

210. Sixtus IV (Xystus) Σίξτος Δ'   25 Aug 1471 – 12 Aug 1484+   1414-1484
   Franciscus della Rovere, filioque-universalism-purgatory

211. Innocent VIII   Ιννοκέντιος Η'   29 Aug 1484 – 25 Jul 1492+   1432-1492
   John Baptist Cibo, filioque-universalism-purgatory

212. Alexander VI   Αλέξανδρος ΣΤ'   11 Aug 1492 – 18 Aug 1503+   1431-1503
   Roderic Borgia, filioque-universalism-purgatory

213. Pius III   Πίος Γ'   1 Oct 1503 – 18 Oct 1503+   1439-1503
   Franciscus Todeschini Piccolomini, filioque-universalism-purgatory

214. Julius II   Ιούλιος Β'   1 Nov 1503 – 21 Feb 1513+   1453-1513
   Julian della Rovere, filioque-universalism-purgatory

215. Leo X   Λέων Ι'   17 Mar 1513 – 1 Dec 1521+   1475-1521
   John de Medici, filioque-universalism-purgatory

216. Hadrian VI   Αδριανός ΣΤ'   9 Jan 1522 – 14 Sep 1523+   1459-1523
   Hadrian Dedal, filioque-universalism-purgatory

217. Clement VII   Κλήμης Ζ'   19 Nov 1523 – 25 Sep 1534+   1478-1534
Julius de Medici, filioque-universalism-purgatory

218. Paul III   Παύλος Γ'   13 Oct 1534 – 10 Nov 1549+   1468-1549
Alexander Farnese, filioque-universalism-purgatory

219. Julius III   Ιούλιος Γ'   8 Feb 1550 – 23 Mar 1555+   1487-1555
John Marius Ciocchi del Monte, filioque-universalism-purgatory

220. Marcellus II   Μάρκελλος Β'   10 Apr 1555 – 1 May 1555+   1501-1555
Marcellus Cervini, filioque-universalism-purgatory

221. Paul IV   Παύλος Δ'   23 May 1555 – 18 Aug 1559+   1476-1559
John Peter Carafa, filioque-universalism-purgatory

222. Pius IV   Πίος Δ'   25 Dec 1559 – 9 Dec 1565+   1499-1565
John Angelo de Medici, filioque-universalism-purgatory

223. Pius V   Πίος Ε'   7 Jan 1566 – 1 May 1572+   1504-1572
Michael Ghislieri, born Anthony, filioque-universalism-purgatory

224. Gregory XIII   Γρηγόριος ΙΓ'   13 May 1572 – 10 Apr 1585+   1502-1585
Hugo Buoncompagni, filioque-universalism-purgatory

225. Sixtus V (Xystus)   Σίξτος Ε'   24 Apr 1585 – 27 Aug 1590+   1520-1590
Felix Peretti, filioque-universalism-purgatory

226. Urban VII   Ουρβανός Ζ'   15 Sep 1590 – 27 Sep 1590+   1521-1590
John Baptist Castagna, filioque-universalism-purgatory

227. Gregory XIV   Γρηγόριος ΙΔ'   5 Dec 1590 – 16 Oct 1591+   1535-1591
Nicholas Sfondrati, filioque-universalism-purgatory

228. Innocent IX   Ιννοκέντιος Θ'   29 Oct 1591 – 30 Dec 1591+   1519-1591
John Anthony Facchinetti, filioque-universalism-purgatory

229. Clement VIII   Κλήμης Η'   3 Feb 1592 – 3 Mar 1605+   1536-1605
Hippolytus Aldobrandini, elected 30 Jan, filioque-universalism-purgatory

230. Leo XI   Λέων ΙΑ'   1 Apr 1605 – 27 Apr 1605+   1535-1605
Alexander Octavian de Medici, filioque-universalism-purgatory

231. Paul V   Παύλος Ε'   16 May 1605 – 28 Jan 1621+   1552-1621
Camillus Borghese, filioque-universalism-purgatory

232. Gregory XV   Γρηγόριος ΙΕ'   9 Feb 1621 – 8 Jul 1623+   1554-1623
Alexander Ludovici, filioque-universalism-purgatory

233. Urban VIII   Ουρβανός Η'   6 Aug 1623 – 29 Jul 1644+   1568-1644
Matthew Barberini, filioque-universalism-purgatory

234. Innocent X   Ιννοκέντιος Ι'   15 Sep 1644 – 7 Jan 1655+   1574-1655
John Baptist Pamfili, filioque-universalism-purgatory

235. Alexander VII   Αλέξανδρος Ζ'   7 Apr 1655 – 22 May 1667+   1599-1667
Fabius Chigi, filioque-universalism-purgatory

236. Clement IX   Κλήμης Θ'   20 Jun 1667 – 9 Dec 1669+   1600-1669
Julius Rospigliosi, filioque-universalism-purgatory

237. Clement X   Κλήμης Ι'   29 Apr 1670 – 22 Jul 1676+   1590-1676
Aemilius Altieri, filioque-universalism-purgatory

238. Innocent XI   Ιννοκέντιος ΙΑ'   21 Sep 1676 – 12 Aug 1689+   1611-1689
Benedict Odescalchi, filioque-universalism-purgatory

239. Alexander VIII   Αλέξανδρος Η'   6 Oct 1689 – 1 Feb 1691+   1610-1691
Peter Ottoboni, filioque-universalism-purgatory

240. Innocent XII   Ιννοκέντιος ΙΒ'   12 Jul 1691 – 27 Sep 1700+   1615-1700
Anthony Pignatelli, filioque-universalism-purgatory

241. Clement XI   Κλήμης ΙΑ'   30 Nov 1700 – 19 Mar 1721+   1649-1721
John Franciscus Albani, elected 23 Nov, filioque-universalism-purgatory

242. Innocent XIII   Ἰννοκέντιος ΙΓ΄   8 May 1721 – 7 Mar 1724+   1655-1724
    Michael Angelus de Conti, filioque-universalism-purgatory
243. Benedict XIII   Βενέδικτος ΙΓ΄   29 May 1724 – 21 Feb 1730+   1649-1730
    Peter Franciscus Orsini, filioque-universalism-purgatory
244. Clement XII   Κλήμης ΙΒ΄   12 Jul 1730 – 6 Feb 1740+   1652-1740
    Laurentius Corsini, filioque-universalism-purgatory
245. Benedict XIV   Βενέδικτος ΙΔ΄   17 Aug 1740 – 3 May 1758+   1675-1758
    Prosper Laurentius Lambertini, filioque-universalism-purgatory
246. Clement XIII   Κλήμης ΙΓ΄   6 Jul 1758 – 2 Feb 1769+   1693-1769
    Charles Rezzonico, filioque-universalism-purgatory
247. Clement XIV   Κλήμης ΙΔ΄   28 May 1769 – 22 Sep 1774+   1705-1774
    John Vincent Anthony Ganganelli, elected 19 May, filioque-universalism-purgatory
248. Pius VI   Πίος ΣΤ΄   22 Feb 1775 – 29 Aug 1799++   1717-1799
    John Angelus Braschi, elected Feb 15, filioque-universalism-purgatory, died in prison
249. Pius VII   Πίος Ζ΄   14 Mar 1800 – 20 Aug 1823+   1742-1823
    Louis Barnabas Chiaramonti, filioque-universalism-purgatory
250. Leo XII   Λέων ΙΒ΄   28 Sep 1823 – 10 Feb 1829+   1760-1829
    Hannibal Sermattei della Genga, filioque-universalism-purgatory
251. Pius VIII   Πίος Η΄   31 Mar 1829 – 30 Nov 1830+   1761-1830
    Franciscus Xavier Castiglioni, filioque-universalism-purgatory
252. Gregory XVI   Γρηγόριος ΙΣΤ΄   2 Feb 1831 – 1 Jun 1846+   1765-1846
    Bartholomew Albert Cappellari, filioque-universalism-purgatory
253. Pius IX   Πίος Θ΄   16 Jun 1846 – 7 Feb 1878+   1792-1878
    John Marius Mastai-Ferretti, filioque-universalism-purgatory, dogmatized teaching of
    immaculate conception on 8 Dec 1854, dogmatized teaching of papal infallibility on 18 Jul 1870
254. Leo XIII   Λέων ΙΓ΄   20 Feb 1878 – 20 Jul 1903+   1810-1903
    Joachim Vincent Pecci, filioque-universalism-purgatory-im.conception-infallibility
255. Pius X   Πίος Ι΄   4 Aug 1903 – 20 Aug 1914+   1835-1914
    Joseph Melchior Sarto, filioque-universalism-purgatory-im.conception-infallibility
256. Benedict XV   Βενέδικτος ΙΕ΄   3 Sep 1914 – 22 Jan 1922+   1854-1922
    Jacobus della Chiesa, filioque-universalism-purgatory-im.conception-infallibility
257. Pius XI   Πίος ΙΑ΄   6 Feb 1922 – 10 Feb 1939+   1857-1939
    Ambrosius Damian Achilles Ratti, filioque-universalism-purgatory-im.conception-infallibility
258. Pius XII   Πίος ΙΒ΄   2 Mar 1939 – 9 Oct 1958+   1876-1958
    Eugene Marius Joseph John Pacelli, filioque-universalism-purgatory-im.conception-infallibility
259. John XXIII   Ἰωάννης ΚΓ΄   28 Oct 1958 – 3 Jun 1963+   1881-1963
    Angelus Joseph Roncalli, filioque-universalism-purgatory-im.conception-infallibility
260. Paul VI   Παύλος ΣΤ΄   21 Jun 1963 – 6 Aug 1978+   1897-1978
    John Baptist Montini, filioque-universalism-purgatory-im.conception-infallibility
261. John Paul I   Ἰωάννης Παύλος Α΄   26 Aug 1978 – 28 Sep 1978+   1912-1978
    Albino Luciani, filioque-universalism-purgatory-im.conception-infallibility
262. John Paul II   Ἰωάννης Παύλος Β΄   16 Oct 1978 – 2 Apr 2005+   1920-2005
    Karel Wojtyła, filioque-universalism-purgatory-im.conception-infallibility
263. Benedict XVI   Βενέδικτος ΙΣΤ΄   19 Apr 2005 –   1927-
    Joseph Alois Ratzinger, filioque-universalism-purgatory-im.conception-infallibility

RECOMMENDATIONS FOR FURTHER READING

J. M. Hussey, *The Orthodox Church in the Byzantine Empire*, Oxford University Press

Steven Runciman, *The Great Church in Captivity: A Study of the Patriarchate of Constantinople from the Eve of the Turkish Conquest to the Greek War of Independence*, Cambridge University Press

Steven Runciman, *The Eastern Schism: A Study of the Papacy and the Eastern Churches During the XIth and XIIth Centuries*, Wipf & Stock Publishers

Timothy (Kallistos) Ware, *The Orthodox Church: New Edition*, Penguin

Kallistos Ware, *The Orthodox Way*, St Vladimir's Seminary

Patriarch Bartholomew, Kallistos Ware, John Chryssavgis, *Encountering the Mystery: Understanding Orthodox Christianity*, Doubleday

Noteworthy Greek publications:

Θρησκευτική και Ηθική Εγκυκλοπαιδεία (Religious and Ethical Encyclopedia) Vol. 1-12, Athens 1966-68, compiled under the auspices of the Greek Orthodox Church, remains a treasure of Orthodox knowledge, with detailed articles on most issues of the Orthodox faith, biographies of numerous Hierarchs, and articles on most Metropolitanates. Although long out-of-print, a copy can be found in most Greek libraries.

The works of *Βασίλειος Σταυρίδης* are highly recommended, especially *Επισκοπική Ιστορία του Οικουμενικού Πατριαρχείου (Episcopal History of the Ecumenical Patriarchate)*, Ekdotikos Oikos Adelfon Kyriakidi, Thessalonica 1996, which contains the history of each Metropolitanate of the Ecumenical Patriarchate that remains inside Turney (with the notable exception of the Metropolitanates of Smyrni, Ankyra, Saranta Ekklisies, Moschonesia, and Vryoula), concise Hierarch catalogs, and detailed bibliography of all (sadly, mostly out-of-print) relevant publications. His highly acclaimed *Οι Οικουμενικοί Πατριάρχαι 1860-Σήμερον (The Ecumenical Patriarchs 1860 - Today)*, Ekdotikos Oikos Adelfon Kyriakidi, 2nd Edition, Thessalonica 2004, contains biographies of unprecedented detail for all Ecumenical Patriarchs since 1860.

Regarding the biographies of pre-1860 Patriarchs, only the work of Μανουήλ I. Γεδεών, *Πατριαρχικοί Πίνακες (Patriarchal Tables*, published in Constantinople during the 1880s) remains in print—2nd Edition, 1996, Syllogos Pros Diadosin Ofelimon Vivlion.

Two good histories of the Ecumenical Patriarchate are: Γεννάδιος (Metropolitan of Ilioupolis and Thira), *Ιστορία του Οικουμενικού Πατριαρχείου (History of the Ecumenical Patriarchate, Vol. 1 Byzantine Era)*, Ekdotikos Oikos Adelfon Kyriakidi, Thessalonica 1st ed. 1986, 2nd ed. 2001; and Βασίλειος Σταυρίδης, *Ιστορία του Οικουμενικού Πατριαρχείου 1453-Σήμερον (History of the Ecumenical Patriarchate, 1453-Present)*, Ekdotikos Oikos Adelfon Kyriakidi, Thessalonica 1st ed. 1987, 2nd ed. 1999.

For the recent and ongoing history of the Ecumenical Patriarchate, one can consult the tri-monthly publication of the Ecumenical Patriarchate *Ορθοδοξία (Orthodoxy)*, which is published in Thessalonica by Patriarchikon Idryma Paterikon Meleton, and the annual publication *Ημερολόγιον του Οικουμενικού Πατριαρχείου (Almanac of the Ecumenical Patriarchate)*, which becomes available every January in relevant Greek bookstores.

www.ingramcontent.com/pod-product-compliance
Lightning Source LLC
Chambersburg PA
CBHW062038090426
42740CB00016B/2947